My Daughter, My Son
An Adolescent's Gender Transition
Experienced by Mother & Child

Betsie Harvie & Luca Harvie

Published by:
Churchill & Son Publishing LLC

I0212739

ISBN 13: 978-0989208611
ISBN 10: 0989208613

Edited by
East Valley Writing Workshop

Special Thanks to
Candice DeBarr
&
Dan Trumpis

Dedication

"You always have to remember - no matter what you're told - that God loves all the flowers, even the wild ones that grow on the side of the highway." - Cyndi Lauper

"No one can make you feel inferior without your consent." -Eleanor Roosevelt

The way a person treats you is a reflection of their character, not your value. It's okay to think you're cool, regardless of anyone else's opinion. You don't need permission to like yourself.

This book is dedicated to anyone who's ever been through some shit in their life. Wherever you are, know this- I may never know you, but I don't need to in order to love you for who you are. This book was made with you in mind. - Luca

Confession

My mother Betsie and I did not use our real last names in this book. It was a decision we made to protect my anonymity at work. You may think this is cowardly of me. You may even be right. But I'm not a celebrity or an artist. I'm a regular Joe with a regular menial job that I depend on to pay my mortgage, receive health insurance and feed my family. I'm inspired by anyone who's GLBTQ and out at work or school. I also don't judge people who aren't out in all areas of their life for fear of retaliation. It's a personal choice we all must face and live with. I look forward to a day where I'm financially stable enough to brave being out 24/7. Until then I hope you can forgive me and respect my being stealth.

Chapter One

Life Isn't Worth Living

By Betsie

The best time of my day was to snuggle into Marie's bed and read her a story before she went to sleep. One particular night had been no exception until I leaned over to kiss her goodnight.

"You know Mom, life isn't worth living if I can't be a boy," Marie's sad little voice whispered in my ear.

"Why on earth would you say that?" I asked confused.

"Because boys get to play all the neat games. They have all the best toys. They play baseball and football. They have all the fun."

"You can play those games."

"But no one will play with me Mom," Marie said despairingly.

"Have you asked them?"

"Yeah. But they always tell me to go play with girls. I don't want to play with the sissy girls. Mommy, would you play with me? Would you buy me a bat and ball?"

"We'll go shopping tomorrow," I promised. With a kiss to her forehead I added, "Now it's time to get some sleep. Love you, Sweetie. See you in the morning."

"Love you too, Mommy."

Wearing jeans and plaid shirts, Marie would rather pretend cops and robbers with the boys than push baby carriages with the girls. She played dress-up with pirate eye patches and swords, not with princess crowns and pretty dresses. Her dolls and teddy bears did nothing more than collect dust. But I always put it down to Marie being a tomboy.

I thought about her haunting words, 'Life isn't worth living'. Their sincerity troubled me. Why would a four-year-old say 'Life isn't worth living?'

The following day I told the school psychologist what Marie said.

"Don't worry, it's just a phase she's going through," he told me.

I wanted to believe him. After all, he had the degree.

As the sun set the next evening, I found myself playing catch at the park with my four-year-old. She was having a great time, and I was actually having fun. A few weeks later the Easter Bunny left a big yellow plastic bat with the understanding that after dinner every night Mom would become pitcher and outfielder.

Spring turned into summer. We took our annual vacation to Story Land. In the fall, Marie's skeleton pajamas were perfect for trick-or-treating. Santa Claus had brought her a new pink bicycle. Marie celebrated her fifth birthday and had been in kindergarten for seven months. Not hearing anything further about being a boy, I'd forgotten those ten words spoken in the spring.

While doing dishes one evening, I heard tiny footsteps running down the hallway. Marie quickly turned the corner into the kitchen and in an instant the flatware drawer beside me flew open.

Grabbing a butter knife, Marie firmly pointed it toward her stomach.

"If you come near me, I'm going to hurt myself," she said.

Her scared brown eyes spoke for themselves.

I was more startled than frightened. I knew Marie couldn't hurt herself physically. Somehow, I managed to talk her into handing me the knife and immediately called her pediatrician for advice. Was this a cry for help or just another phase she would outgrow?

Thus began our many years of counseling and my countless nights of lonely, tear-soaked pillows.

"Life isn't worth living if I can't be a boy."

Although it would take years to connect the dots back to those ten words spoken by my four-year-old, they had set in motion a journey of heartache, triumph, discovery of how much courage my child possessed, and the strength I would draw from this courage.

Life Isn't Worth Living

By Marie

I've known as far back as I can recall. There was no epiphany. It was always just there; an uncomfortable anxiety itching underneath my skin. I felt I was living in one of those pictures at the back of a *Highlights for Kids* magazine; the section where you have to figure out what's wrong with the picture. Except even when I looked at the picture and circled what was out of place with my green crayon, I couldn't close the magazine and walk away. For me there was no escape from a world of black and white nonsense.

Mom always told me when I grew up I could be anything I wanted to be. My first choices were a dinosaur or Karate Master Kangaroo. When those dreams fell through, I decided to be a doctor. The part I never verbalized was in my mind I was a boy dinosaur, a boy kung-fu kangaroo or a male doctor. It didn't occur to me gender wasn't something I could choose. When I played with my friends it was never with girls and dolls. I always played sports with boys. If we played imagination games, I always imagined myself as a boy and my friends went along with this un-phased. It grew hard to hide my resentment when all my friends used a bathroom where I wasn't allowed. I assumed for a while I would outgrow being Marie the girl just like a caterpillar becomes a butterfly. It was only natural I too would transform into the physical person I was destined to be. Ask a person when they started believing in Santa and they probably won't be able to remember. Ask them when they **stopped** believing and you may have to brace yourself for some drama.

When I realized I would never be a boy, I still hadn't had the Santa bomb dropped on me. However, my new understanding of anatomy was crushing. I fell into a deep depression. What was the point in anything? Why try to succeed? Why make friends? Why behave? Why get out of bed? Why live? These questions swirled around in my tiny skull. There were no answers. I felt betrayed – betrayed by my parents, my body, even God. The world was suddenly full of injustice.

My moods swung wildly. Sometimes I was so sad I couldn't speak. I wanted to withdraw and be alone in my dark misery. I'd sit in a corner of my pre-school classroom and just stare at the wall. This drove the teachers bonkers. A child my age suffering from depression was unthinkable in the 80s. Trying to make a five-year-old last through more than five minutes of time-out is a physical feat. My voluntary stillness befuddled everyone.

I knew as soon as I was able, I would kill myself. Knowing my death was in my hands made me free and whimsical. At these times I could ignore rules and convention and carry on with a devil-may-care indifference to consequences.

Occasionally I'd lose patience waiting for a way to die and grow weary of being sad. That's when I would rage. My anger could seethe for days. I was totally unreasonable.

I was conscious of the fact my problem was socially taboo. When my mother, teachers, or therapists asked what was wrong, I'd always answer vaguely with something like, 'everything' or 'the world'.

Looking back, I wish I had been brave enough to speak up about what was really wrong. I might have saved myself a decade of heartache. But at age five, I was too scared of losing my mother's love. She was my only protector. I knew I was a freak. I just wasn't ready for everyone to have positive proof yet.

I was incapable of keeping my complex emotions in check, but I was good at keeping my answers for my issues generic. Conveniently, in this lifetime there's no shortage of excuses to be depressed. Orphans, starvation, poverty, war, AIDS, the South African apartheid – I was getting good at using current event headlines as a scapegoat for my behaviors. Becoming more enlightened to others' tragedies made me feel less alone.

The children at my elementary school couldn't possibly understand the hell I lived in. God had chosen to make me an outcast with no choice but to kill myself or endure never-ending pain.

Maybe I was a little too dramatic. Even by children's standards I had a vivid imagination, but as outlandish and over the top as my descriptions may be, at the time they were my reality.

I remember Mom always doing her best to make me happy. I don't remember telling her life wasn't worth living if I couldn't be a boy. I do remember playing ball with her. I remember she was my favorite person and my best friend. I wish I could remember exactly what was going through my mind the first time I grabbed a knife and tried to be done with it all over twenty years ago. I remember trying to move fast. If Mom caught me, I'd lose my nerve because she'd cry and make me feel guilty. That's exactly what happened. I was afraid stabbing myself would hurt, but mostly I was afraid of the look on my mother's face. I was afraid of scaring her and making her sad. I'll never forget the panic, hurt and confusion I saw on her face. I wish it had been the last time I caused her such fear and deep hurt, but in 1989 I was just getting started.

Chapter Two

The Night Our World Stood Still

By Betsie

Marie was seven now and in the second grade. She still showed signs of deep depression, often crying for no reason. My husband Brooks and I decided to pull her out of school for a week and take her to Disney World. We thought a week of fantasy for children would snap her out of her constant sorrow.

Disney World worked for the time we were there – or maybe Marie was being a good actor for our sakes. As soon as we arrived back home, she reverted to her talk of death and even what she wanted on her tombstone.

I sought help once again. Marie was assigned another children's therapist. His name was Rick, a young, slight, pleasant man. Marie seemed to like him immediately and saw him on a regular basis. However, her moods of sadness and hopelessness never changed for any length of time.

One evening, as we returned home from a friend's house, snow began blowing so hard it was creating white-out conditions. My nerves were strung tight as I tried to maneuver the car without colliding with another auto. Fussing, Marie kept trying to get my attention.

"You need to knock this off!" I yelled at her with white knuckles glued to the steering wheel. "I need to concentrate."

It was a freak ten minute snow squall and I had gotten caught in it.

Why not, this had been my life for the past two years. Why should today be any different? I thought.

When we arrived home, Marie was still giving me a hard time. I lost control and spanked her a little harder than normal.

"I'm sorry," I yelled as she ran from me.

Silently we trudged up the stairs and into our apartment. We shed our winter clothing. With a slam of her bedroom door, Marie disappeared. Minutes later, I heard a chair being dragged towards the kitchen sink. My gut told me to run in that direction. I reached the kitchen just in time to see my little eight-year-old reach over the kitchen sink and grab one of the sharpest knives from the knife rack.

"You can watch me slit my throat or jump off the balcony. I don't want to live any longer," Marie cried, moving the knife to her throat.

"Come on, Honey, give Mommy the knife," I pleaded. "Someone is going to get hurt."

I was terrified. One wrong word or move from me, and this would all come to an ugly end. As fear took over, I was thrust into a Salvadore Dali painting; nothing was as it should be. The hands on the clock became motionless as time started melting away. As abruptly as the fear began, it came to halt. A bizarre calmness took its place. I should have been yelling frantically. Somehow my words were quiet and composed as I pleaded for Marie to put down the knife

"I don't want to live, Mommy. I just don't want to live," Marie sobbed repeatedly.

I kept telling Marie how much she was loved and how sad we would be without her. This went on for one minute or one hour. I couldn't make a conscious reference to time. Every second had been focused on the Cutco knife in Marie's grasp.

All at once, yet in slow motion, Marie gently placed the knife in my hand. I immediately dropped it into the kitchen sink and grabbed her as she jumped off the chair. I pulled her close.

"It's all right. It will be all right," I whispered.

Could she feel my heart thumping as she rested her head on my chest? Someone was pounding on a drum and it was going boom, boom, boom to the rhythm of the ringing in my head. Without warning, my nerves returned, washing over me like a flood.

Holding Marie in my arms, I quickly called Rick, her counselor, for guidance.

"This is an emergency," I nervously explained to the receptionist.

Within minutes Rick was on the line.

"We need to come and see you right now! Marie just took a sharp knife to her throat and threatened to kill herself. Can we come in and see you or should I take her to the hospital?"

"First you need to calm down," Rick's firm voice answered. "I know it won't be easy but showing her how frantic you are will make the situation worse. Second, find all the sharp objects you can and remove them from the house. Come in first thing tomorrow morning."

Then he added, "Don't let her out of your sight. This includes lying across her on her bed if necessary."

After a quick phone call to Brooks, we moved towards the couch.

"Come sit by Mommy. I promise we'll figure this out. You know we don't want anything to happen to you. Can't you tell me why you are so sad?"

Snuggled in my arms and with tears in her eyes Marie cried, "I don't know why. Nothing feels right. I have no friends. No one will play with me. I just don't know why."

"I'm sorry, Sweetheart, but things will get better," I promised her again, trying to believe my own words.

I stroked her hair as we stayed snuggled together on the couch too exhausted to speak.

For a year and a half I had been listening to Marie's teachers tell me what a smart child I had. Even fought to have her skip kindergarten and go directly into first grade. But the school committee wouldn't allow it. Every paper she brought home from school was marked "excellent." In the second grade Marie's reading and math skills were that of a fourth grader. Everyone knew of her superior intelligence; it was just the norm and we expected nothing less of her.

"Keep her challenged," Rick would say. "She'll be all right."

But Marie was far from being all right. Later that night I slept on the floor just outside her open bedroom door. If she tried to hurt herself again she would have to climb over me first. Sleep never came. My thoughts kept returning to my little girl.

What was going through that young, pained mind of hers? Why was she so unhappy? Where had I gone wrong? Why were my hugs and kisses not enough? Would this ever end?

I had so many questions with no answers. It was just two weeks after her eighth birthday and a second grader should not have been living in this much hell.

The Mentor Program

Brooks sat calmly waiting in the small area outside Rick's office while I nervously paced the hallways. Marie's dad always acted as if nothing was wrong, always going through the motions with no emotions. After an eternity, Rick's door finally opened. Marie emerged with some crayons and paper.

"Take a seat and draw me some more pictures," Rick told her. "I need to speak with your parents."

"This is a picture she drew for me," Rick said as he showed us a very dark, ugly drawing.

I had never seen Marie draw anything like it before. Even in the second grade she had quite an eye for art. Her drawings were always bright and happy; at least the ones I had seen.

"See how it's all in black?" Rick continued. "Although she had her choice of colors she chose to use only black. The figure with the sword in him is dead. She also told me she will not promise not to hurt herself. This above everything else bothers me. I definitely need some help."

Rick's supervisor, Dave, joined us. Suddenly the small office seemed very crowded. We started discussing our options and what action we should take. I felt I was going to be sick as I listened intently to what Rick had to say.

"I've discussed this with Dave. Because of Marie's age, we see no benefit to committing her," Rick informed us.

"*Committing her?*" Rick's words rang in my ears.

"There's a program operated through another hospital," Rick continued. "Although they usually don't take anyone this young, they've agreed to help. The program is run through the Boston Regional Medical Center. It's called the Mentor Program. Marie will live with a family where she can be watched twenty-four hours a day for two weeks. During that time they'll bring her to the Cambridge offices for further tests. Sorry Betsie, we don't feel she'll be safe at home. It will be impossible for you or Brooks to watch her twenty-four hours a day. The husband and wife team she'll stay with have been trained for this and have been mentoring for years."

"Will I be able to visit her?" I asked choking back the tears.

"Well today is Tuesday. She can go tomorrow. Next Friday she'll be back at the Cambridge offices for more tests. You'll see Marie when you go in for a consultation. As long as we all concur it will not be detrimental to her you can take her out on Sunday."

How in the world could seeing her own mother be detrimental to her?

I knew this was best for my little girl, but I didn't like the idea. It took me a few minutes before signing on the dotted line. In the end, this wasn't about me. It was about my angel, and I would go to the ends of the earth to protect her. Marie was called back into Rick's office.

After explaining to her what was going to happen, Marie signed a contract stating she wouldn't hurt herself. Apprehensive but hopeful, we took Marie home.

Physically and mentally exhausted, I spent another night on the hallway floor. Trepidation had taken over sadness. I could no longer find the tears to cry. Numbness finally set in. I fell into a restless sleep. In the morning I would have to be brave as I put my little girl's life into some strangers' hands.

The sun shining through her bedroom window the following morning did little to break the tension as I packed Marie's bag. I wondered if strangers would do a better job than I had making my child happy. My love for my daughter had not been enough. My heart was breaking.

Locking the door behind us, we left for Boston Regional Medical Center. I questioned whether or not we would ever feel safe again. We followed the very well written directions to unfamiliar territory. When we arrived, everything about me felt unfamiliar. I wanted to throw up but there was nothing in my stomach. I wanted to cry but couldn't find my tears. I wanted to feel some sense of normalcy but my head wasn't attached to my body.

I held Marie's hand as we opened the beautifully carved, heavy oak doors. I didn't know it then, but I would learn to hate those old doors. I felt like I was moving in a dream, falling one step behind for every two steps forward. We must have walked a mile before the hallway ended in a large, semi-private waiting area. Rick's small stature was swallowed up by the overstuffed chair. He motioned us over.

After asking Marie how she was doing, Rick asked Brooks and me to move into a room I swear was once used as a broom-closet. He then asked Marie to wait in the hallway by the door and gave her some markers to color with.

"I called Marie's school and spoke with her teacher. She should be here soon. I wanted to be sure we were all working on this together," Rick updated us. "Are you doing okay?" he asked me with genuine concern.

Just then a young woman tapped on the open door and said, "Hi. I'm Kate from the Mentor Program. Are you Rick?"

Rick brought Kate up to speed about the events two nights earlier. Kate promised to take good care of Marie and then told us she had to get going. She had to be home before her son got out of school. It had been a much longer drive than she anticipated.

I didn't even have time to form an opinion of this woman.

All too soon, it was time to say goodbye to my little girl. I was having a difficult time believing this was happening. Inside, my broken heart cried as I held Marie tightly and kissed her goodbye. I was trembling as I watched her walk out of my sight holding a stranger's hand. Tears were now in over-flow mode.

"She'll be all right," Rick promised as he patted my back. I no longer believed him.

Marie's teacher, Mrs. Manning, arrived. I loved Mrs. Manning. She was always giving Marie extra work to do and had a genuine love for her students. I was eventually able to catch my breath and thank her for coming.

"Hi, I'm Rick, Marie's therapist. We spoke briefly yesterday afternoon," said Rick. "Thanks so much for coming. I want to be sure we were all on the same page with this. Was there any hint of anything wrong at school?" he was quick to ask.

"No. Marie is a great student. I'm still trying to digest the fact she did something like this."

"Well, she'll be gone for two weeks. Will this be a problem with the school?"

"No. Not at all. I'll put some work together to keep her busy, but she's so far ahead of the rest of the class it will not be a problem. I'd like to help in any way I can," Mrs. Manning replied.

We thanked Mrs. Manning once again as the three of us walked towards the door together. I don't remember any further conversation. I was sorry she had come all this way for approximately three minutes of conversation. Rick stayed behind to complete paperwork. The walk back to the old oak doors seemed somewhat shorter than I had remembered. I knew I was in motion physically but this wreck of a mother had broken down mentally.

After shaking Mrs. Manning's hand goodbye, we walked to our own cars. Brooks and I were speechless, each immersed in our own thoughts during the long drive home. I couldn't wait to get back to familiar surroundings.

I had promised my boss I would go to work that afternoon. It was a promise I had to break. I crawled into bed well before noon and did not re-emerge until the sun had gone down. Brooks had already left for the three to eleven pm shift. I was glad for the quiet.

My mind wouldn't shut down. I couldn't help wondering if Marie was okay. *How was I ever going to get through the next week and a half? Would she be happy to see me or hate me forever for sending her away?*

Thinking of my parents was the last thing that went through my mind. Although I could have used a hug from my mom, I was glad she was not there to experience this.

Our First Visit With Marie

I awoke Friday morning as excited as a five-year-old on Christmas morning. After a very long ten days, I was going to see my little girl at the Mentor offices in Cambridge. I wanted to wrap my arms around Marie, tell her everything was okay, and steal her away. I hadn't had a full night's sleep since watching her walk away with that Kate woman. I believe I gained five pounds trying to find comfort in food.

As Brooks and I rode Boston's subway system on a busy Friday morning, my optimistic mood soon changed to one of pessimism. It had taken us forty-five minutes from the time we parked the car in Revere, took the blue line to the green line and the green line to the red line. I thought I would go out of my mind waiting on the platform for the next train to come. The red line was not one of the busiest lines on the MBTA, and the trains were few and far between. *Rapid Transit my ass!* I thought, as I constantly checked my watch, pacing back and forth. After reading the map and seeing all the stops before ours, I realized we weren't going to make it in time.

My thoughts kept returning to Marie. *Did she think I had abandoned her? Would they wait for me?*

When our half hour ride from hell was over, I tried to compose myself as we exited the Alewife T stop. We turned left like the directions said and walked for about fifteen minutes fighting the morning crowds and traffic lights. The building they described was nowhere in sight.

We turned around and headed back to the subway station. Rain started to fall from dark clouds that had gathered overhead.

Another fifteen minutes of walking, this time in the rain, and we were back to the exit of the subway station. Before walking aimlessly in another direction, we took a look around to see if the two-story, yellow brick building they had described was within eyesight. Sure enough, it stood straight ahead, over a little bridge and to the right. Maybe they had meant the subway station was to their left, not to take a left. What moron had given me those directions? The dark clouds overhead moved into my brain and gale winds began to blow.

The tightness in your chest is just nerves, I kept telling myself.

Brooks and I were soaked when we opened the doors to the Mentor offices forty-five minutes late. Tears welled up in my eyes as we checked in with the receptionist. I was terrified Marie had already left.

"We were concerned you weren't coming," a stern male voice said as he entered the waiting room.

"Well, the directions you gave me were wrong. Is Marie still here or did I miss her?" I frantically asked.

"She's still here, but they have to leave soon."

At that moment the waiting room doors burst open. I saw a big smile running towards me. Like a magic act, the smile that disappeared when she left with Kate ten days earlier had reappeared. It melted the fears I had of Marie hating me for sending her away.

We sat down to have our brief moment together. Marie was excited to tell me about the past few days.

"Mommy, they live in this neat house with a yard. I get to play with their son, Logan. Isn't that a cool name? They even have a swing set in the basement!"

Marie's excitement was in such contrast to the anxiety building up inside me all morning.

"Mommy, I miss you," she said, hugging me tight.

I wished I could whisper in her ear and tell her how much I had missed her. I wanted her to know my heart broke when she walked away with Kate and how I had cried for days. But I had been warned not to put any undue pressure on her. So instead, my words were light and cheerful.

"I missed you too, Sweetheart. Maybe we can see a movie on Sunday. Would you like that? I'll come early so we can have lunch first. Mommy can't wait," I added, holding her tight.

"Come give Daddy a hug. Daddy misses you too," Brooks said, holding out his arms.

They got in a quick hug just as Kate came into the room.

"Sorry, Mr. and Mrs. Harvie, but I do need to get going. Give Mommy and Daddy a kiss goodbye, Marie. Mommy will come and see you in a few days. Sorry, but I really do need to get home. Don't worry about Marie. She's doing just fine and is a pleasure to have in our home."

I regretfully gave Marie a kiss goodbye. The gale winds I felt blowing in my brain were upgraded to a tropical depression. Once again my heart had not been given enough time to digest saying goodbye.

"Mr. and Mrs. Harvie, come on in so we can talk," the same male voice said, abruptly giving me the clue hugging Marie was cutting into his precious time.

I blew Marie another kiss goodbye as he ushered us into his cluttered office. I could tell this middle-aged, heavy set psychiatrist was going to be all matter-of-fact with no personality thrown in. The first words out of his mouth proved me right.

"I'm sure you know Marie is very intelligent; much more so than most second graders. Our tests are inconclusive but she'll be back next week for an I.Q. test. After all the tests are completed, I'll have more information for you. She has done well with Kate but I'm sure she wants to go home. I'll discuss that with you next week."

"Today is the third time she has come here. Hasn't she said anything? Anything at all to help us understand why she grabbed that knife? Has she said anything to Kate?" I asked frantically.

"I don't have anything conclusive to tell you. I know you came here looking for answers. I don't have any right now. You just need to be patient."

We had shown up late. It seemed we had already taken up too much of his time. After escorting us out of his office, he asked the receptionist to give us driving directions for the following week. He would be damned if we were going to mess him up the next time. Our ten

ten minutes of time were over.

"What the hell? Can you believe that shit?" I asked Brooks angrily as we headed back for another hour of riding the subway. "Two hours to get here, we see Marie for five minutes, and they have no answers. None!"

It was still raining as we traveled back home. But the storm raging in my brain was eventually downgraded to a drizzle with calm winds. I was somewhat relieved. I could see Marie was happy and in good hands.

That afternoon I paid a visit to Mrs. Manning's classroom.

"Thanks so much for coming to our meeting last week. I felt bad you had to leave so soon. I'm not sure what Rick was looking for," I said.

"You're very welcome. I had to tie up some loose ends before leaving the school and was running late. And Rick seemed to be in a hurry."

"Well, it meant a lot to me."

"I love having Marie in my classroom. She's a very bright little girl. I've put together some homework for her. Actually, it's mostly busy work. She doesn't have to complete any of this. I'm also giving her a copy of *Matilda*. It's a fourth grade book, but I know she can read it. It's about a smart little girl just a little older than Marie. I think she'll relate to Matilda's character. Sorry she missed our Valentine's party. Here are the Valentine cards from her classmates."

"Thanks. I'm seeing her Sunday and can't wait. Thanks again for everything."

Later that night I called my sister to ask if she would drive with me to the Mentor office for a trial run. I had always been a nervous driver; the thought of driving into Cambridge gave me a headache. I wanted to know right where we were going when we had to drive in on Thursday morning. We would not be late this time. The directions looked so easy I wished I had known about them earlier in the day; it may have helped prevent Tropical Storm Betsie from forming.

Sunday Finally Arrived

Sunday had not come soon enough. Missing Marie, searching for answers, and worrying about the future had consumed me over the past week and a half. Not a moment had gone by that I hadn't worried about my little girl. I wanted to know why she had taken a knife to her throat. Why in the world did she want to kill herself? Would she do anything like that again? The events of that night kept looping over and over in my brain like a rat running a squeaky wheel and going nowhere. Getting some answers, any answers, would have helped relieve some of the apprehensiveness I was feeling.

To add more stress to an already tense situation, I was a nervous driver and had never driven to Amesbury by myself. What would happen if I were to get lost? What about the car breaking down? Would the grey clouds hanging around all day produce a snow squall like the one I got caught in a week and a half ago? At least I didn't have to listen to Brooks' chatter today. I was grateful he had to work, leaving this day for Marie and me.

With the radio blaring, counting to three, and taking a deep breath, I turned onto Route 95. I hoped the sound of the radio would drown out the uneasy thoughts in my head. Forty minutes later, when I saw the Whittier Memorial Bridge, I knew I was almost there.

I breathed a sigh of relief as I pulled into the driveway of the model two-story house with the white picket fence.

Don't you dare start crying. Don't you dare start crying, I kept saying over and over in my head. *Keep it all together.*

I walked past the swing set and up the stairs. Before I had a chance to knock, the door flew open.

"Hi Mommy, I was watching for you," Marie said laughing.

"Hi Sweetie," I said kneeling to give her a hug.

"Hello again, Mrs. Harvie. How was your drive?" Kate asked as I scanned her immaculate living room. "You must have had a pretty rough week. I know this is difficult, but things will get better. Are you and Marie going out for lunch?"

"Yup. And I was wondering if there was a movie theater around here."

Kate gave me driving directions, and Marie and I were off to lunch and a movie. My stomach was doing flip-flops. I felt anxious around my own daughter! I was so afraid of saying or doing something to upset her.

The moment I was able to park the car, I leaned over to give Marie a hug. Some of that sick to my stomach, anxious feeling slipped away. We hugged so tightly Marie could barely breathe. I didn't want to be the first to release my hold. I wanted the moment to last forever. When we finally did pull apart, I couldn't wait to give her the gift I had brought from her dad and me.

"Here's a Valentine present from Mommy and Daddy. We thought you'd like these hugging monkeys. Aren't they funny?" I asked hoping to set the mood for the rest of the afternoon.

"Oh Mom, I love them!"

"Are you having a good time, Hon?"

"I really like playing with Logan and his mom is very nice. She gave me a kite for Valentine's Day. Can I hang it in my bedroom when I get home?"

"Of course you can."

"I don't want to talk to that guy anymore, Mommy. He asks me lots of stupid questions."

"Just one more time. You'll be home in a few more days."

During lunch we opened Marie's Valentine cards and had a few laughs reading them. I gave her the book *Matilda* and told her it was a gift from her teacher. Marie loved books and seemed happy with the gift. We sat there eating our burgers and fries while she told me all about ice-skating and how well she had done for a beginner. I let her know how much I loved skating when I was her age. We were just mother and daughter enjoying a typical lunch at Burger King.

Lunch over, we ventured back out into the cold February afternoon.

Following Kate's directions I easily found the movie theater. We were able to enjoy each other's company without a lot of talking. I had a lot of questions but the answers would have to wait.

Halfway through the movie Marie rested her head on my shoulder. It was the innocent calming I so desperately needed. The movie ended all too soon. Once again I was torn in two when I had to drive Marie back to Kate's. I wanted her with me. But I also wanted her safe. Why couldn't she be safe in our home?

"Come give Mommy a kiss goodbye. I love you, Sweetie. Be good and I'll see you in a few days," I said, disguising my sadness.

"I love you too, Mommy."

With a smile painted on my face, I blew Marie another kiss goodbye and started the ignition. As I backed out of the driveway, I quickly realized I wasn't going to make it home. I don't know where the tears came from, but they were there, making driving impossible. Within minutes I found myself pulling into a grocery store parking lot. I hoped no one was watching as I parked in the back away from the traffic and shut off the ignition. My hand shook as I fumbled for the lever to recline my seat. Closing my eyes, I allowed the tears to flow freely.

I don't remember falling asleep. When I finally opened my eyes, the sun had gone down. I knew I had to get going. I was still in foreign surroundings; following directions in the dark would be worse than in full daylight. Starting the ignition once again, I wondered if I would ever find the compass direction to lead my family safely home.

Marie Came Home

Marie had been gone for fifteen days. After visiting with her on Sunday, I stopped worrying about how she was doing at Kate's. However, I didn't stop worrying about what might happen in the future. I couldn't wait to get her home, but I had the feeling home was never going to be the same again.

Thanks to my sister Louise making the long drive in with me the previous weekend, Brooks and I were able to drive right to the Mentor offices for our last visit. The sun was shining, and I was in a better mood. I was looking forward to learning why Marie was so unhappy. This time there were no tears as we walked up the steps and entered through the glass doors.

It didn't take long before Mr. No Personality called us into his office. "Well, all of our tests are complete, and I do have some answers for you. Marie's I.Q. is 138; high for an eight-year-old. The reason for all her unhappiness is she thinks too big. Marie worries about the world instead of immediate challenges. You may want to find something she enjoys doing outside of school. Something she can take pride in. We believe with further counseling and keeping her occupied, she should be fine."

What the hell? Hadn't I heard this over a year ago? This was the conclusion from a team of specialists?!

"But an eight-year-old doesn't try to kill herself because she's smart. Besides her I.Q. test, what were all the other tests for?" I asked, shocking him with my loud comeback.

"The rest of the tests were to see where she is socially. We also spoke with her at length. She gave us no indication of anything going on at school or at home. However, I would suggest you keep her away from the news. She takes things too personally. I'm releasing her back to Rick's care. Kate will bring her to Boston Regional tomorrow."

I needed something more. I couldn't believe the past two weeks from hell had been for nothing. We had been keeping Marie challenged most of her life. Look where that had brought us. I tried arguing there was something deeper. But he had already made up his mind and wouldn't listen. After all, he was the specialist! That was it! Marie would come home tomorrow, and I knew nothing more than I did two weeks earlier.

The trunk of my car was now home to all the sharp objects collected in our house. Still, it was no guarantee Marie wouldn't try something else. Uneasiness started gnawing inside me.

Friday morning our trip to Boston Regional Medical Center was a joyful one for me. I was bringing Marie home. Our home where she belonged. I opened the beautiful, old oak doors for what I thought would be my last time. My steps were faster and the floor didn't move beneath my feet. Rick was there to release Marie from Kate's care and into my arms. Holding Marie tightly, I naively believed nothing would separate us again.

On our way home, Marie, Brooks, and I stopped to enjoy a rare lunch out. Marie was in good spirits. I wondered what kind of a mother I had been. Strangers were able to rediscover her smile when I was not. It should not be work for a mother to keep a smile on her child's face, but I promised myself I would I work as hard as I possibly could.

Marie's therapy session with Rick the following week was just one more blow to my struggling family.

"I'm sorry to have to tell you this, but I'm leaving the hospital," Rick informed us.

"You've got to be kidding! What will happen to Marie?" I asked, feeling like I had been punched in the gut.

"Next week I'll introduce you to her new therapist. She's well qualified and has been practicing for over ten years. I know she'll be a good fit."

"Do you have to leave now? Couldn't you stay a little longer? Marie can't start over again with someone new. Is there any way we can go with you?"

"I think I told you at the beginning of our sessions I'm still in school. This was my internship. Please believe me, it's also difficult for me."

"I don't remember you telling us that. I have to say this really sucks."

"I wish I could stay. I've grown attached to my patients. Especially Marie. But Mrs. King has been fully briefed. She is totally up to speed with Marie's history. She'll do a great job."

We met Mrs. King during our next visit. I immediately didn't like her. She was a fish working in a fish bowl. I was ignored as I tapped on the glass trying to get some attention. Swimming away from me while I was speaking annoyed me. She talked incessantly, only coming up for air when absolutely necessary. Was she capable of listening to my daughter through all of her own chatter?

"Isn't there anyone else we can see? I don't like her. I don't have any confidence in her. I can't see how this is going to work," I whispered to Rick.

"I know you've all been through a terrible ordeal. But you have to give Mrs. King a chance. She's very good. Mrs. King is the only therapist here who can take on another case. You're in good hands."

Rick was trying to reassure me. All I heard was, "We really don't care." My psyche said *run*, but my insurance company said *"stay"*.

"Okay, I'll try my best," I lied.

Marie saw Mrs. King for a few more months. Nothing else came of her knife episode. We were told it was time to end her therapy.

I was sitting in the lobby waiting for Marie's last visit with Mrs. King to be over when I heard laughter coming from the hallway. Poking my head around the corner, I witnessed Marie and Mrs. King tossing a football. Was Mrs. King onto something? Looking back, I wish I had paid more attention to what was really happening with that football.

You would think I learned nothing from the knife episode. Not true. I learned to walk on egg shells around Marie, never saying what was truly on my mind for fear of disturbing her. I did not want another trip back through hell if I could avoid it.

Marie's teachers kept her busy. The principal of her school let her eat lunch with him if she was having a bad day. Thank you, Mr. Manning. I kept her challenged with trips to the library, museums, and playing board games. Brooks and I supported her many forms of art. As difficult as those two weeks had been, after a few months we had put it all behind us and had become comfortable with our lives.

The Night Our World Stood Still

By Marie

I remember thinking how young and stupid I was when I grabbed that butter knife. I would never make such an amateur mistake like that again. On television it looked like it hurt when people got stabbed, but having your throat slit was usually quick and quiet.

I felt sorry for myself; sorry I had to do this. But I couldn't carry on. I was sad thinking of my little body slumped on the floor, skin pale from blood loss. Blood would be soaking my hair and clothes. I wasn't going to leave a note. I still wanted to keep my being a boy to myself. Maybe with me out of the way Mom could have another kid– a normal kid. Then she could be happy.

I was so miserable and so alone. I didn't have any real friends. The kids in my grade didn't really pick on me. I thought they were stupid and boring. I wanted a human connection deeper than any second grader could give me. I wanted someone to see me for who I really was. I wanted a lot of things. When you're that young everything happens slowly. I couldn't wait any longer for something that might never come – something I couldn't even put into words. I dragged a chair over to the sink and grabbed the big knife. But I was too slow. Once again I was confronted by Mom. She made me feel ashamed of what I had done just by looking at me. I doubted I could drag the knife all the way across my throat before she could stop me. And I was not prepared to turn the knife on her to buy myself more time. My mind was reeling. I thought if I could get her to back up, I could make a run through the door and jump off the balcony. It was a long way to run before getting grabbed. I was running out of options unless I was willing to point a weapon at my own mother, which I was not.

I felt defeated and embarrassed. Mom phoned my dad at work and Rick, my counselor. Now more people knew I was a real whacko. That was even more embarrassing. Fatigued by failure, I figured I'd play possum and rest a bit. I could wait until Mom went to sleep and throw myself off the balcony or maybe even out of my bedroom window if I could figure out how to get the screen off. I still didn't want to live to see the next day. Knowing I'd have to explain myself and my actions to my counselor made living sound even less appealing. To my disappointment, however, Mom spent the night on the floor outside my bedroom door leaving me little choice in the matter.

The Mentor Program

Having breakfast with people who thwarted your suicide attempt the night before makes for an awkward morning. I should know. I've had to do it more than once. Being driven by my parents to a hospital to talk to a therapist or counselor is also awkward. No matter how many times I took rides like that, it never felt like a normal thing to do.

Normal families drove to soccer games or ice-cream parlors, maybe even to the library or a mall. They didn't routinely drive to psychiatric treatment facilities.

Normal moms had to take a day off from work because their kid had a cold or tummy ache. My mother took time off to take me to emergency mental health evaluations and appointments. I think these drives eventually became routine for my family. For me they remained routinely awkward.

You can hide a lot of things about yourself from people. I couldn't hide the fact I was crazy from the one person who had to make the appointments and shuttle me back and forth from them. No matter how many times my mother told me it would be alright, I knew it wasn't all right. Knowing she also knew made me feel like shit.

The waiting room in children's psychiatric treatment facilities are uncomfortable and sad. Sure there are lots of cool toys to play with, but that didn't distract me from sizing up the other kids. I still wondered who was biggest fruitcake or trouble maker. I wondered why they were there. What problems could they possibly have? They were all so young. There were never many kids, but I wasn't the youngest. I wondered if any of them were like me. They didn't appear to be, but then again on the outside I didn't appear to be like me either.

When I went to talk with Rick I knew I couldn't lie my way out of whatever consequence were already waiting for me. I knew he knew everything that happened the night before. I heard Mom tell him. What she didn't tell him was the reason I did what I did because she didn't know either. I couldn't hide my actions. I could hide my motives. They were going to send me away no matter what I said, so I chose to say nothing.

That actually could have been a great opportunity for me to try and articulate some of what was going on inside me and get some genuine help. Instead, my inner turmoil was so overwhelming it crippled my judgment.

I felt proud because with all the poking and prodding I had still managed to keep some of me to myself. After all, isn't a person entitled to secrets? Shouldn't thoughts and feelings be private if you choose them to be?

They could force me to do a lot of things, but they couldn't force me to share my secrets. Giving them the run-around was my small revenge for subjecting me to all the bru-ha-ha. I couldn't stop it from happening, but I could make damn sure it was all for nothing. I know now this way of viewing the situation was a mistake. I made a lot of bad decisions back then.

Talking was out of the question. I had nothing to say. When asked if I'd promise not to hurt myself again I answered, "No!"

By the way, that's a very demeaning thing to ask a person. I didn't owe anybody anything. My body was my own. No one had any right to ask me to do or not to do something to it. I hated it when people took the dignity of making personal decisions pertaining to me away from me.

It should be an inalienable human right to decide things about the care of your own body.

I wouldn't talk about what was going on, so Rick asked me to draw a picture. When you're in child therapy, lots of people ask you to draw lots of pictures. It may sound like fun, but it's very annoying unless they provide markers that smell like fruit, which Rick's office did not. He gave me a boring but reliable Crayola eight-pack. I drew a picture of a dead person with a sword in him. The person could have been me, Rick, my dad, or a personification of the rigmarole I was being put through. I can't remember. Apparently it made an impression.

I knew instantly I'd made a mistake. Usually when someone threatens to, or actually hurts themselves, it's a cry for attention. Not me. I really did hate myself that much and would have preferred to be left alone about it.

When Rick came back, he explained to me I would be going away for a little while. I would be going far away from anyone or anything I knew. I'd be forced to live with complete strangers who were going to spy on me. They would shuttle me back and forth to more treatment centers for a variety of tests. Somehow this was for my own good. The only good I could see was getting out of school for awhile. As a last ditch effort to avoid having to live with people I'd never met, I agreed to sign some bogus contract. It didn't work.

The next day I was taken to Boston Regional Medical Center. The ride there seemed so long I remember thinking it must have been a hundred miles from home. It was more like twenty-five. I have a vague memory of sitting in a hallway alone amusing myself with paper and markers again. Mom was in a meeting with Rick and some strangers. I would have been mortified knowing anyone from my school was there. I don't remember saying goodbye to Mom. I don't remember if Dad was even there.

Living with Strangers

I remember the drive with my mentor, Kate, to her house. It felt like another hundred miles away. I already missed Mom. I spent two weeks with Kate, her husband Bob, their son Logan who was in the second grade, and their daughter Sara who was four years old. They were all nice enough. That was the problem; they were all just nice enough.

I had a hard time sleeping. Other than the occasional sleep-over, this was the first time I'd had to go to bed without Mom giving me a kiss goodnight.

At first things weren't too bad. The family had been doing the mentor thing for a while so that helped make it less awkward. Logan and

Sara were used to strangers coming and spending a few weeks in their house. I was taken aback by how large and luxurious their house was. The mentor family's house was set up to illicit imagination and play. I felt as though I had been invited to stay in a Disney castle.

At home I lived in a small two bedroom apartment with an eat-in kitchen and a bedroom view of a parking lot.

Kate and Bob's house had three bedrooms, two bathrooms, a dining room, office, den, two-car garage and a finished basement with an indoor swing set and sandbox. They had three TV's and their cable package included the Disney channel.

Their living room had a working fireplace; their den had a Nintendo system. No one in my family had half the luxuries these people had. I had always known we weren't rich, but no one we knew was so I had never really had it rubbed in my face. I was beginning to realize my family was poor.

I started to fantasize maybe this family might adopt me, and I could stay forever.

I'm not sure what a mentor was supposed to do in this situation. I was only there for two weeks. Kate never asked me why I had wanted to kill myself. In fact she made no attempt at probing my psyche whatsoever. She didn't ask me questions beyond what I would like for lunch or my shoe size so she could rent me ice-skates. We didn't talk much.

Kate was a stay at home mom. While I amused myself by watching cartoons on the Disney channel or playing with Sara, Kate would be doing chores or watching soaps. Logan went to school during the day and Bob went to work. I had schoolwork sent to me. But I never did any of it. No one ever checked on my progress or complained. As long as I was quiet, I was free to do as I pleased most of the time. This suited me just fine.

Halfway through the first week Kate took me to an office full of stuffy shirts and condescending beards so they could ask me questions. They talked to me like I was a child. It annoyed me. They treated me as if they knew the answers before asking the questions. I just nodded and uh-huhed my way through it. Letting them pat themselves on the back and inflate their own egos was the fastest way out of there.

Logan, Sara and I each received a bag of presents from Kate and Bob for Valentine's Day. Inside were a couple of small toys, bathroom stuff and a kite. I was pretty psyched until I realized I got the same things Sara got. There were unicorn shaped pencil erasers, froo-froo bath soaps from Avon and a pink kite with a white carousel unicorn on it. Logan's pencil erasers were shaped like different planes, his bath stuff was way less girly, and his kite was blue with a fighter plane on it. I was jealous but managed to feign gratitude. I was grateful to receive presents but these people didn't get me at all. I never used the erasers or bath soaps. I kept the kite but I never flew it. I said it was because I didn't want it to get ruined. In reality, I was embarrassed to be seen in public with it. No one in my family would have given me something so feminine. I guess I had taken that for granted. I had never known anything else so the situation threw me.

A Visit With My Parents

During one of my appointments in Cambridge I was going to see my parents. It had been about a week since I'd seen them but to me it felt like months. I didn't understand why I had to meet them in the office instead of someplace normal like a park or restaurant. I wasn't happy about the prospect of being spied on while I talked to them.

It was raining outside. My parents were running late. I listened to the rain as my feet dangled from a chair, swinging back and forth. I tried to block out the pessimism of Kate and Dr. Stuffyshirt McBeardface. They thought my parents weren't going to show up. I knew Mom wouldn't leave me hanging.

When Mom and Dad came through the door they were both soaking wet and Mom looked frazzled. I was so happy to see her I literally leapt into her lap. We only had a few minutes. I tried to tell her as much as I could about what I'd been up to so she wouldn't worry about me later. My moment was shattered when Kate said we had to leave.

The big rush to get back home was so Kate could cook dinner. It wouldn't do for Bob to have to boil the spaghetti himself. Now granted, my father never made dinner for me once in my entire life. The only cooking he'll do for himself is whatever can be microwaved. But still. I was pulled out of my mother's arms so Kate could boil noodles.

I was mad but I knew there was nothing I could do about it. I really didn't know these people. They seemed nice but I didn't know what they'd do if they were mad at me. Would they hit me? Would they tell McBeardface bad things about me? Mom was coming Sunday to take me out to lunch and a movie. Could they cancel that? I decided it was better to keep quiet.

Sunday Finally Arrived

On Sunday Mom took me out to lunch at Burger King. I excitedly told her about the fun things I'd been doing with the Mentor family. They had taken me ice-skating a couple of times. Even though it was new to me I had a knack for it. Kate had also taken us to a maritime museum I thought was kind of cool. The following week we were going to a children's science museum I had never been to.

I spent time complaining about the jerks from the Mentor office who talked down to me and were really condescending. I shouldn't have to explain myself to strangers.

Here's a tip if you're a psycho-analyst of any kind and you're trying to examine someone for their own good. Try being polite and friendly. Contrary to popular belief, children don't instinctively trust any adult who comes along. I wasn't there long enough to build a trusting relationship with any of those doctors. If they had treated me respectfully, I might have responded more openly. I've never been the kind of person to respect authority for authority's sake. I think they took it for granted I would. When you're a kid it doesn't seem like any of this could possibly be for your own benefit

Therapy never made me feel better. It made me feel worse. I was a freak with freak problems. People wanted to single me out and study me like a bug under glass. If all of this was being done just for me why wasn't I allowed to say "no thank you" and walk away? Mom assured me I only had to meet with the Mentor Program doctors one more time so I dropped the issue.

Mom took me to see the movie *White Fang*. For 100 minutes things were quiet inside me.

Going Home

I had to go back to the Mentor Program Offices for an I.Q. test. Sometimes you can find I.Q. tests online. They take around twenty minutes to fill out. It's kind of fun. Actual I.Q. tests take a few hours and are not so fun.

I soon lost patience and wanted to be left alone. Instead I was shown picture after picture and told to make up a story to accompany them. It may sound flattering to have someone hanging on your every word, diligently copying down what you say verbatim. I found it highly irritating and creepy. I felt like no matter how many characters or plot twists I threw at him, he wanted more. It was exhausting. By the end, every picture I was shown led to a story about grizzly homicides. McBeardface never flinched.

At the end of the day, after Kate had taken me back to her house, I found myself in their basement with Logan. I had started in my room where I wanted to be alone. Logan came in and started bugging me. I told him to get out but he told me that before the Mentor Program this had been his room so he didn't have to leave it. I left and went downstairs to the basement and started playing with some Legos. He came down and started grabbing at the Legos too and although there was a bucket full of them this really pissed me off. We started calling each other names and eventually I hit him. I punched him right in his stupid mouth. I was so sick of this little rich blonde egomaniac in front of me. Logan went to a nice school where he had lots of friends. He lived in a big house with a big yard. He had lots of expensive toys and a mom who stayed home and a dad who actually wanted to spend time with him. His little sister adored him. He'd never need therapy or feel like a freak. His family would never look at him like they were afraid of him. I noticed right before I punched him that I kind of hated him. I knew he wouldn't want to be my friend anymore and that made me glad.

Logan was a tattle-tail. He told Kate I hit him. She sent me to my room for a time out. She followed me and took away my copy of *Matilda* and anything else she thought I might amuse myself with. I was to sit on the bed for fifteen minutes and think about what I'd done.

I sat there and thought about everything I'd seen and experienced that week. It slowly dawned on me Kate and Bob were probably getting paid for me to be there. Judging by all the nice stuff they owned, I started thinking maybe they were getting paid a lot.

After fifteen minutes, Kate came back and told me I could get up. I said "uh-huh" and continued to sit there. The idea I was just a cash cow for this family made me mad. I figured out why Kate didn't ask me anything about myself or check up on my homework. She didn't care. None of them did.

Kate came back later to tell me dinner was ready. I told her I wasn't hungry. She told me I needed to stop pouting and I was being ridiculous. This only infuriated me more. I rolled over and gave my back to her. She left and I went to sleep for the night with my legs tightly curled across my growling tummy.

As much as I was beginning to loathe my Mentor family, when it was time for Mom to take me home, I didn't want to go. I realized I wasn't going to be happy in either home. I also realized no one cared how I felt or what I wanted. So I put on a happy face and shoved my feelings down as far as they would go.

I'd like to say I didn't learn anything from the Mentor Program and it didn't change my life in any way, but that's not true. I was learning to become even more adept at hiding what was inside me. My daily performances were Oscar worthy. Oh, and I was learning to trust authority figures and adults in general even less. So yay Mentor Program!

I actually liked Rick. I may not have been completely forthcoming with him, but I felt I wanted to be. Even after the Mentor Program I wanted to trust Rick. A few days after I came home and I thought maybe the dust would start to settle, I learned Rick was moving on. I felt betrayed. I meant nothing to Rick. My future meant nothing to Rick. He was going to move on and never look back. How can you trust people that only care about your problems when your checks clear and it's convenient for them? I call bullshit.

The next therapist was a plump older woman with a shrill voice. We'd mostly play games instead of talking. She only asked me to draw pictures once. I drew a picture of my pet guinea pig. She actually laughed at it and said it looked like I drew a furry potato. Maybe I was too sensitive. Okay, I know I was too sensitive, but I definitely got the impression she was laughing at me and not with me.

Laughter is only the best medicine if you're the one doing the laughing. I was relieved when my parents stopped making me see her.

Chapter Three

Running Away

By Marie

In the summer of 1991 my older cousins and I went to a swanky overnight summer camp for two weeks. I felt anything they did, I had to do. And I mean **HAD TO!** I thought the sun really did shine directly out of my older cousins' asses. This camp had everything; archery, horseback riding, canoeing, sports, campfires and, most importantly, no parents.

As usual, most of the kids my age at the camp accepted me the way I was, tomboy to the tenth power. Some of the older kids, however, gave me a difficult time. There were fist fights and tears. It's amazing how thirteen to sixteen year olds have no qualms about literally beating an eight-year-old bloody. At the time, I wasn't amazed though. I was used to it. When you're as androgynous as I was, no one took it easy on you in a fight just because you were a girl. I knew better than to expect any pity. For the past two years people had been trying to beat the abnormalities out of me. I just kept on being different.

A few months before I left for camp my grandmother died. She had been the only grandparent I had known because the other three had passed away before I was born. Unbeknownst to me, while I was away at camp my parents moved us into her condo. I had known before I went to camp that we would be moving, I even packed a few boxes. I hadn't expected Mom and Dad to move while I was away. When I left for camp I had left my childhood home forever. When Mom picked me up from camp and took me to our new home, I was in shock.

Grandma's condo was much larger than our apartment. I had the master bedroom. My parents put a nineteen-inch color television in the room hooked up to cable and a VCR. I still didn't have the Disney Channel, but I had HBO in my bedroom. They bought me a bunk bed so I could sleep on the top bunk every night and have a bed for my friends for sleepovers. I was finally the spoiled child I had been accused of being for years.

This was exciting until I realized there were no other kids in the building. I was now miles away from my friends and my cousins instead of just a short walk away.

My parents told me not to tell anyone at school where I'd moved. We now lived two towns over. I had no right going to my school. Being forced to change schools would have been a crushing blow. I kept my mouth shut about the move so I could stay in the familiar school with my few friends.

In the beginning of the third grade I would walk to my after-school daycare center when the school day was over. It wasn't very far, and was the same place I'd gone to pre-school. I thought it would be fun. I had a lot of fond memories of pre-school there. The instructors were always coming up with extra stuff to keep me busy. They all thought I was smart.

Going back there didn't turn out to be fun at all. It was a Catholic Charities Center on the line of two cities so most of the kids didn't go to my school. In pre-school I had friends. Now I didn't know anyone. A lot of the kids went to parochial school during the day, and most of the kids who didn't still went to catechism and other Catholic classes in the afternoons. When CCD was in session, I was one of a small handful who didn't attend and was immediately ostracized by the other kids. Since I was in a core group of third to fifth graders, this was my introduction to pretty and popular girls.

Obviously they didn't welcome me into their club. I was used to being picked on for not being girly enough. Older kids had been calling me *he-she* for awhile. Now I was being called *ugly*. They would call me ugly all afternoon and throw things at me until my mother came to pick me up.

Before going to Catholic Charities after school, I had never thought of myself as ugly. I was tall for my age with dark blonde hair, big brown eyes, an athletic build, and a nice smile when I cared to use it. I knew I wasn't feminine, but in an androgynous way I still thought I was an attractive person.

Now I had to accept the fact I would never wake up as a boy and look at myself as Marie. Marie couldn't be a parallel stranger to me anymore like the parasitic twin I thought I could escape from if I ignored her long enough. At one point I had named my inner male self Frederick because that's what Mom told me she would have named me if I was born a boy. Frederick was who I saw when I thought about myself. When I was alone or with my close friends, Frederick's mouth was what I spoke through and his eyes I looked through. Marie was always nearby. When people would address her, I would hide inside Frederick and we would be invisible. When Marie wasn't being addressed, Frederick and I would ignore her. It was confusing having three people share one body. Marie was the girl, Frederick was the boy and I was the nameless go-between. But that was before I realized no matter how real Frederick felt to me, he would never be real to the world. That was before the big knife and the Mentor program. Now Frederick was gone. I was nameless inside Marie.

I took a good look at Marie in the mirror and decided I agreed with all the kids who were making fun of me. Marie was ugly. I was ugly. With the loss of Frederick, I was now alone and ugly. I sucked my thumb like a baby and cried a lot. I hated being Marie.

At Catholic Charities the pretty and popular girls had made throwing things at me so trendy older kids who used to ignore me started throwing sticks and rocks at me. I had to run from school to daycare to avoid the unsupervised torment from kids who were much bigger than me and vastly outnumbered me. I couldn't tell the teachers because I didn't want to be a tattle-tale. I couldn't tell Mom because I was too embarrassed. I complained to Mom the daycare program was stupid. I hated it and everyone there. She stopped making me go. Now when I got out of school, I walked around the block to where no one from school would see me. Dad would pick me up and drive me home.

It didn't take long before afternoons with Dad became unbearable. Sometimes his friends would be in the car when he came to get me. They'd already be stoned, reeking of pot and body odor, talking a bunch of chauvinistic nonsense. On those days, I knew I'd be in my bedroom from the time I got home until Mom got out of work. Dad and his friends would be watching adult movies in the living room, and the condo security guard always stopped me from playing outside.

I couldn't wait for Mom to get home to end my hunger and my boredom. I knew better than to ask Dad for an afternoon snack. I hated his friends so much I wouldn't leave my room for a drink even if I was thirsty. If I did come out Dad and his friends would offer me tobacco and alcohol and laugh as I choked or stumbled around buzzed. Worse still was the way some of Dad's friends looked at me. I knew I was an ugly girl, but when they looked at me, it felt creepy.

I decided to run away during the first week back to school after Christmas break. I was sick of everyone and everything at that point. Before Christmas I had been getting into a lot of fights at school. At home I had the worst Christmas of my life.

It was the first and thankfully the last time my family celebrated Christmas at our condo. All of my aunts, uncles and cousins were there. My aunt Louise had given me a box of electronic musical instruments that were insanely cool at the time. I was enthralled with the drum sticks called Hot Sticks, which were motion activated. I opened the box on the floor between the television and the Christmas tree. Sitting on the floor, I was trying to figure out where the batteries went when Dad came over and told me I needed to pick up the mess I'd made. It seemed ridiculous since half the floor was covered in boxes and wrapping paper from everyone else, but I knew Dad. He was actually angry with something one of my aunts had said to him, and he dealt with it by yelling at me. I got up, took the instruments into my bedroom, and came back to the living room to scoop the wrapping paper into the box. Dad came over again and said, "I told you pick this shit up!" Then he hit me so hard across my face, I spun around and landed on the box and the rest of my presents. Being hit by Dad was always embarrassing.

But having a room full of spectators made it much worse. No one made a move to help me up or say anything to Dad about what he had done. It made me feel awful.

I ran out of the room pinching my bleeding nose so it wouldn't run into my mouth as I hiccupped from crying. Hiding in my bathroom with the door locked, what surprised me most was how long it took for anyone to check up on me. Mom came to the door but I wouldn't let her in because I couldn't tell if she was concerned for my health or upset that I was making a scene. Sometimes when Dad hit me or yelled at me Mom would fight with him because she didn't like him to treat me that way. Other times she'd blame me. It was hard to predict whose side she'd be on. My older cousins came to see how I was doing without any ulterior motive. Ellen washed my face and Will made up stories about Dad getting his butt kicked by my favorite WWF wrestlers which almost made me smile. My cousins drifted out after awhile. I guess Christmas in a bathroom wasn't fun for them either.

I spent the rest of the night curled up in the tub with my raggedy stuffed Pound Puppy Red until it was bedtime.

My first attempt at running away was pretty ambitious for a third grader. For two weeks I pocketed the thirty-five cents Mom gave me every day to buy chocolate milk. It would be my money for food. On a Friday morning I packed a flashlight and a clean pair of underwear and socks in my backpack. I also snuck a roll of toilet paper in case I had to go to the bathroom in the woods or something. I didn't leave a note behind or act differently. I let Mom drive me to school as usual and kissed her goodbye as if it wasn't for the last time.

All day at school I couldn't concentrate. I kept checking and re-checking the items in my backpack. I'd added a five dollar bill left over from a Christmas card to my stash of money and wrapped it up in a plastic sandwich baggy. I'd thought about waiting for January so I'd have birthday money too. Or waiting for summer so I wouldn't be so cold. But I couldn't wait that long. Besides, leaving from school would give me the best head start.

When school let out, I knew where Dad would be parked waiting for me. I left through a side door and ran so fast in the opposite direction I didn't have time to look back. After I had three or four blocks between me and the school, I slowed down so I wouldn't draw attention to myself. There weren't any other kids walking this far away so I was sure to stick out. I didn't really know where I was going. I knew where my

Aunt Louise's house was and figured that's where Dad would go after looking in the school yard. I just kept walking in the opposite direction.

After what felt like hours, my stomach started growling. I was disappointed at how soon I became hungry and tired. I stopped someplace for a slice of pizza. I was surprised how much money I spent on one meal. I thought I'd better just eat candy from the ten-cent machines from now on.

The sun had gone down while I was in the pizza place. Now it was cold. I kept walking to stay warm, but in the dark I started getting confused. Soon I was going in circles. There were no other people out walking. All the stores nearby were closed. I had no one to ask for directions. I figured I had better stick out my thumb and try to hitch a ride somewhere or else I'd have to sleep on the sidewalk. Maybe a trucker would pull over who was driving all night. Then I could sleep in the passenger seat of the cab and wake up someplace new.

I stuck my thumb out with high hopes. Lots of cars beeped at me but didn't stop. I was starting to get discouraged, but my little feet couldn't go any further. I knew if a car didn't stop soon, I was going to have to give up and find a payphone to call Mom. I started working on an apology in my head. I also worked on some lies as a backup. Before I gave up, a maroon Pontiac pulled over. A lady in her forties with a page haircut smiled at me. She rolled down the passenger window and started talking to me.

"Sweetie, are you lost?"

"Um, I think so."

"Where are you going?"

"I don't know"

"You don't know?"

The way she talked to me I knew she wasn't going to be cool about the situation. She probably had kids of her own and thought I needed help. I was afraid if I told her I was running away she'd call the police.

"I'm trying to get home," I told her.

"Where's home?"

I shrugged.

"I was supposed to go to my aunt's house after school but decided to walk home instead," I said, lying, shivering and shuffling my feet.

"Why don't you get in the car? We can call your mommy to pick you up."

I sighed.

"Okay" I answered, defeated.

I got into the stranger's car. Luckily, she wasn't a psycho kidnapper. She drove me to her work so we could use her office phone. No one had cell phones in 1992. We didn't talk much. She could probably tell I was full of it. I think I made her uncomfortable. I didn't have much to say since I was very tired and figured I was in deep shit.

When we got to her office she gave me a bottle of Veryfine Apple Juice from a vending machine. I sipped it as she looked through a phone book for the Children's Protective Services phone number. I sat there embarrassed as she told another stranger over the phone she had picked up a runaway child hitchhiking. I was right about being in deep shit. She asked me for my name, parents' names, home address, phone number, and what school I attended. She gave the information to the CPS agent on the phone. When that was done, she dialed my home phone. No one answered. This was before answering machines were common, so she hung up. I told her my aunt Louise's number. It turned out Mom was already there.

My uncle, Aunt Louise's husband, came to pick me up. I spent the whole ride back to his house listening to him tell me how stupid I was to hitchhike. I was just a little girl. There were a lot of sick bastards out there. Then he told me how he hitchhiked when he was a teenager, but it was okay because he was a big guy and carried a knife. I took this as another example of how girls were inferior and incapable of doing what boys could do. I hadn't learned anything.

Mom was glad to see me because she had been so scared. She was also mad at me. My cousins Will and Ellen wouldn't talk to me. Dad was just pissed.

Aunt Louise made me dinner. I ate it at her kitchen table while Mom, Dad and my uncle continued peppering me with questions and insults to my intelligence. They were sick of being lied to about what motivated my antics, but I knew they couldn't handle the truth. For my family's sake as well as my own, I kept answering "I don't know."

Running Away
A Letter to My Child
By Betsie

My Dearest,

I have written and re-written about the terror I felt not knowing where you were the day you ran away. I wrote about how I collapsed after learning you had been thumbing a ride and I may have lost you forever. Those three hours of fear, however, were nothing compared to the fear you must have endured on a daily basis. To think I may have contributed to that fear is inconceivable.

Saying I'm sorry seems so little, even if it is felt with every fiber of my being. I hid behind my own insecurities when you needed me the most. Just like you were humiliated over who you were becoming, I am humiliated to learn who I truly was. I let you suffer because I was too afraid to walk away from your father. I was worried about what people would say. I was terrified of having no money. Living in a shelter was scarier to me than anything your father could have done. It was just easier to remember the good times. I let myself believe your father's occasional temper was not that bad.

You were right. I could not have handled this back then and I am struggling to handle it now. In fact, this is so difficult for me, I would like to quit now and not go any further. I won't. I have quit on you too many times in the past. Your words show me in black and white I was not the mother I thought I was. Each time I read them, I cry some more.

Learning how much you were bullied by older children saddens me. Learning how much you were bullied by your father sickens me. Was I aware of what was going on in the afternoons with your dad and pushed it aside for convenience sake? I hope not.

Hearing you say you believed you were ugly deeply wounded my soul. Will that wound ever heal? You should have felt comfortable telling me anything and knowing I would have listened. I guess that's what hurts me the most. Did you try to tell me and I just didn't listen? Maybe together we could have lessened some of your pain.

I know we had told you about moving to the condo. Maybe you didn't realize it was going to happen so quickly. Your dad and I fought a battle with attorneys for two years to keep you away from that place. The party suing your grandmother's estate won the battle and we were forced to move in. I knew moving into a building full of rich, stuck-up, snobby people would be tough on you. It was a cold, uncaring building where children were not allowed to be seen. A color TV and VCR certainly could not replace friends. I'm not sure who hated living there more, you or me. As you may recall, I referred to that horrible place as "Hell House."

I do remember an incident on Christmas day, but for the life of me I cannot remember the details. Was I in the room when your dad hit you? Did I do nothing? I would hope I came to the bathroom door to check up on you and not because you were making a scene. I'm angry with my family for not defending you, but I am mostly angry with myself. I know I am fully to blame for creating a day which you will always look back upon with sadness.

I never truly understood what motivated you to run away. It took a great deal of courage for you to tell me the truth. You no longer have to carry that burden by yourself. Could I have stopped the bullying from your peers? Probably not. However, I should have stopped the bullying happening in your own home. Letting you down is a personal demon I will forever struggle with. I hope someday we can discuss how much I failed you, without me crying. It will take awhile.

I have always regretted losing your respect but I am eternally grateful for your love and forgiveness.

Love,

Mom

Chapter Four

An Unmarked Grave

By Marie

After trying to run away, it was decided Dad wouldn't be picking me up from school anymore. I felt I had won some small victory. Now I would be walking with my friend Andrew to his house after school. We'd hang out until Mom came and picked me up after work. I thought this was going to kick ass.

For a while things were cool. Andrew and I would play in the snow until we got cold, then we'd go inside and watch television or play video games. Andrew got a Super Nintendo for Christmas; we were really good at Super Mario Brothers Three.

Most of the time Andrew's mother Dianna wasn't home. His step-dad worked a lot, so he was hardly home either. Andrew shared a room with his older step-brother Bobby, who was fourteen. I liked Bobby because he had a huge Garbage Pail Kids card collection and a lot of R-rated movies he let us watch.

I thought Bobby was really cool. He smoked cigarettes and treated Andrew and me as equals. It's always flattering when older kids want to hang out with you.

One day some of Bobby's friends came to the door and he blew them off to hang out with Andrew and me. It made me feel important. We decided to play basketball with an indoor Nerf hoop in Andrew and Bobby's bedroom.

When I scored a basket, Bobby patted me on the behind. I tried hard not to tense up and let Bobby see how uncomfortable he had made me feel. I wanted him to think I was cool. So I tried to silence the alarms going off in my head. I told myself it probably didn't mean anything to him. After all, I was only nine. I had been confirmed ugly many times over. It was probably a sports thing. Coaches pat guys on the butt all the time.

But then he did it again. And again. And again. I started getting weirded out. But I still didn't want to say anything, so I suggested we watch television. We sprawled out on the floor to watch some old Three Stooges tapes.

Bobby got up and grabbed two pillows. He handed one to Andrew and laid the other one behind himself. He then told me to come and lean against him so I'd be comfortable.

Andrew didn't act like this was unusual in anyway. At the time I was used to sharing a blanket on a couch with my older cousin Will when we watched television, so this didn't seem *that* strange. Bobby put his arm around me and told me of all Andrew's friends, I was his favorite.

I thought to myself, *Wow, finally someone who gets me. Someone mature and cool wants to be my friend and hang out with me. He's like the older brother I always wanted.*

The next day Andrew and I were in his room playing video games when Bobby came in with a plate of Pepperoni Bagel Bites to share. I thought he was so thoughtful and nice to make food for us. Dad would never have made snacks for me or my friends.

Bobby hooked up his Game Genie and showed us some cool tricks on a few games. He let me have a turn on a racing game. I knew he liked me more than Andrew because he always let me have the first turn. Bobby probably wished he was my step-brother instead of Andrew's.

When Andrew's turn to play came, Bobby whispered to me, "Come here, I want to show you something."

We got up and Andrew asked where we were going.

"To talk video game strategy," Bobby coolly answered.

I thought, *Cool! He's going to tell me something secret about video games so I can beat Andrew!*

We left the room and walked across the hall to their parent's bedroom. Bobby shut the door behind us and sat down on the bed. I tried to sit next to him.

"No, you need to sit on the floor for me to show you." I sat on the floor.

"No, no. You need to be on your knees. Here, turn around and get on your knees and face me."

I thought it was weird because I was expecting him to have a magazine or even some drawings or a spare video game controller. Something. But I did what he told me to do. I kneeled there still thinking he probably had something in his back pocket he'd show me any second.

Bobby undid his pants and pulled them down to his knees. I just kneeled there like a moron, staring at his underwear. They were red plaid and long and loose. I had only seen briefs before so these were intriguing. They looked so comfortable. I would learn later that they were boxer shorts.

He asked, "Do you want to touch it?"

"Sure," I answered.

I reached out to touch his underwear. I didn't understand what this had to do with video games but they were flannel and snuggly.

"Not my underwear!"

"Oh."

He grabbed my hand and shoved it inside his boxers.

My first thought was *What the hell is all this curly scruffy stuff down here? Is he hiding a dishwashing Brillo Pad in his drawers? Will steel wool help me become better at Street Fighter II Turbo?*

Then he put my hand on his penis.

Mom had explained the mechanics of sex to me awhile back when I asked why boys and girls have different parts. Not surprisingly, Mom hadn't told me about hand jobs, or foreplay of any kind. I wasn't sure what was going on with Bobby. Someone had come into my daycare the year before and explained to us the difference between a good touch and a bad touch and how if someone touches your privates you should tell a parent or teacher. But they didn't say anything about what to do if someone makes you touch them. I guess they didn't want to explain handsies or blowsies to elementary school kids.

I thought this might be wrong and Bobby would tell on me later for touching him. But it was so confusing because he initiated it. And I was very curious about penises. I secretly wanted one of my own so badly, I wanted to explore it and see what I was missing.

Maybe Bobby had sensed I wanted to know more about penises. Maybe he was just being friendly and letting me satiate my curiosity, but didn't want to talk about it so as not to embarrass me.

My brain was trying to process all of this in the span of about two seconds. Before I could make up my mind, I found my hand wrapping around the middle of the shaft of his penis all on its own. I didn't realize I was doing it until I felt this intense heat in the palm of my hand that drew my eyes down. It was so hot it was like he had a fever in his penis. I had never felt anything like it before. It was hard too, like holding a salami. I had expected it to be softer. Then again, at that age, adults will tell you sex is when a man puts his penis in a woman's vagina, but no one wants to tell a young girl about erections.

Bobby pulled my hand out of his underwear and shifted around so his penis was sticking out of the unbuttoned hole at his crotch. Now that I could see it, I was taken aback. It was kind of ugly. The skin was brown and the tip of it looked like an alien nightmare. This was the first time I'd ever seen an uncircumcised penis. I didn't even know what a circumcision was, so I thought Bobby's penis was a mutant.

"Go on" he said.

I just looked at him.

"You know you want to."

I had no idea what he expected me to do.

"Put it in your mouth."

"Um, no."

I started to back up, but he grabbed my shoulders.

"You'll like it, I promise."

I shook my head.

Bobby grabbed a handful of my hair and forced my face down to his penis. It was pressing against my mouth and cheek. I shut my eyes, afraid of it poking them and took a deep breath through my nose. Up close his penis smelled musty, sort of like my Mentor family's basement.

I thought *Oh God*, and gagged.

That slight parting of my lips was all Bobby needed to force his penis inside my mouth. It tasted like sweat and stale urine. He brushed the inside of my cheek with it. I couldn't breathe. I was so upset I forgot how to breathe through my nose and started suffocating on my own whimpers and gags. It was all too disgusting. I was afraid he'd pee in my mouth like I was a human toilet. My eyes burned with tears I couldn't shed because my eyelids were squeezed shut so tight.

When I thought I was going to puke or pass out, Andrew started knocking on the door. Bobby was distracted enough to let go of my hair. I jumped up and ran across the room. By the time I had the door unlocked, Bobby had his pants pulled back up. I opened the door and pushed past Andrew to cross the hallway and get into the bathroom.

"What were you guys doing?" I heard Andrew ask Bobby.

"Nothing. I was showing Marie some techniques."

I didn't want to see myself in the bathroom mirror. I just stared at the water swirling down the sink drain and rubbed toothpaste on my tongue with my finger, willing myself not to cry. I didn't understand why Bobby was suddenly so mean and scary. I thought we were buddies.

When I came out of the bathroom, Bobby was gone. Andrew didn't seem to know what had happened. It was so humiliating I was glad he didn't know. We drank Kool-Aid and did homework until Mom came to get me.

Back when I was in pre-school and Dad was alone with me in the mornings, he'd watch Playboy videos in the living room until it was time to drop me off at school instead of helping me get ready. When I wasn't dressed on time with my shoes tied and everything, he'd come in my room, pull my pants down and spank me with a wooden hair brush. By the age of four I was the only kid in my pre-school group who could completely dress themselves, including tying my shoes and zipping my coat. When Mom picked me up at Andrew's house that day, I felt the same embarrassment I used to feel when I'd show up at pre-school with a sore bottom. I was hurt, but I didn't want to talk about it.

On the car ride home I felt a little nauseous thinking about what had happened. But I decided it still wasn't as bad as an afternoon with Dad. Bobby hadn't really hurt me much. He was probably teasing me, trying to gross me out. It's a good thing years of bullying had made me tough. I figured I'd get over it.

The next day was a Friday. I remember sitting in my third grade homeroom being so grateful it was almost the weekend. It was also February fourteenth. I was starting to hate Valentine's Day. I couldn't eat any of my candy because I was nauseous. I kept fidgeting and tapping my pencil. I couldn't concentrate. I kept watching the hands on the clock tick away.

When Andrew and I got to his house, I was relieved to find we were alone. We played outside for a while with some other neighborhood kids and eventually drifted inside for a snack. We were drinking Seven Up and eating cold pizza when Bobby walked in.

I tensed up so bad I had to stop eating and drinking so neither of them would see my hands shaking. I silently watched in disgust as Bobby made himself a mayonnaise sandwich and chewed it with his mouth open, talking to Andrew about some cartoon show.

Bobby asked what Andrew and I were up to. Andrew and I shrugged. Bobby suggested we play hide and seek. All kinds of red flags and alarms shot around inside my head. But I didn't say anything. I figured I had made my bed by choosing to come here instead of going home with Dad. Now I had to lie in it.

I longed for the days when I could walk to my Aunt Louise's house and hang out with Will and Ellen again. But Ellen was afraid to be in charge of me. I had run off and hid down the street one day when Will hit her and I got scared. Maybe hide and seek wasn't a bad idea. Maybe I could hide in one spot until Mom came to pick me up.

Bobby suggested Andrew be it first. I should have seen that coming. It was the best way to keep Andrew and me apart.

When Andrew started counting, Bobby grabbed my hand and dragged me back into his parent's bedroom. I was so afraid I couldn't move. And I was too embarrassed to yell for help. I was terrified by how weak and defenseless I was compared to Bobby, who was at least fourteen inches taller than me and outweighed me by fifty pounds.

Usually when bigger and older kids picked on me and tried to beat me up, I would fight back viciously – even if it resulted in my getting my ass kicked harder. I wouldn't go down quietly. Yet with Bobby I was the perfect docile victim. If he had punched me I would have fought back. But this was different. I didn't know what he was trying to do so I didn't know how to respond.

Bobby pulled me down onto the floor behind the bed with him and covered us with a sheet.

"Shhh" he said.

I laid there on my back with him hovering over me in claustrophobic semi-darkness, my heart thundering in my chest.

"If we're quiet Andrew won't find us," Bobby assured me as he slid his hand under my shirt to caress my non-existent breasts.

I was contemplating whether this actually counted as a bad touch. My chest was as flat as a pancake, so he wasn't really touching my breasts because the only thing I had were pale pink pre-pubescent nipples. I think my stomach stuck out farther than my chest.

It didn't feel good, nor did it hurt. It just felt weird. Why was Bobby touching me like this? Didn't he know I was ugly? Couldn't he tell I was barely even a girl?

That's what I was thinking when Bobby unbuttoned my red corduroy pants, put his hand in my underwear, and reminded me at that moment I was definitely a girl.

"Don't" I finally managed to squeak.

"Oh come on, you've been leading me on for way too long to say no now."

Had I been leading him on? What did that even mean? Was this my fault?

"Oww," I whimpered as Bobby forced a finger into my vagina.

"Shhh, it'll only hurt for a second. Then it'll feel good."

"No. Don't. It hurts."

I started squirming. Bobby pressed his weight on me and pinned me down with his sheer size.

"Just kiss me and I'll stop."

"What?"

"One kiss and I'll stop."

I thought *Gross! Kiss a boy?!*

But I was out of options unless I wanted to scream so Andrew would find us. I didn't want Andrew to see me like this so I puckered up and kissed Bobby's lips.

"No, a real kiss!"

He pressed his face to mine and tried to French kiss me. I clamped my mouth shut as Bobby licked my mouth, trying to force his tongue past my lips. It was like being kissed by a dog. But instead of smelling like dog drool, I was now covered in slime smelling like mayonnaise.

"Let me up! I'm going to be sick!"

I started dry heaving and Bobby rolled off me. I scrambled out from under the sheet and ran from the room into the bathroom, trying to fight back vomit for the second day in a row.

My vagina felt like something inside was on fire. There was also this weird pressure inside that felt like I had to pee, but I wasn't sure. Outside in the hall I could hear Andrew ask Bobby why we weren't hiding anymore.

"I don't know what happened. We had a great hiding place but suddenly Marie felt sick. It was probably the pizza you guys ate."

"I feel fine," Andrew replied.

"I'll check on Marie. Ask her what's wrong."

"Dude, she's in the bathroom! You can't go in there!"

"It'll be okay. I just want to check on her!"

I was on the toilet yelling, "Don't come in!"

Bobby opened the door. I jumped up and tried to pull my pants up but Bobby grabbed my hands.

"Are you okay?"

"No! It hurts!"

"Let me see."

"What? No!"

"Trust me. I just want to see. I'm sorry I hurt you. Just let me make sure nothing's wrong."

"It hurts inside. You can't see that."

"Let me make sure you're not bleeding."

He said all this as if I had a choice anyway. He was standing between me and the door.

"Just look at it. Don't touch it!"

"I won't touch it, I promise."

Bobby spun me around and bent me towards the toilet seat. I was looking in the toilet bowl water for any traces of blood or fire I might have peed out. Suddenly I felt something hard and hot poking me in the vagina. It was as if Satan was jabbing me in my privates with one of his pokers.

I tried to get up, but Bobby pushed me back down. I was struggling to keep from falling into the toilet while he was struggling to get inside me.

I rolled to the right figuring I'd rather smash my face on the tile floor than let this go on. My action caught Bobby off guard. He stumbled behind me and had to grab the wall and the toilet so he wouldn't fall over.

Once free of his grip, I lunged for the bathroom door and rolled into the hallway, landing on a surprised Andrew. I pulled up my twisted pants with one hand, wiping my tears with the other. Bobby had slammed the bathroom door shut behind me. Andrew asked what happened.

"Nothing," I said. "I just didn't want him to see me pee! It's private!"

I gathered my stuff and stood watch by the front door for Mom to pull up. I didn't blame Andrew, but I was glad he wasn't in my grade at school. I knew I couldn't be his friend anymore.

Being sexually abused forced me to further accept I was a girl. It's hard to pretend you don't have a vagina when there's burning, stabbing pain shooting through it for a day. I had never felt so feminine in my life or hated it more. I blamed the existence of my vagina for leading Bobby on. I blamed myself for not being able to do anything about it.

If I thought I was depressed before, then there were no words for the anguish I felt now. I imagine it's how a parent feels when they mourn the death of a child, except I was the mourner and the deceased at the same time.

My innocence was now completely dead, having died a twisted cruel death. My childhood met its end in silence. I buried it in an unmarked grave that received no flowers or mourners. The rest of the world kept carrying on as usual. No one noticed, and I didn't want to share.

An Unmarked Grave

The Garden School

By Betsie

"Hey Sweetie, how was your day?" I asked Marie as I reached the top of Dianna's stairs.

"Fine. I want to leave. Can we please get going?"

Marie picked up her backpack and ran down the stairs.

"I'll be right down. Thanks again, Dianna. See you next week."

Dodging the rain drops, I quickly opened the car door and asked, "Why are you in such a hurry? What's going on?"

"I never want to go back there again. Please, please don't make me go back," Marie begged.

"Did something happen? Was Andrew mean to you? Did Dianna do anything to you?"

"No, I just can't go back."

Marie was scared. Something happened but she wouldn't confide in me. Andrew was her best friend. Dianna had become my close friend. The more I attempted to get answers, the more she withdrew. I just hoped over time she would let me know.

I called my sister for help.

"Louise, I hate to ask, but can Marie come to your house after school for a few weeks? Something happened at Andrew's and I don't dare send her back. I wouldn't ask but I have nowhere else to turn."

"Okay, we'll see how things go. I'm sure Ellen won't have a problem watching her as long as she promises not to run away again. Do you know what happened at Andrew's?"

"No, but she's afraid of something. She just won't tell me."

I spent the next few days calling local afterschool programs only to be told time and time again "Sorry, we have no openings." Frustrated, I broadened my search and started looking at other towns. I spotted an ad for The Garden School. They were a full time private school but also had an afterschool program. It said they had a bus to pick kids up after their regular school hours and bring them to The Garden School's afterschool program. I gave them a call.

"We don't usually pick kids up that far way," Mr. Gary one of the co-owners told me. "We would be willing to make an exception if you're willing to send Marie to our summer program."

Feeling as though I had no other options, I agreed to their terms. Heaven only knew how I was going to pay for this. The following week we visited the school.

The Garden School was a little bit further than I thought, and we were running a little late. Mr. Gary met us at the door and gave us a tour of the building. Everywhere we looked, kids were busy and laughing. As we turned the corner Marie's face lit up.

"Mom, do you see the swimming pool? Do the kids swim all year?" Marie asked excitedly.

"The kids go swimming once a week after school and then almost daily during the summer. They love it," Mr. Gary told us.

Marie was an excellent swimmer. The pool was all she needed to see. She would start in two weeks.

Marie had been attending The Garden School's afterschool program for about a month. Things were finally settling down when I received a call from her regular school.

"Mrs. Harvie, this is Cheryl from the principal's office. Is there any way you can stop by the school in the next few days? We need to speak with you."

Like everything else in my life, as I got one issue settled another one came along. I decided to stop in the following day to get whatever it was over with.

"Thanks for stopping by," Mr. Manning said meeting me at the door. "We know you moved to another town last year and have been driving Marie to school every morning. You do realize we don't participate in school choice. I'll let her finish out this year but unfortunately she can't attend the fourth grade here."

"But she just got accepted to your accelerated classes in the fall. This is exactly what she needs. We've waited years for this. You know her and what she's been through. There's no way she's ready to start another school. Isn't there anything we can do?"

"I'm sorry. My hands are tied. If it were up to me, I'd let her stay."

I knew writing to the school-board would be a long shot. But this was my daughter. I wanted something to go right. I wanted her to stay in a school where she was comfortable. Knowing they would do the right thing, I included transcripts from Boston Regional Medical Center. I poured my heart out. I made sure they were aware of the suicide attempt at the age of eight and how the teachers had worked with us to turn a bad situation around. Her physician wrote a note stating how imperative it was she be allowed to stay.

Their reply came quickly. I was met with closed ears, minds and doors. They would not budge on their policy.

Hearing Marie had been the first student accepted to the new accelerated program for the fourth grade gave us a thrilling ride to the top of this roller coaster. Having an uncaring school committee made us free-fall back to the bottom. Not wanting to deal with the sharp curves ahead, the only thing that made sense was to have Marie stay at The Garden School for the fourth grade. She had made a few friends in the afterschool program and was comfortable with the teachers. I called the school the following morning.

"Mr. Gary, is there any chance Marie can attend your school for the fourth grade?"

"Well, we don't pick up kids that far away for our school program."

"I could drop her off before I go to work. She already knows most of the kids and the teachers."

"As long as you can drive her, we would love to have her attend. Will you be able to afford the tuition?"

"Do you accept credit cards? I don't have that kind of cash," I said, feeling the dollar signs suffocating me.

"We do. It will be an easy transition for her and you already know about our curriculum and teaching methods."

When I picked Marie up after school I couldn't wait to ask her.

"So, do you think you would like to attend The Garden School for the fourth grade? The two Jennifers will be there. I think it would be a lot of fun."

"Do you mean it? I can go there all year? Wait till I tell the other kids," she replied with more excitement than I had heard in quite some time.

The Assault

It was after midnight when familiar sounds coming from Marie's bedroom woke me once again.

"Marie, why are you crying?" I asked my sleepy little girl.

"I had a bad dream."

"Do you want to tell me about it?"

"I can't remember. I just want to go back to sleep."

"Are you sure there isn't something going on? You've been having bad dreams for a few weeks now. This is not the first time you've awakened crying. You know our deal. If something is bothering you, you have to let me know."

"No. I just want to go back to bed."

"Maybe you can tell me in the morning. I'll stay here until you fall asleep."

Although Marie seemed happy with her new school and had made some friends, this wasn't the first time she had awakened with nightmares. I couldn't let this go on any longer. Maybe someone else could get her to talk.

About a week later, I couldn't believe I was driving to another therapy session. I thought those days were far behind us. Pulling into a parking space in this beautiful old part of town brought back memories of a high school student who believed she would conquer the world. Whatever happened to that young woman?

It was difficult writing all of Marie's history in the small amount of space given. I had just finished on the back side of the paper when the receptionist said they were ready.

The therapist's office was on the third floor of an old sea captain's house. I stood at the bottom of the beautiful, winding staircase, in awe at the amount of stairs I would have to climb.

"Come on Mom!" Marie called back as I stopped on the second floor landing to catch my breath.

It seemed like I hiked to the top of the Bunker Hill Monument before finally arriving on the third floor.

Meeting Gabrielle was a breath of fresh air. I liked her immediately. She was young and got down to Marie's level, mentally and physically. Although I was only allowed in the room for a short period of time, it seemed to me the first session went well. I was very encouraged.

A few weeks later I received a phone call from The Garden School.

"Mrs. Harvie, Marie has been crying again during school. I know she started seeing someone and thought you should know," Mr. Gary alerted me.

It had been about a year since Marie stopped going to Andrew's after school. She was now in the fourth grade. I don't remember exactly when the nightmares and crying started, but she was now crying in school. I couldn't take it any longer. When I picked her up from school,

I snapped. We were both settled in the car and driving home, when out of nowhere I yelled at her.

"Marie, I've had enough. You have to tell me why you're crying all the time. You need to trust me it will be okay. I can hear anything.

Just tell me!"

Without warning, Marie blurted out, "Bobby took advantage of me."

"What do you mean? Did he take something that belonged to you?"

With her head bent down and her hands over her mouth, she answered, "No, he touched me in my private place."

Jesus Christ!

Her words were like a hammer to glass. In that moment, I knew our lives had been shattered. Some fragments damaged beyond repair.

Knowing I had to get off the road, I quickly pulled into a nearby Walgreen's parking lot. Unfastening my seat belt, I leaned over and threw my arms around my little girl.

"I'm so sorry Honey, I'm so, so sorry," I said, trying to catch my breath.

Her beautiful brown eyes were red with tears.

Still looking down, she whispered, "Bobby attacked me when I went to use Dianna's bathroom. My pants were down. He came in and took off his pants. Mom, he touched my private parts. I didn't want to say anything because you and Dianna are friends. I didn't want to hurt you. That's why I couldn't go back to her house. I was so scared. Are you mad at me Mommy?"

I couldn't breathe. I couldn't think. I just held her tighter.

"Of course I'm not mad at you. Don't worry about Dianna and me."

My head started pounding. I had never felt so helpless.

"What the hell did Bobby do?" I asked.

"I don't want to talk about it."

"If you can't tell me, do you think you can tell Gabrielle?"

"I don't know."

With those few short words Marie shut down and became very quiet. She was not going to say another word. I drove through rush hour traffic telling her over and over again everything would be okay. When we arrived home I didn't remember how we got there.

I babbled at dinner, finding it impossible to stop asking questions to which there were no answers. All this time I knew something was wrong. But this never made my list of possibilities. We spent the rest of the night sitting quietly on the couch watching television.

When Marie was settled in bed, I told her, "You know Gabrielle needs to know about this. I'll go with you tomorrow. We'll tell her together. Your dad needs to know. I'll tell him as soon as he gets home."

"Okay," she sniffled.

"You let Mom and Dad take care of this. You did the right thing letting me know. Now, no more bad dreams. Bobby can't hurt you anymore. I'll stay right here until you fall asleep."

My faith in God shattered as I kissed Marie goodnight. I questioned His very existence. If this was another test, I failed miserably. Hadn't I been tested enough losing both parents at a young age? Hadn't Marie's knife episode and running away tested me? No more tests! No loving, caring God would let this happen to my little girl. I was tired of battling with my feelings. If I did believe in Him, I would have to hate Him. I was not prepared to hate God. Not believing was just easier.

Waiting for Brooks to come home, I felt like the space shuttle getting ready for launch. My body was filled with a nervous energy. How was I going to tell him? I paced from the bedroom to the kitchen, the kitchen to the living room and back to the bedroom.

The monumental weight of my anger, sadness, and guilt started slowing me down. Making my way to the kitchen table, I turned off the lights, put my head in my hands and sobbed.

As soon as I heard the living room door open, I yelled to Brooks almost hysterically.

"Hon, I need to talk with you!"

Turning on the kitchen lights, I motioned for him to take a seat.

"Marie finally told me what has been bothering her for the past few months. Do you remember the day I picked her up from Dianna's and she insisted she never go there again?"

"Did Andrew do something to her?" he asked, with an unfamiliar anger in his voice.

"No, I guess when Marie was in Dianna's bathroom, Bobby went in before she could get her pants up. She said he also pulled his pants down. At some point he touched her vagina. She won't tell me what that means. I can only imagine. That's all she told me and then stopped talking."

The shaking and tears I thought I had under control started again. The more questions Brooks had for me, the fewer answers I had.

"She didn't want to say anything because she didn't want to hurt me and Dianna. Why did I ever let her go to Andrew's?"

"You know we have to tell the police," Brooks said.

"I know, but I don't want them accusing us of putting words in her mouth. I think we should wait until she sees Gabrielle. I told Marie I would go in the room with her tomorrow while she tells her."

"I wish I could get my hands on that kid. I'd be in jail."

"He's only fifteen. I think the best we can hope for is three years," I said, wiping tears from my cheeks. "I'd like to know where the hell Dianna was and what the hell Bobby did to her!"

Around eleven pm, I checked on Marie one more time before turning on the television. My stomach was in knots. My brain hurt.

I kept thinking *"If I only hadn't let her go to Andrew's."*

I wished I could turn off the faucet but the washer was broken.

"Did you sleep any better last night, Honey?" I asked Marie as she shuffled down the hallway.

"I don't remember having any bad dreams. What did Dad say when you told him?"

"He's angry with Bobby. You have to know you did nothing wrong. I promise when we see Gabrielle tonight I'll be right there with you. Don't say anything at school. It's better the kids don't know."

"Hi, Dad," Marie said quietly. "Mom said she told you what happened. You aren't mad at me are you?"

"No, of course not," he said, giving her a hug. "It took a lot of courage to tell us. But like Mom said, don't say anything at school. Let us handle this."

"Okay."

Sitting in the parking lot at work, I tried to compose myself enough to walk into the building. Crying since dropping Marie off at school had left me with the hic-ups and a swollen face. I was a mess!

When I was asked why I was so upset it was difficult not to blurt it out. I wanted to discuss this with Gabrielle and the police before I was asked a lot of questions I couldn't answer. The day dragged on and on.

The conversation at dinner was strained as I struggled to find words to comfort my daughter.

"You know you're a very brave little girl. Everything will be okay. Bobby can't hurt you again."

I must have repeated those phrases a dozen times. I kept returning to that afternoon at Andrew's house while Marie kept changing the subject. She clearly did not want to discuss being molested.

As we sat there in the stillness I kept hearing my mother-in-law's voice when she told me, "You know you're not a very strong person physically or emotionally."

I'll have to prove her wrong, I thought.

Marie's silence was deafening during the drive to our appointment with Gabrielle. She was deep in thought. I was silent, realizing my words were not enough to help either of us.

As always, Marie was the first to reach the top of the third floor.

"Are you ready? Let's go," I said, finally reaching the top of the stairs.

"Marie and I have something to tell you. I'm going to try to remain quiet and let her do most of the talking," I said, barely able to get the words out.

When I get nervous I stutter and my face turns red. At that moment my face was scarlet.

Although Marie told Gabrielle everything she had previously told me, and then some, it was not enough for me to know what went on in that bathroom.

"I didn't want to call the police until you had a chance to speak with her," I told Gabrielle. "I'm calling them as soon as we get home. Is there anything else we should do?"

"No, you did the right thing. This is just the beginning though. You know it's going to get worse for all of you before this is over. I'll be here for Marie through all of it. She's going to need a good support system."

"Thanks, I'll keep you informed."

"I'll see you next week. In the meantime, call me with any concerns. Goodnight."

"You did a wonderful job, Sweetheart. Would you like to get a treat before going home?"

"Can I get a lemon-lime slushy?" Marie asked, as if I didn't see that coming.

Once I knew Marie was sleeping, I made the dreaded phone call to the police station. They informed me I had to contact the station in the town where the assault happened. Standing in the kitchen doorway, phone cord twirled in my fingers, I made the second call.

"I need to make a report of my child being molested a few months ago at a friend's house," I heard the words, not believing I was the one speaking them.

"How old is your daughter?"

"She's nine."

"Hold on. I'll have our officer in charge of juvenile affairs speak with you."

"Hello, this is Officer Randall. How may I help you?" a friendly voice answered back.

"This is Mrs. Harvie. My nine-year-old daughter was molested by a friend's step-son.

"Can you give me his name, address and phone number? Is your daughter able to speak with me tomorrow afternoon?"

Giving the officer as many details as I could, we set up the appointment for the following afternoon.

"Mrs. Harvie, don't call Bobby's mother. She may head him off, making it difficult for us to pick him up."

"I promise. Thanks. We'll see you tomorrow."

Sitting at the kitchen table with my head in my hands, I tried to grasp the meaning of the phone call I had made. This happened to other families, not mine. Sliding my elbows onto the cold glass-top table, I leaned over and rested my head on my hands, too distraught to cry. I stayed in that position for about an hour until Brooks got home from work.

"We have to go to the district attorney's office tomorrow and meet with a police officer and a special unit from the prosecutor's office," I whispered to Brooks. "They need to speak with Marie and see if there's enough information to arrest Bobby. I'll leave work early and pick her up from school. Someone has to keep working to pay our bills, so I'll take her myself."

"I think I should be there," Brooks answered back.

"I still have vacation days left. I can take them in hours if I want to. You'll miss too much pay. Besides, this is just the beginning."

When I went to bed I tried counting sheep but the big bad wolf kept dragging them away. When Mr. Wolf was finally apprehended I was able to fall into an agitated sleep. Bobby's grinning face kept creeping into my dreams as if to taunt me.

"Just you wait, you little bastard. I'm going to wipe that grin off your face!" I screamed in silence.

District Attorney's Office

Trying to find a parking space in the middle of the day in a busy downtown only added to my anxiety. I hoped Marie couldn't tell how my insides felt. Maybe she felt the same way. If she did, she wasn't showing it.

Checking in with the receptionist, we were told to take a seat in the business only, waiting room. Our anxiety was relieved a little as it became a game trying not to slip off the large, plastic seat cushions.

Hearing footsteps approaching the doorway, we looked up to see Officer Randall and Mrs. Dunn, a representative from the prosecutor's office, enter the waiting area together.

They introduced themselves.

Mrs. Dunn informed me, "Mrs. Harvie, I'm terribly sorry, but because of the sensitivity of this matter, Marie has to come with us by herself. Sometimes it's easier for the victim to talk if the parents aren't present in the room. I hope you understand."

"I do."

I turned to Marie to reassure her.

"I'll be right here, Sweetheart. Just tell them everything you've told us. Okay?"

Marie looked every bit her young age as she took Mrs. Dunn's hand and followed Officer Randall. The three of them disappeared behind closed doors.

My brain went into hiding as I stared out the second floor window to the busy street below. I wasn't aware of anything in motion except my gentle swaying as if holding my baby in my arms. Thirty minutes passed when the clicking sound of a door handle brought me out of my trance.

Mrs. Dunn was speaking to Marie.

"You did a great job. Don't be afraid of him anymore. He can't hurt you."

"Mrs. Harvie, you have a remarkable daughter. She was able to give us enough detail to arrest this kid. There's no way this didn't happen."

"Officer Randall will pick up Bobby tomorrow. What happened in that house constitutes rape."

Rape! Although I had known this all along, hearing the word spoken out loud confirmed my fears. As the room started spinning I reached for Marie, throwing my arm around her shoulder. I needed her near me as much as I needed her to support me. I could see Mrs. Dunn's lips moving but couldn't understand what she was saying. It took a minute for blood to return to my head.

"I'll set up an appointment for you to meet with an Assistant District Attorney," Mrs. Dunn continued. "Marie will be assigned a court advocate to help her through all of this. Are you okay?

Okay? No. I was not okay.

"I'm fine. This is a lot to take in. Is anyone going to tell me what happened in that house?"

"We can't because Marie is our client. It will depend on how much Marie wants to tell you and whether or not it goes to trial. Do you have any questions for me?"

"I guess not at this moment, but I'm sure I'll have plenty as we go along and all of this sinks in. Rape. I thought that's what you were going to say. But hearing it is difficult. Is there anything else we need to do?"

"My part is done for now. Someone else will contact you with the next appointment. You have a brave little girl."

After completing his paperwork, Officer Randall joined the conversation.

"I'm going to pick Bobby up at school tomorrow. This way we know where he is and we shouldn't have any problems. Again, don't contact his mother. I know this is difficult for you, but we want his arrest to go smoothly. I'll call you tomorrow when it is all over."

"What happens from there?" I asked.

"Bobby will be brought in and read the charges against him. The following morning he'll see a juvenile judge who'll set bail for him. Because of the rape charge, Bobby is entitled to a trial by jury. If he decides to go that route, I'll be there to testify on Marie's behalf. Otherwise I'm done. The courts will keep you updated from here. I'll call you tomorrow."

Officer Randall was late for another appointment. Checking his watch, he departed down the steps two stairs at a time.

"I'm so proud of you," I said, giving Marie another hug before heading down the stairs.

"You know Mom and Dad will help you through this. Gabrielle will be there for you. Anytime you want to talk, even in the middle of the night, we'll listen. It's getting late. Want to go to Pappa Gino's for pizza?"

With a faint smile, we headed for some comfort food.

Bobby's Arrest

I took up space at work the following day, but got very little accomplished. Watching the clock became my job. Ten am. Eleven am. One pm. Why was Officer Randall not calling me? When my phone finally rang, I hesitated answering it.

"Mrs. Harvie, it all went well. Bobby is at the police station with his dad and step-mom. He'll be let go tonight, but has to appear before a judge in the morning. At that time bail will be set. Please don't hesitate to give me a call if there is anything else I can do for you."

I thanked Officer Randall for all his help. What took seven hours to hear was over in thirty seconds.

"Don't cry. Just don't cry," I kept telling myself.

If I ran to the ladies room every time I felt like crying, I would have dug my own path in the carpet. Eventually the well would have to run dry.

This news did not make me as happy as I thought it would. Nothing was going to ease the pain I felt for my daughter.

Marie showed very little emotion when I told her Bobby had been picked up. I almost wished she would go back to crying. She was holding so much in.

The following day I was back at my desk and actually trying to get some work accomplished when my phone rang.

"Mrs. Harvie, this is Officer Randall. I have some bad news. Bobby didn't show up for his hearing this morning. I promise I'll do everything I can to find him. Do you think there's any possibility he'll go to your house?"

"Bobby doesn't know where we live. We moved two towns over. I doubt he'll find us. Marie has someone with her twenty-four hours a day. I think we'll be okay. What happens now?"

"We've issued an APB for his arrest. Not showing up for his hearing will weigh against him when he does go before a judge. Judges don't like this sort of thing. That's all I know for the moment. Again, I'll call you."

What the hell was going on? Now I had to play another waiting game.

Later that same day, Officer Randall called me again.

"I wanted you to know we picked up Bobby at a friend's house. This time he was not released to his parents. He'll be before the judge in the morning."

"Thanks," was all I could manage.

That night, just after tucking Marie into bed, my phone rang.

"Hi, Betsie. This is Dianna. Do you have a minute?"

"Of course," I said.

"I wanted to tell you how sorry I am you and Marie have to go through all of this. We're not going to bail Bobby out of juvenile. He's been a real trouble maker at home this year. A few months ago he stole a leather jacket from Filene's and was let off real easy. Not this time. I've even been afraid to be alone in the house with him. We wanted you to know we'll support Marie."

Kicking the trash can out of my way, I leaned against the wall and then sank to the floor.

"I'm so sorry I couldn't call you. The police and the prosecutor's office told me not to have any contact with you. I feel terrible for you and your husband."

"I know you can't talk with me. I just wanted you to know I'm on your side."

"It's going to be a long haul for all of us. Dianna, thanks so much. You take care."

I pulled my legs to my chest and cowered in the corner. I wished I could fast forward life and have all this in my past.

I was worn out physically and mentally. There were not enough hours in the day to get everything accomplished. We still had to meet with the Assistant D.A. and Marie still had her therapy sessions. It wasn't just all the running around; getting Marie to school fifteen miles away, getting to work on time, picking Marie up from school, and getting her to therapy. It was the constant nagging, knowing something happened in that bathroom that would forever change my little girl's life. I gently sobbed into my knees.

The Assistant D.A.

Marie, Brooks and I found our way into the courthouse to meet the Assistant District Attorney assigned to our case. Our nerves were growing as we waited an hour while he enjoyed his liquid lunch at the local watering hole. Standing together in the hallway, Marie and I watched in horror as this large, overweight man staggered towards us. Using his cane for balance, he was trying not to walk into the wall.

I had to step back from his alcohol breath as he introduced himself. We made our introductions short while he jotted down some notes.

"Let's go see the courtroom so Marie will be familiar with it in case we go trial," he said with a slight slur of words.

Walking down the steps sideways one at a time, he only made it to the first floor landing, too drunk to go any further.

"My arthritis you know," I heard him say as I looked back to see him leaning against the wall. "You two go ahead."

Holding Marie's hand, we completed our walk down the two flights of stairs. Opening the door we found a very large, cold, dark courtroom. This was real. We were not actors in a television show. The feeling of intimidation was overwhelming. Too panic-stricken to actually walk in, after about a minute we turned around and walked back up the stairs to our waiting drunk.

"When do we get assigned an advocate?" I asked, hoping we would not have to deal with this intoxicated ass again.

"You'll get to meet her in a few weeks. She's finishing up a case and couldn't be with us today."

"We're looking forward to meeting her. If I have any further questions, I'll save them for our next meeting."

"See you in a few weeks," he said as we turned to leave.

"Not if I can help it," I said under my breath.

There was no way this drunk was going to represent us in court.

A few nights later I was up late watching Paul Newman play an intoxicated attorney in the movie *The Verdict*. Marie woke up as she often did and cuddled up with me on the couch.

"Mom, are all attorneys drunk?" she asked.

"No, Honey. This is just a movie."

"Our attorney was drunk."

"I know. But I'm sure our next one won't be."

Marie eventually fell asleep. I finished watching the movie. In the end, Paul Newman's character may have redeemed himself, but I wasn't about to allow our assigned drunk another chance.

When our advocate called the following week I let her know how totally disgusted we were with the Assistant D.A.

"I'm sorry, Mrs. Harvie. Everyone knows he has a drinking problem, but he has seniority, and they won't let him go," Susan replied.

"That's not my problem. I won't deal with him. I'm anxious to meet you, but I want someone else representing us."

"I'll see what I can do. I've set up an appointment with you for next Thursday. Will that be a problem?"

"No. My boss is great and has given me all the time I need. Thanks for your help."

Having Susan as our court appointed advocate was a blessing. She was able to bring us back into the courtroom and explained how everything would go if the case went to trial. Thanks to her, our next

Assistant D.A. was young, well dressed and professional. He put us at ease.

The Victim Has No Rights

It took months before we heard from our advocate again. Marie completed the fourth grade at The Garden School and stayed for another summer. She was now in fifth grade at the public school.

Bobby's date to appear before the judge had been set. It would be a closed hearing. Gabrielle wouldn't be allowed to be there for Marie. Officer Randall would testify for us. Bobby was going to proceed with a trial by jury.

I knew Bobby wasn't doing this for himself. He was trying to punish Marie for speaking up. The more difficult he would make this, the more we would have to fight back.

We were asked to show up at the courthouse at nine am. The hearing would be at ten. Of course, in the world of the legal system nothing goes as planned.

Making Marie, Brooks, and me sit in the hallway outside the courtroom across from Dianna and her husband was a nightmare. Dianna and I had become enemies through no fault of our own. We were each too afraid to make eye contact with one another. Instead we spent most of our time searching the floor for answers. We found none.

Brooks couldn't hold in his anger and seemed to want to pick a fight. He yelled across the hallway at Bobby's dad.

"Do you have any idea what that fucked up kid of yours has done to my daughter?"

Bobby's dad never even looked up.

"Look, Brooks, we're all suffering," were the only words Dianna spoke.

A long, unsettling hour went by before our advocate showed up. She quickly moved us into another room so we could relax a little and go over the proceedings one more time.

"Sorry I'm so late," the Assistant D.A. said. "Bobby is still going for a trial by jury. His attorney and I have been talking. We're trying to get him to plead to a lesser charge so a rape conviction doesn't appear on his record. Because of his age, both charges would carry the same sentence. He would be in juvenile until the age of eighteen."

"What is the lesser charge?" I asked.

"Indecent assault."

"And it puts him away for the same amount of time?"

"That's right. His attorney is speaking to his parents right now to see if they can convince him. I also have to make sure it's okay with you. It would keep Marie off the witness stand."

Marie, Brooks, and I all agreed.

"Well, we have to go. They're calling our case. Now remember, let me do all the talking."

Entering the courtroom, I spotted Bobby's parents seated on the opposite side of the aisle. My doctor had put me on a mild tranquilizer to help me through this, but my pounding heart hadn't gotten the message. We took our seats.

Juvenile court was called into session. The clerk read the charges out loud. Bobby's attorney stood to address the court.

"Your honor, my client is not present. No one went to detention to pick him up."

What a freaking circus! The defendant wasn't even present. The angry ringmaster gave the clown one hour to produce him. We were dismissed for lunch.

Brooks was able to eat in any situation. Marie and I just picked at our food. As we approached the courthouse forty-five minutes later, we noticed the juvenile van parked in the driveway. In honor of attending this circus, my food started doing somersaults in my stomach.

Our attorney met us inside the doorway.

"I'm sorry. Bobby's father wasn't able to convince him to accept a plea. The only thing the judge will do today is set a date for the trial."

We took our seats in the same places as before. The door in the back of the courtroom opened and four teenage boys came in handcuffed together. Bobby's eyes met mine. The little bastard grinned just like in my nightmares! Maybe I couldn't wipe that grin off his face, but I was sure when the judge's gavel came down it would disappear.

It was difficult listening to the judge take his time explaining the charges to Bobby and making sure he understood them completely.

When asked if he still wanted to proceed with a trial by jury, Bobby answered "Yes."

Going through his calendar, the judge set a date for the trial.

Now I was willing to move mountains to be there for my daughter, but I was hoping our advocate could help me with the court date.

"I don't have any more vacation time. Today is my last day," I whispered in her ear. "Is there any way of getting that date changed?"

Our advocate stood to speak with the judge and explained my situation.

"Mrs. Harvie, you do understand you don't need to be here. Bobby is entitled to a swift trial," the judge told me.

You have got to be f'n kidding! **I didn't need to be present** *when my ten-year-old was questioned about being raped! I take back what I said about him being the ringmaster. He was the jackass in this circus. What was wrong with this situation? Where were Marie's rights? The defendant had been given the center ring in this show. The victim had been left on the sidelines like a spectator.*

I was too angry to give Bobby the satisfaction of seeing me have a nervous breakdown. From where we were sitting we could hear Bobby's attorney whispering to him, but couldn't make out what was being said. The judge was about the call the session over when Bobby's attorney stood to address the court.

"Your honor, Bobby has agreed to accept the charges of indecent assault and will forgo a trial by jury."

We were stunned. Bobby could have agreed to those charges weeks earlier but wanted to drag Marie through hell. He had succeeded.

The judge ordered him to juvenile until his eighteenth birthday. That wiped the grin off his face!

Follow Up:

Those two years of my life may be in the past, but even as I write this twenty-odd years later, they are never in the distant past.

Marie had been seeing Gabrielle for seven months when Bobby had his day in court. She continued seeing her for a few more weeks.

Dianna and I never spoke to one another again.

Marie was nine and in the third grade when Bobby raped her. She was ten in the fourth grade when she finally told us. By the time Bobby was sentenced, Marie was in the fifth grade. Because we never did go to trial, I never knew what happened in that bathroom until the writing of this book. It shook me to my core.

Two and a half years into Bobby's three year sentence, the day before Thanksgiving, I received a call from a representative within the juvenile court system.

"Mrs. Harvie, we want you to know Bobby is being released tomorrow. We need to know if you want to get a restraining order against him."

"I don't think Bobby would know how to find us. A restraining order might make things worse and we've all been through enough," I answered.

An Unmarked Grave

A Confusing Time

By Marie

I had a lot of friends during the fourth grade at The Garden School. For my birthday that year, my parents booked a couple of hotel rooms at the Marriot so I could have a pool party in January. It was over the top extravagant for someone who was turning ten. We pretty much took over the pool from the time we arrived until it closed at ten p.m. It was the most amazing party I had ever been to, and it had been for me! I felt like the luckiest kid alive.

This was so much different than being the ugly, unpopular girl the year before. I finally felt like I could be myself, which was liberating. It was also so different I almost didn't recognize myself. I was becoming a new person. I was strong, charismatic, popular, athletic, and funny. I finally had friends who saw me for who I was.

Years later I found out two of the boys who went to The Garden

School with me were flaming homosexuals (okay - we all had our suspicions at the time, but it was later confirmed). My three best female friends turned out to be lesbians. Maybe they intuitively saw who I really was with their budding gaydar. Whatever the reason, I found myself happily accepted. I loved it.

Two weeks later was Valentine's Day. I hated that holiday. I hated how I was going along, minding my own business, and suddenly these stupid crepe-paper hearts were everywhere. It reminded me no matter how much I thought I fit in, I was different. Not because I was ugly or weird, but because I was dirty. I was unclean. In my mind everything that had happened a year earlier with Bobby was my fault for putting myself in the situation. I let him do those things to me. Something like this never would have happened to my alter ego Frederick. I hated myself again.

I struggled to act normal. I'd be hanging out with my friends, listening to Michael Jackson or Kriss Kross, smoking cigarettes and trying to pretend everything was fine. But I was afraid any minute they'd smell the thick dirt caked up under my skin. I was becoming paranoid and having trouble sleeping. I started to cry whenever I was alone. Since I couldn't talk about what was wrong without implicating myself as a whore, I started trying to eat away my feelings. I quickly became fat and started hating myself for that too. Living with myself was becoming harder by the day.

It was a confusing time for me. I couldn't decide if I was a victim of sexual abuse or not. I wasn't even sure if I was still a virgin or not.

At first I hoped what Bobby had done didn't really count. Since I didn't aspire to wear a white wedding dress anyway, I kind of thought it didn't matter in the end. Now I viewed myself as damaged. Then again if something is ugly, does it matter if you break it? I guess it didn't matter too much, but it still hurt.

I couldn't let go of the idea if I had been born a boy like I knew I was supposed to have been, then no one would ever have taken advantage of me the way Bobby did. If I were a boy, I would have been stronger, less naïve, more popular at my old school, less weird and depressed. If I were a boy, I would have been happy.

It's so frustrating to have a problem and know the solution yet understand the answer isn't a viable choice. I wanted to scream, and sometimes I did. I wanted to fight, and sometimes I did that too. Certain adults started accusing me of being a selfish, spoiled brat. I had everything a kid could want; a loving mom, roof over my head, good school, lots of friends, and an expensive birthday party. To them I showed my appreciation by throwing fits and acting up. Mom was always quick to defend me though. She never gave up believing there was a reason for my behavior other than me just being rotten.

I started seeing yet another counselor. If you included school counselors and therapists, this was the fifth person assigned to me long-term. Gabrielle was probably the coolest of them all. She was sort of young and hip. I'd complain to her about Dad or whatever else was bothering me that day. But I never opened up about myself. I was adept at throwing out crumbs to keep people busy or distracted any time they tried to analyze me.

The only time I had heard the term "transsexual" was in a line from the *Rocky Horror Picture Show* and I didn't really understand it. However, I had recently seen a movie on the *Lifetime* channel about a teenage girl who was in love with another teenage girl. She was a lesbian. The kids at her high school and her parents gave her hell about it. Her mother cried for half the movie. This was inspirational and frightening. When it came to crushes, I had always had them on other girls. I never said it out loud or acted on it for fear of being laughed at and simultaneously beaten to death. Now here was someone on television with a similar situation. I still felt I was meant to be a boy. But the idea I might be gay was sprouting in my mind. At least being gay would be a verbal identity. I wouldn't have to be alone anymore. I knew other gays would be few and far between but at least they were out there.

Seeing the reaction of the television family toward their gay daughter distressed me. I didn't want Mom to hate me or be ashamed of me. I was barely ten. On top of being ugly, gay, and damaged, how could I survive without Mom's love? All my friends and the rest of my family would surely turn their back on me if they found out I was gay.

These were big questions. I felt I had no one I could trust to ask. The consequences were too dire to risk asking the wrong person. I was trying to handle my feelings of being abused, feeling unworthy of friendship or love, self disgust and loathing, and identity crisis. I had an immense fear of being ousted from my family and home if any of these things were to be revealed.

The anxiety was causing me to have extreme stomach pains. It hurt so much I even had to have an ultrasound. In the end my pain was attributed to nerves. I knew that would be the outcome. I was still trying to be covert about my problems and my stress. I secretly hoped they would find a cancerous tumor to deflect attention from my mental distress, but no such luck.

I started to crack under the pressure. I was caught crying more and more often by my teachers at school or Mom at home. I was being sloppy, but I was too tired to do better. Finally one afternoon Mom had me pinned in the car and kept at me for an explanation. I was so exasperated I almost blurted out 'I think I'm gay!' but at the last second my brain's self preservation mode kicked in. I said I was sexually abused instead. I knew this would have big consequences but at least no one would throw me out on the street or stop loving me.

Mom was very worried about me. I felt guilty about upsetting her. The next few days she was tightly wound. Her eyes were constantly red, her cheeks puffy and she was overly attentive. She was brimming with nervous energy. I knew I should have kept my big mouth shut.

Mom made me promise to tell Gabrielle what Bobby had done. I didn't give her many details and I certainly left out what I felt was my part of compliance in the encounter. Everyone assumed I was a victim. I didn't protest. The way everyone took to the news of my being sexually abused was kind of like watching sharks feed. I had provided the adults in my life the tiniest scrap of a scapegoat for my behavior. They tore at it in a feeding frenzy. I knew my secret identity crisis could be safe for years to come.

The way my family and teachers looked at me, and the hush when I entered a room, made me feel awful. I hated the attention. I hated how everyone knew one of my secrets. But I still managed to find relief in the hope maybe the rest of my secrets needn't ever be shared.

I was so sick of people telling me how brave I was; it was enough to make a person puke. If the praise wasn't lip service, it still wasn't deserved. If I had been brave, I would have done whatever it took to fight Bobby off of me or to hurt him back. I knew I wasn't brave. I had let myself be intimidated. Now I had to let myself be humiliated by telling strangers what happened to me.

The first were a pair of police officers from my home town. They came to my house to take my statement. I had to sit on my dead grandmother's yellow velvet sofa and tell a policewoman how I had let Bobby put his penis in my mouth and how he had hurt me in my privates.

The whole time I was talking, I could feel the dirt inside me making its way out through my pores and encrusting my skin. I should have felt lighter, as if I had a load off my mind or burden off my shoulders. Instead I felt heavier. Then the policewoman told me I was brave. I wanted to hit her across the face with a lamp.

When Bobby was arrested, I didn't feel any better. He went to the same high school as my cousins Will and Ellen. Bobby's girlfriend got in a fight with Ellen. The girlfriend told Ellen I had ruined Bobby's life. Ellen stood up for me. I was grateful, but I knew the situation was causing a lot of embarrassment and stress for my cousins in a very public forum. I felt devastatingly guilty about Will and Ellen having to bear the brunt of the gossip and angst unleashed because of me. I couldn't even rally the courage to tell my cousins I was sorry for what they were going through because they were related to me. It was too painful to admit aloud I understood what was going on. I hadn't told any of my friends. No one at my school knew what was going on.

Worse, I wondered if I really had ruined Bobby's life. I was very confused. Everyone I knew blamed Bobby for what happened. Bobby and his ilk blamed me. I didn't know who to blame. I think it's difficult for victims of abuse to navigate emotions of shame and guilt and try to suppress the intangible and utterly human desire to please everyone around us. It's what makes us such easy targets for manipulative predators.

Before Bobby was arrested, I had been interviewed by people from the Police Department and the D.A.'s office. It was sort of scary, having to talk about what happened in a cold room with a two-way mirror. Mom hadn't been allowed in the room. I was in an unfamiliar and uncomfortable setting having to tell strangers about the most frightening and intimate thing that ever happened to me. The police officer and attorney were very nice to me, but the experience left me feeling naked and ashamed.

I had expected meeting the Assistant D.A. representing me to be a similar experience. I was wrong. But I was justified in my suspicion it would suck. The courthouse seemed big and cold. It felt like a museum dedicated to the preservation of the *memory* of justice, rather than a place where justice was still actively served. The ceilings were enormous.

Everywhere we went, our shoes made clicking echoes on the stone floors. The attorney reminded me of Santa Claus if Santa wore a three piece suit, had a shorter beard and drank buttered rum instead of milk. I kept at least five feet between us lest his drunken ass should stumble and fall on me. He was supposed to be prepping me about courtroom etiquette and familiarizing me with the proceedings so I wouldn't be nervous or afraid when the day came. Instead he mumbled some incoherent nonsense and let Mom and me briefly explore an empty courtroom on our own. It wasn't a comforting experience.

By the time our day in juvenile court arrived, I had a court appointed advocate and a new attorney. The proceedings were scheduled for first thing in the morning, but nothing ever goes according to plan in a courthouse. All morning people were making phone calls and running around trying to get Bobby to plea to a lesser charge so I wouldn't have to testify in open court. I was too nauseous to eat and too antsy to read or do anything to pass the time. My advocate kept bringing me bottle after bottle of orange juice. It didn't mix well with the bile in my stomach.

Almost three hours after we had arrived, we were finally brought into a courtroom. I was terrified. When I looked around, the entire room was full of strangers except for Bobby's dad and stepmother.

I was afraid to have to get up in front of these people and talk about my sexual defilement. Strangely I didn't see Bobby. As it turned out, he wasn't there. No one remembered to bring him over from the detention center. Obviously, knowing such diligent and capable people were handling this delicate situation only strengthened my faith in the legal system (insert sarcasm here).

The court was adjourned for lunch. When we returned, Bobby was there, larger than life and grinning his ass off. He insisted that he wanted the whole thing to proceed with a trial by jury. I had been hoping this would all be concluded in one day. The judge came back with a date a few months out. I heard Mom whisper to my advocate she wouldn't be able to get any more time off from work. I was paralyzed with fear. The thought Mom wouldn't be by my side at a time when I was so vulnerable made the room spin and turn black around the edges.

The judge announced to Mom her presence wasn't required. His voice was totally void of any empathy. Now I knew why people kept telling me I was brave. When you're a victim, you have to subject yourself to such public degradation at the feet of people who have sworn oaths to uphold justice while they look on with tired indifference. I didn't know if I could continue this fight much longer.

Thankfully, at the last minute Bobby decided to plead no contest to the lesser charges. I felt relieved at avoiding having to testify. I didn't feel victorious. Sometimes even when you win, you don't. Bobby going to a juvenile detention center didn't undo what was done. He wasn't a Catholic priest so I didn't score a big payday. I was still hurt and confused and had to just keep moving forward with my head down and my mouth shut.

Navigating Murky Emotions

To this day I've never openly discussed my attack to a therapist or any kind of survivors group. I've never discussed the details with anyone in my family or my friends, not even my wife. I've never written down what happened to me or my feelings about it until this very moment.

Living my life now as a twenty-plus man, I feel uncomfortable trying to equate myself with other victims of sexual trauma. I don't think I'd fit in well with a men's group; at the time it happened I was a girl. I don't feel I'd fit in a women's group either.

Other than my parents, whom I definitely didn't feel comfortable discussing this with, I get the impression from the rest of my family if I tried to talk about it I'd just be complaining. That's how they've made me feel about any problem I had growing up. No one ever treated me as if something actually traumatic ever happened to me – as if I were a legitimate victim.

Yet I felt victimized. I felt damaged. It's a confusing way to feel when people keep telling you there's nothing wrong with you other than your attitude. Most of my pain and shame I've managed to shove down inside me for the past two decades. It surfaces sometimes. I keep it to myself and try to move forward.

It's ridiculous after seven years of marriage my wife will sometimes touch me or even just lean over me in a way that reminds me of Bobby and I'm too embarrassed to tell her. But there it is. She doesn't know why I'll suddenly lose interest in intimacy, start cracking jokes, or worse, picking fights. I suppose I'll have to tell her sometime. I just don't know where I'll find the words. I know she'll understand. I guess I'm afraid she'll look at me with pity.

Funny. I spent the first half of my life wishing people would be sympathetic toward me. Now it would injure my pride. The idea of someone feeling sorry for me fills me with sickness and rage. I actually feel sorrier for people who have to navigate my murky emotions than I do for myself.

Chapter Five

The Nightmare of Fifth Grade

By Betsie

Marie had a very difficult time transitioning into the fifth grade at our local school. The town was very small and the school had well defined cliques. They teased Marie for her short hair, choice of clothes and, of course, her weight.

My heart broke each day when she came home with new stories of being teased. One afternoon she called me at work so distraught she could barely speak. While riding the bus home, a student spit in her face. I immediately called the school principal. The following day the student was suspended from the bus for a week. However, the rest of my accusations always fell on deaf ears.

Marie became an emotional eater. Although we tried many diets, nothing worked. It was a vicious cycle. The kids would harass her for her weight; she would come home and consume more comfort food.

The principal and her teachers refused to admit they had a bullying problem, leaving me helpless in stopping her out of control, downward spiral.

The Nightmare of Fifth Grade

By Marie

Somewhere between giving my initial statement to the police about Bobby and the trial itself, I completed the fourth grade and had one of the best summers of my life. Then I was sent back to the public school in the town I actually lived in for fifth grade. Public school was horrible; a living nightmare. We lived in a small town where all the other kids had known each other since diapers. I was an interloper on their extremely cliquey turf.

I stood out for a number of reasons the other students were quick to remind me of at every opportunity. I was fat, my haircut was a boy's haircut and my clothes were ugly. I was ugly and poor. These kids all lived in very nice homes. Most of their moms didn't have to work and their parents were members of a country club. It was difficult for me to make friends. I terribly missed my old school and all of my old friends.

I was very naïve when it came to making friends. I'd never had a *frenemy* before. Usually if people didn't like me they were up front about it. They'd either call me names or hit me when a teacher wasn't looking. There were a few kids at this school, however, who pretended to like me. They would gain my confidence and learn things to use later and hurt me.

I had missed a few days of school leading up to the trial. Whenever I was asked about it I'd say I was sick or I didn't feel like talking about it. Unfortunately, I made the mistake of confiding in a classmate I thought was my friend. I told her about the trial. The next thing I knew I was out on the playground at recess and all the popular kids from my grade and the next grade up had me surrounded. They shouted things like "God, you're so ugly! Who would want to rape you? You're so fat you should have been grateful for the attention! You probably enjoyed it! You're the fattest whore I've ever seen!"

I tried hard not to cry in front of them. I didn't want to run away because I thought it would be undignified. I'd always been taught when you're being bullied and don't let them see they're bothering you they'll just leave you alone. But that's complete bullshit. If modern media has taught us anything, its bullies won't leave you alone until you kill yourself. And no, they don't mature when they grow up.

So I sat there like an idiot while over a dozen preteens screamed the most horrible things you can imagine at me. No other students or teachers came to my aid. I had to wait it out until the bell rang and it was time to go back in. Some of the kids lingered to throw mud and rocks at me.

I stayed outside, frozen to the spot in terror and shock. I willed myself not to cry. The effort made my breathing ragged and my body tremble. My pulse sped up. I could feel my face getting hot from my rising blood pressure. I tried to compose myself. Instead I slipped into a slightly catatonic state, staring at the clouds in the sky and losing track of time.

Eventually I made my way inside and upstairs to the nurse's office where I vomited profusely. I finally allowed myself to cry until Mom came and picked me up. I said I felt nauseous and my stomach hurt, which was true enough. I stayed home from school the next day. If it were possible, I would have stayed home the rest of the school year.

I can't count how many times I begged Mom not to send me back. At home I'd lock myself in my room and cry and cry, reliving all the hurtful things the other kids said or did to me during the day.

Mostly they'd call me fat, which I hated because it was true. They'd call me a loser or a dyke, too. In gym class I was always picked last. On team assignments no one wanted me in their group.

I had no friends to stick with for protection. I was pushed down the stairs twice and had my lunch stolen out of my desk. The sixth graders would kick me, punch me, spit on me, and tear up my homework on the bus. I was scared and miserable all the time.

The couple of friendships I did manage to start up were brief. Two girls who lived nearby tried to be my friend. They thought I was funny and kind of rebellious. Unfortunately, they came over my house after school too many times when Dad was home. He'd say creepy and inappropriate things to my friends about how they had pretty mouths or how nice and flat their stomachs were. He'd tell them they had good figures or they should be models. In hindsight I'm glad they had the self-esteem and wherewithal to understand the innuendos and walk away. Dad was scaring off my friends. After a while I stopped trying to make new ones.

I finished the fifth grade with fewer friends than when I started. I didn't see or talk to my friends from The Garden School. It was too difficult to maintain long-distance friendships. However, I was still very close to my best friends Jenny and Jen.

One afternoon Dad announced Jen's breasts were developing nicely. She asked Mom to drive her home. We never hung out again. That left Jenny. She spent the night at my house almost every weekend. She was my best and closest friend.

For every friend I lost, I think I gained at least one pound of body fat. I was becoming enormous. At barely five feet tall, I weighed between 150 – 160 pounds. I started getting little fat girl boobies. I hated them and I hated me.

Chapter Six

Gym Class

By Betsie

"Mrs. Harvie, you need to come and pick Marie up from school," the principal was telling me.

"What's wrong?" I nervously asked.

"She was in gym class and all of a sudden went into this sort of stupor. She won't talk to me or anyone else. She's sitting in my office with her jacket over her head and shaking. You need to come and get her."

By now I was a pro at dropping what I was doing and running to Marie's rescue. However, it never got any easier. I instantly became nauseous; the feeling of flying ants picnicking in my stomach.

I found Marie in the principal's office, sitting on a chair with her jacket over her head. She was trembling like someone fighting off chills associated with the flu

"She still refuses to talk," the principal said. "You can take her out to your car but she should take the jacket off her head. You don't want the kids to stare. Make it look like she just doesn't feel well."

Driving home I knew my life was about to go into a tail-spin once again. I kept thinking *Maybe Marie should be in therapy the rest of her life. Every time we stop, something else happens.*

As I sat on my bed leaning against the headboard, Marie lay across the bed, resting her head on my lap. Her constant trembling had calmed down but at least once a minute her body would give a quick shake. I knew she had to get back into therapy. I was at my rope's end and this time I wanted someone willing to put a sixth grader on anti-depressants. We needed to try something different. Therapy alone never worked.

I called my insurance company demanding a referral to a pediatric psychiatrist.

Now I was the one shaking as I dialed the new phone number, only to be connected to an answering machine. Frustrated, I left a message conveying the urgency of my call.

Stroking Marie's hair, we silently stayed on my bed until we both fell asleep.

I jumped when the phone rang.

"Mrs. Harvie, this is Dr. Burke. I got your message."

"Thanks for calling me back. Before we go any further, I need to know if you work with adolescents and if anti-depressants work for kids."

"I only work with adolescents, but I do have to tell you, I hesitate putting them on any type of drug. I have time next week. Bring Marie in and let's see what's going on."

As I sat there staring into space I wondered, as Marie's mother, what was I not seeing? I thought we were close yet I felt as though I didn't know her at all. I also started questioning whether or not attending school was important. Marie's life was more valuable than learning the three R's. Maybe we should try something called home-schooling. How would I pull that off? There was no way I could stay home. We needed health insurance to help pay for therapy. Well that took all of three seconds to decide. Regretfully, I had to continue working, and Marie would have to go back to school.

The following day, Marie seemed to relax a little as I kept her home from school and I stayed home from work. It was Friday and we would have the weekend to further decompress. I wished she would tell me what frightened her so much in gym class, but she was barely speaking. Seeing her in this state was disturbing. As I tried my best to keep her occupied, my thoughts kept creeping back to the same thing. ***What the hell happened in that gym class!***

Without any answers, Monday came and it broke my heart to have to send her back to school. What would happen today? Would she be able to handle it? When would my work phone ring with bad news?

No phone calls. We both made it through the day.

Marie and I took an immediate dislike to Dr. Burke. He looked like a store mannequin with his black hair and mustache perfectly trimmed. His nails were impeccably manicured, and his posture was flawless as he sat in his overstuffed chair, clipboard in hand.

Robotic sounds came out from his lips when his mouth moved. He wanted to see Marie one more time before deciding to put her on any drugs. I was amazed. He had actually heard some of our concerns.

After the second visit, because of Marie's past, Dr. Burke agreed to put her on an anti-depressant. I was glad he was listening yet sad my twelve year old was going to be put on drugs. Drugs I had insisted on!

It only took a few months to realize the anti-depressants did little to affect Marie's mood swings. We agreed to take her off the drugs but continued with the therapy.

Then I heard the same dreaded words I had heard with Rick, "Mrs. Fish" and Gabrielle.

"Mr. and Mrs. Harvie, there isn't anything else I can do for Marie. It's time to stop therapy. Marie should be fine. I think this was a onetime episode."

This news was devastating. My hopes of finding answers to Marie's sadness were shattered. Once again, all this time had been wasted. Nothing had changed.

In a few months, Marie would be graduating elementary school and heading off to middle school. Would her problems get bigger the higher the grade level? I could hardly wait!

Sixteen years ago, in my quest to get answers, I repeatedly questioned Marie's teacher and the principal of the school. The answer was always the same. No one knew anything.

I begged Marie to tell me. At the time, it was too much for her.

Over the years, this would become another life experience faded into the background of everyday living.

I'm outraged knowing the gym teacher knew all along what happened that day. My daughter went through hell because the teacher didn't have the guts to speak up. I'd love to get her alone in that gym.

Gym Class

By Marie

Gym class was always a struggle. I was always picked last for every team, every sport, for two years straight. It hurt. Even if I managed to score a basket, goal, or point in whatever we were playing, my reluctant teammates would never congratulate me.

The worst gym classes were always the ones where you had to run a mile or do a bunch of sit ups and pull ups to see if you met federal fitness guidelines or some such bullshit. I couldn't run a mile. I couldn't do a single pull up. When the obstacle course came I knew I was going to embarrass myself in front of a crowded gymnasium. Part of my problem in gym was I never wore clothes that fit right. I was always trying to hide my fat rolls and boobies by wearing heavy dark clothes that were way too big for me. The other part of the equation was my now categorical obesity. I'd always gotten an A in gym class for effort. I figured I might as well try. Sure I'd have the slowest time out of everyone in the class. Sure all the kids would watch me and laugh at my fat jiggling the whole time. But I had to do it.

So with my adrenaline pumping, when the teacher blew her whistle, I took off at a sprint. I tripped over the first hurdle and belly flopped onto the hard gym floor, skidding to a stop on my face. God damn that hurt! Before the teacher could even ask if I was okay the room erupted into boisterous laughter. I rolled onto my side and through dusty tears I saw the entire class laughing at me. It was more than I could bear. My heart sunk so low it felt like it fell out of my ass. I'd never run away before when people made fun of me. I always stood my ground like a defiant criminal facing a firing squad with his chin up.

Not this time. I didn't run so much as limp, but I left the class and collapsed on a stairway in uncontrollable, hysterical sobs. It all came out. The anxiety and self-hatred I'd been bottling up for months. How could I let myself get so fat? How could I let people treat me this way? Why was I even here? Is this all there is to life? People putting you down at every turn. Teacher, principals, adults everywhere who look on, watching you drown in a sea of violence and hatred, without ever offering you a hand?

I refused to talk. I sat and cried until I ran out of tears. Then I sat and shook, my body heaving, not ready to accept that I couldn't cry anymore. The sadness in me was overwhelming. I was so alone. Everything seemed so bleak.

Mom picked me up from school. How embarrassing for her. Now I was going to be sent to see someone with a doctorate in psychology. Great. How could I be such a giant fuck up? A one person shit storm? I was only twelve years old for crying out loud!

Before I went to bed I prayed God wouldn't make me wake up ever again.

Chapter Seven

Space Camp

By Betsie

Letting Marie attend Space Camp was a double-edge sword. She wanted to go. I *didn't* want her to go. I tried to get caught up in her excitement but knowing her past made it difficult.

My nagging anxiety was constantly asking, *"What will happen if something goes wrong and she's in Huntsville, Alabama?"* I wouldn't be able to drop everything and run to her rescue.

Brooks kept telling me to stop worrying and let her have a good time. Although the reps from Space Camp and the escort service from the airline assured me Marie would be okay, it took months for me to make up my mind. With a great deal of hesitation, I put her on the plane at Logan Airport.

My week of peace and quiet had turned into a week of worrying and no sleep. I was glad it was finally over. Brooks and I were once again at Logan Airport. This time we were waiting for Marie's flight to arrive.

I nervously watched plane after plane land and thought *"Please, please, please, let this have been a good week."*

The ramp doors opened and there she was. Oh my God! Were my eyes playing tricks on me? What in the world was on her face?

A smile! Marie was beaming!

Not wanting to embarrass her, I quickly brushed away my warm tears of joy.

Marie was wearing the blue NASA flight suit she insisted on owning. It wasn't part of the original fees and I had to wire extra funds to Space Camp for her to purchase it. The smile on her face was worth every penny. There was a large medallion with a drawing of a space shuttle hanging around her neck. She looked like a very happy astronaut in training.

A crowd gathered as we hugged and kissed our junior astronaut. As the saying goes, "It was a *Kodak* moment."

On the way home Marie couldn't stop talking about the wonderful time she had. There had been no teasing, no bullying, no being picked last for a team. I listened to every word, even the ones repeated over and over again. I didn't want to miss a minute of it.

That night when I went to bed I put my worrying away until the next crisis.

Space Camp

By Marie

Going on anti-depressants wasn't as life changing as I'd hoped it would be. I thought I'd be happy or at least less anxious. I thought I'd have more energy too. I'd read in a magazine that some young adults on Zoloft lost weight as a side effect. I was hoping the same would happen to me. A little blue magic pill that could make me thin and happy. Yeah, right. Nothing changed for me except I gained even more weight.

The first time I actually felt happy all year was when I pestered my parents into sending me to Space Camp in Huntsville, Alabama during Spring Break. I don't remember how the idea even came to me, but once I saw the VHS tape they mailed me, I was obsessed with the notion of going.

It was a little scary going off on my own. That week there were over five hundred kids in Space Camp alone. There were also three levels of Space Academy and two Aviation Challenges on site at the same time. Altogether, there were about fifteen hundred kids running around the campus at any given time. That did not include the tourists and visitors for the attractions open to the public, and the giant staff. My mouth hung open the entire first day.

There weren't many other fat kids, but strangely enough no one gave me a hard time about being fat. No one picked on me for being ugly or weird either. I was nervous about having to sleep in a room full of girls on bunk beds. The last time this happened was three years earlier at the overnight summer camp where I had been picked on and beat up.

I woke up every morning at five a.m. so I could have the community showers to myself. I was nowhere near comfortable enough with my body to shower with other girls. Then I'd sneak back into bed and sleep another ninety minutes and get up with everyone else at seven a.m. The only other awkwardness all week was stopping by the nurse's station every morning to get my daily dose of prescription Zoloft before breakfast.

We did all kinds of awesome shit the entire week. Everyone on my team seemed so cool. They were all nice to me. No one ever told me to shut up or butt out if I tried to join a conversation. They listened to my input on group projects and laughed at all my jokes. I was having a ball.

At the end of the week we had a graduation ceremony in the morning for all the Space Camp attendees. My team won a special award for having the highest scores in all kinds of things. We also won a team spirit award for working together so well. I had never been part of a group that respected everyone so highly, including me.

The last award given out was for the Outstanding Trainee of the week. It only went to one attendee out of over five hundred kids. The person who was presenting the award gave a nice speech about how the recipient had been watched closely all week. Not only did this person excel in all the physical and academic challenges of the week, but he or she had gone above and beyond to coach their teammates about good citizenship, the importance of including everyone, and valuing what every team member could bring to the table. This person was instrumental in making their team perform together successfully.

Wow, I thought, *this person is probably on my team since we just won a team award.*

I was so busy looking around wondering who it could be I didn't hear the presenter announce my name. Then all I could hear was thunderous applause. I still didn't know who had won the award and was wondering why everyone on my team was looking at me. A counselor clapped me on the back and told me to go up to the stage and get the award.

What? I thought. *Are you crazy?*

Then I looked around. It slowly dawned on me all these people were clapping for me. Oh my God!

It was a long walk to the podium and people kept clapping the whole time. I had my picture taken by a professional photographer when I received the medal. It was surreal.

It may not sound like a big deal, but I'd never had this many people applaud me for anything before or since. It was also nice to be noticed for something real, something that mattered. It was genuine because I hadn't even known I was being watched. I was just being myself and apparently I kicked ass.

Chapter Eight

End of Sixth Grade

By Betsie

Wow! Marie had made it through sixth grade! A graduation dinner was coming up and she wanted no part of it.

"If you don't attend, you'll regret it later," I told her.

Was I telling her that for her sake or mine? Besides being proud of my daughter, we had been through a lot over the past five years and damn it, I deserved to celebrate!

Of course there had to be major drama as to what Marie would wear. I knew if she had it her way, she'd be wearing a shirt and tie. After quite a struggle we settled on a pair of skorts. Not quite shorts but not a skirt either. This outfit was the farthest from dressy. Not my choice.

The night of graduation arrived and the three of us left for the yacht club. Stepping inside the main ballroom it was hard not to miss all the girls wearing their pretty new dresses. Most of the boys were wearing jackets and ties. Marie stood out. I was just happy to be there.

Before dinner my attention was drawn to a commotion coming from the outside balcony. The boys were seeing who could spit the furthest. Marie was right there spitting with the best of them.

During the awards portion of the ceremony Marie was called up on stage three times. She received an award for being on the Student Council and one for the school newspaper. At the end of the evening Marie received a special award. She was one of two students who had achieved all A's on her report card from the second through sixth grades. An A in every subject, every quarter for five years. Even more of an accomplishment when you consider everything she had lived through over the past five years.

Brooks and I were very proud of our daughter. Regardless of her choice of attire, or the fact she had participated in a spitting contest, I was thrilled to be there with Marie, celebrating Marie.

End of Sixth Grade

By Marie

Sixth grade was coming to an end. At school there would be a chorus concert for the parents followed by the conclusion of the D.A.R.E. essay contest. In a couple of weeks there would be a graduation ceremony at the yacht club. And finally a school dance for all the graduating sixth graders in the tri-town area. Whoopity doo.

At the end of the D.A.R.E. program there was an essay writing contest. The grand prize was a $50 bond. I wrote an essay on the power of "NO" and how I carried this power inside me at all times. Naturally, I won the contest. Seriously though, if I could have spent that $50 on drugs or alcohol I would have. It's just so hard to make dealer contacts in elementary school.

I should have written an essay about how, if people were serious about stopping underage kids from self-medicating, they'd go after the root of the problem instead of chastising good kids who made bad decisions. If creative kids weren't systematically stifled or learning disabilities, domestic violence and bullying weren't ignored or swept under the rug, self-medicating wouldn't seem like the only solution for unbearable pain, boredom, depression and fear.

I absolutely did not want to go to my sixth grade commencement ceremony. I didn't care how many awards they were going to give me. There was no way in hell I was going to put on a dress. It would have been like putting a dress on a big ugly warthog. I wasn't girly. I wasn't pretty. I wasn't thin. My hair was short. I was the fourth tallest kid in the entire grade. I looked like a huge monster compared to the rest of my classmates. Putting on a dress would only exacerbate my flaws.

Mom insisted if I didn't go I'd regret it for the rest of my life. I didn't care. I could see though, this meant a lot to Mom. She was proud of me. God knows why, because I sure wasn't. You'd think she'd be as embarrassed to be seen with me in public as I was to be there. Love must really be blind. I owed Mom. She had done a lot for me and sacrificed a lot so I could have opportunities such as Space Camp. I had given her a lot of grief over the past few years and figured I owed her something to look forward to.

Mom took me shopping for something nice to wear to the ceremony. We had to shop in a women's plus size store. I hated my life. I chose something that looked like overalls with a multi colored pin striped button up shirt and a pair of sandals. I looked awful, but at least it wasn't a dress.

At the commencement my parents and I sat at a table with my buddy Pete, his parents, Pete's friend Steve and Steve's parents. Pete and Steve wore button up shirts with ties. They looked sharp. I looked like a dumpster with legs. I wished I could have dressed like them. I was so jealous. I did manage to have a good time despite my animosity toward most of the people there, and my outfit. I doubt I'd regret it if I hadn't gone, but I don't regret going either.

The dance was a big, scary deal. I had never been to a school dance before and this dance was for all the sixth graders of the tri-town schools. I wouldn't know over two thirds of the people in the room.

I had tons of apprehensions before I walked in, but oddly nothing bad happened to me. I wore a home-made tie-dye shirt and blue overalls which was appropriate because most of the other kids were dressed casually too. I spotted Pete and Steve and pretty much clung to them.

Thankfully no slow songs were played so I didn't have to feel bad about not being asked to dance a slow dance. I'm sure I would have felt worse if I had been picked. Slow dancing with a guy would have felt gay and awkward to me.

There was a lip syncing contest which Pete, Steve and I entered. We sang and danced to "Hakuna Matata" from the *Lion King*. I was Simba. We won first place but I attribute that to no students being allowed to vote, only teachers. I laughed a few times and went home unscathed. Not bad.

Chapter Nine

Middle School

By Betsie

My heart ached each morning as I watched Marie trudge along to the bus stop. With her head bent down she watched every step as though it would be her last. I knew she was miserable but I wanted her to try. I remembered how scared I was when I started middle school.

"*I got through it, so will she,*" I mistakenly thought.

Middle school came with a lot more homework than elementary school but with Marie's intelligence that shouldn't have been a problem. It was. She was having difficulty getting her homework done. It seemed as though she couldn't concentrate. This was not Marie!

Every time I tried talking to her she would insist things were fine. I walked a fine line between being helpful and nagging and I certainly wasn't being helpful. So I stopped nagging.

A month had gone by when I got a wakeup call as Marie tried to pass me in our small galley-like kitchen.

"Where did these bruises come from?" I asked, grabbing her arm.

"Kids push me into lockers and water fountains between classes."

"Why in the world are they doing that? Aren't any adults watching the hallways?"

"They don't care. Mom, I don't want to go back. The bus ride is hell. My day is hell. Please don't make me go back."

"You need to tell me what's going on or I can't help. I can call the school but I need to know what to say."

The conversation was getting loud.

"I'm just tired of being pushed around between classes."

"But you're still not telling me why you're being pushed around."

"I don't know! Maybe because I'm fat and have no friends!" Marie yelled back.

"I'll drive you in the morning if it makes your day any better," I said examining her arm. "But I don't like these bruises."

So I started driving Marie to school. But this was only part of the equation. What about the bullying? I called the school and spoke with the assistant principal.

"This is Mrs. Harvie. My daughter Marie has been coming home with bruises and says she's deliberately being pushed into lockers between classes. Don't you have adults watching these kids?"

"Mrs. Harvie, I'm sorry Marie is having a difficult time but we can't watch all the kids all the time."

"She has specific names."

"Unless we see it happen there's nothing we can do."

"You can't even talk with these kids?"

"I'm sorry."

Letting my anger get the best of me, I yelled into the phone.

"Well, I guess Marie will have to walk down the middle of the hallway and run like hell when the other kids approach."

I slammed down the receiver. What bullshit! This asshole wasn't even willing to listen. No wonder Marie didn't want to go back.

I continued driving her for the next few weeks, worrying from the time I dropped her off until I got home from work. That made for some very long days. I so desperately wanted to believe whatever she was going through was typical seventh grade stuff.

We were now about six weeks into the school year. That morning had started out like any other. Dropping her off at school I wished I could give her a hug, but God forbid. Twelve year olds did not hug their moms in public.

Just like always, I worried about her all day. How many lockers would she be pushed into today? Was any part of her day okay?

After speaking with Marie tonight I'll call the school again and ask for a person-to-person talk with the principal, I reasoned in my head.

When I arrived home from work I soon discovered how horrible and unordinary this day had been.

I opened the living room door as Marie ran past me to get to her bedroom. She was holding a green towel wrapped around her right wrist.

"Marie what are you doing?" I shouted before she had a chance to open her bedroom door.

Slowly walking back towards me, she un-wrapped her wrist.

"Jesus Christ, Marie. What have you done?" I screamed, dropping everything from my arms.

"I tried to cut my wrist. I guess I didn't do a very good job," she chuckled.

"Why on earth?"

"Because I'd rather be dead than go back to that school!" she yelled, pulling her arm away.

"Okay, I've had enough!" I yelled back, my anger not helping the situation.

I took a deep breath and attempted to calm down before I spoke again.

"We need to have your wrist looked at. I don't think it's too deep but we'll have it checked out."

I knew the cut wasn't too deep. However, I was so scared I didn't want her in the house. What would she do next?

I called Brooks and explained the situation. He would meet us at North Shore Children's Hospital.

It wasn't easy remaining calm as I drove the ten miles to the hospital. I knew there would be lots of questions. Questions that would be directed towards my parenting skills. Questions to which I had no specific answers. Would Marie have to spend time in a mental health facility? My nerves kept creeping closer to the surface.

"Why on earth did you do that?" I asked again, not able to keep my mouth shut.

"Mom, you don't get it. I've been trying to tell you for weeks. I can't go back there!"

"Okay, okay, I get it! You don't have to go back. Please promise me you won't do anything like this again."

"I can't."

"What the hell does that mean?"

"I don't know. I just can't promise," she said as I pulled into the hospital parking lot.

What the hell *did* that mean? Her comment scared me more than her cutting her wrist!

Thank God we were at the hospital.

As I had suspected, Marie's wrist was fine. But it wasn't Marie's wrist I was worried about.

There were so many intake questions.

"Has she ever done anything like this before? When? How? Has she been in therapy before? When? With who? What school does she attend? What grade?"

The questions went on and on.

"Why do you want to hurt yourself? Do your mom and dad mistreat you? Do any family members or friends touch you inappropriately?"

My head felt like a volcano. I wished it would erupt and let out some of the pressure.

The emergency psychologist was called in. Finally, someone who would listen!

With my brain ready to explode and all the commotion going on, I can't tell you a thing about this person. I know we discussed Marie's past in detail, and talked about having her admitted to a mental health facility. I remember him making call after call to see if he could find her a bed.

In the end, there were no juvenile beds anywhere in the states of Massachusetts, New Hampshire, or Rhode Island.

"It's so sad," I said to Brooks. "I thought our daughter was the only one who had these problems."

Marie was admitted to North Shore Children's Hospital under a suicide watch. This wasn't something the hospital usually did, and they were not equipped to handle it. We had to wait until they could find an overnight nurse who would sit in Marie's room with her for the night.

It was past midnight when I gave my daughter a kiss goodnight. I was sure she was as scared as I was thinking about what the next day would bring.

Brooks and I had arrived in separate cars so I had a quiet half hour drive home by myself. My brain was too fried to think of anything but the driving. Once we did arrive home, we did very little talking.

The room started spinning when I finally climbed into bed and I actually fell into a deep sleep. The morning came all too soon.

Brooks and I drove to the hospital together, completely expecting Marie to be transferred to a juvenile facility. Instead, to our disbelief, she was released back to our care. They still couldn't find her a bed. The hospital didn't want her going to an adult facility and our insurance wouldn't cover another night in the hospital.

No one had freakin listened!

My life felt like a board game. I kept rolling the dice, moved a few squares forward, received no help and was sent back to start over. I never collected the $200.00 or a free pass to get out of jail. I kept taking "chances" only to pull the wrong card.

"I want to see Marie in my office first thing in the morning," the psychologist said. "If you have any issues tonight, don't hesitate to bring her here or call 911."

"I guess I can sleep in her room tonight, but what about the future? Do you think it's safe to bring her home? This can't keep going on."

"Let's take it one step at a time."

This was so frustrating. One step at a time. That's what we had been doing for the past five years. Couldn't we just for once take three steps into the future and get some answers? Was it wrong of me not to want to bring Marie home? Obviously I was failing as a parent. Now the system was failing her as well. What good would bringing her home do?

But by mid-morning there we were, leaving the hospital and bringing Marie with us.

I was anxious all day and couldn't let Marie out of my sight, not even to use the bathroom. I had to stand outside the bathroom door.

Now that I had promised her she didn't have to return to middle school, what in the world was I going to do? I called the school and made an appointment for me to see the principal that very afternoon. Brooks stayed home with Marie.

I found this principal arrogant and useless. He would make no concessions to keep my daughter safe. Not even after a suicide attempt. He then went on to tell me Marie was a trouble maker and had been making threatening phone calls to one of her class mates. So, my appointment really had nothing to do with Marie cutting herself. No wonder I got in to see him so quickly. This was the first I had heard of these accusations, and didn't believe them for a minute. When I asked for more details he said they were confidential.

You've got to be kidding! You're going to accuse my child of something and then not provide any details? No names. Dates. Anything! My guess was it was the other way around and the other student spoke up first to head the blame in another direction. After about fifteen minutes, I walked out of his office even more disillusioned than when I walked in.

As soon as I arrived home, I had to find out the truth about the phone calls.

"Marie, the principal told me you've been making threatening phone calls to one of your class-mates. Is this true?"

"She wouldn't leave me alone. I told her I was going to tell her boyfriend the two of were together. She freaked out. Let's just say she started it and I finished it."

"Okay, this is a lot to process. I don't know what we're going to do about school. The principal said you can't go back until this mess is straightened out. Next week I'll look into other options. I'm doing all I can. Will you promise me you won't hurt yourself?"

"If I don't ever have to go back to that school, then I promise."

My brain constantly felt like it was working overtime. I swear, even in my sleep I was trying to figure this mess out. I knew we had to put Marie back into a private school but where? I didn't know of any private middle schools.

Maybe I'd just run away.

Middle School

By Marie

(Mom, sorry if some of this surprises you.)

I was hopeful the Tri-Town dance at the end of sixth grade was an indication of what to expect at middle school. It wasn't.

The campus was so large I got lost daily during my first two weeks. My locker was so far away from my classes, and the time in-between so short, I had to carry all my books with me all the time. The bag must have weighed forty pounds.

In gym class you were expected to change into a gym outfit in the locker room. You'd think being in an all-girls locker room would be exciting for someone who's attracted to girls. It wasn't. It was scary. No one looked like me. The other students were comfortable with their bodies. I didn't dare look at another girl in the locker room. I was already labeled a dyke before going in. I was afraid if I even looked up to see which locker was mine I'd be crucified. The first week I "forgot" my gym clothes. After that I skulked around the hallways during gym period and never went back.

At first things didn't seem so bad. Other than being called a fat dyke in the hallways I was kind of left alone. I didn't have any classes with anyone I knew from sixth grade so I sort of had a fresh start. Lonely but fresh.

Then something changed. In computer class I was assigned a seat next to a really pretty and popular girl named Jessica. I thought she'd be mean to me, but every time I said a curse word under my breath or reacted sarcastically to something the teacher said, she giggled. I liked the sound of her giggling so I tried harder to crack jokes or offer up my witty insights on things and she'd laugh even more.

I saw her in the hall one day between classes and she passed me a note. It was a full page long. I wrote her a note back and the next day she gave me a three page letter that I read during Spanish class instead of learning to conjugate verbs. The letter didn't contain anything emotional. It was more like a one sided conversation. She wrote about her day, what she liked or didn't like about certain classes, what TV shows she watched the night before and whatever else crossed her mind. It was flattering to think as she wrote all this, she was thinking about me. Thinking about how I'd react or reply to her thoughts. Within days I had developed a pretty big crush. I was also failing Spanish.

Except for computer class and note passing, Jessica and I didn't talk much. Her friends and boyfriend were at the top of the popularity pyramid so it would be utterly inappropriate for us to associate together in public view. We had both openly conceded this to one another. I made Jessica a mix tape of music to listen to on her walkman so she could think of me when we weren't together. To my astonishment not only did she listen to it, she gave me her phone number.

After school we'd talk on the phone for hours. I was falling behind in a lot of my homework. One day on the phone Jessica asked me if I was gay. She said a lot of people were saying that about me. I could have denied it. Hell, I could have just told her I was gay. But I wasn't gay. I had never even heard the term transgendered before and I didn't understand what a transsexual was. So I told her a lie with some partial truth in it. I told Jessica I had been born a hermaphrodite and my parents had decided I should be a girl, but when I turned eighteen I was going to have surgery to fix it because I should have been a boy. That was a big lie. But it was the only thing I could think of that had some medical validity so I wouldn't sound crazy. To my amazement not only did Jessica buy it, she thanked me for telling her. Then she asked me what my name would be after I had the surgery. Mom had told me if I had been born a boy my name would have been Frederick Brooks. I decided Frederick was too old fashioned and Brooks was too girly. So I shortened Brooks to Brock and told Jessica that's what my name would be. She said she thought I'd be a cute guy.

Then things got weird. The next day at school I was hiding in the library during recess as usual. I was standing in front of a big window watching the gray clouds and rain outside and enjoying the musty smell of the encyclopedias next to me. Jessica came up behind me and whispered, "Brock."

I turned around and she smiled.

"I wanted to be the first to see you respond to your real name."

She hugged me and ran her fingers through my short hair. Then the bell rang and she left. I felt so happy it was like my insides had melted to goo. I had the worst nervous pains in my stomach and I could hardly breathe, but I couldn't stop smiling, either.

At lunch, Jessica and her friends had started sitting at the table behind where my sort of friends, the nerds and geeks, and I sat. I was afraid to look up from my food because making eye contact with popular kids was a death wish, but I kept catching Jessica glancing at me. I knew this was why they were all suddenly sitting there.

The next day Jessica caught up to me in the halls before computer class and grabbed my hand. We held hands between classes the rest of the week. Then things got complicated.

Jessica's boyfriend Kevin had been following her around and had seen us holding hands. He was furious. Jessica called me on the phone crying and said we couldn't be near one another in school anymore. Her boyfriend was jealous and scared her, but she couldn't break up with him because she was afraid of what the fallout would do to her reputation.

Fortunately for me, her boyfriend was smaller than I was and not much of a physical threat. Unfortunately, he had many friends, some of them larger than me. I started getting pushed into lockers and shoved against drinking fountains by Kevin's friends. A few times I had tried to go to the bathroom during class and Kevin and two or three other guys had been in the hallway waiting for me. He was stalking me and having his friends kick my ass. I started not using the restroom all day, holding it for upwards of six hours until I got home. It was distracting and painful.

At lunch Kevin and his friends started throwing food at me. Jessica wouldn't even look at me anymore. She asked the teacher to re-assign her seat in computer class so she wouldn't have to sit next to me.

Then one night, she called me crying again. She told me she had told Kevin about me being Brock. She kept apologizing over and over. Apparently he had been badgering her about what was up with me and wouldn't let it drop. He had threatened her, so she told him. I freaked out. *Really freaked out.* I screamed things at Jessica like "How could you?" "I can't ever go back to school now!" "I'm going to have to kill myself and it's all your fault!"

I hung up the phone and looked around the kitchen to see what we had for pills. I settled on Advil and took about twenty of them. Then I went back into my room and pulled out an X-acto knife meant for art projects, and tested how deep I could press the thin blade into my wrist.

Jessica's mother phoned our house. She said Jessica was hysterical and wanted to know what I had said to her. That's when Mom found me.

I spent the night in a children's hospital under a twenty-four hour suicide watch. I couldn't wear my own clothes. I had to wear a hospital gown so I couldn't hide things in my pockets. I couldn't even use the restroom unless I kept the door open. The next day I was released back to my parents because there wasn't a single bed available in an adolescent mental health unit for 100 miles.

There was no fucking way I was copping to what had actually happened between Jessica and me. Apparently she wasn't telling the truth either. The junior high principal and vice principal were adamant I not return to school. I felt the same, so I kept my mouth shut. I wasn't expelled, just strongly urged to leave. Cool. If I hadn't been so depressed and confused about what had happened with Jessica I probably would have been thrilled. Instead I was embarrassed and relieved.

Chapter Ten

Washington Street School

By Betsie

Well I guess I had overreacted to Marie cutting her wrist. At least that's what everyone was saying. My family wanted no part of discussing it. They felt Marie was just throwing a tantrum and getting her way. "You know she was trying to get attention," they were saying. And once again Marie convinced her therapist if she could change schools, she would be fine. He bought it. I didn't know why. Was it because she hadn't cut her wrist deeply enough?

But what if I had not come home when I did? Would she have gotten the knife down to a vein? Would I have found her bleeding to death? None of this mattered. I had overreacted.

So now I had the task of finding Marie a middle school. The majority of the schools were K – sixth grade. However, there was one that jumped out, K – eighth grade. It wasn't the distance that grabbed my attention. It's what the ad said. *"We demand respect from our students."* Just what I was looking for!

It was Saturday but Marie and I couldn't wait to check it out. With a high level of excitement, we took a ride to find the school.

"Well, this should be the place," I said to Marie.

We were both looking around but saw no indication of a school. In my pacing, I must have walked past the hidden door with the small sign on it four or five times before noticing it.

"This is a funny place for a school," I said, taking a few steps back and looking up. "The school is upstairs over the restaurant. I'll call them on Monday, and if the cost is reasonable, hopefully we can come back for a visit."

"Mom, why can't I stay home? You could get all the books and teach me."

"Because I'm not a teacher. Besides, you need to be around other kids."

"Okay, I just know we already have a lot of bills."

"You let me worry about the bills. While we're here, why don't we get some lunch?"

I called The Washington Street School and found out it was run by two women.

"I'm looking for a place where my daughter can learn and feel safe," I said.

"Mrs. Harvie, we don't tolerate bullies. The students don't have to be the best of friends but they do have to respect one another. Academically we challenge the kids. They're expected to do a lot of extra work."

I liked this already.

We discussed the fees and they were agreeable. Well, I guess they had to be. I had no choice. Although the school was already six weeks into the semester, they agreed to give Marie a trial period. That's all I could have asked for.

"Come in when you get out of work tomorrow. Someone is always here. I think you'll be very impressed."

Could she sense the smile on my face?

"Thanks, see you tomorrow."

I immediately called Marie. This was the first time in days we had left her alone and I had been a nervous wreck. I could call her now to say it was to give her information but actually it was to check up on her.

"Well, we're going to visit the school tomorrow. The woman I spoke with said they don't tolerate bullies. You won't have to make a lot of friends but you won't be coming home with bruises either."

Over dinner, we discussed this new possibility. The more we talked about it, the more excited Marie became. I felt this school would give us both a new beginning. She would get the education she deserved and I could stop worrying about the trouble she could get into after school.

That night the sleeping dragon didn't stir. There was nothing breathing fire down my neck. Unfortunately, the dragon was only sleeping and would have to come out of its slumber sooner or later.

The following day Marie and I went to visit the school.

"Hi, I'm Miss Elizabeth, one of the co-owners. You must be Mrs. Harvie and Marie. Come on, I'll show you around."

Marie and I followed Miss Elizabeth around the large, open room as she showed us where each subject was taught. There were no walls on the "class-rooms."

"This is very impressive," I said, trying to get a few words in.

Miss Elizabeth and Marie were doing all the talking. At least Marie seemed comfortable.

"The only other subject you haven't seen is PE. In the spring we play softball at the park. In the fall and winter we go swimming at the local YMCA. It's just down the street."

Did I hear swimming? Swimming was what Marie liked best about The Garden School. She would fit right in.

"Well, if you're all set Marie can start anytime," I informed Miss Elizabeth.

"You'll need to get Marie's school transcripts first. We need to know where she stands. As soon as we have them, she can start."

Marie spent a little more time looking around, making mental notes.

"Thanks for your time. I'll have everything ready by the end of the week," I said, closing the door behind us.

"Well, what did you think?" I asked Marie.

"I liked it okay. I'll need a new bathing suit though. It's too late in the season to get one. Do you think Auntie Louise would make me one?"

"Let's stop by her house and ask," she's just five minutes away.

"Of course I will," Louise said. "What kind of bathing suit do you want?"

"I want something that looks like shorts and has long sleeves."

The long sleeves had me concerned. Why would anyone want to swim in long sleeves? It made no sense. Marie should have been trying to blend in, not stick out as someone weird.

"You won't be able to swim in anything like that. They may not even let you into the pool," I said.

"If its bathing suit material, I don't see why they would say anything," Louise said, always coming to Marie's rescue.

It was settled. Marie would start another school the following week. The bathing suit issue however, should have been a hint to me.

Marie went through seventh grade without many issues, just typical pre-teen stuff. She made a friend and they attended Aviation Challenge together.

Actually, having Marie attend The Washington Street School made my life a hell of a lot easier. I ended up changing jobs and working right across the street from the school. It was nice being able to walk to and from work with Marie each day. There was something peaceful about starting and ending my day that way. I especially liked the times we walked as light snow fell, giving the busy city a quiet, eerie feeling. All-in-all it was a good school year.

Unfortunately toward the end of the seventh grade, we were drowning in debt once again. We never had the funds to send Marie to a private school, but at the time, we did what we had to.

Marie and I attended a seminar on home-schooling and decided it was time to give it a try. It seemed perfect for her. She could be home by herself and learn at her own pace. No bullying to worry about.

The public school supported our home-school efforts but would not supply any books or curriculum. I had to send a sampling of Marie's work to the Superintendent of Schools every quarter. The internet was now running full force and we even had it in our house! Thankfully I found an on-line school based out of Minnesota that helped with the curriculum. They also had great ideas on how to achieve the credits Marie would need to graduate

I couldn't "teach" algebra. Marie became the first eighth grader to attend the local community college. Her assessment tests for math and English were above average for incoming college students.

Once again, our adventure was about to take another fork in the road.

Marie's First Job

At the end of the seventh grade and before home-schooling, Marie started her first job. The mother of one of the students of The Washington Street School was going to start a business with a guided horse and buggy ride in down town Salem and asked Marie to join her.

Ruth was wonderful. She had no problem letting Marie dress as a boy. My sister Louise made Marie an authentic looking 1700's footman's costume and Ruth provided her with a top hat.

Marie went by the nickname of Luca. I visited her one day at the job and she looked happy having her picture taken by tourists as she stood beside a huge Belgian horse. I swear, if I didn't know it was my daughter standing there, I would have believed it was my son.

I don't know why there were no red flags as Marie was dressing as a male. Maybe because she had been wearing men's clothes most of her life. Playing a male role in public however, should have been a big clue.

Washington Street School

By Marie

I changed schools before Halloween. The whole fiasco of public middle school hadn't even lasted six weeks. In less than forty days I'd gone through one of the most traumatic highs and lows of my life. I entered The Washington Street School more damaged and jaded than I'd ever been. I deliberately acted strange and weird around the other students to keep them at arm's length. After Jessica, I had been scared back into the proverbial closet and would have been content to be left alone in there.

I had my first period during the seventh grade. It was disgusting. I refused to go to school all week, feeling too unclean to be in public.

Experiencing such a radical and unwelcome physiological change made me feel like a foreigner vacationing in my own body. I don't think it was a surprise or more unpleasant because I still viewed myself as a boy on the inside. I think most girls regard their first menses with disdain streaked with horror. I wasn't stupid. I knew my body was female and this was an unavoidable eventuality. Still, when it happened I felt dirty and ashamed. I stayed home alone and spent hours looking in the mirror and thinking, *"Who are you? Who the hell are you?!"* Thankfully it was just the one. It didn't happen again for another year.

I took my PSAT that year and almost had a perfect score, the highest in the school's history. I also went back to Huntsville Alabama for Space Academy with Corey, the only person in school who was remotely my friend. We had a great time. For one week I had lots of friends again.

The Washington Street School played soccer and basketball in the spring and fall, and in the winter we swam at the YMCA. I was so overweight that even though I was tall, 5'7" now, at over 200 pounds, I couldn't run fast enough to be good at basketball anymore.

I was still a very strong swimmer, but my custom bathing suit, a two piece with shorts and long sleeves, definitely made me stand out in a negative way. I was uncomfortable and disassociated from my own body. It was nice not to be called a fat dyke at school, but I could tell everyone was thinking it. The kids at the Washington Street School had been very cordial to me, but by the end of the school year I was ready to move on.

My First Job

In the summer between seventh grade and starting home-schooling for eighth grade, I began my first job. One of the parents of a classmate at The Washington Street School was starting her own business and had asked me if I was interested in working with her. It was a horse-drawn carriage, historical tour guide business in Salem. Salem, Massachusetts had been a tourist destination for many years but it was just on the edge of booming. This was a great idea.

Ruth bought a huge Belgian work horse and a working replica of an eighteenth century horse buggy that could take two workers and six passengers. My Aunt Louise made me a very authentic looking costume to be a footman and I spent hours in the library learning about Salem history. The guided tours focused on the shipping industry and revolutionary politics that made Salem home to the first millionaire in the country and the location of President Washington's inauguration parade. Ruth taught me how to groom and tack a horse, and while she drove the buggy I gave the tourists the low down.

This was a lot of responsibility for a thirteen year old. I worked strictly for tips, so an eight hour day would typically earn me less than $40, often less than $20. It wasn't the money I loved about the job. It was my uniform and my name.

This was my first real experience encompassing a male role in public life. My work uniform was a frilly white shirt, blue button up vest, breeches with silver buttons at the knees and a top hat. My name at work was Luca, a nickname I had been transitioning into for a while.

Origins of Luca

The origins of Luca started with Luka. A pair of teenage girls had moved into the same condo complex that I lived in. I was sort of friends with them until I dropped out of public school. At one point while we were friends, I had brought them into my condo to show them a large dent in the wall where Dad had thrown a bicycle at my head.

The older girl had laughed and said "We should call you *Luka*, like the song by Suzanne Vega!" Then she started singing, "My name is Luka, I live on the second floor. I live upstairs from you. Yes, I think you've seen me before."

I interjected, "But technically I live on the fifth floor."

She continued, "If you hear something late at night, some kind of trouble, some kind of fight!"

Her sister joined in, "Just don't ask me what it was!"

It was a song about child abuse. A week later Mom heard one of the sisters calling me Luka and thought it was cute. My little cousin started calling me Luka-Boo and it stuck. I guess I didn't really choose my name, it chose me. If I had chosen my own name I would have picked an old family name like Luder or named myself Gavin after Gavin Rossdale, my favorite male rock vocalist. I changed the spelling of Luka to Luca to try and lose the child abuse connotations.

Lake Winnipesaukee

The summer came to an end with a trip to Lake Winnipesaukee with Mom and Dad. The night before we left, I finished off Mom's prescription of Tylenol with Codeine, chased down with a dozen or so Advils. I fell asleep on the floor of my shower, fully dressed, with the hot water running. The next day I puked my guts out all the way to the lake, wondering why I was still alive. If the drugs didn't stop my heart, I thought they'd at least damage my liver or kidneys.

This was the most dehydrated and pain-fueled delirious I'd ever been. I couldn't keep anything down: no food, no water. My throat burned. My back and stomach muscles ached furiously from the projectile vomiting. My head throbbed. My body trembled and was covered in cold sweat. Yet I lived on, watching the highway scenery zoom by.

This was how my life was. Every minute of every day I teetered on the edge of grasping something better for myself or falling into oblivion. The slightest thing could tip the scales at any moment. I was engulfed in depression day and night. Even when I was happy, I was sad. When I got what I wanted, it seemed like a lot of effort for nothing. Everything was meaningless. So much so, it wasn't even worth trying to explain. Nothing equals nothing.

So there I was, alone in a cramped motel room with a threadbare mauve carpet, orange drapes pulled shut, and cigarette burns on the bedspread. As I sat in that muggy, semi-dark room watching reruns of *My So Called Life* and listening to an overtaxed air conditioner choke out its last breath, Mom and Dad were out in the beautiful day trying to pretend I didn't ruin their vacation. I thought I was starting to make them hate me. I wondered if I cared.

On the last day of the trip I was finally well enough to leave the room. I had gone so many days without eating or drinking more than a few sips of water, my clothes were hanging off me. I looked at my reflection in a store front window. My features were gaunt and my skin pasty. I thought I looked great. My most successful diet ever!

I talked Mom into paying a psychic to read tarot cards for me. I went through the beaded curtains and into the back room alone. There sat a plump, graying lady, chain-smoking Pal Mal's. She told me my future. I was going to grow up to be a strong man. I'd never make a lot of money, but the next girl I met would be my soul mate. I hadn't told her my gender so I thought her predictions were eerily cool.

Chapter Eleven

Trapped!

By Betsie

"C'mon Marie, at least talk to me," I pleaded as I knocked on Marie's bathroom door. "You've been in there for over an hour. Just talk to me."

No reply.

"I want to know what's going on. I need to know you're okay."

Still no reply, but I could hear Marie crying.

I stopped knocking and sat on the floor outside the bathroom door.

"I promise I'll listen. I can handle anything."

Why was she not answering me?

It had been a year and a half since Marie had done anything to hurt herself. Initially I hadn't even given it a thought. Suddenly my mind was brought back to the cutting of the wrist incident. It gave me the chills. What if Marie had done something to hurt herself and needed help? Panic set in.

Jumping to my feet, I started banging on the door.

"Open up this God Damn door or I'm going to kick it in!"

I had enough adrenaline in me to do it!

I could hear some movements and a few moments later the door gradually opened. Marie's eyes were red and swollen and she was shaking. Dressed in her usual dark clothes and heavy boots she slowly turned around and went back to sitting in the bathtub.

She wouldn't look up at me. Gulping for air, she tried to speak but it was difficult.

I tried to reassure her.

"No matter what you tell me, I promise I'll understand."

Fully clothed, Marie continued to stare at her boots.

Finally able to catch her breath she shouted, "I'm in the wrong body! I'm supposed to be a boy but I'm trapped in a girl's body!"

Her words should have shocked and confused me. They didn't. I thought I was going to hear "Mom, I'm gay." I'd been preparing myself for that moment for years. Marie and I had even discussed it at one point, but she insisted she wasn't gay. Although her words were difficult to hear, they didn't surprise me.

I couldn't imagine the hell she was going through.

I walked toward the tub. Marie stood up and I threw my arms around her, holding her with all my strength.

"But you're only thirteen. Are you sure?"

"I've known for a long time," she cried. "I just didn't know how to tell you. Mom, I can't go on this way anymore."

"I don't know where to go from here," I told her. "But I'll do my best to get you some answers."

While Marie went back to sitting in the tub, I sat on the side. We talked and cried, cried and talked until there were no more words to say or tears to flow. All those years of searching for an answer had been summed up in two sentences. I was scared to death, but at the same time, relieved. Now I had the information, what the hell was I supposed to do with it?

Later that night I told Brooks what Marie had said. He didn't seem surprised either. He took it all very calmly. Our concern was for our daughter. Fear of the unknown made us afraid for our daughter's life.

Marie continued her regular routines for the week but she was in pain and needed answers. I didn't know where to turn. A few days later I read an article published in our small weekly paper about a doctor from Ipswich, Massachusetts who was helping a family dealing with gender issues. I told Marie if she wanted to see this doctor, I would take her, but she needed to make the appointment herself.

Within a week we were off on another journey, searching for answers. I believed Marie would speak more openly and not be embarrassed if I were not in the room, so I went back to the car. As I think back, that was probably the wrong decision. Who knows, maybe a small part of me was in denial and I wasn't prepared to hear what the doctor had to say.

Being too anxious and nervous to sit in the car, I started to walk around the parking lot. There was a quiet crispness in the air. A perfect fall morning in New England. Immediately my ears were drawn to the sound of a small trickling brook. On my way to investigate I found myself shuffling through an artist's pallet of colored leaves. One maple leaf, having gently fallen to the side of the path, beckoned me. Picking it up, I was in awe at its beauty. The soft yellow at the base gradually changed to a brilliant orange. An explosion of deep red painted its tips. Only Mother Nature herself could take the ordinary greens of yesterday and transform them into something so remarkable. As I stood there holding this incredible gift, I couldn't help but wonder if Marie would undergo such an amazing transformation.

Marie was disappointed yet excited when she arrived back at the car. Although she didn't get the life changing information she was eager to hear, she had pamphlets that would hopefully send her in the right direction.

As Marie was absorbed in the literature, we drove home in silence. Every once in a while she would read something out loud and I thought, *"What the hell are we getting ourselves into?"*

Marie made an appointment right away to see a peer counselor. Once again, pushing aside my fear of driving to unknown places, I fastened my seatbelt and headed into the unknown, physically and emotionally.

Meeting Vanessa was a life altering experience. Finally! Someone who understood! Finally! Someone who could help **me**!

The three of us sat down. Speaking slowly and confidently, Vanessa turned to Marie.

"Do you know how special you are? Do you realize most people use only one side of their brain? You actually use both sides. I bet you're pretty smart in school, right?"

"I guess."

Then Vanessa turned to address me.

"And Mrs. Harvie, I want you to know you've done nothing wrong."

"I've done nothing wrong." No one had ever told me that before. Although no one had ever come out and blamed me for Marie's actions, I had always blamed myself. Maybe I wasn't such a bad mother after all.

Vanessa continued, "This isn't easy for Luca or his family."

"His?" Why did this shock me? I knew why we were there. What had I expected? Hearing the word spoken out loud made this transgender thing very real. I was too stunned to answer back.

Taking a large book, Vanessa threw it to the floor, the loud sound echoing in the small room. It brought my mind back to the conversation.

"This book is what it is, you can't change it. Just like Luca is who he is. You can't change him. He's been a boy since birth."

All of a sudden I went from having a daughter for thirteen years to having a son for one minute. This wasn't something I could accept right away.

Marie and Vanessa talked a little more. I listened.

"I know this great therapist," Vanessa said, handing me a business card. "Diane will not only help Luca find his true self, she will work with the family, helping you to understand all this."

We stayed a little longer as Vanessa answered more of Marie's questions. The conversation was sensitive and informative, not embarrassing.

The hour passed quickly and all of a sudden we had to leave the first place Marie had truly felt safe.

I didn't know it then, but closing the door behind me, I was about to embark on my own journey. Like Dorothy, I would meet my own Wizardess of Oz, encounter many characters along the way, be terrified, endure hardships I never thought possible, witness incredible courage, and awaken in a new yet familiar world.

Wizardess of Oz

With Vanessa's recommendation and high hopes, I made an appointment to see Diane, a transgender therapist.

I felt right at home stepping into Diane's waiting area. After all, I'd played that scene many times before. However, someone had changed the props for Act Two A small dose of optimism had been carefully placed in the room.

Soft lights and peaceful music gave a pleasant calmness to the room. Diane's many books and magazines held stories of encouragement and laughter. She had put a lot of thought into making her clients feel welcome. I liked this woman even before I met her.

An inner door opened and a soft, friendly voice greeted us. Diane was tall, with short sandy blonde hair. Smartly dressed but comfortable. Something about her relaxed mannerism told me everything would be okay.

The overstuffed couch and cheerful curtains made the room very inviting. Fresh flowers placed on the coffee table and dimmed lights gave a feeling of warmth.

I appreciated Diane's sensitivity as she asked us many questions, most of them directed toward Marie. Marie had waited years to be asked the right questions, to be able to give the right answers. To my surprise, with very little hesitation, she was answering them truthfully. I began to understand my daughter's actions more and more.

I told Diane about the words Marie spoke as a four year old.

"Life is not worth living if I can't be a boy."

Although Marie's words were not a surprise to Diane, to my surprise, they were very common among transgendered children, even as young as four years old.

"Gender identity is Luca's internal sense of being male," Diane said. "He has probably felt this way from a very early age. It has nothing to do with his physical sex at birth. From what you have told me so far, Luca seems to be displaying behaviors different from his physical assigned sex. Sexual orientation is different. It's our attraction to the same or opposite sex. Luca can be transgendered and be gay or heterosexual. His sexual orientation has nothing to do with his gender."

Towards the end of our meeting, Diane asked Marie to leave the room so she could speak with Brooks and me.

"This will be a long journey," she informed us. "And by long, I mean a few years. Before any surgery, I have to be sure there's no doubt Luca is actually a boy. Most of my clients lose their families over this. I'm happy to see all of you here."

"I can't imagine losing Marie," I replied. "I would rather have a live son than a dead daughter."

Diane called Marie back into the room.

"I want to make sure you understand there will be no quick answers, fixes or changes. You've taken the first step, but there will be many more to go. Luca, it has been a pleasure meeting you and your family."

After speaking with Diane for just fifty minutes I knew we had finally found the right therapist. Our Wizardess of Oz. With our first step, Marie and I were off on our journey of self-discovery.

"Now remember," Diane said. "Others will react to this change by how you react. If you're comfortable telling them, they'll be comfortable hearing it."

Just how comfortable would I be? No one in my family had ever heard the word transgender. How would I work that into a conversation? It was a long ride home and tomorrow would be another day.

Telling Others

"Now remember, if you're comfortable, others will be," I heard Diane's words again.

Not being prepared to face my family with Marie's news, I made the numerous calls to let them know. They were very supportive.

However, my sister Jean and her husband wanted to come and talk to Brooks and me. I understood. It would be up to them to tell their twelve year old daughter her cousin Marie was actually her cousin Luca. They wanted to be armed with the right information.

Because nothing had been easy in the past, my mind was fearful Jean and her husband Gary would not be supportive. Was this what Diane meant about losing your family? I didn't want to have to choose between my sister and my son.

After a few minutes of talking, my anxiety eased. Our conversation had broken the ice.

"I don't understand a lot of this," Jean said. "But we love Luca. That won't change."

How could I have doubted my sister? I was actually grateful for her visit. I was now armed with the confidence needed to speak openly to others about Luca.

I had to find the right moments to tell my supervisor and co-workers. I couldn't blame them for their numerous questions. "How long do you think she knew?" "Aren't you scared?" "But she's only thirteen, how can she be sure?" Never feeling afraid or embarrassed, I answered the best I could. I found their questions came from their compassion and the wanting to understand.

Trapped

By Marie

The internet changed everything. Dad had bought a refurbished Cannon computer and Mom had let me install AOL 3.0. AOL was great. It allowed me the anonymity to finally be myself. I could go into chat-rooms and lie my ass off about all kinds of things. I lied about my name, my gender and what I looked like. I had entire online relationships from just friends to romantic cyber-involvements that lasted weeks, sometimes even months, based on lies. Strangely when I lied about who I was, I felt most like myself.

That's how I met my first girlfriend, Michelle. It was October, 1996. We met in a random AOL chatroom for French speaking people, although neither of us spoke French. I noticed she was a sixteen year old girl from Arizona and started a private message chat with her under the guise of a sixteen year old boy. We genuinely had a lot in common and chatted for hours before I asked for her phone number. I had never felt this connected to another person. I had to hear her voice. I knew it was risky calling. My own voice, though deep, was obviously feminine. Still, I had to hear her.

She had the most beautiful voice I had ever heard. It suited her. She said hello and told me she had something to tell me.

"I lied about my age. I'm only thirteen."

I laughed and admitted I was only thirteen too. I knew right away there was something special between us. I may have lied to Michelle about my name and gender, but it didn't feel like a lie. I felt she was the only person who knew the real me. We talked online and on the phone for hours a day every day for almost two years. I wasn't just in love with her, I was in love with how she thought of me. My relationship with her allowed me to explore myself as a man from the safety of my own bedroom.

So flash forward a few months. It's late autumn, 1996. Homeschooling was going great. I slept in late every day and still managed to get all my work done before Mom got home. I was also in love with Michelle and experiencing a real relationship for the first time, even if it was from a distance.

You'd think with all these good things going for me I'd be happy. Instead my misery had compounded. Being home alone during the day or talking to Michelle from the sanctity of my bedroom was like living in another world. It made my time outside this world all the more unbearable. My plan was to hide in my parent's condo until I turned eighteen and then run away to California and start life over as a man. But now I'd tasted how it might feel to be perceived as a man. I didn't know if I could wait another five years for my life to begin.

It was a Saturday morning and I had locked myself in my bathroom. Fully dressed in a men's plaid hoodie, jeans and boots I sat in my tub listening to Bush's *Razorblade Suitcase* on my portable CD player. I was weighing my options and crying because they all sucked. Wait. Don't wait. Tell someone. Say nothing. Live. Don't bother. Run away. Stay put. Stay in this tub forever Open the door. Mom was pounding on it and screaming. Just ignore her. You need to figure this out. Fuck it. I couldn't think through her yelling so I let her in.

I really let her in. Into my world. Into my pain and confusion. Showed her the raw bleeding roots of my problems and then stared at my boots so I wouldn't have to see her reaction. Pathetic. Go ahead Mom, let's see you try and fix this.

The following week Mom brought home a torn newspaper article about a pediatric doctor helping a young transgendered child right here in Massachusetts. The child was a small boy, younger than twelve, who insisted he was a girl. Instead of treating the child as a psycho, this doctor and the child's parents were treating him like a girl. He wore dresses and they used female pronouns for him. Wow. I needed to meet this doctor! Mom said she'd drive me to see him, but I had to call and make the appointment myself. No problem.

My hands were slightly trembling and my breath was coming fast as I dialed the doctor's office. I tried to sound grown-up and manly, but my voice came out high and nervously pinched when the receptionist asked the nature of the appointment.

"Isawanarticleinthenewspaperwiththedoctorinitabouttransgenderism andIthinkImightbetransgenderedtoo," I blurted out as quickly as possible.

"What?"

"I saw an article in the newspaper with the doctor about transgenderism and I think I might be transgendered too," I said a touch more slowly.

The days leading up to the appointment stretched on and on. When the day finally came I was ready. I was filled with nervous excitement. Instead of chattering away like a happy monkey I kept my mouth shut, painfully aware of how awkward this was for Mom.

The day was cold but Mom stayed in the car. I waited in the waiting room alone. I thought maybe I'd see other trans people waiting too.

Instead, the crowd was like any other family practitioner's. It was a little disappointing.

When I was called in, I gathered all my strength and tried my best to articulate to the doctor what was going on. He was kind and patient but professed he was no expert on gender disorders. I was confused and deflated by this news. I had shown up expecting a miracle, a solution. He did give me some literature and pamphlets though. Finally I had something tangible to hold on to. Up until now life had been so confusing. But here was a map! Progress!

Vanessa was more than a trans peer counselor, she was my compass. She was a fifty-five year old tall, stout, trans woman with red hair and beautiful nails. She was the first openly trans person I met. There's a stereotype that many trans women are beastly. Vanessa was effervescent. Her vivaciousness was contagious. She brought me out of my shell. Mom too. Vanessa was the first person to tell me there was nothing wrong with me. She said it with such assuredness and conviction, I believed her. She let me browse through her bookshelves where I saw pictures of other trans men. On the floor of her office, curled up with a copy of

Body Alchemy, I started to dream I could have a future.

She introduced me to the gender spectrum, but most importantly she showed me that maybe, just maybe, I could like myself.

Vanessa was a great peer counselor, but she wasn't a psychologist. She couldn't diagnose me or recommend me for gender altering treatments and surgeries. Thankfully Vanessa gave me the name of the best trans therapist in the world, Diane Ellaborn.

Diane was the first therapist I was honest with. She asked me tons of questions, some of them embarrassing, and I answered truthfully. I told her how, from preschool on up, I'd lived every day aware that I was in the wrong body. It was much easier to confide in Diane than in Mom. Diane didn't judge me or cry when I told her the truth about things.

Changing genders is a long, long process. The prospect of spending years in therapy before I could have surgery was frustrating and fatiguing. I was glad Diane was working with me and not against me. Instead of trying to convince me I was someone I wasn't, Diane helped to bring the real me all the way to the surface. Vanessa was my compass and Diane was my flashlight in the dark. I now had the tools I needed to begin my journey. Everything else would come from inside me.

Telling Others

Dad didn't take my being trans as well as I'd hoped. I understood why Mom cried so much, but Dad's refusal to accept was beyond me. He had never given a crap about anything I did before, so why was this so different? It's not like I was, or had ever been, Daddy's little girl. We didn't have a relationship like that. He never reacted violently toward me, but it took a long time for him to come around to accepting it and even longer to stop "forgetting" and "slipping up" with the pronouns in public.

I was terrified of how the rest of my family would accept the news. I have a small family. No grandparents, four aunts, three uncles and six cousins. My two youngest cousins were too little to tell. I think for a long time they grew up thinking I was a biological guy.

Mom told my aunts over the phone, who told their husbands and children. This spared me a face-to-face confrontation. I don't think I could have handled that. The acceptance and love of my family was vital to me. I would have lost all sense of self-worth if they had rejected me.

Fortunately, my entire family seemed to take the revelation well. I was one lucky ducky. My uncle, Gary and cousin, Will were the only ones who questioned me about it, but it was more for information than confrontation. If anyone else had a problem or question they kept it to themselves and never made me feel self-conscious around them. My six year old cousin took it the hardest. She was too young to understand but too old not to notice what was going on. I felt bad for her but didn't know how to broach the subject. She was exceedingly bright for her age and within two years she accepted the situation with adult candor, but for a while she was pretty hostile toward me.

The only person I had to tell was my friend Jenny. We were still friends since The Garden School, even though she lived two cities over. I asked Mom for some money so Jenny and I could go to the mall on a Friday night for pizza and a movie. I wanted to tell her in a public place so she couldn't make a scene. She was also dependent on a ride home from Mom so I knew Jenny wouldn't haul off and ditch me if she was upset.

I was scared to tell her. Jenny knew I was attracted to girls, but this was different. We were seated in a crowded food court with our elbows on a grimy table, Cokes and pepperoni pizza between us, when I told her I had something to tell her that wouldn't be easy to hear. She perked up and looked at me. I looked down at the congealing grease on my cooling dinner, afraid to see her face.

"So you know how I'm really butch and always wearing guys clothes and changing my name from Marie to Luca and stuff? Well that's because I'm transgendered. I'm going to start taking testosterone and eventually have sex change surgery to be a guy. I hope we can still be friends."

"You asshole!" Jenny leaned over and punched me. "I can't believe you thought I wouldn't want to be your friend because of something so trivial. It's not a surprise you know."

"It's not?"

"No, it's not. Tool."

"OK. Um. Cool. Thanks."

Jenny snorted, the way only Latina chicks can, seeming to say so much with a simple exhalation of breath, then moved on to the rest of her pizza.

Chapter Twelve

Pronouns

By Betsie

First let me say I'm sorry if switching between Marie, Luca, she, he, hers, his, is confusing. That's how it was, confusing.

I had been calling Luca Marie for thirteen years. It was difficult to change. Luca's pain permeating through me each time I made the mistake of calling him Marie in public became my own pain. I hated myself for it.

Going to the mall was the worst. We could be shopping, having lunch, or on our way to a movie and all of a sudden Luca would have to be Marie depending on who we bumped into. I was constantly on guard, switching between the two in an instant. It was exhausting.

Watching Luca use a public men's room was terrifying. After all, he still had female plumbing and a part of me still thought of him as my little girl. Fearing for his life, I would stand as close to the men's room door as possible, straining to hear every sound. It scared me to death not knowing who else was in there.

Having Brooks around Luca in public was embarrassing. For whatever reason, Brooks would constantly use the wrong pronoun. Although it was embarrassing for me, it was extremely hurtful for Luca. For the longest time, Luca and I did everything in our power to keep Brooks from tagging along.

The friend who attended Space Academy with Luca asked him to attend Aviation Challenge with him. How would Luca pull that off? Physically he was still a girl and would have to stay in a girl's dorm. But he really wanted to go. So for one week, Marie attended Aviation Challenge but with the nick-name of Luca. When Luca returned, he didn't want to talk about it.

I relentlessly argued with Luca for not giving his father a chance. Why couldn't he see how difficult this was for Brooks? Then I turned around and argued with Brooks for not trying harder. If I felt Luca's pain, why didn't he?

Uncertainty had wrapped its arms around me and held on tightly. It was hard to shake. I wanted to believe in God just so I could have someone to blame for my feeling of helplessness. It wasn't as if I could say "Luca, I know what you're going through. Everything will be okay." I didn't have a clue as to what inner turmoil Luca was going through and I doubted everything would be okay.

As I struggled with all of this happening too fast, Luca struggled with it not happening fast enough. I watched Luca become more and more withdrawn. Marie's happiness over transitioning was battling Luca's sadness. Luca's sadness was winning the battle.

Pronouns

By Luca

I think the only thing harder than coming out of the closet was jumping back in. For the first six months or so of transitioning I'd have to do this from time to time. I'd completely stopped using the name Marie and was Luca full time, but if someone recognized me in a public place and shouted out, "Hey Marie!" what was I supposed to do? Ignore them? I had to answer. I tried ignoring people a couple of times, but it's amazing how even casual acquaintances will climb stairs or forge pedestrian and automobile traffic just to make sure you acknowledge them. I even tried denying who I was once but the girl looked at me like I was mental.

Situations like this were awkward for a few reasons. When you're in public trying to pass as a guy and someone *outs* you it can really screw up your day. Forget using a bathroom now until you get home. Using men's rooms was iffy for the first year of transitioning anyway for personal safety reasons. But if people think you're on the fence about your gender they lump you into the sex pervert category and now women's bathrooms are off limits too. People with young children look at you funny. I don't know if they were afraid I'd be a bad influence on their kids, confuse them, or molest them. Whatever the reason, it hurt to see instant distrust in people's faces.

In April of 1997 Corey from The Washington Street School asked if I wanted to go back with him to Huntsville, to attend Aviation Challenge for a week. It took me a while to make a decision. In the end I went because I wanted to go so badly. I thought the sacrifices I'd have to make would be worth it. No male pronouns. No being openly attracted to girls. No binding and hiding my breasts, I'd have to wear a bra. I was glad my hair was still long. It would help me look more feminine if I styled it right. Crap.

I had a fun week at Aviation Challenge. It's a little different than Space Academy. It's more Air Force oriented than Space Program. I got to ride in one of those G-Force machines that spin you around until you practically shit your pants. Corey and I got to go up in a four person airplane with an instructor and actually log flying hours. It was very cool.

The group vibe this time was much different than it had been before. At Aviation Challenge all the kids were fourteen to sixteen years old so the atmosphere was charged with hormones. The sexual innuendos were non-stop. This was eye opening for me as to how I was supposed to act as a teenage boy.

I definitely stood out as the only a-sexual of the group, but no one made fun of me or questioned me. The guys didn't view me as competition so friendships were easily made. And the hot girls actually flocked to me. They thought I was hilarious and made deep observations. Also, I didn't have a penis so they felt safe around me. Once again I knew better than to try and use the bathroom or showers at the same time as the other girls.

The hardest part of the week, besides hiding who I really was, was going so long without talking to Michelle. We were used to talking almost four hours a day. At Aviation Challenge I could barely manage a five-minute pay-phone call without my friends interrupting me, wanting me to rejoin the group. Michelle cried every day I was away and she spent most of our time on the phone crying as well. I felt guilty having so much fun while she missed me so much. It was also hard going to sleep without her telling me she loved me and blowing kisses through the phone at me. At home it was our nightly routine.

Coming home from Aviation Challenge was difficult. On the one hand I could go back to being a guy. On the other hand I was mostly alone again. I didn't maintain my friendship with Corey because I was afraid to tell him I was trans and I couldn't stay in the closet just for him. I had the email addresses of two girls I was friends with at Aviation Challenge and decided to tell them electronically, and from a great distance, that I was trans. One of them was cool with it and stayed my friend/pen pal for years, even after I had fully transitioned. The other one totally bugged out. She was pissed off and grossed out. She swore at me and called me some nasty names, then blocked me from ever contacting her again. That's about the reaction I had expected, and honestly about what I deserved. I wished I hadn't had to lie to anyone in the first place, but springing heavy shit like that on a fourteen year old isn't cool either. It was a lose-lose situation. I could either be the victim, villain, or both.

I still had Jenny, but I only saw her every few weekends now that she was in high school. I had Michelle too, but I couldn't see her. I could hear her through the phone for a few precious hours a day, but I couldn't reach out and hold her. I missed the group dynamic of Aviation Challenge where I was never alone. All week I'd had such a great time, but leaving all that behind had left me feeling so empty I couldn't even tell Mom and Dad about all the fun I'd had. Instead, I lay on my bed, fully clothed, not caring that my grubby sneakers were on the comforter, listening to the Foo Fighters *Monkey Wrench* on repeat, hugging myself and crying.

I was desperately lonely all the time. I wanted my transition to speed up so I could go out and make friends. Now that I was a teenager I craved peer acceptance more than ever. My life felt more like purgatory with every passing day.

Chapter Thirteen

Michelle

By Betsie

Luca had been talking to Michelle through instant chats and by phone almost daily. Now she and her parents would be vacationing in Massachusetts and Luca asked if I would drive him to Lexington to meet her. The only thing I knew about her family was they were affluent residents of Scottsdale, Arizona.

Growing up in a small coastal town where my grandmother was a maid to the wealthy had always made me feel like an outcast. We literally lived on the wrong side of the tracks. Now I was being asked to spend an afternoon with the Scottsdale elite. This wasn't exactly the way I wanted to spend my Sunday afternoon. But, since Luca had been so depressed, I said yes.

The day was hot. We were both on edge. What if I screwed up? I was fully aware of what was at stake. Calling Luca *Marie* would not only be embarrassing for everyone but could be the end of Luca's and Michelle's friendship. It was one thing to have a short conversation with someone and remember Luca's name. It was something completely different trying to keep it up for a prolonged period of time. I was still fairly new at this and through no fault of Luca's, I had been thrown into a very challenging position.

A van pulled into the parking lot, and Luca just knew it was Michelle. Luca became quiet and his body tensed as we walked slowly toward the van. This was his cue to be a man.

"Remember Mom, I'm Luca," he reminded me once more.

After convincing Michele to exit the van (she was as nervous as Luca), Luca and Michelle quickly disappeared leaving me alone with her mom and dad. For about a half hour we browsed an antique shop making uncomfortable conversation. I had nothing in common with Michelle's wealthy parents. They dressed in designer clothes. I dressed in Walmart. Michelle's mom had the gaudy diamond ring. I'd never owned a diamond. While they drove a Lexus LS400, I drove a Ford Escort. They lived in a million dollar home. We lived in a condo that didn't belong to us. Although Michelle's parents were never rude or made me feel second class, we couldn't seem to find any common ground.

Being tested, and knowing how critical it was for me to pass, gave me a headache. I had no chance to relax. With no more antique shops to wander through, we decided to go to Friendly's for lunch. Michelle's parents, her younger sister, and I sat there with our grilled cheese sandwiches and awkward conversation for about an hour before Luca and Michelle showed their faces.

Actually I don't remember seeing Michelle's face. A tiny nose peeked out from long black hair that covered both sides of her face. Her eyes played hide and seek, mostly hide. It was extremely annoying. She reminded me of a China doll on display.

I was angry at first when I noticed Luca and Michelle holding hands under the table. Luca's grin and lack of appetite told me there was more to this friendship than he had divulged. I had been lied to once again. But seeing how happy Luca was quickly dissolved that anger. I was happy watching him being happy. Something I didn't get to see too much of.

Michelle begged her parents to stay a little longer. Thankfully it was time for them and me to go home.

Michelle

By Luca

Michelle's dad had grown up in western Massachusetts. Even though their family lived in Scottsdale Arizona now, Michelle had an aunt and uncle still living in Massachusetts. Michelle and I wanted to be together so badly she actually convinced her parents to vacation in Massachusetts for the first time in decades. They were staying with family in Sturbridge but would drive to Lexington to meet Mom and me so Michelle and I could have a few hours together.

I was excited but also scared shitless, because I had lied about my weight and gender. I told Mom that Michelle knew I was trans but her parents didn't, and Michelle and I had agreed it was best to keep it a secret. That was a lie, Michelle didn't know I was trans either, but I had to stress the importance of not slipping up with pronouns around them. Dad wasn't coming. He was still far too unreliable to not accidently (or deliberately) *out* me. Mom said she'd try her best.

We met in a public parking lot near a Starbucks. I felt like such an asshole standing there in the hot May sun dressed all in black with long sleeves and boots. I had a long chain attached to my wallet, three studs in each ear, and a long crazy bleached Mohawk. Michelle's parents must have thought I looked like a bum punk.

At first Michelle refused to come out of the minivan her parents had rented. This wasn't helping my confidence. At the urging of her younger sister, I stuck my head in to talk to her. She was all the way in the back, partially obscured by shadows.

"So, are you not coming out because I'm ugly?"

"No!" she gasped. "I'm nervous!"

"Well I'm hella scared, and you're not helping." I noticed her Discman. "What are you listening to?"

"Veruca Salt."

"Which album?"

"*Eight Arm to Hold You*. I love *Don't Make Me Prove It*."

"Me too. It's not as good as *Shutterbug* or *Earthcrosser* though. Want to come out now? Our parents are staring."

She crawled out of the back of the van and stepped into the sun. It was like being struck by lightning. I had never seen a girl so perfect and beautiful. I couldn't move, couldn't breathe. I think my heart might have even stopped beating. It was the longest single moment of my life. I had to shake my head to clear the angelic symphony ringing in my ears.

Michelle reached out to take my hand,   and when our fingertips touched I felt more alive than ever before. I felt like every cell in my body wasfull of electricity. The sun shined more radiantly, colors were brighter, the breeze more aromatic. The world was more beautiful because Michelle was in it.

I felt bad leaving Mom alone with Michelle's parents and sister. I had known Michelle for months, but the rest of her family were basically strangers. Our families had little in common, and Mom wasn't good at small talk to begin with, but my need to be alone with Michelle trumped Mom's need to avoid awkwardness.

Michelle and I were as alone as we could be. Neither of us were old enough to drive or lived nearby so we settled on hiding in an alley behind a Friendly's restaurant for a couple hours. If Michelle was disappointed in my physical appearance, she never let it show. It seemed that she burned to touch me as greatly as I her. We probably spent two hours alone in that alley but it felt like fifteen minutes or less. We didn't talk much. We just held each other as if we were drowning and the other were a life preserver. It was desperate, nervous, and comfortable all at the same time.

I had never been touched that way before, intimately and romantically by another person. I was glad to be loved and touched as a man, lucky to be loved by a divine girl who was the center of my universe. She had the bluest eyes I had ever seen. Sapphire with silvery flecks of cerulean, and in them I saw a future where I could be happy. Michelle had to constantly remind me to breathe. She was so awe inspiring to me, I kept accidentally holding my breath.

I was certain she could feel I was using a binder and could see I didn't have an Adam's apple, but she never let on if she could. I had found all the acceptance I would ever need in Michelle's arms.

When we finally left the alley behind Friendly's and went inside to meet our families for lunch, I couldn't bring myself to eat. Being with Michelle left my stomach constantly feeling like I was at the peak of the biggest drop on a roller coaster. I savored the excited feeling as I sipped my Sprite.

When it was time for her family to depart and drive back to Sturbridge, Michelle clung to me and cried. Her tears coming so fast they spilled down my neck and collected on the collar of my shirt. She was trembling, externalizing every quake I held in.

The air conditioning in the car made the wet spots on my shirt from Michelle's tears cold against my skin. That afternoon Michelle had been my first real kiss. It was an experience so new and sensational I could feel the ghost of her tongue in my mouth all the way home. I knew now I could make it to eighteen. I had almost three years to finish transitioning before Michelle graduated high school and we could start our lives together. I was no longer in limbo, I was on a path.

Chapter Fourteen

FTM Convention

By Betsie

There was a female-to-male convention coming up in Boston and because of Luca's age, if he wanted to attend, a parent had to attend. Ugh. But I was willing to be there to support him. Maybe there would be other parents there for me to talk with.

Looking over the program, I realized the majority of workshops would be geared to the trans person. They also made it clear outsiders would not be allowed in most of the rooms. Fine. I didn't want to see a bunch of naked female/male bodies anyway. Although there would be a few hours Luca and I could spend together, I would be by myself for the most part of each day.

I was blown away by the hundreds of people attending. They were all female to male and in various stages of transitioning. Some of the men, although in their forties or fifties, were just starting their journeys. Others, in their early twenties, were completely transitioned and starting an even newer journey. I have to admit though, for the majority, I would never have guessed they had once been female. At the age of fourteen, I believe Luca was the youngest one attending. He may have fit right in but I was extremely uncomfortable. It was all too weird for me. I tried to envision my Luca as an adult male but my mind would have no part of it.

There were no workshops geared specifically towards parents. Too bad. It was a missed opportunity for parents to share what we were each going through. It would have meant a lot to me to have a better understanding of what to expect in the coming days, months, and years.

In the two days of wandering hallways I only bumped into one other parent. She was even younger than me but her son was three years older than Luca. She was also one of Diane's clients and we would see each other a few more times in the future. I was very disappointed.

There was one workshop Luca and I did attend together. It was frightening. Dr. Spack was very thorough as he explained the pros and cons of starting testosterone therapy. Luca's voice would become deeper and he would grow facial hair. Luca would stop having periods. All pros. All changes for Luca to look forward to.

The cons. Luca's cholesterol would definitely increase. His blood pressure would go up. If he wore the testosterone patch he couldn't have any intimate relations with anyone who might come in contact with the patch. Their voices would change and they could also grow unwanted facial hair. If he didn't wear the patch, he would have to learn to give himself injections. These needles were thick and would have to be placed in a muscle. I wasn't looking forward to the pros or the cons and knew I would never be prepared for this.

I had been set adrift, wandering hallways full of strangers and closed doors. Even if I had known everyone there I still would have felt lost at sea. I was alone in my thoughts and had to get through this on my own.

Towards the end of the second day I found my way into an auditorium where they were showing a video on the different female to male surgeries. I wasn't supposed to be in the room but it was a large, dark auditorium and no one noticed me sitting in the back. I had thankfully missed most of the video and the part I did see I wished I hadn't.

To mold a penis, so much skin was taken from the inner fore-arm it left the patient open to infections and massive scarring. I couldn't imagine anyone deliberately wanting to do this to their body. That's all I needed to see. All five minutes worth. I left the auditorium.

I had been hoping the convention would lead to some contacts of my own. Some other parents to talk to. Someone else who understood what I was going through. Although that didn't happen, Luca was able to make a few contacts, giving me comfort knowing he would not be going through this alone.

Support Group

Luca had met a very nice couple at the Transgender Convention who lived two towns away. Twice a month they held a support group in their apartment. Of course in order for Luca to get there I would have to drive.

I didn't mind the driving, it was the staying.

The group was actually for the transgendered person and their partner. Although everyone there always made me feel welcome, they couldn't make me feel comfortable. The group would split into two rooms, one for the female who was becoming a male and one for their partner. I was grouped with the partners. So for two hours I sat in a room with six to eight lesbians listening to them complain about the person they came with. Most of them had all fallen in love with another lesbian and were not sure they wanted to stay in a relationship with a man. The ones who had made the commitment to stay were trying to deal with anger issues. Not just their own anger over how their partner could do this to them but with angry outbursts from the trans person who was once so lovable.

I couldn't relate.

I don't remember saying much. I didn't understand the dynamics of being in a lesbian relationship and couldn't understand how they could stop loving the person they had come with. My son may have been changing but he was still my child. Stop loving him? I would never stop loving him. Never.

Dr. Spack had talked about the mood swings experienced when a person starts taking testosterone but I didn't remember him mentioning anger issues. I didn't know what to say to this wonderful group of women who were trying so hard to understand their partners.

Once in a while the group would meet early on a Saturday or Sunday and then go out for dinner or to the movies. When I did let Luca go, I never tagged along. I would either catch a different movie at the same time or walk around the mall by myself for an hour or two. This was Luca's time. Luca's time to feel comfortable with who he was.

Something I couldn't provide him.

Transgender Convention

By Luca

Diane informed us of an upcoming FTM (female to male) convention in Boston. I was super excited. Two whole days of workshops, learning, and maybe making friends with other trans men!

Mom and I took the train into Boston wicked early. Besides pictures, I hadn't seen any other trans guys. Now suddenly I was in a building with hundreds of them! How cool! They were all so different too. Tall, short, young, old, fat, skinny and every race and religion you could think of. Some had beards or sideburns, some had bald spots. Some dudes were very masculine and handsome, others were far less along in transitioning and still slightly feminine looking. Some still had breasts, others had had their breasts removed and sported pectoral muscles instead. Some guys were sharply dressed in shirts and ties, but most were casually dressed in tee shirts or polos. There were preps, gangsters, bikers, sports fans, and hippies. I was the only metal-head goth present. But with such a wide variety of people I fit right in, although at the age of fourteen I was the youngest trans man there.

For the first half of the day I didn't speak to anyone. Mom and I had separated early to attend different workshops. I can't remember the first few workshops I attended. I was too busy staring at all the other men and dreaming about what kind of man I would grow into. So many possibilities were right before my eyes. It was amazing and inspiring. I didn't know anyone's name but I felt less alone just being near them.

After a little while I stopped being shy and opened up more. The men who talked to me were all nice and treated me as an equal. It felt good. Most of them commented on how young I was and said positive and encouraging things, like how they wished they had started when they were my age. They told me how brave I was and how cool it was that Mom supported me and was there that day. It was the first time in my life I felt lucky about my situation. My life wasn't ideal, but when it was, I'd have a lot of happy years ahead of me instead of wasted years behind me.

It was nice not to feel sorry for myself.

One of the workshops about hormones was headed by an endocrinologist named Dr. Spack. I listened intently as he talked about the human endocrine system, the primary functions hormones play in our bodies and some of the fundamental differences between testosterone and estrogen/progesterone. I was surprised to learn my body already produced small amounts of testosterone on its own.

Then Dr. Spack talked about what happens when FTM's (female to male) start taking testosterone; what changes may occur, would occur and why they occurred. It was fun learning about voices deepening, body hair thickening, muscle mass increasing and most importantly menstruation stopping. It was less fun hearing about bald spots, back hair, hypertension and higher levels of LDL cholesterol. But I was ready to take the bad with the good. Dr. Spack gave out his office number and address. I copied them down in a little spiral notebook. An FTM friendly and knowledgeable doctor was an important resource.

The next day I went to a workshop headed up by three trans men about different top surgery options. They removed their shirts and stood vulnerable and unashamed before an audience so we could see the differences between them. Two of them had thick body hair on their chests, stomachs and backs. The third hardly had a "happy trail." They supposed genetics played a role in the variances since they had all been on testosterone over three years.

The tall Asian man spoke first. He had had keyhole surgery, where a small incision is made near the arm pit and the breasts are liposuctioned from there. There was no visible scarring but his nipples had not been resized or re-grafted (re-grafting is when they change the placement of the nipples by cutting them off and re-attaching them at another site) so they looked a bit large and lopsided in his slightly saggy chest.

The second man's surgeon had resized his nipples and used that as his liposuction site. After the surgery this guy had hit the gym hardcore for a number of years. His chest was smooth, his pectoral muscles hard and tight. He looked amazing. He looked so natural and attractive that he could go topless at any public beach and turn heads. No one would suspect he was trans or had had any surgery.

The third man looked more about how I suspected I'd look some day. He had been over-weight with large breasts before surgery so liposuction alone wouldn't do it. He'd had a double mastectomy with nipple resizing and re-grafting. He'd also had a lot of extra skin cut off. His chest was flat but his scars were almost half an inch wide. Red angry scars that went from armpit to armpit. He said he didn't mind the scars.

His chest hair hid them pretty well and when he wore a shirt no one could tell. Since I was overweight and large breasted I figured this was my future and worried how it would affect intimacy. With scars like that even after top and bottom surgery I wouldn't be able to hide that I was trans from a lover. In the dark their fingers would feel the deep biting scars.

After lunch there was a workshop closed to anyone who wasn't an FTM about bottom surgery. At first the workshop conductor was iffy about letting me in because of my age but conceded after talking to me for a bit. There was a man who hadn't had any surgery, one who'd had a radial forearm phalloplasty, one who'd had a metoidioplasty and a bio man (biological) volunteer. All four of them stood at the front of the room completely nude and talked about their junk.

The man who hadn't had any surgery didn't plan to in the future. He said he was satisfied with what testosterone had done for him over the years. His breasts were large and hairy with hard purple nipples. They swung freely as he spoke and looked quite out of place. I would have felt sorry for this awkwardness but couldn't bring myself to judge him in the face of such courage. He'd brought a clitoris pump with him and demonstrated its use for us. I'd never even heard of such a thing. I knew what a penis pump was from the *Austin Powers* movie, but a clitoris pump was news to me. It was already enlarged from taking testosterone, but with the pump it grew to about three inches. The clitoris was red and swollen, looking sore, but the man assured us it felt fine. He said it would stay this way long enough to penetrate a woman's vagina for intercourse. It was all too weird for me but he seemed very pleased.

The guy who'd had a forearm phalloplasty probably had the biggest dick in the room, possibly the building and city block as well. It was huge. Even soft it was over 9 inches. He admitted he had to wear briefs to keep it in place, having to practically roll it up to fit it in his underwear. The surgeons had taken a skin graft from his arm to create the phallus which left him horribly scarred from wrist to elbow. He looked like a shark had bitten his arm and skimmed off some of the fat and muscle tissue with its teeth. The results were scary. His penis however looked good. It was smooth, and aside from the size, appeared normal. He could urinate through it and achieve erections all on his own. Testicles were created using the labia skin and silicone implants. At a later date he planned to have a penile pump implanted so he could achieve stronger erections. This was intriguing to me but I supposed having to take time out from fooling around to inflate your dick might be unromantic. Curiously his clitoris had been moved down between the base of his penis and the top of his testicles. The man was able to achieve orgasms from there. It was a lot to process mentally and emotionally. I didn't know what I had expected a surgically created penis to look like or how it would function but it seemed sacrifice and compromise would be part of the package.

The last man to talk was the one who'd had a metoidioplasty. This is where the clitoris is freed and moved a little higher on the pubis, the urethra is extended to allow urination from there, the vagina is essentially sewn shut and testicles are formed from the labia. The results are practically scar free, sensitivity is maintained, standing urination is possible and the package looks incredibly realistic. It's also far less risky and expensive compared to a phalloplasty. The only drawback is that your penis is tiny. Really tiny. Size isn't everything but I knew I was too vain to opt for this. Still it was interesting.

After that I sat in on some documentary screenings and joined up with Mom for the closing ceremonies. I had made a few contacts over the weekend with other trans guys. One guy named Tucker was only seventeen and the closest to my own age. Another guy named Michael was about twenty years older than me but he ran an FTM support group out of his apartment on weekends and lived very close to me. The whole weekend had been a little overwhelming, but I definitely felt like I was less of a freak since there were thousands of other men from all walks of life going through the same ordeal as me.

Support Group

Mom and I went to the support group at Michael and Jillian's apartment a few times. It was actually two groups, one for the men and another for their partners. Poor Mom had to sit with a bunch of lesbians venting about their relationship problems now that their girlfriends were their boyfriends. That kind of situation is complicated to the max. I'm not sure what kind of support Mom had to offer but I'll bet she tried.

Likewise most of the things the other trans men talked about I couldn't relate to because of our age differences, but I enjoyed their company. I was the only guy there not dating a lesbian. Because I was still the age of a junior high school student I hadn't had the opportunity to mistakenly come out as a lesbian and start dating as one. I told them about Michelle though. They were all extremely impressed that I had a straight girlfriend who was cool with me being trans. That was a lie of course. Despite everything, I still hadn't come clean to Michelle. I felt bad lying to people who had been so honest and nice to me, but lying was becoming natural for me. Sad but true.

Sometimes they'd invite me out to a movie or dinner with the guys after group. I couldn't always go because it was hard for Mom to drive home and then pick me up later. But when I could go I was thrilled to be included. It felt good to be around people who saw me for who I was and treated me accordingly. It also felt amazing to have adults treat me as a contemporary.

I was glad to have the group to talk to when I started taking testosterone. My family had been accepting of me but they never expressed happiness at any of the changes I went through. The other trans guys were there for me in a very special way to congratulate me on what they knew was a large and important victory. They also teased me about my voice, acne and other subtle changes. It wasn't hurtful teasing. Instead it actually made me feel good someone else noticed the minute differences in my appearance.

Chapter Fifteen

A New Beginning

By Betsie

I guess you could say Luca had been waiting for this day most of his life. Legally changing his name was the first step in the transitioning process. Although we had been discussing this for weeks and I knew I was ready, I was so unprepared.

I was ready for my son to start living the life he so deserved but I was unprepared to lose my daughter. Although I had lost Marie years earlier, this day would somehow make it official.

I had made it through my denial and anger stages and thought I was headed towards my acceptance stage. Boy was I wrong!

We had worked hard for Luca to be able to start his first year of high school with his new name. All high school transcripts had to be consistent, no changing names half way through. The court document had been sent in months earlier with a request to have his name changed before school started in September.

The weeks of waiting took a toll on me. The more I tried to be happy for my son, the more depressed I became. I was slowly watching as more and more of my daughter disappeared before my eyes. Soon she would be gone. I cried when I carefully tucked away all family photos of our little girl. They were now just memories.

We finally had our court date and Brooks, Marie and I were sitting outside the courtroom waiting for the clerk to give us instructions. A young woman opened the door and speaking to the entire crowd, informed us we would all be called into the courtroom together. The judge would then call us up one by one. In front of all these strangers, we would have to tell the judge the reason for wanting to change names. He had the authority to approve or deny our request.

I was already a nervous wreck and hearing this made me want to vomit. I couldn't control my shaking legs and my slight headache became worse and worse by each long minute. My clenched fists were turning my fingers white.

We were supposed to be called in at 9. It was now 9:15.

"*What the hell is taking this judge so long?*" I was thinking as the door opened. As she entered the hallway, the same young clerk called our names. I knew this was going to be difficult. Everything I had gone through with Marie had been difficult. Why should this be any different?

Without ever having to see the judge, the clerk pulled us aside and handed Luca the precious document he had been waiting for. Signed, sealed and delivered, Luca's life had officially begun and Marie's had officially ended. My daughter would not be returning.

Luca so much deserved that day to be one of celebration. To mark the occasion, we planned on having lunch out on the Rockmore, a floating restaurant in Salem Harbor. But I robbed my son that day. Instead of celebrating with him on what should have been the happiest day of his life, I went home and cried myself to sleep, mourning one the saddest days of mine.

Diane had talked to Brooks and me about mourning the death of our daughter. It is a natural process parents go through as their child transitions. Because I still had my child, I couldn't wrap my head around what she meant. I thought, "*Okay, my daughter will be gone, but I will have a son in her place. How can I mourn someone I have still have?*"

But when the clerk handed Luca that piece of paper, I knew immediately what Diane had been talking about. It hit me hard. I don't know what to say to other parents going through this. At some point you *will* mourn the death of your child. There is no right or wrong time or right or wrong way.

Testosterone

Let's talk about testosterone. Let's talk about mood swings and anger!

Luca had waited almost a year for Diane to recommend hormone therapy. He was as excited as I was apprehensive. There was no way anyone could forewarn me of what was to come.

Luca was agitated all the time. If I thought he had been impossible to live with before starting testosterone, it was nothing compared to this time in his life. If you have had teenagers or you can remember when you were a teenager going through puberty, take your raging hormones and increase them by ten. He was still producing female hormones and getting shots of male hormones. The male hormones were determined to win the battle.

Everything was right, everything was wrong, all in the same moment. He would make me laugh and then cry within minutes. I would get a hug and then be told to go to hell. The poor neighbors would hear doors slamming all the time. Sometimes by Luca. Sometimes by me. His anger would rage out of control as he broke bottles out on the balcony (a neighbor called the police) or destroyed items meaning a lot to him. I know some of you are still saying, yeah but all teenagers go through this. Yes, but at least they ease into it gradually. This all happened within weeks, not giving Luca time to learn how to handle his emotions.

There were times when Luca's arms would be all bloody. Out of desperation, he was cutting himself. Diane explained to me, Luca was hurting so much emotionally, cutting himself took the emotional hurt and transposed it to a physical pain he could deal with. More than once I called the police out of fear he had hurt himself. I always regretted doing this. It only embarrassed Luca and added to the pain he was already feeling.

Knowing the reason he was cutting himself did not make it any easier to see. One night, as I felt I was losing my sanity, Brooks came home from work just before I called the police. He took Luca out for a drive to Hampton Beach, giving me time to calm down and re-think my actions.

Luca so desperately wanted his dad and me to trust him. But he was making it so difficult.

Thank God for my sister Louise. She had the loving touch necessary to give Luca the shots he needed every other week. Poor kid. He had to drop his pants for his aunt. I'm sure this added to his frustration.

I remember calling the house one day and a strange voice answered the phone. I almost hung up, thinking I had the wrong number.

"It's me," Luca said.

Luca's voice had deepened overnight. I didn't know if I should laugh or cry.

Falling asleep at night was almost impossible. Alone with my thoughts, I started doubting our actions. Was this the right thing to be doing? Would Luca ever calm down and be the lovable person he used to be? What about the spike in blood pressure and cholesterol? Would it be worth it in the end? Would he make it to his next birthday? Would I ever stop crying?

Besides the emotional toll this was taking on all three of us, there was the financial toll I worried about. Our health insurance didn't cover Luca's weekly, bi-weekly and then monthly appointments with Diane. Because Luca's pediatrician refused to go along with his treatment, we had to pay for the testosterone and needles. I had to pay cash each month to Dr. Spack because our insurance wouldn't cover his bill either.

Then you had the traveling. If I remember correctly Dr. Spack's office was in Newton. Diane's office was in Wayland. Depending on the traffic, it was a forty-five minute to one hour drive each way. I panicked every time I got close to Boston.

I was drowning emotionally and financially. I was exhausted from no sleep, working full time, worrying full time, arguing full time, and all the driving, driving, driving.

I kept saying, "I want to have the nervous breakdown I'm entitled to."

People around me would think I was being funny. I wasn't. Sometimes I thought I should be locked up in a padded room.

Actually, my doctor made me go to counseling by myself but it added to my stress. Another appointment to keep. Another co-payment to make. I only went a few times.

A New Beginning

By Luca

The name change happened in August of 1997. This was a super huge deal for me. Waking up that morning and looking in the mirror while brushing my teeth, I knew in just a few hours I'd be embracing Luca full time.

I was worried the judge would give us a hard time or the court employees would be rude. I was trying to ignore my anxiety about having to possibly out myself before a room full of potentially hostile and judgmental strangers. I definitely had a preconceived notion that all judges were unsympathetic and void of any humanity. The last time I'd been in a courthouse had been because of Bobby and things hadn't gone so great so I was worried. Seated on a very uncomfortable bench in a hot hallway, I kept listening to *Paradise in Me* by K's Choice on my discman while battling my nausea. After what felt like tens of hours, a court employee came over and told Mom a judge had signed off on my name change without having to speak to us. We could sign the papers and leave. I was immensely relieved.

The anxiety and tension of the morning took most of the celebratory spirit out of me. We went from the courthouse to the social security administration office so I could change my name on my social security card. I felt so proud when they printed off my new card with my new name on it. I've never signed a document so slowly and deliberately in my life.

It had been a long morning and we were supposed to go out for lunch at this restaurant I really liked that floated out in the harbor. You had to take a water taxi to get to it. But instead we went home because Mom had a headache. I didn't have anyone I could call who would be happy for me so I kept the news to myself and spent the afternoon alone in my room, examining my social security card from time to time.

Testosterone

After almost a year of therapy Diane had recommended me for hormone treatment. My primary care pediatrician expressly denounced

Diane's recommendation. In fact my pediatrician did not believe gender identity disorder to be real. It's hurtful when your trusted childhood doctor thinks you're off your nut and possibly some sort of sexual deviant in the making. It sucks even more when your insurance company refuses to send you to another primary care doctor. So now every time you have a cold or flu you also have to hear a lecture about how the path you're taking in life is wrong in God's eyes.

I was glad I had kept the contact information for Dr. Spack. His office was over an hour drive away and our insurance wouldn't cover the visits or drugs because my pediatrician refused to issue a referral. Still, seeing him always filled me with comfort and joy. Probably because I didn't have to do the driving or pay the bills. That was Mom's problem.

Starting testosterone was a really big deal for me. I was so excited I was able to overlook my fear of needles and accept the injections gladly. Aunt Louise had been to nursing school and worked as a phlebotomist for the American Red Cross. Every two weeks Mom would drive me over to her house and Louise would stick the hugest needle I've ever seen, 21 gauge, an inch and a half into my thigh muscle. The liquid medicine was thick and the injection site would sting for almost an hour. Just looking at needles filled me with terror so I was deeply appreciative of Louise doing this for me. When I was depressed or angry I'd sometimes cut myself with box cutters or broken glass, but the thought of sticking myself with a sterile needle made me woozy.

I started out on 2cc's of testosterone every other week. Menses had occurred late in life for me and even after it began my periods came infrequently. Still, whenever it happened I'd feel dirty and ashamed. I'd hate my body and curse it for punishing me. I wouldn't leave the house until it passed, feeling too unclean to be in public. Thankfully the testosterone put an end to all my menstruation within a few months.

The acne brought on from testosterone was impressive. Before taking T (testosterone) I'd only had like three pimples in my life. Now I had at least three a week, sometimes three a day. I'd get them on my face, shoulders and upper arms. Yuck!

My voice started to slowly change. It never turned into a deep sexy bass but people stopped thinking I was a woman over the phone. I didn't get thicker body hair or start growing facial hair but most high school freshmen don't have beards or hairy chests so I was OK with that. My metabolism increased. I felt more energetic and stronger. I also craved red meat like I was a freaking lion on the Serengeti. My blood pressure spiked right off but given my weight, diet, and lack of exercise, I was sure my lifestyle would have caused a similar increase in time.

The only real drawback was the mood swings. I didn't get periods anymore but my hormone levels would spike and wane drastically between injections. It was like PMSing every two weeks instead of once a month. I'd start out angry, horny and really stand-offish and ten days later be emotionally sensitive, needy and clingy.

Before taking T I had already been diagnosed as manic depressive. I'm not sure if I really had a chemical imbalance in my brain or if my life sucked to a point where the stress broke me. Either way the hormone ups and downs exacerbated my mental frailty. I made a lot of bad decisions and picked a lot of fights. The anger I had built up over the years fed on the T and grew into this vicious, seething, dragon-like creature inside me that would explode into a fiery rage burning so hot it was blinding.

There was more going on than just the T. I was still "homeschooling" and the long stretches of isolation were taking their toll as well. I'd sort of stopped doing any school work. I still went to NSCC for Algebra. I was also auditing an aviation class. Sometimes if Dad had a day off during the week we'd go to art or history museums in Boston or Salem. Other than that I'd spend my days watching MTV, reading, or chatting online since AOL was now unlimited.

So despite finally getting to take T, having other trans people to confide in, and having some hope for my future, I was still fat, hated my body, lonely, bored, emotionally unbalanced and wasting my time dulling my intelligence with television.

With so many things happening to me beyond my emotional maturity and comprehension, I was very fortunate to have Diane in my life. For the most part she really helped me keep it together. It's hard to explain how even when you get what you want you're still not okay. I had really, really, wanted and needed to get on testosterone. But I wanted and needed a lot of other things too. Diane understood me even when I didn't.

Chapter Sixteen

The Balloon Pops

By Betsie

I had to be out of my mind! If you've ever driven into Boston's Logan International Airport, you know you don't drive there unless you absolutely have to. Yet there I was.

It was just after Christmas and Luca's friend Michelle and her family were coming to Massachusetts for a week. His excitement was so contagious, he convinced me to drive him to the airport to surprise her. I knew driving into the airport for a five minute visit was a crazy idea, but once again Christmas day had been pretty terrible for Luca and this was my way of saying I was sorry.

Since my first meeting with Michelle's parents had not gone well, I had no interest in speaking with them again. Luca would have to meet Michelle all on his own. This left me sitting alone in a busy airport watching snow swirling around and around.

Just like the snowflake riding on the back of the wind to unknown destinations, I day-dreamed about traveling to my own unknown destinations. Having already navigated through rough seas, did I dare look forward to smooth sailing ahead?

When Luca finally returned he was glowing. I couldn't remember a time when I had seen him so happy.

The following week, Luca went in and out of Boston every day, spending as much time with Michelle as possible. Brooks would drive him to the Salem train station every morning to drop him off and I would drive to the Revere subway station every evening to pick him up. I didn't mind. It was as if I had a different child. There was no fighting. No arguing. Just a smile on his face every day.

Like a balloon that's been inflated with air, Michelle's visit had filled Luca's heart with happiness. But at some point balloons deflate. When Michelle left, Luca's heart was punctured. Day after day I watched as it slowly seeped its happiness, until it had vanished.

Once again, the situation at home was extremely strained. Having a hysterectomy in February of 1998 only added more steam to the pressure cooker we were living in. Three days after I came home from the hospital, Brooks had a heart attack.

I thought Luca would explode with anger as the three of us were now trapped in a prison called home. With no way of leaving, there may as well have been bars on the windows. Visitors were few and far between. The cold, snowy days dragged on and on.

February turned to March and I had been fighting one infection after another and not healing. Brooks still had not been given the okay to drive. Snow and ice lingered.

"Mom, can I please go sit in the car and listen to the radio?" Luca begged. "I've been cooped up in this house for six weeks!"

"I don't think so."

"C'mon Mom. I need some fresh air!"

"You promise the car won't move."

"I promise," Luca replied. "I just need to get out of the house."

I knew the past few weeks had been hell for Luca. I wanted so much to believe him. I handed him the car keys.

Within minutes I could hear music blasting. Looking out the window, I could see Luca dancing in his seat, singing along. I could stop checking and worrying.

All of a sudden I heard the engine start. Running out the door in my bare feet, I was too scared to be conscious of the wintery conditions. It didn't take long before Luca pulled out of the parking space and was heading out of the parking lot.

"Someone call the police!" I yelled at the top of my lungs.

No one heard me.

Running on the snow and ice, I caught up to Luca and started pounding on the windows.

"What the hell are you doing?" I screamed.

"I don't know. I have to get away from here. I can't take this anymore."

I was terrified.

"Someone call the police!" I screamed again.

Again, either no one heard or they chose not to respond.

Luca was only fifteen. If he left the parking lot, especially with all the black ice, he and someone else would be hurt.

"Roll down this God damn window!" I demanded, banging the window with both fists.

After a lot more yelling and some crying thrown in, Luca finally rolled down the window but would not turn off the engine.

As I reached in to grab the car keys, Luca rolled up the window, forcing me to pull back my arms. Unfortunately the window went up a lot faster than he had expected, trapping my arms between the glass and the rubber of the window frame. Luca looked into my horrified eyes and rolled down the window just enough to get my arms out.

Getting so caught up in the situation, I had forgotten I was standing on ice and snow. Numbness had set into my feet and I was freezing, but I wasn't about to let go of his shirt. Although I believed my right arm was broken, I tried not to let my pain show.

Keeping my arm in the window, I took the chance Luca would not try to pull away. He would never intentionally hurt me.

I couldn't hold back the tears any longer. I was hurting physically and emotionally.

"You know I love you," I was barely able to say. "I'm sorry you've had to deal with all of this."

"But mom, it isn't fair. You had the surgery I want."

"I'm sorry Hon. Diane says we're really close to getting you upper surgery. You won't get that surgery by running away. Please move over and let me park the car."

Time was as frozen as that grey winter's day. It was a long agonizing minute before Luca put the car in park and let me slide in.

Once inside the house we headed for his bedroom. Luca was hurting. He needed to see Diane but we lived too far away to ask someone else to drive. There was nothing I could do but hold my child and tell him to hang in there a little bit longer.

Thankfully, my arm wasn't broken, just very badly bruised. A few weeks later at my final doctor's appointment, my arms were still a hauntingly purplish grey. My doctor wanted to know if Brooks had hurt me.

"No," I told him. "My son didn't see me reach into the back seat of the car to get some packages and he rolled up the window. I couldn't get my arms out quick enough."

This hadn't been the first time I didn't tell the truth about my child and I was sure it wouldn't be the last.

The Balloon Pops

By Luca

Christmas 1997 had been interesting. My cousin Will had a job at the mall selling T shirts from a cart and now had money to spend on Christmas. He got me an album of Anthrax B sides and Tool's first album *Opiate* on CD. He also got me a Tool t shirt I'd had my eye on for months. It was black with a white skeletal alien fetus on the back. He spoiled me hardcore that year.

Then I made the mistake of putting the t shirt on. I was wearing it at the dinner table with my entire family when Dad told me to take it off.

I said, "Why? It doesn't have any profanity on it or anything."

He said the image was inappropriate to wear in front of my cousin's grandmother. The grandmother said she didn't care.

I said, "What's inappropriate about an alien fetus? It's just a drawing."

Then Dad slapped me across the face for saying fetus at the dinner table. Once again my whole family sat there and said nothing to either defend or condemn me. I still have no clue what the big deal was, only it seemed every holiday where wine was present I ended up getting hit. Will grabbed his keys and we left immediately. I walked around his neighborhood for a little while to cool off. It didn't seem to matter that I only had a denim jacket over a t shirt to protect me from the wind and snow. I had my rage to keep me warm.

With Christmas behind me I was looking forward to New Year's Eve. Michelle's family would be spending five whole nights in Boston, including New Year's Eve, and I'd be seeing her every day of their vacation.

I was waiting at Logan Airport when their plane arrived. I had convinced Mom to let me go all the way into Boston just so I could say hi to Michelle while her family waited for their luggage. The plane's landing had been delayed due to snow on the runway. I waited in the baggage claim area for almost an hour, freezing my butt off whenever the doors to the outside opened. Instead of wearing a winter jacket I was in jeans and a turtleneck. At fourteen years old looking cool was more important than practicality.

Seeing Michelle warmed me to my core. All of my anxiety, insecurity, self-loathing and any other thoughts or feelings I had seeped out of me. All the other people in the room disappeared. My vision of the world narrowed down to just her. Floating down toward me her lovely image stunned the breath out of me. She ran to me and threw her arms around me. My body exploded into painful bursts of intense heat. It felt like I'd been swimming in cold dark water so long I had become numb to it. Then Michelle pulled me out, and as her heat penetrated me it stung, the contrast of temperatures extreme. Being with her was like having the whole Earth spun off its axis. She even changed the effects of gravity. My shoulders felt heavy, my feet light as a feather. Then she was gone. Michelle and her family were in a limo to their hotel before I could even see or think straight.

Over the next few days Michelle and I spent a lot of time together in Boston and Salem. I spent time with her mother and sister too. The four of us went to the Peabody Essex Museum together. Michelle and I went off on our own. We meandered slowly, holding hands and pressing our bodies close together whenever we stopped to look at something. There were many stolen kisses.

Eventually we were alone in a dimly lit room staring at a landscape painting. Michelle had her back to me, pressing the length of her body against my front. The smell of her hair was intoxicating. With my arms around her I slid my hand down the front of her jeans and inside her satin panties. Yup. We were those horny indecent teenagers that you hate. Sorry. I skipped second base and went straight to third in a public history museum.

It never stopped amazing me that Michelle wanted me. I think it amazed strangers on the street too. We were quite an odd pair. A fat guy with crazy bleached hair in cheap clothes with this stunning, perfectly put together girl. It's not Cupid making me say Michelle was beautiful. The girl was a knockout. As an adult she's modeled professionally. As a teenager she had long thick silken black hair, porcelain skin, striking blue eyes, full breasts, thin waist and round hips. Men ages ten to sixty would stop dead in their tracks for a second look at her everywhere we went. If I had been more confident in myself I would have reveled in their jealousy.

If Michelle's family thought anything was off about me they never showed it. I couldn't get a handle on what Michelle had figured. I wore a binder the whole time I was around her. It was a thick medical binder meant to go around a person's waist after surgery. It was Mom's from when she'd had her appendix out years earlier. Not only did the tight Velcro flatten my chest, it also made it hard. I packed around Michelle too. For anyone who doesn't know, packing is when you put something down the front of your pants to resemble a male package. Sometimes in movies people will use rolled up socks. In *Spinal Tap* the bass player used a cucumber to simulate a large rigid phallus. For me I used an un-lubricated condom stuffed with cotton balls. I felt this had more of a penis like shape with a soft texture. These were the days before realistic flesh-like silicone packies were available for purchase in adult stores. Besides, even if they had been available I was still only fourteen.

We spent one afternoon alone at my house. We didn't leave my room until it was time for Michelle to go back to her hotel. It was my first time completely alone with her in a private setting. As soon as my door was closed and locked she took her shirt off and hugged me. Once again she had to remind me to breathe which made her laugh. Then she clung to me and cried which scared me. She said she was crying because she was so happy to be with me and sad because she knew it couldn't last. I didn't know what to say. No one had ever cared for me like this before. No one had ever hugged me while topless before either. It was sexual but felt so natural at the same time.

I wished I could have taken off my clothes too and had nothing between us but our skin. I wasn't going to strip because of the binder, but even if Michelle knew what it was hiding and was okay with it, I don't think I would have been.

When your insides and outsides don't match it's hard to get a lover who accepts you. But I think it can be harder still to accept yourself. I didn't want my first uninhibited sexual encounter to be with this body. It would have ruined everything for me. I was also unhappy with my weight. My gelatinous body disgusted me. If Michelle had the chance to love me, stretch marks and all, I would have resented her. There was so much I wasn't ready to come to terms with about myself and someone else accepting my flaws would have blown a hole in my cocoon of self-hatred. I wasn't ready for that. I wasn't ready to love myself so I kept Michelle at arm's length, physically and emotionally, when we made love.

Since I wouldn't take my clothes off beyond stripping down to a t-shirt and boxer-briefs, I didn't have a penis, and I wouldn't tell Michelle I didn't have a penis, lovemaking was complicated. Michelle knew I wasn't happy with my weight and that I'd been sexually abused as a child so she cut me a lot of slack. She didn't push or pry. We went slowly. Every touch was timid and tender. We were also both fourteen and virgins so it's not like it was going to be great or anything anyway. Neither of us knew what we were doing.

When Michelle was nude I was taken aback by her beauty and her confidence. She wasn't narcissistic about how good looking she was, but she wasn't shy about it either. I was very jealous of how at peace she was with herself. At that moment I would have given anything to be more attractive, more capable. I wanted to be the kind of lover she deserved and it pained me deeply that I couldn't be.

Michelle let me touch her wherever I wanted, however I wanted. She would have given me anything, everything. I explored her body thoroughly with my eyes, fingers and mouth. I committed everything about her to memory in one afternoon; every curve, every goose bump, her different smells, textures and tastes. Underneath our clothes we both had female bodies but they were nothing alike.

When Michelle's family left Boston to go back to Arizona I was too devastated to cry. The entire visit had been bittersweet but being with Michelle was the happiest I'd ever been. At the time it was the best week of my life. I tried to hold on to that but you can't hug a memory.

Michelle and I were together one more time before we broke up. She spent the night at my house and took a bus from Boston to Sturbridge the next afternoon. In the day we fooled around while listening to Veruca Salt's *American Thighs* and Marcy Playground's *Opium* on repeat.

At night Michelle and I fell asleep together on my bed but I ended up on the floor after my arm fell asleep. I kept the binder on all through her visit. My skin was screaming by the time she left. Binding is ineffectual unless it's tight. I was so insecure I pulled that sucker extra tight before Velcro-ing it in place. Most of the time it made breathing difficult and pinched the skin under my armpits. After thirty hours straight, I had painful red sores all over my upper torso. I wanted to control my appearance so desperately, pain was hardly a deterrent.

Since my bedroom had its own private bathroom Michelle eagerly let me watch her shower the next morning. She asked me to join her but I had to be content to watch. It was the most sensual thing I'd ever seen and it hurt to be on the sidelines.

Two months later Michelle broke up with me. It was over the phone but when you live 2,600 miles apart that's the best you can get. Sometimes I wish she had sent me a letter so I wouldn't be haunted by the sound of her somber goodbye.

It wasn't surprising when it happened. We'd been growing apart for a while. She was in high school, beautiful and popular. Attractive boys with lean bodies and fast cars had been calling on her for a while. What's more, they were there. I couldn't compete. When I first felt her pulling away I became emotionally manipulative, bordering on abusive. I didn't know how else to keep her paying attention to me. I thought having Michelle feel sorry for me was better than her forgetting me. And when she'd finally had enough of my crap and broke up with me, the only thing that surprised me was my heart kept beating as if it hadn't heard the news.

I couldn't comprehend why I didn't just die after she hung up the phone. I couldn't imagine a future anymore without Michelle in it. She had been my everything. For months I had planned my future, my vision of myself, around her. The man I would become would be her boyfriend and eventually her husband. Without her I had nothing. Was nothing. So why did my lungs continue to draw air? Why didn't I just fade away?

I convinced myself Michelle's new boyfriend Alan had come between us. That Michelle had never loved me as I loved her. I told myself my fault in the breakup had been being fat and being trans. I cursed the heavens for not letting me be the kind of man she wanted. It was God's fault I'd lost the love of my life, my soul mate.

It took me over ten years, long after I'd gotten over her and moved on, to realize what really broke up Michelle and me. It wasn't her new boyfriend. It wasn't that she hadn't loved me. It wasn't the distance or our compatibility. It wasn't my weight. I could have gone on a diet. It probably wasn't my emotional neediness that ended up suffocating her or even that I was trans. It was the lies.

Michelle turned out to be a full blown bisexual. She's also a decent person who's far less shallow than I made her out to be. If I had been honest with her from the start things may have turned out differently. I know in my heart that if I could have been honest I wouldn't have been so insecure or felt the need to constantly chip away at Michelle's self-esteem to keep her at my level of self-hatred. I'll never know if she would have accepted me for who I really am, and that's the real tragedy. Worse, it was a tragedy completely of my own making.

To this day I can't go to Faneuil Hall in Boston or walk past the Peabody Essex Museum in Salem without thinking of Michelle.

We've spoken a few times over the past years. I've never met another person who I've had so much in common with, someone who gets me without my having to say a word. But to this day I think my lies and cheap shots have made it impossible for us to successfully communicate and although I'm no longer in love with her I occasionally miss our friendship.

I don't know if there's really a good time to have someone break up with you, but Michelle couldn't have picked a worse time to dump me

In the beginning of spring Mom had a hysterectomy. Her stomach looked disgusting with staples holding together a long infected incision. The infection had made her very ill and due to other complications she came home with a catheter. She said it felt like she was pissing knives. For days her skin was waxy from sweat, her body racked with pain. It took much longer for her to heal than originally expected. Still I found myself jealous of her. I wished my ovaries had cysts and tumors so I could have all that junk cut out of me too.

While Mom was recuperating the household cooking and cleaning became my responsibility. Dad's only chore was to scoop the poop out of the cat litter box at night. The first time he bent over with that little plastic kitty crap shovel and a baggy he had a heart attack. Now I had two parents laid up in bed needing me to do shit constantly. Not that asking if I'd make a bowl of soup or take out the trash was demanding, but to a spoiled, lazy, rebellious teenager it felt that way. I was too young to drive so I was effectively trapped in isolation with them. This was when Michelle chose to break up with me. The stress mounted quickly and I overreacted.

Chapter Seventeen

A Sunday Drive

By Betsie

In May of 1998 Brooks had finally been given the okay to drive and I was almost completely healed. On a beautiful Sunday afternoon Brooks, Luca and I decided to drive along the coast of Ipswich, Massachusetts.

Stopping at a local beach to stretch our legs, the warm sun and cool breezes lifted our spirits. I wanted to linger, breathing in the peacefulness of the day.

After satisfying our craving for Chinese food with a nice lunch out, we headed for home.

As Brooks slowed down for a stop sign, without warning the back door opened and Luca jumped out of the car.

"Stop the car!" I shouted to Brooks.

The car barely had time to stop before I jumped out.

"Let me go Mom! You have to let me go!" Luca yelled, as he started running on near-by railroad tracks.

Not knowing if he was trying to run away or run into an oncoming train terrified me. There was no time to think, only react.

"Luca, please stop!" I shouted. "Why the hell are you doing this?"

Luca kept running. I began chasing.

When I was finally out of breath, Luca stopped in the middle of the tracks and turned around.

"Don't come any closer. I'll just start running."

"Why the hell are you running down the tracks? Where do you think you're going?"

"I don't know. I just don't want to go home."

"We won't go home. Where do you want to go?" I yelled back.

"I don't know."

Luca began to cry.

"Well at least get off the tracks before we get hurt."

"I can't," Luca yelled back as he turned and started running.

It didn't matter that the intense pain in my side got sharper with every pounding step on the railroad pilings. I pursued Luca.

Luca was as out of breath as I was and slowed down enough to allow me to catch up with him. Grabbing his right arm with all my strength, and yanking back, he eventually stopped.

I could now see the headlight of a train off in the distance.

Luca pulled back with everything he had. We battled a tug-of-war before I was finally able to get him off the tracks.

By this time, Brooks had driven the car through the parking lot and was holding open the back seat door. Luca was fighting us with all his might and it took Brooks and me both to push him into the car.

Jumping into the back seat and grabbing Luca's wrist, I yelled to Brooks, "Drive to the Children's Hospital."

"What do you think they're going to do?"

"I don't know, but I don't know what else to do!"

Luca wanted to jump out of the car and struggled with me all the way to the hospital. I held him so tightly both my hands were severely cramped by the time we got there. I couldn't hold him another minute.

Exhausted, there was no way I could go through another tug-of-war so Brooks went into the emergency room to get some help.

With my thoughts always directed on keeping Luca from jumping out of a moving car, I hadn't had the chance to process my feelings.

Now, sitting in the car in the hospital parking lot, I had a few seconds to go over the events of the day. Why did Luca want to hurt himself again? He was back to seeing Diane and I thought things were going well. His name was legally changed. He was on testosterone. Upper surgery was in sight. Why was he doing this to me? Why did he always have to ruin a good day?

Brooks returned with two large males. Luca was defeated.

All of a sudden, like a switch had been turned off, Luca quieted down and calmly walked into the hospital. Sitting motionless while being bombarded with questions, he never answered back. He may have been sitting there physically, but Luca's mind was somewhere else.

I tried desperately to get in touch with Diane. No answer.

It was going to be a long night. This time Luca was admitted to Boston Regional Medical Center. Just before midnight, Brooks and I were walking through the beautiful old oak doors we had walked through when Luca was eight years old. Instead of leaving with a stranger, this time Luca would be spending three weeks in the adolescent psych ward.

Fifteen hours earlier, what started out as a lovely Sunday drive by the shore quickly turned to a voyage back through hell. Swimming against my ocean of tears was futile. There was no way I could reach a safe harbor. In a few hours dawn would break, but I wouldn't welcome the light of day.

Luca had now been a patient at Boston Regional for almost one month. One more night to go. The insurance company said he had to leave whether he was ready or not. I knew he wasn't ready.

Walking down the familiar grey hallways, a small child about seven years old caught my attention. He looked lost standing in the doorway to his room, head bent, exploring the floor. Tears came to my eyes as I thought about his poor mother. Would she have years of appointments and disappointments searching for answers? Would she give up on living, just going through motions, chasing anything that was vaguely familiar? Would she worry each day, wondering when she returned from work whether her son would be dead or alive? Would she come so close to a nervous breakdown she was holding on for dear life?

Entering Luca's room quickly brought my thoughts back to my own reality. Due to his special circumstances, Luca had been given a private room. Each day before leaving, he would bind his breasts so none of the other patients knew he had them.

We had been experiencing a very warm, moist May and Luca had developed a sore under his left arm from the chafing of elastic pulled tightly against his skin. During my visit the previous evening, Luca showed me how red, puss filled and infected his sore had become. Asking for help, I became infuriated with the incompetent nursing staff when I was told it was not in their job description to change bandages.

The psychiatrist had told Luca not to put the binder back on. This wasn't an option. Although I knew Luca wasn't ready to leave, as I cleaned his wound the best I could, I just wanted him home where he could at least feel comfortable in his own skin.

Before Luca could be released I had to meet with the psychiatrist heading up the adolescent ward. Walking into his overcrowded office, Luca and I took seats together opposite the small, well groomed gentleman with the messy desk. I felt very uncomfortable as his slender black eyes stared me down.

"Mrs. Harvie," he began. "As you know, Marie shows compulsive and addictive behaviors."

"His name is Luca," I interrupted.

"*What an ass,*" I was thinking. Luca had done nothing but complain about this idiot for weeks. After one sentence, I could understand why. I wanted to scream.

We had legally changed Luca's name nine months earlier. Where did he get off calling Luca *Marie*? Was that even legal?

"We also feel Marie needs to go back to school," he continued.

"How in the world is that going to happen? Luca is still in the process of transitioning. There's no way in hell I'll allow him to go back to his old high school."

"You'll have to contact the school and work that out. A lot of the kids here pass through alternative schools. I'm sure your school district has one. Call your special ed department."

Then he pointed an insulting finger in my face.

"Mrs. Harvie, you'll be very sorry if you pursue this transgendered notion any further. Marie is too young to make this decision. This Diane person doesn't know what she's talking about."

Was this jerk going to undo everything we had worked so hard for? Did we have to sit here any longer and listen to this shit? I was so angry at this ass I wanted to throw something at him. Knowing how much authority he held as head of the psychiatric ward, I somehow controlled my anger.

Grabbing the papers off his desk I said, "Just give me the papers to sign to get Luca out of here tomorrow."

Leaving Luca pleading with me not to leave him there another night, unraveled my confidence. I felt the hallways closing in on me. As I walked towards the elevators, once again I felt the absence of my mother. I needed her wisdom. I was so confused. Who was I supposed to listen to? Was my child too young to understand his own feelings?

The elevator door opened and I stepped out onto the deck of the SS Titanic. My ship was sinking and there were no lifeboats waiting for me at the exit. My legs became heavy as I waded through the muck in the hallways. My chest tightened. I couldn't get enough air in my lungs. The ten foot tall, heavy doors I had admired in the past became an obstacle to get through.

With a force of adrenalin, I pushed open the old, beautifully carved doors and gasped for air. Regaining my land legs, I slowly retreated to my car. Taking deep breaths I was able to salvage my composure and my thinking became coherent.

I had let my head take over in there when I should have let my heart lead the way. I was sure Luca knew exactly what he wanted and needed. From then on, I only listened to and trusted Diane and my son.

I now had searching for a school thrown in with appointments with the endocrinologist, appointments with Diane, and holding down a full time job. My life was like a yo-yo. Up one day, down the next. I wondered when the string would snap, causing me to curl up into a ball and roll away.

A Sunday Drive

By Luca

I'm not sure how I ended up at the hospital. I don't remember if I threatened to hurt myself or actually tried something and failed. I've been told I jumped out of a car and ran onto active train tracks but Mom coaxed me back before a train reached us. It sounds familiar but the memory is like mist in my head.

I was admitted to a high security juvenile psychiatric ward. I'd never been locked up anywhere against my will before. Everywhere I turned there was another locked door. Dining room, art room, isolation rooms, living room, patient rooms, supply closet, bathrooms and exits, all locked.

My pockets were searched and my disposable lighter taken away. They took my belt and shoe laces. I had to take off my necklaces, take all the studs out of my ears and turn over my Discman. I wanted to point out if I was really determined to hang myself I wouldn't need a belt or shoe laces, I could twist a long sleeve shirt or pants and hang them over a shower rod just as easily. But I decided a smart ass comment like that wouldn't get me my belt back but rather cost me my pants. These people weren't playing around.

After they'd taken all my belongings, I was given a bed in a room with a kid named Steve. Steve was a year younger than me, a mean-ass skater townie who was hyper and funny as hell.

At first I was afraid of everyone and everything. I didn't want to leave my room. When I poked my head out the door, the hallways seemed to grow longer the more I stared at them. But my roommate Steve seemed normal so this encouraged me a bit.

Other than obvious anger and behavior management issues I couldn't understand why Steve was there. The more I interacted with the other patients I noticed no one really seemed suicidal or depressed. One or two were, but mostly everyone there was just angry.

The mental health system could be a catch-all for kids and teens that act out. They didn't have separate treatment facilities for drug rehab and mental health for patients under eighteen so we were all lumped together.

I suppose whatever your issue was it could be traced back to a mental or personality disorder if you dug deep enough. It also made for a pretty good threat. If you've ever been in the system they could hold that over you until the end of days. You put one toe over the line and instead of juvenile detention you'll end up back in a mental health hospital where all civil liberties disappear in the name of protecting you from yourself. It wasn't just bullshit. When you saw the system in operation it was terrifying.

They could hold me for days without letting me contact my parents or guardian under the pretense of observation. I couldn't contact my family or friends unless a doctor approved it. They decided whether or not I received mail and they read all of it first. When I finally got to use a phone it was monitored. They decided what and when I ate, drank, slept, pottied, and bathed. You were not allowed to alter your appearance by cutting your hair, painting your nails or wearing makeup, even if you left the facility for a scheduled family visit. It could be construed as acting out and result in loss of privileges. All music, books, movies and television shows had to be parental guidance free and doctor approved. Any medicine they prescribed had to be taken. I wasn't allowed to raise my voice or swear. I couldn't have caffeine or candy. The list went on and on. It was horrible not being able to make personal choices for myself or express my personality. Having Big Brother looking down on me 24/7 was exhausting and frustrating.

As soon as another bed was available I was moved to my own room. I had entered the hospital wearing my binder under my clothes and except for when I showered I hadn't taken it off. Not even to sleep because I was never alone. I missed rooming with Steve and he was pissy when I was moved, but the sores the binder created were starting to get infected after three days of no relief.

All of the staff seemed to be cool with me being trans except the doctors, who I only met with in private. The art therapist and general staff all used male pronouns for me. None of the other patients knew I was trans. This was my first time being Luca, the man, in a large peer setting. It was intense and encompassing because of the literal confinement, but as far as peer interaction went I was very well accepted. My social skills were a little rusty but it wasn't an issue with this crowd.

When I'd earned phone privileges I called Michelle. I think she tried to be nice to me because of the circumstance but made it very clear we were still broken up and never getting back together. I was scared and miserable but Michelle was glowing because Alan had asked her to his prom. I decided not to call Michelle anymore. This was probably a huge relief to her.

I still had it in my head that Michelle had left me for Alan because he was more attractive than me, not because I was a pathetic, parasitic, douche-bag. I couldn't speed up my surgery date but I decided to take control of my body in the only way left to me. I was going to lose weight.

When I stood up straight I was 5'7" and weighed 244 pounds. I was grossly fat. I didn't understand nutrition and I was confined to spaces too small to exercise. My solution was to stop eating. I drank water and apple juice but didn't eat a single thing for three days. After two days I'd lost all my privileges because your food intake is monitored. I wasn't allowed to talk on the phone, watch TV or leave my room except for meals or therapy until I ate something. After the third day I was so lonely and bored I decided to come up with a new plan.

I ate every scrap of food they put in front of me and drank tons of water. Then when meal time was over and we had bathroom breaks, since the bathrooms were one at a time, I'd go in and shove my finger down my throat and puke all that food right back up. No one suspected anything because fat boys aren't bulimic, just skinny girls. I started losing weight pretty quickly and started feeling better about my self-image.

It was nice to control what food stayed in my body because nothing else was my choice. I was prescribed a sleeping pill at night, Trazadone, which I became addicted to. I wasn't allowed to have testosterone injections anymore because my primary psychologist didn't believe I was trans. He was from India and because of religious reasons believed gay, lesbian and trans people suffered from serious mental illness induced by Western liberal godlessness. He was scary. I was only forced to meet with him twice but both meetings were intensely traumatic for me.

In the first meeting he insisted on calling me Marie, even though I'd legally been Luca for almost a year, and reminded me that physically I was a girl. This was very uncomfortable for me. He told me my other therapist Diane was a quack and she'd poisoned my mind with nonsense. My mother and endocrinologist had poisoned my body, and my godlessness had poisoned my spirit. It was his opinion that my gender confusion was the root of all my problems. I walked out.

The second meeting with him I skipped but it cost me my TV watching and rec-room privileges. Finally I was literally dragged into an office to meet with him. I had to listen to his spiel about how, if I would accept I'm a girl, I'd see how pretty I was. At this point I realized he wasn't just a bigot, but he was actually the crazy person in the room. I'm not being mean to myself. I wasn't pretty to begin with and taking T hadn't made me prettier. It had been months since anyone in public had confused me for a girl. My face, voice, body language and mannerisms were unmistakably male. If you couldn't see that about me you either weren't looking at me or not even seeing me when you did. I got up and left the room. This guy was screwing with my head. He followed me out into the hall. I ran to my room.

The doctor chased me, calling out "Marie! Stop! Get back here this instant!"

His yelling caught the attention of the general floor staff. Two of which came running to my room to see what the commotion was. He cornered me in my room. I screamed for him to get out. A female staff member who was friendly to me asked me gently from the doorway what was wrong.

"I want him out of my room! I want to be alone. I need some space!"

I thought this would help get him out. In the psych programs anytime you feel you're getting too worked up you're allowed to voluntarily remove yourself from the situation until you calm down. It's called "taking space" and unless it's medicine time you can take space whenever you want or need. I've always found these personal time outs to be helpful actually, especially in anger management.

"Okay Doctor, you need to leave now," the staff member closest to him said.

He ignored her and kept yelling to me.

"Marie! You need to stop this! You're never getting out of here until you accept that you're a girl! I don't know why this is so hard for you. You're beautiful and smart…"

My fist connecting with his mouth cut him off. At that point I wasn't just mad but scared. All his shouting with the door open may have outed me to all the other patients. In this situation it wouldn't just be devastating but possibly dangerous.

The two staff members rushed me, putting themselves between me and the doctor. I put my arms down at my sides and stood very still, tears sliding out of the corners of my eyes. The male staff member pushed the doctor out into the hall and stood in my doorway until the doctor walked off. The female staff member asked me if I was okay. I nodded.

"I'm sorry. I didn't mean to hit him. When I felt myself getting mad I left his office. But he followed me and wouldn't get out of my face."

"No honey, it's alright. He had no right to follow you into your room or say those things to you. Are you going to calm down and stay calm if I leave the room?"

I nodded, glad she was on my side.

"Okay I'll be back. You're not in trouble but I need you to stay calm."

She left and closed the door behind her. I peeked through the small shatter-proof glass window and saw her march down to the nurse's station where the doctor was holding a gauze compress to his bleeding lip. She went inside and they started yelling at each other. But since they were in a sound proof room it was like watching a muted television. I went back and slumped on my bed, praying none of the other patients had heard him call me Marie.

I should have been in a full body restraint jacket on the padded floor of an isolation room for two to four hours for hitting someone, especially a doctor. Instead I was confined to my room for the rest of the day. I guess the two staff members who had helped me had pointed the finger at the doctor for causing the trouble. I doubt any professional misconduct reports were filed, but I was removed from his patient list.

They didn't let me call Mom or Diane to tell them what happened. I had to tell Mom in person on my first visit that wasn't supervised. Aunt Louise had come along for the visit too. Together we snuck into a handicapped bathroom outside the hospital cafeteria so she could give me an injection of T. I had been very scared up until Louise came. If I went much longer without T I might start a menstruation cycle again. I was not in a state where I could have handled that mentally.

The doctor who directed the psych maximum security ward didn't believe I was trans either. He at least did believe gender identity disorder was a genuine affliction and treated multiple M2F's in his private practice. He didn't believe anyone as young as me could understand themselves well enough to know if they're actually trans or not. To be fair I can see how people could have their doubts about me. Many young people go through all kinds of phases. But I never doubted myself. My insistence that I truly was a man was unwavering.

Knowing yourself and your mind yet being unable to convince others of what they cannot see is frustrating. It's frightening when the person you're trying desperately to convince is in a position of power over you and their belief or disbelief may have direct and dire consequences for you. When the person you're trying to convince won't listen to a word you say because before even meeting you he's already made assumptions about your intelligence, candor and mental capacities, it's insulting and dehumanizing. How can you win a battle when not only have you been disarmed, but the bare essence of who you are has been erased from the battlefield? It's like a ghost trying to win an argument with a wall.

Minimum Security Psych Ward

In the midst of all the turmoil and upheaval of the psychiatric ward I did manage to make some friends. The teens in these situations have a lot of fucked up shit going on in their lives and although we didn't share the same problems, our feelings and experiences were similar. These teens were more my peers than anyone I'd met before, and I hit it off straight away with most of them. We bonded during some of the most stressful and vulnerable times in our lives. Some of them are still my friends more than ten years later.

I had mixed feelings about being moved from maximum security to the minimum security ward two floors up.

On the one hand I had a lot more personal freedoms and some of my friends had already been moved up there. On the other hand it was new, and I was becoming very comfortable in the maximum security ward. In fact I was thriving. I hadn't cried at all in weeks. My anger was mostly under control. I was losing weight and never lonely or bored. I laughed all the time. I didn't want to leave my friends or my comfort zone behind. That's how it is in the system though. You start doing well and they kick you out. Makes sense.

In minimum security everyone gets their own room and bathroom. The phones you use are un-monitored payphones and available anytime that isn't bed time. The dining area had cabinets and refrigerators so you could store your own food and snacks, although the hospital still provided three meals and one snack a day. You got to order from a menu rather than eat whatever they felt like serving you. The craft supplies were never locked. Neither were the cleaning supplies, and we had access to laundry facilities. If a parent or guardian signed a form, you were allowed to smoke cigarettes. Caffeine and junk food were no longer off limits. Entertainment wasn't regulated, mail wasn't opened. We could even mingle in each other's rooms if the doors were kept open. I got my belt and shoe laces back. Jewelry was okay, and hairstyles didn't require approval. I could listen to CDs again instead of just the radio or cassette tapes. In minimum security no one was afraid you'd snap a CD in half and try to cut yourself with it. We were allowed writing tools that weren't felt tipped markers, and the scissors were real scissors, not paper cutting scissors. There were no isolation rooms or straight-jackets. If things got that out of hand you were sent back downstairs. The exits weren't locked, just alarmed.

Monday through Friday we left the hospital from 8am to 4pm for outpatient treatment at an offsite location. If we behaved and weren't on a restriction list there were weekly outings on Tuesday and Thursday nights. This might be anything from mini-golf and ice-cream to a movie or shopping at a local mall. Every Saturday and Sunday if you weren't on restriction you had automatic day passes good from nine am to nine pm. Before, if Mom came to get me I could leave for two to four hours if a doctor approved it and only once a week. Now I could be out almost all weekend.

I missed some of my friends from maximum security like Justin who had been locked up for trying to dig a guy's eye out with a claw hammer in shop class. As Dad would say, at least he wasn't a young Republican. Justin and I identified with each other's extreme anger issues. He confided in me once that he hated the way he was. Every morning he woke up angry and didn't know why. All day he walked around looking for excuses to fight with people. He felt like he didn't know anyone and no one knew him because his anger was like a wall around him. I seriously understood.

At the outpatient facility I met even more new people because the program wasn't exclusively for hospital patients. We were split into different groups by age, seven to twelve year olds in one room, thirteen to seventeen in another. At any time there were only a dozen or so of us in either group. The entire day was very structured. We'd have group therapy in the morning, then a break and snack. Two hours of school-work, lunch and drug testing. Free time was punctuated with individual therapy, and late afternoons would alternate activities depending on the day of the week. We'd have art therapy, outings and trust building exercises, addiction and recovery meetings, anger management, or men's or women's group.

I actually liked and trusted the entire staff of the outpatient day treatment program. They were insightful, understanding, caring and even funny at times. No one gave me crap about being trans or tried to out me. I felt very comfortable there.

Group therapy was intimidating. I wasn't willing to talk about being trans and I was embarrassed at still being broken up over Michelle, so I didn't have much to say to the group. Listening to some of the other kids though was heart breaking. A lot of them had an absent or abusive dad. Some had neglectful or alcoholic mothers. One of the girls, Lisa, had been pregnant and miscarried while in the maximum security ward. I remembered her wailing as she was loaded on a gurney and wheeled past my room when it happened. Her jeans had been soaked in blood. In her wake, the smell was like fresh road kill in the summer and left the back of my throat tasting like old pennies. I didn't tell her that.

Samantha, a girl I was close to, could press her nose flat against her face because avid cocaine use had burned out the cartilage before she was sixteen. Tristan, another sixteen year old, had a cast on his leg from being shot in the knee by his father while protecting his mother. Jose was a fifteen year old alcoholic who would often drink to the point of blacking out and wake up tens of miles away from home. He was also anorexic, finding it difficult to eat while drinking so heavily. I found that intriguing. Eric was in a street gang. Jane, only thirteen years old, came to the group with dark bruises around her neck. She'd tried to hang herself and very nearly succeeded. Joseph had accidentally OD'd on a sheet of acid that was in his sock during a rainstorm. He had seizures for two days. Now he lost track of time constantly and huge chunks of his long term memory were gone.

Even more shocking and disturbing were the things people wouldn't say in group but they'd tell you one on one if you were friends long enough. Sexual abuse and rape were sadly common amongst the girls. Some of the boys, too.

Rowena, who I developed a massive crush on, told me after we'd both been released from the hospital that she was there because she'd had an abortion so as not to ruin her life with an unwanted teenage pregnancy. Now she struggled with the guilt of killing her baby. Mostly she drowned her pain in Lithium and Southern Comfort. She was only in the tenth grade. It amazed me the things people would open up and tell me. I guess eventually it's too much to keep to oneself.

I'd smoked weed with Dad and his friends since I was a kid and too young to know any better. I'd also developed a craving for alcohol that was strong enough I'd willingly gone to parties with Dad at his friends' houses many times over the past two years. While his friends were distracted luring teenage girls, some of them former class-mates of mine, into sexual relationships with drugs and alcohol, I'd make off with a six pack of Rolling Rock in one hand and a four pack of Bartle and James wine coolers in the other. Finding a quiet place I'd drink alone. I always brought my backpack with me to sneak a few beers home. I thought watching grown men corrupt young girls had given me an f'd up perspective, but most of the people I met in day treatment made me feel like I led a quaint sheltered life. Their lives were so full of trauma, struggle and grief, my heart broke every day just being around them. On the other hand I was somewhat jealous of how much they'd lived and seen. It's probably not a good sign when you're in awe of addicts.

Halfway through my first week in minimum security I was prescribed Paxil. That stuff sent me flying. When they upped the dose I started acting like one of the witch's flying monkeys. I couldn't sit still. I was constantly jumping around. My hands shook. I developed a stutter. It felt like in my brain things were moving at a million miles an hour while outside my body everything was in slow motion. My mind would be forming new thoughts faster than I could speak them. The medicine might have affected me so strongly because I was still deliberately vomiting three times a day. I'd also discovered that with ten teaspoons of sugar per cup I had a taste for coffee. Within a couple of weeks I was tolerating the Paxil much better. The world was full of richer colors and more sensational textures than it had been before.

It was a very curious drug. I did feel somewhat happier taking it. That might also have been because I was constantly surrounded by friends and immersed in love and acceptance. I did feel terrible about not telling anyone I was trans. If people don't like you for who you are then they're not your true friends. I knew that, but better fake friends than no friends. And they didn't feel like fake friends. I was definitely the non-genuine one of the bunch. But guilt aside, I loved being popular and being Luca. I liked being happy. I liked that it didn't hurt anymore that Michelle had cast me aside, or that Dad was a prick and Mom always took his side. The faces of all my childhood bullies, even Bobby and that religious zealot from maximum security didn't haunt me any longer. I had let go of everything and was living in the moment.

Then one day Justin, my hammer wielding angry buddy who had been moved to minimum security, was being sent back to maximum security because he was still too dangerous. I was devastated. I was so excited when he'd been put in the room next to me upstairs. We always teamed up for projects and activities. We were very close. Now he was being sent back and I didn't think I'd ever see him again. I knew that by the time he was ready for minimum security again I'd be long gone.

But the weird thing was I didn't feel sad. I watched out the window as they handcuffed him to a stretcher and loaded him in an ambulance. I knew I'd never see my friend again, but still I didn't feel sad. I even tried listening to sad music and thinking about how sad I should be. All I felt was tired, but not too tired. I knew it was the Paxil. It created a fog around my heart. I knew I should be upset about the loss of half my range of emotions. I was now incomplete as a person because of it, but I'd become too complacent and indifferent to care.

While in day treatment I was diagnosed with some new mental and personality disorders. My manic depression was now bipolar disorder. I also had an addictive personality and a lack of impulse control. I suffered from massive anxiety and compulsively lied. I would often mistake my own lies for truth which I suppose made me delusional. No one noticed and I kept it to myself. They still hadn't noticed the bulimia either, but they did notice the scars on my arms and legs from cutting myself for years. I agreed. Then to my shock and horror it wasn't only suggested, but made mandatory as part of my treatment, I return to school. Crap. What had I gotten myself into now?

Chapter Eighteen

Medford's Finest

By Betsie

It was Memorial Day weekend and my family was getting together. I loved our big cookouts and thought Luca would enjoy the beautiful sunshine and being around his family. Brooks had to work so Louise and I picked him up at Boston Regional.

Things were going well. Luca was upstairs playing with the other kids. Everyone seemed to be having a good time. About every half hour I would call upstairs to be sure he was okay.

We had been at my sister's house about two hours when I went to check on him again. Calling upstairs and getting no answer made me sick to my stomach.

I ran upstairs to be sure he heard me.

My heart began racing as I checked in the two bedrooms and Luca wasn't there.

"Where's Luca?" I asked the kids.

"He got mad and went downstairs a while ago," my niece informed me.

I couldn't believe this was happening. Where should I even start looking? Besides the park around the corner, nothing in the area was familiar. What was he going to do now?

My sister Louise and I jumped in her car and started driving towards downtown Medford. Another sister went walking in the opposite direction. I felt the burning of stomach acid as we drove slowly, scanning everything around us. The foul tasting liquid reached my mouth by the time we spotted him.

"*What the hell has he done now?*" I thought when I noticed the police officer.

"Are you alright?" I frantically asked.

"I'm waiting for the other officer to come back out. He has to get his coffee and donuts. He promised he'd help me."

Showing off his authority, the younger officer asked, "Is this your son?"

"Yup," I answered, intimidated by the tone of his voice.

This officer was angry. Luca had clearly bothered him.

Trying to calm down, I turned my attention back to Luca.

"Why did you leave Dorothy's house?"

"I want to go back to the hospital before I hurt myself," he answered.

"Why? What happened?"

"Nothing. I want Dad to come get me and bring me back to the hospital."

The older officer finally came out of Dunkin Donuts. He was more soft-spoken than Officer Macho and Luca pleaded with him to take him back to the hospital. Informing us he was getting off duty, we were told we had to deal with the young officer already helping us.

I was fuming. Medford's finest? Bullshit! This officer's donuts and the other officer's time were more important than listening to my child. I may have been angry at Luca for leaving, but these officers had no right ignoring him. I wanted to scream at them, "*Listen to him. Just listen to him!*"

Officer Macho wouldn't listen to either of us.

"I can't get involved in family problems," the officer told Luca.

And with that, he grabbed Luca's arm and escorted him to Louise's car.

I had really been looking forward to Memorial Day. After all those forty mile round trip hospital visits, didn't I deserve to spend some time with my sisters? Didn't I deserve to have a good day? I was hurt and angry. I couldn't seem to get past the fact Luca had ruined **my** day.

I often felt if Luca loved me he wouldn't pull the shit he pulled. He must have been blaming me for something. If he loved me, he would know how much his actions hurt me.

During a family therapy session I said to Diane, "It seems Luca does everything he can to ruin my day. Cutting himself. Running away. The trip to Ipswich. Making me worry sick on Memorial Day. Why does he keep doing this shit to me?"

"Luca does these things to himself and without malice towards you. He doesn't sit there and think *"Maybe I shouldn't do this. It will make mom mad."* It's up to you how you chose to handle these situations," was Diane's reply.

That was a turning point for me. I was slowly able to stop blaming Luca for my hurt.

Luca and I have discussed the actions of these two Medford Police officers many times. Each time, I have voiced my anger at them for putting donuts and time higher on their priority list than listening to my son.

But who am I to criticize? It has taken me years to understand the real reason Luca left my sister's house. Spending an afternoon with my family was higher on **MY** priority list than spending time alone with my son. Luca's anxiety had been caused by my selfishness. When I look back on that day, I still get angry. But it's no longer just with the police officers, but with myself. It wasn't up to them to listen to my child. It was up to me.

Medford's Finest

By Luca

At the end of May Mom picked me up from the hospital to take me to a family cookout for Memorial Day. I felt estranged from my family. They looked at me like I was a lunatic. It was difficult being around them, given the circumstances.

One of my younger cousins in particular had really been stressing me out. She followed me around all day asking why I was crazy and when was I going to cut myself again. My entire body cried out with a desire to kick her in the face. Part of me wanted to hit everyone there. They all either walked on eggshells around me like I was made of glass and filled with violence, or made snide comments with smiles that didn't reach their eyes. I could feel them judging me from the moment I walked through the door. It felt like hundreds of tiny insects biting my skin.

It was so much easier in the hospital. Whenever I felt myself losing control I could walk away, take space and be alone until my emotions subsided. In the real world it's not so simple.

There was no place to be alone at my Aunt Dorothy's house. I had expressly told her I needed to be alone for a few minutes to calm down. She told me in no uncertain terms it was her house, not mine. No one would be banned from any part of it for any amount of time because she didn't wish it so. That included bratty cousins deliberately tormenting me to see how long they could get away with it. So I left.

I started walking, without much of a plan. I was over twenty miles away from home and penniless. I knew I needed help. I didn't want to actually run away. I wanted to go back to the hospital where I had friends and could find comfort or at least solace. Mom had driven by a Dunkin Donuts on the way over. On a holiday weekend I figured that was the best place to find a police officer and ask for help.

Sure enough, less than a mile down the road was the Dunkin Donuts and pulling into the parking lot just as I arrived was a cop car. I ran up to the officer and told him I needed help. He looked me up and down and told me he was on a break.

"Stay out here and I'll talk to you when I get out."

I watched him waddle into Dunks and nervously shifted my weight from one foot to the other. I was looking up and down the street at passing cars, worried someone from my family would be looking for me, when I spotted a second cop car on its way over.

This cop was built like a linebacker. He climbed out of his cruiser and asked me why I was hanging around the first cop car.

"I need help. The other officer told me he'd help me after he got his coffee and donuts so I'm waiting for him to come back."

"Uh huh. And what exactly do you need help with?"

"I don't have any money and I need someone to call my father and tell him to come get me."

Just then Aunt Louise and Mom pulled up in Louise's car. Great.

"Luca!" Mom shouted.

"Who's that?" The officer asked.

"That's my mom and aunt but I don't want to go back with them!"

"That's your mom? Did you run away?"

"Not really. I thought about it but decided it'd be safer to have my dad come get me. I don't know where I am but he'll know because he's been here before. I want him to give me a ride back to the hospital where I live."

"Come here for a sec." The officer beckoned me over against the side of the building.

"Here's the deal. You're going to walk over to that car and go home with your family. If you run off again and I have to take time out of my busy day to deal with your bullshit I'm going to arrest you. Are we clear?"

"Then arrest me! I'm not going back with them!"

He reached out and squeezed my upper arm, not in a friendly way, more of an *ow my bones are being ground to dust,* way. He used his hold on me to steer me over to my aunt's car. The door to the backseat was open and he shoved me in.

After the cop talked to Mom for a minute, while the first cop looked on with a mouthful of powdered munchkins, I was driven back to my other aunt's house. I sat on a couch while Mom and half my family reamed me out. Then Mom drove me back to the hospital.

I learned from that experience that I couldn't reach out to anyone for help or sympathy anymore. Outside the hospital I was alone.

I was released from the hospital weeks before I was through with outpatient treatment. I didn't want to go home at all. My first night home I went to bed without supper at six in the afternoon. I couldn't bring myself to watch TV or listen to music. I was so depressed I lay on my bed fully clothed, too depressed to even take off my shoes I cried for a while then watched the light fade in my room as the sun set. My last thought before I fell asleep was, "God, how am I going to make it through the entire weekend here all alone?"

Being at home was hard. Jenny, my only friend left from before the hospital, was busy living her own life two towns over. We hadn't talked or hung out much in a long, long time. My online friends couldn't compare to having people there with me to talk to or goof around with like at the hospital. Online chatting was zero consolation now.

On Saturday I tried calling some of my friends who had already been released from the hospital. I talked to a few of them on the phone. No one could hang out because they all lived twenty plus miles away and unlike me, they'd had friends waiting for them at home so they already had plans.

Eventually I resigned myself to watching a Daria marathon on MTV and chatting on-line. I talked to a girl named Charlotte from a tiny hick town in upstate New York. I'd been talking to her for a few months now. She was only thirteen and a devout Catholic. She used to tell me I was making Jesus cry because I had a potty mouth and drank and abused over-the-counter medications. Teasing her always put me in a better mood. Somewhere along the way I had become sort of a mean person.

I've never been so excited for a weekend to be over in my life. I couldn't wait to go back to the day center on Monday as an outpatient and to be with my friends again.

Chapter Nineteen

The Race Is On

By Betsie

"I'd like to speak with Luca alone and then with the two of you," Diane informed Brooks and me as we stepped into the waiting area.

While waiting our turn, I sat amusing myself with one of Diane's many books of jokes written by children. Making me chuckle, I thought back to a time when Luca laughed at silly jokes. Those days seemed so long ago.

"Okay, you can come in now," Diane told us.

Brooks put down his *Psychology Today* as I finished reading one more joke.

"What are we discussing today?" I asked, sinking into the over-stuffed chair that had become mine during our visits.

"Well, you remember we've been discussing Luca returning to public school in the fall. I've set up an appointment with the special ed department within your school district. They have some ideas I think you'll be pleased with. It's just a matter of finding the right fit"

Then Dianne shocked the three of us.

"I'm also giving my permission for Luca to have upper surgery. I know you've been waiting a long time for this. Sometimes not so patiently."

"Oh my God! Oh my God!" Luca shouted, almost jumping out of his seat.

Luca had won the lottery. The biggest prize ever handed out.

I was stunned. This had completely taken me off guard. It took a few minutes to sink in. We were supposed to be months away from surgery.

"Are you sure he's ready for this after everything that's happened?" I questioned.

"I think it's time," Diane answered. "Here's the name of a doctor in New York I recommend to a lot of my clients. In fact, do you remember

Thomas? He and his mom are going there in a few weeks."

"This is really going to happen," I said, trying to put my thoughts together.

"How soon can we go?" Luca asked.

"First you'll need to get a letter of recommendation from another psychologist. I'm recommending one I know will be willing to help. He's also trans."

"How about this surgeon in New York? Is he real expensive?" I asked. "Does he take credit cards?"

"Give the surgeon's office a call. The receptionist will be able to answer most of your questions. Let me know next week how you make out," Diane said as the three of us headed back to the car.

"I can't go back to school until after I have the surgery," Luca said. "The kids can't know who I am. Please, please call the surgeon tomorrow."

"I promise. I have some money in my 401K and will draw it out. Then we only have to put the balance on a credit card," I answered. "Maybe we can also have some fun in New York. I can't wait to hear what the school has to say," I said bouncing from one subject to another.

"Can we fly to New York?" Luca asked excitedly.

"I don't think so," Brooks chimed in. Up until this point he had been very quiet. I don't think he was as emotionally overwhelmed by the idea of surgery as I was. It was the cost. Like me, although he knew this was a necessity, he also knew it was one we couldn't afford. "We'll have to discuss some of this later," he added.

"I think we'll have to take the bus," I answered. "We need to keep the expenses down. A lot will depend on when the surgeon can see us. I'll get a lot of questions answered after I call Dr. Johnson. This is going to be a lot to put together."

The following morning I made the phone call to Dr. Johnson's office. The receptionist was quite surprised when she heard Luca's age.

"Fifteen? I don't think Dr. Johnson has ever done this surgery on anyone that young. I'll have to have him call you back. How are you going to pay for this?"

"I'll have $5,000 in cash and the rest will have to go on a credit card."

"We'll make the financial arrangements as soon as we know your credit card will clear. The surgery will be about $9,000. It can be a little more or less depending on how long the surgery takes and whether or not you want to stay at the clinic the first night."

"We'll want to stay at the clinic."

"I have all your information. Dr. Johnson will get in touch with you."

Well, that was that. Now all we could do was wait and see if Dr. Johnson was even willing to see Luca. Along with the surgery there would be bus fare, train fare, ten nights hotel in Manhattan and food. It was overwhelming.

I never thought I would say this, but I was grateful to have another meeting to look forward to the following day. At least pondering the possibility of Luca going back to school was keeping my mind off of waiting for Dr. Johnson's phone call.

Walking through the hallways of his previous middle school, Luca was watching for signs of former classmates. I was watching for the primitive assistant principal from two years earlier. Brooks was just being his obnoxious self.

Checking in at the front desk, we were escorted to a small, marginally furnished room. The straggly plant sitting atop the filing cabinet was begging for water. Feeling like a student about to be reprimanded, I was pleasantly surprised when Mr. Cummings walked into the room. He greeted us with a welcoming smile and introduced his assistant, Kimberly.

"Well I hear Luca needs to come back to school after a few years of home-schooling. My goal is to find a suitable school for all of us. This school will pay for Luca to attend another school within our system. I have two in mind that should work very nicely."

Looking at Luca's transcripts Mr. Cummings added, "I can see you're entering the tenth grade but placed twelfth grade in your Iowa Test. Do you like math?"

"It's okay," Luca replied. "I took classes at the community college."

"How were your other schools before home-schooling?"

"Well, I hated this one," Luca replied with a smirk.

Mr. Cummings chuckled.

"Kimberly and I are here to be sure your next experience is a good one. Once you check out the two schools you can let me know which one you like best and we'll arrange for transportation."

"Will I actually have a say in what school I attend?" Luca asked. "Will you make sure there are no other kids from this school attending the school I pick?"

"We'll do our best but I can't guarantee anything. I understand you changed your name. Diane also informed us you'll probably be having surgery before starting back. That will make it easier. Mrs. Harvie, here are the two schools, the principals' names and phone numbers. I suggest you call them as soon as possible so we can get this going."

"Do you have a preference?" I asked.

"I like the one in Ipswich. It has few discipline problems. The other one is a little bit closer but smaller. Let me know by the end of next week."

I once got so lost going from my house to an ice rink and back (a trip I had made dozens of times) I ended up on the highway heading for the state of New York. So it was no surprise to me I was lost trying to find school number one in Ipswich.

Backtracking, I discovered where I had missed my turn. It looked as if only wagon wheels had traversed the packed-down dirt road. Rays of light struggled to break through the forest of pine trees.

"Do school buses actually travel down this narrow path?" I was thinking just

as I came to an opening with a circular drive.

"Follow the path across from the tennis courts," my notes reminded me.

Standing in the middle of the driveway, I scrutinized the ominous old mansion before me. I could imagine horse-drawn carriages pulling up to the old wooden door. Ivy crept up the walls, trying its best to cover the deteriorating old red brick. Oversized black windows had probably once been adorned with beautiful drapes. Naked, they now just stared down at me.

Pulling on a large metal handle, the door opened easily. The wide hallway and tall ceiling gave me a feeling of uneasiness. Drab, green painted walls had never experienced the warmth of sunshine. A worn pathway leading to the principal's office could be seen in the dull, gray tile floor.

"Turn around and run!" the voice in my head murmured.

Too late.

"Hello, you must be Mrs. Harvie," a male voice called from down the hall. "Come on in. I'm Principal Goodman. Mr. Cummings has told me all about Luca. Let's take a walk around the property and then I can answer your questions."

We walked through the quiet hallways and back outside to the tennis courts. Overall I had been pretty impressed with the school. But then the principal said something that shocked me.

"All the students know why each other are here. Of course I'll have to tell them Luca's background."

Jesus Christ! He couldn't have dropped a bigger bomb on me.

"There's no way the other kids can know his background," I said, trying to keep my composure. "It will undo everything we've done over the past two years. He has to enter as a male and be treated as a male."

"I'm sorry you feel that way. If Luca attends this school the other students will have to know. I feel it helps with discipline problems."

"I don't see how this is going to work. Thanks for your time."

Walking as quickly as I could to my car, I didn't want students seeing tears welling up in my eyes. I was crushed. My hopes had been shattered. If this was Mr. Cummings's first choice I was scared to death thinking about the second.

Wiping my eyes while reflecting on all the downfalls of attending this school made me miss the turn-off that would have headed me in the direction of work. Traveling in the wrong direction for a few minutes actually brought me to a highway I knew well.

Cruising down Route One gave me time to review just how horrible this place was.

Did Mr. Cummings know of the principal's rule? If so, did he believe we would be okay with it?

I was glad Luca hadn't come with me this time but he was going to want to see school number two. What would we do if the next experience was as bad as this one?

The Race Is On

By Luca

My school advocate had been busy tracking down a school for me. It turned out there were only two of them near me with any openings. One was mostly for recovering drug addicts and I pushed for this one because those kids knew how to have fun. The other was a straight up alternative school one town over from where I lived. I was worried the alternative school would either have kids who may have known me as Marie or developmentally disabled students. I knew I had problems but I didn't see how riding the short-bus would help.

Mom went to look at my first choice of schools during the day while I was in treatment. Apparently the principal insisted the other students would have to know I was trans. This scared me and disappointed me greatly.

Since I was living at home again, I was back to seeing Diane on Thursday nights after dinner. Despite being recently released from a mental hospital she gave me the go ahead to have top surgery. I was over the moon but I couldn't tell anyone about my good news. I'd long ago stopped attending the trans support meetings. I couldn't tell any of my friends, not even the online ones, because none of them knew I was trans and that's how I wanted to keep it. But I definitely felt as though a huge weight had been lifted from me. Now, wearing my painful sweat and blood stained binder all day didn't seem so bad. I knew there was an end in sight.

I still needed a second letter of recommendation to take to the surgeon. I knew it was for my own good but seeing as no woman ever needed a mental health professional to recommend her for a breast enlargement, I felt needing a letter for a reduction was insulting.

I was nervous. Because I was so young and had recently had a stint in a mental hospital it didn't look good. Just because this guy was a long time post op trans man himself, didn't mean he'd risk his credibility on me. I laid all my cards on the table and answered his questions honestly. The interview was two hours long. At the end when he told me he was going to recommend me for surgery I felt like I'd completed and won a marathon. I can't tell you how amazing it was to talk to a professional that understood how it felt to be me. All the way home my legs felt like rubber but my head was in the clouds. For once it was a happy exhaustion.

Diane gave us the name of a surgeon in New York City who she thought would be willing to operate on someone as young as me. He performed a lot of top surgeries for trans men. I couldn't believe I was finally going to get my surgery and I'd get to see New York. How lucky could one guy be? I'm surprised I wasn't shitting four leaf clovers and horseshoes.

I felt awful that Mom and Dad would have to put my surgery on a credit card. You can't imagine how much debt they took on over the years for me. It was staggering and depressing. But I absolutely needed this surgery. I needed it to live as much as any organ donation recipient or dialysis patient. I was glad Mom was still on my side. And Dad. The looming debt made it bittersweet, but still sweet.

I shared my joyous news with my outpatient advocate. She and the other staff members who knew about me were happy for me. Then I found out if the alternative school accepted me I was going to have to attend summer school there starting in July. I was mortified. This was totally bogus. Summer school was for dipshits. I wasn't stupid. I had passed all my state scholastic tests with flying colors while homeschooling. What it boiled down to, as part of my release plan, I wasn't to be left alone for any extended amount of time. I had no one to blame but myself which really pissed me off.

Now the race was on to be released from outpatient treatment and get to New York for my surgery before I had to start summer school.

Chapter Twenty

Kendal Tanner

By Betsie

After my experience with Mr. Cumming's choice of school number one, I was very apprehensive about calling school number two. But it had to be done.

Our conversation was brief, but when Principal Tanner told me where the school was located I answered, "I thought that building was condemned years ago."

So it was all set. We would visit Principal Tanner and the old building with weather worn bricks, torn shades and cracked windows, the following afternoon.

I hadn't even taken my hand off the receiver when the phone rang again.

"This is Doctor Johnson calling from New York. I got your message. I've spoken with Diane and she feels strongly this surgery needs to be done. I'm not sure myself about operating on someone fifteen years old. Is there any way you and Luca could come to New York so we can meet and discuss this further?"

"If we make the trip to New York, it has to be for the surgery. Could we just come a day early? I should have the money in two weeks. The trip would have to be after that."

"Mrs. Harvie, I have to tell you it won't just be up to me. The anesthesiologist will also have to agree. The office manager will call you back with the time and directions. I'm looking forward to meeting Luca. Diane says he is quite the young man."

"Thanks. This will mean a lot to him."

I tried to be as excited as Luca about the surgery but now I was more scared than anything. I knew many things could go wrong during any surgery and this would be a long one. However, I was more scared of how I would react when it was over. Would I be able to be as strong as my son or fall to pieces?

Would I have the confidence to stand up to the skeptics who would say, "How could you do this to your fifteen year old? Are you crazy? He's too young to know what he wants or needs."

But it really wasn't the skeptics I was so afraid of. It was me. I wasn't ready.

Before leaving work early (again) I gave Luca a call to be sure he would be waiting for me. Like a duck in a shooting gallery, I did a lot of flying in one direction, only to be turned around and pointed in another. Today I wished I could sprout wings and actually fly. I had some great news.

I thought I would burst as I waited for Luca to buckle his seat belt.

"Are you ready for this?" I blurted out. "Dr. Johnson's office called. We leave for New York three weeks from today."

If Luca screamed any louder my windshield would have cracked.

"It's all arranged. We're going to see him on a Friday and if he approves, he'll do the surgery on Monday morning. We'll also have to convince the anesthesiologist."

"They'll do it. They have to."

"Maybe we can see some of New York over the weekend."

"I can't believe it. I'm finally going to have the chance to be me."

"It will all work out," I said as we pulled up to the school.

Parking alongside the old building, I was shocked students actually attended classes there. Cardboard taped to broken windows definitely wouldn't keep old man winter out when he came calling.

"I don't know," I said to Luca as we walked up concrete steps with cracks that had abided there for years.

"This place is cool," Luca laughed.

An echo answered our knock on the locked door leading us to believe no one was left inside. The turning of a key let us know we were mistaken.

The door swung open and we were greeted by a warm smile as wide as Alice's Cheshire Cat. His six foot plus stature would have been intimidating if it were not for his kind eyes.

"Come on in. Sorry the door was locked," Principal Tanner said. "I'm here by myself. Didn't want anyone wandering in. Why don't we have a seat in my office so we can go over a few things."

For a man of his size, his voice surprised me. It was soft and calming.

"Did you bring Luca's Iowa test with you? I need to know where to place him in the fall."

"I think I have everything you need. Mr. Cummings sent a list of classes Luca will need in order to graduate. Did he explain Luca's circumstances?"

"Mr. Cummings told me as much as I need to know. I've already spoken with the assistant principal and one of the school's counselors. We feel the only people who need to know about Luca are the teachers. Luca, it will be up to you to tell whoever you wish. I have to let the teachers know in case of an emergency."

Now I absolutely loved this guy. If it hadn't been inappropriate, I would have reached across the desk given him a hug.

"Would you like to take a tour of the school?" Principal Tanner continued. "We have things here other schools don't have. You can work in the coffee shop as one of your classes. We also have a wood-working room."

"Can I make furniture or is it just small stuff?" Luca asked.

"Our wood is donated so it depends on what we get. I've seen some pretty large items made Sorry it's all cleaned up. The kids have taken everything home."

Leaving the wood-working room behind, the three of us walked back up the uneven, creaking wood stairs.

"The kids love our drama teacher," Mr. Tanner said. "Do you like drama?"

"Will I be able to be in something or just work behind the scenes?"

"It would depend on what the teacher is working on. Well, what do you think? Will we see you in the fall?"

"I guess."

"Luca is going to have his surgery in a few weeks," I told Principal Tanner. "The next time you see him, Luca will look a little bit different."

"Well that's exciting news. Good luck to both of you. Luca, I look forward to seeing you in the fall."

The old school door groaned behind us as Mr. Tanner said goodbye. I was left wondering *"What just happened here? Did I come face to face with a guardian angel?"*

There was no feeling lost this time.

Kendal Tanner

By Luca

Mom had made arrangements for us to visit the alternative high school together. I was nervous. What if this principal was a dickhead like the last one? What if some students recognized me? What if all the students were mean or stupid? But I was running out of time and choices. If this place was a total shithole full of scumbags then my only other option was the school where the principal would make damn sure everyone knew I was trans. I'd never make any friends or get any dates under those circumstances and I might go back to getting my ass kicked routinely. I dreaded the thought of coming so far just to go back to a situation where I was the outsider who was constantly bullied.

On the ride over to the school Mom gave me the news about booking a surgery date. Her excitement was almost as cool as the news itself. She seemed so happy she could bust. This was much different than her reaction to my name being changed. I was touched. She was smiling. It had been so long since she smiled I didn't want her to stop. Of course, she did stop smiling when we pulled up at the school and I groaned,

"What a dump."

The grounds keeping left much to be desired. Some of the windows had web shaped cracks from rocks being thrown at them. Anywhere there was metal there was rust. Paint flaked, cement was cracked and peppered with dandelion sprouts, graffiti sprawled, the foundation groaned and the architecture was just plain ugly. All in all it looked as sweet as halitosis smells.

Walking up the steps I was sure the building would collapse on us any moment. The doors were locked and when Mom knocked we heard a large echo on the other side. When the door opened the biggest, bushiest man I'd ever seen met us with a huge grin. His size and beard reminded me of *Sweetums* from the Muppets. I wanted to be scared but found myself smiling back at him instead.

His name was Kendal Tanner and he was the principal of the New Horizons alternative high-school program. It was impossible to be sad or afraid in Kendal's presence. Sitting with him in his office I knew everything was going to be okay.

The inside of the building didn't look much better than the outside. It was a good sized school. In addition to New Horizons it held four other alternative education programs. New Horizons was the largest program, taking up half the classrooms in the building and the main entryway offices.

After Kendal assured me that no one from my home town or the towns immediately surrounding it were currently enrolled at New Horizons, he took us a brief tour. The school may not have put much money into building maintenance but they invested heavily in other areas like wood shop and field trips. That was cool with me.

Some of the other students were learning disabled, but mostly the students were removed from public schools for behavior problems. In short, instead of being locked up with drug addicts, I was going to be surrounded by drug dealers, violent criminals and a few misfits. But New Horizons also had a zero tolerance policy for bullying. That made me feel better about the situation.

What sealed the deal for me was that Kendal didn't want to out me. I was glad he understood how sensitive my situation was. I just wanted to have a normal high-school experience. Well, as normal as I could get under the circumstances. This was a chance to start over. I wanted it to be fun, not miserable and dangerous. I think outing me against my will would have made school feel like a punishment rather than an opportunity.

As mom and I headed home, I actually felt good about the situation. I was very lucky to have met Kendal. I was lucky to have a proposed surgery date that would have me mostly healed before summer school started. I was luckier still to have an awesome mom who'd stuck by me through all the crap I'd pulled in the last few months and who fought so hard for me to have opportunities and a future. I farted rainbows and gold coins all the way home.

Chapter Twenty-One

They're Gone

By Betsie

It had been a long bus ride from Boston to New York. Excitement started building as we rode through the busy streets of Midtown Manhattan on our way to the New York Port Authority Bus Terminal. Traffic was slow and I felt like a kid wanting to say "Are we there yet?"

We departed the terminal around two pm. It didn't take long to realize eighty degree heat in New York City felt a lot hotter than along the New England coastline. We were on a budget and there would be no money for cabs. With no idea as to what we were getting ourselves into, we started walking from Eighth Avenue toward Fortieth Street and Fifth Avenue. Dragging our luggage behind us, the three short blocks on the map became an exercise in physical fitness. The shade of Bryant Park was a welcome relief. We had one more block to go.

Arriving at the corner of Fortieth Street and Fifth Avenue, you could have wrung the sweat out of our clothes. Riding up the elevator to the tenth floor of the hotel was excruciatingly slow. Finally, we reached our air-conditioned room.

We had decided most of our entertainment would be in the form of eating out. After all, we had to eat anyway. Right away, Luca wanted to visit Planet Hollywood.

"I promise we'll go as soon as I've rested," I told him. "Why don't you go downstairs and try to get directions."

Exhaustion took hold. I quickly fell asleep.

About an hour later, feeling rested I threw on a change of clothes. I was ready to rock and roll. Luca had been able to get a map from the front desk. I would end up using that map until you could no longer distinguish the streets.

Although the sun had gone to bed, the city had retained its heat. Neither of us objected to the long walk though. We had quickly fallen in love with New York City.

Arriving at Planet Hollywood we were surprised by the very long line. Adding our name to the restaurant's list, we headed to the gift shop. I had promised Luca he could have one souvenir of our trip. He purchased a nice black and white men's shirt to celebrate the new figure he'd have when we got home. We arrived back at the restaurant in time to hear our name called. After enjoying our first fun meal together in New York, we headed for the lights of Times Square.

There was a certain vibration to this "Crossroads of the World." Everyone was either in a hurry to get somewhere or tourists like ourselves, standing with our mouths open in awe. Luca thought it was pretty cool to be standing across the street from the MTV Studios.

It was getting late and the next day would be an early one. We would be meeting

Dr. Johnson at nine am. Taking our time, we walked back to the hotel, discussing the possibilities of what we would do after Luca's doctor's appointment.

From our hotel room we could see the top of the Empire State Building, its blue light blinking like a beacon of hope. We planned to go Sunday night. The last thing we would do before surgery.

Although we were on the tenth floor, I found it difficult to fall asleep against the honking of taxi horns. I tried putting the idea the surgeon would say *"no"* to the back of my mind but somehow it was always there. It was like a two year old asking, *"But why Mommy?"* with every answer you gave. *"But why? But why?"*

Friday morning we walked our twenty blocks to 66th Street, marveling at the architecture of the buildings and the size of Grand Central Station. Passing a church displaying a rainbow flag gave us both a sense everything would be okay.

We walked for an hour before reaching our destination. Entering the lobby, we were greeted by marble pillars, what looked like antique vases, and porcelain figurines. I'd never seen such opulence at a surgeon's office, but then again I'd never been on Park Avenue in New York before.

My breakfast was doing flip-flops as we took our seats in Dr. Johnson's office.

The door slowly opened and the doctor appeared with a jovial grin.

With introductions over, Dr. Johnson asked Luca, "So why do you believe you need this surgery? Once it's done, there's no turning back. No changing your mind. I have to reduce the breast and re-position the nipple. Some patients lose the feeling in the nipple and it never comes back. Are you prepared for this?"

Without hesitation Luca replied, "I've waited my lifetime for this. I can't keep putting on a binder to leave my house. My breasts feel foreign to me. I want to go back to school but can't the way I am. I know there's no turning back. This is not something I want but something I need to survive."

"The anesthesiologist has arrived," Dr. Johnson said. "Let's call him in and see if we can get him on board with this."

Dr. Johnson left the room for about two minutes. A very long two minutes. Luca had pleaded his case and it sounded like Dr. Johnson had listened. But what about the anesthesiologist? Without him, Luca's life would not change. Did we come this far only to be sent back home? It wasn't the miles I was worried about. We had come so far emotionally.

Dr. Johnson appeared with a much younger gentleman. This gentleman's stern mannerisms were the complete opposite of Dr. Johnson's cheerfulness.

"This is Luca and his mom," Dr. Johnson said. "I'm a little concerned about his age but I'm leaning toward going ahead with the surgery. What do you think?"

"I'm also concerned about your age," the anesthesiologist said as he faced Luca. "Being a minor your mom will have to give us consent for the surgery. It's a long procedure and one that can't be reversed. There can be complications with any surgery. Are you both ready for this?"

"We've lived in hell for the past eight years," I told both doctors.

"He's a great kid and deserves a chance at life. He can't live without the surgery. I'll sign anything you want."

"Give us a minute. We'll be right back."

It was very intimidating waiting for an answer that would change my child's life forever.

In actuality it would be my signature that would change my child's life forever. My palms began to sweat. The stillness in the room was broken only by the rapid pounding of my heart.

I grabbed Luca's hand as footsteps approached, hoping to hear the words we had journeyed so far for.

Dr. Johnson entered the room alone.

"We'll see you Monday morning at 8:30. Be on time. Nothing to eat after eight pm Sunday night. Bring a button down shirt to wear when you leave. Mom, if you're staying here at the clinic, wear comfortable clothes."

We finalized the arrangements and stepped out into the sunshine of New York City. Standing at the crosswalk of 66th Street and Park Avenue, I didn't know if I should laugh or cry. Don't get me wrong. I was happy my son would be getting the surgery he needed. But without warning came a very physical, heavy feeling. At that very moment, I knew part of me was about to cease to exist.

I was glad the light changed, forcing me to move forward.

"Let's find Central Park," I said, trying to leave my feelings behind.

What a pleasure! The sun had not been up long enough to heat up the city and the trees provided lovely shade. Having no idea how far we had walked, we found ourselves at the entrance to the Central Park Zoo. Admission wasn't much so we went in. This fun diversion helped me forget the reason we had come to New York. Time passed quickly and before we knew it we were on Fifth Avenue trying to decide where to go for lunch.

Hearing of a restaurant inside Saks Fifth Avenue we decided to check it out.

Entering the doors, we quickly got directions to the restaurant. We got off at each floor, picking up objects and trying to guess their cost. Our guesses on everything from men's Florsheim shoes to chocolate-dipped apples weren't even close.

Waiting to be seated at the restaurant, I wondered if we had made a mistake. I really couldn't afford the prices. But it was the one thing I had wanted to do so we went for it. When they said they had a table for two, they meant one and a half. The table could not have been more than one foot square. Luca ordered off the children's menu. Something called "sliders." When they served him three hamburgers the size of half-dollars, Luca and I both had a good laugh.

After a few more hours of walking, I needed a rest. We sauntered back to the hotel for a nap before heading out for dinner and a second trip to Times Square.

Saturday and Sunday we checked out as much of the city as we could. Sunday evening we strolled the short distance from the hotel to the Empire State Building.

The line was like a large snake, coiled around and around and in no hurry to move. Waiting for our turn gave us a chance to talk about the memorabilia from Planet Hollywood, the exciting lights of Times Square and the beauty of Rockefeller Center. We had enjoyed the different aromas of the street vendors with their cinnamon roasted almonds, grilled sausages and wonderfully fresh croissants. We had eaten hot pastrami on rye with a half-sour pickle from the local deli and had gone back a second time.

Wishing we could have done more than just window shopping at Macy's and Saks, we had to be content knowing we had driven the sales people crazy. We talked about the excitement of Broadway and the possibility of returning to see a play, giving us something to look forward to.

Our turn finally came. The sun had set and when the elevator doors opened I was not disappointed. What a view! The skyline sparkled for as far as one could see. Taking our time, we captured every moment. Even in the dark you could see all the way to the Hudson River. The pattern of lights on the Chrysler Building reminded me of a Spanish dancer showing off her skirt.

Sadly, the evening had to come to an end and it was time to head back towards the elevators. As we made our last turn, Luca called out, "Look Mom, fireworks! Look over there! They're celebrating something."

How absolutely miraculous we had been there at that particular moment. New York City was celebrating Luca's rebirth with us. What an incredible night!

The sun rose and with it came the honking of the taxi cabs. This time I was grateful to have so many in one place. Flagging one down, we took the short ride to the surgeon's office. For two years I had been waiting for and fearing this day.

"Now Luca, it is not too late," the surgeon said once again. "Are you sure you want to proceed?"

"Let's do it!" Luca replied.

Giving Luca a kiss on the forehead, he disappeared behind closed doors while I was given the task of waiting patiently. Opening my book, I was hoping the words on the page would calm me down. They didn't. So I closed the book and my eyes. However, rumbling in my stomach soon reminded me I had not eaten since the previous night.

The busy sounds of the city gave me little comfort as I tried to steer my thoughts away from the clinic. I felt guilty leaving but also realized it would be hours before those closed doors would open again. Finding a small corner grocery/deli, I purchased a bagel and cream cheese and inhaled it along with my orange juice. Finishing breakfast, I quickly retraced my steps. I was in a hurry to get back to my waiting game.

Luca's surgery was the only thing going on in the clinic that day so I was alone in the waiting room. This was one time I wished I had a busy-body stranger to help pass the time. Leaning back in the chair I closed my eyes once again and listened to the bubbling sounds of the fish tank. My sleep had not lasted long when the nurse came to inform me it would be a few more hours.

I decided to revisit the deli I had walked to earlier. After lunch, I slowly walked along the beautiful street with the brick sidewalk, admiring the well-kept houses with their window boxes in bloom. The city looked much different than it had a few hours earlier.

Returning to the clinic, I took out my embroidery but my eyes couldn't focus between the small lines. I dosed on and off over the next two to three hours, before the nurse made another appearance.

"The surgery is over and Luca is being prepped for the recovery room. You'll be able to see him shortly."

I thought I'd be a basket case when given this news. But now a strange, unexpected calmness caught me off guard.

Entering the recovery room I was in complete control. There were no tears. No regrets. Just a feeling of relief. It was over. We had done the right thing.

Barely able to bring his arms to his chest Luca whispered, "Mom, are they gone?"

"They're gone Honey," I whispered back, leaning over to give him a kiss.

I can still feel that very moment. All my suppressed emotions came flooding in like a tsunami. Joy for my son being given another chance. Sadness my daughter had never been given that chance. Relief part of Luca's past had ended. Scared to death his future was beginning. Peace knowing we had made the right decision. Anger at watching him suffer through this. But most of all I was proud. Proud knowing my fifteen year old son would be paving the way for other trans youth who would follow in his footsteps. Proud of my son for standing firm in his convictions, helping to make the decision for surgery that much easier for me.

Of course I had been there when my daughter was born but I witnessed unbelievable courage and strength when my son was reborn. Luca had chosen me to experience this moment with him and a powerful bond formed between us. Fourteen years later, it still overwhelms me

When I made the arrangements and said I would be spending the night at the clinic I never realized it meant just Luca and me. Once Luca was stabilized, everyone left. They had given me Dr. Johnson's home phone number in case of an emergency. Thankfully Luca was too out of it to realize how scared I was.

It didn't take long before Luca needed to pee. He had been cut from one arm pit to the other and had almost one hundred stitches. I knew I had to help him up, but I was so afraid of hurting him. This wasn't what I had bargained for. I thought a nurse would have been with us for the night. Through groans and tears, we struggled for what seemed to be an hour before Luca finally made it into the bathroom.

After getting Luca settled back in bed he was able to sleep a little bit. I had been given a blanket and was told to sleep on the couch in the waiting room. Even if I had been in the room with Luca, I had not planned on getting much sleep. But sleeping on a couch, in a waiting room at street level, in a strange, busy part of New York City made it completely impossible. Having the blinds pulled shut and the door locked, didn't seem to make a difference. We were alone.

Somehow, together we had made it through that agonizing night. Dr. Johnson checked Luca over and we were sent back to our hotel room for three days. Asking the taxi driver to take it easy was a waste of breath. It was not in his vocabulary. Go. Stop. Gun the engine. Slam on the brakes. Luca was in excruciating pain and this was a five-minute ride of pure torture.

After the taxi ride from hell we slowly walked into the hotel. I hadn't checked out the day before so we could go right to our room. We were both in desperate need of sleep. Neither of us were able to fall into a deep sleep but at least we slept on and off for a few hours. That's actually how it would be for the next three days.

Dr. Johnson checked Luca out for the last time and we headed for the train station and the long ride home. Luca still had drainage tubes which were very visible. As I dragged the luggage, I had to stay close to him making sure no one bumped the tubes. It was grueling.

Finally. We were seated on the train and heading for home. Seven days earlier I had brought my daughter to New York City. On this beautiful day in June I was taking my son home. A new beginning for each of us.

Dr. Johnson had supplied me with a letter to take to our local town hall to have Luca's name and sex changed on his birth certificate. After filling out a form, the clerk sent it into the Boston office.

Calling a few weeks later, I asked the clerk if I could get a copy of Luca's certificate. It was in. I could have driven over on my lunch break but thought Luca would like to come with me.

Walking up to the clerk and giving her the date of birth and the name, Luca's certificate was presented to us. After checking it over and agreeing it was correct, I purchased a few sealed originals.

Once we were back in the car I asked Luca, "Did you notice anything wrong with your new birth certificate?"

"Yea," he answered, hugging the precious piece of paper. "I thought it was supposed to say "amended" on it. It doesn't. It's like Marie never existed."

I just left it at that.

Of course I still have Marie's original birth certificate. When I look at it though, it feels like it was someone else's life. Someone else's baby girl with the pretty name. The sensation that came over me as I stood on the corner of 66th Street and Park Avenue in New York all those years ago has come true. Sadly, a part of me has been lost forever.

It's difficult to put into words how I felt losing my daughter. When a parent loses a child due to death, I would imagine there is an overwhelming sense of loss. Something final.

But in my case, I still had my child. Once I grieved for my daughter it was more like she just faded away. Not physically buried but buried into the back of my mind.

They're Gone

By Luca

The first leg of the bus trip went by quickly. Even Connecticut seemed to fly by. When we hit the New York state line time started to slow. I checked my watch constantly, tapped my foot and sighed.

When we reached the city my mouth hung open like a fly trap. I thought I was hot shit because I could find my way around Boston on foot, and that was a big city. But compared to Manhattan, Boston was a podunk and compared to these city dwellers, I was a hick.

Everywhere in Manhattan was crowded. Walking down the sidewalk was like trying to walk through Quincy Market at lunch time three days before Christmas. Boston is filled with amazing sights, but Manhattan is also full of amazing sights, beautiful and startling sounds, and interesting aromas. Mom and I were quickly swept away in the ocean of people.

We didn't have a lot of money for cab rides and were far too intimidated by the bustling public transportation system. So we hoofed it. That tiny island didn't seem so tiny with a back pack and suitcase in tow. Sweat poured down my back and greased up my butt-crack all the way to the hotel.

By the time we reached the hotel I'd gotten a second wind. This was the swankiest place I'd ever stayed in. A bell hop actually took our luggage and showed us to our room. It finally hit me. This trip wasn't going to be scary. It was going to be amazing!

The air-conditioning in the room was running full blast and brought much needed instant relief. My bulimia had paid off and I'd gone from 240 to 220 pounds, but I was still too fat to be carrying luggage through a sweltering city.

I immediately looked out the window to see the view from our room. We were so high up, and the buildings so close together, I couldn't see the ground. I stood on a chair and with my forehead resting against the glass still couldn't see down past five floors. It was surreal.

I got some maps and pamphlets from the lobby. The bellhop and door-man were very nice and talked to me for a bit. The door-man suggested Planet Hollywood for dinner and showed me how to get there on the map. I was definitely in tourist mode and could hardly contain my excitement.

Mom and I could hear the music and see the flashing lights of the restaurant from half a block away. Unfortunately we could see the line too. After elbowing our way through other tourists to get our name on the list, we meandered into the gift shop. I spotted a black and silver Planet Hollywood hockey-style jersey behind the counter that looked cool and flashy. It was very expensive, and I was a little apprehensive about picking out my one souvenir at the first place we went, but I thought I'd look macho in the jersey after I'd healed from my surgery.

After dinner we walked over to Times Square. It was exciting to see all the billboards and the MTV studios (this was back when MTV still played music videos and broadcast live shows from Times Square during the week). All the lights were beautiful, even the giant McDonalds signs.

The next morning we set off for my consultation. The walk to the surgeon's office seemed to take forever. It was nice seeing Grand Central Station and most of Park Avenue, but my feet were getting sore and my guts were getting twisty.

I knew I had to convince the surgeon of my comprehension and necessity or he wouldn't perform the surgery. He couldn't say no, I'd come too far to accept *no* as an answer. I was going to get what I wanted, what I needed. I'd have to fight for it one last time.

The inside of the surgeon's office was beautifully and tastefully decorated. The artwork looked museum quality. The air conditioning was running even though it was barely after nine am. New York was muggier than Boston and the long walk combined with my nerves had created a lot of sweat that gelled uncomfortably to my skin as I twisted my hands and tapped my feet in the waiting area.

When the surgeon came out to greet us he was older than I had expected him to be. I was the youngest transsexual who'd come into his office and he was concerned about my age. He looked over the letters of recommendation from Diane and the other therapist which explained why I was a good candidate for surgery. I did my best to explain to him how I needed this surgery so my life could begin. Trying to hide my chest so I could get by in the world was painful and exhausting. Without surgery I'd never be able to let my guard down. Never be comfortable around anyone. Learning and making friends when I went back to school would be all but impossible. I'd been living as a boy for over a year but still those things on my chest had made me an outcast, a social leper. I wanted a chance to not hate myself for something beyond my control.

The anesthesiologist joined us and was not only concerned about my age, but also my weight. Nowadays, it seems someone who's 5'8" and 220 pounds is practically average, but in 1998 I was still obese. It would take a lot of drugs to knock out someone my size. He'd have to monitor the entire surgery and continuously anesthetize me to keep me under.

After the surgeon and anesthesiologist agreed to go ahead with the surgery I got an examination. This was the moment I'd actually been dreading. Exposing my body to the surgeon and a nurse was nauseating. The nurse took photos. I felt dirty. They may have examined hundreds, even thousands of patients a year, but this was all new to me. No one had seen or touched me since Bobby. I held my breath and tried to push him out of my mind. I was panicking enough already.

When the exam was done and I was bound and dressed again, the surgeon discussed the procedure and possible side effects with me and Mom. All the binding I'd done over the past two years had created gangrenous tissue sores below my armpits. I'd become accustomed to the pain they caused, but unaware of how dangerous they were. The red and yellow skin around them would have to be removed, along with fat and muscle tissue below. Having dead and diseased tissue not attached to my breasts but still needing to be removed complicated things.

Every time my breasts were mentioned I felt uncomfortable. I knew I was there to get rid of them because they felt like hideous aliens permanently attached to my torso and ruining my life, but even at a time like this it was hard for me to verbally express or accept ownership of them.

My breast tissues alone weren't very big. It was my weight that made them the size they were. They were too large, and my skin too ruined from binding, for a keyhole surgery to work. The surgeon would have to perform a double mastectomy, with some lipo, and resize and graft my nipples back on with stitches. I would have enormous scars and possible nerve damage, up to complete loss of my nipples. I didn't care though. If that's what it took to be free of these monsters then so be it. On Monday I'd enter that operating room freely and gladly.

We left the surgeon's office and headed for Central Park. It was exciting to be in a place where so many movies were filmed. It could also be both enchanting and disgusting, depending on the time of day and area you're in. I thought the Central Park Zoo was a blast. In my adult life I've become one of those animal loving, pretentious a-holes who believes zoos are mostly just cruel. But as a teenage animal lover I was thrilled at the unexpected impromptu zoo visit. I talked Mom into buying me a green zoo T shirt with a gecko on it. I think she agreed because one, it wasn't black, and two, I was a spoiled only child who didn't know what the word "no" meant.

On Saturday, after breakfast we walked outside the hotel doors and were bombarded by loud dance music, throngs of excited crowds covering the sidewalks, rainbow flags as far as the eye could see and drag queens on parade floats taking up all of 5th Avenue. We'd accidentally stumbled onto the New York City Gay Pride Parade! I'd never seen so many gays in one place. I'd never been to a gay pride anything. Being just fifteen years old and seeing thousands of people showing their pride and love for the gay community was enough to make my head spin and my heart burst.

This was my first time seeing drag queens, leather daddies, ass-less chaps, dykes on bikes and gays and lesbians in wedding attire. It may not sound like an event you'd want to be at with your mother, but I couldn't think of a single person I'd rather have shared this experience with.

Mom bought me a small rainbow flag which I still have to this day. Remembering when I got it always makes me smile.

Lots of nice drag queens and leather daddies in the crowd posed so we could take their picture. I got my picture taken with a convertible full of drag queens in outrageous dresses, wigs, big sunglasses and feather boas. They were so friendly and beautiful.

Most of the churches we walked past on our way to the Metropolitan Museum of Art had gay pride flags flown out front for the entire day. I felt I wanted to stay here for the rest of my life.

Over the weekend we visited the MET, the Chrysler Building, the Hard Rock Café, and Rockefeller Center. We strolled Broadway, stood outside Radio City Music Hall, visited Times Square every night and finished off at the Empire State Building. The best time to be at the top of this landmark skyscraper is at night when the whole city is lit up. I couldn't imagine a better city to be reborn in.

I awakened in the recovery room to the sound of my own sobbing. When you're anesthetized it's like traveling through time. One second I was in an operating room with a hair net and an IV, the next second I was crying my eyes out in a room I'd never seen before and in more pain than I thought possible. My face and hair were soaked with tears. The notion that I had been crying in my sleep creeped me out.

A nurse came by to check on me and I asked her why I was crying. She told me it was probably a side effect of the anesthesia. I'd been under for almost ten hours. That baffled me. I thought I'd be in surgery for four hours, six tops. The complications from years of binding gave the surgeon a difficult time. Once he opened me up he found the tissue damage was deeper and more widespread than initially estimated. The incision on my torso was over thirty inches from end to end. They had to cover more than two and a half feet to remove my breasts and cut off the irreparable skin, stretching and sewing together what was left. The stitches numbered in the hundreds. My arms were held above my head with weighted sandbags for most of it. This was partially why my pain was so deep. My chest and shoulder muscles had been strained. I had two tubes ten inches deep inside me to help drain fluid. This news nauseated me. I was too bandaged to see what I looked like. There was also a new binder made of spandex covering me from my shoulders to my waist. It was itchy. I had to pee. I didn't want Mom to see me until I could make myself stop crying. I didn't want her to be scared that I was unhappy or in pain. I was actually over the moon with happiness and triumph. I just couldn't show it yet.

Mom and I were left alone in the clinic overnight. I hadn't eaten anything since dinner the night before, but the nausea made it impossible for me to hold anything down except two or three animal crackers and enough gingerale to wash them down. I tried some chicken soup Mom had brought from a deli around the corner but it came back up on me.

The only pain killer I was allowed was 500mg of Tylenol every six hours. It might as well have been two sugar cubes. The pain was excruciating. I had to be propped up with pillows; it hurt too much to lie down. I couldn't sleep because I was used to sleeping on my side or stomach, never on my back or sitting up.

I was exhausted but couldn't get comfortable enough to sleep. I was hungry but looking at food made me gag. I was bored but couldn't concentrate on anything past my pain. And I hadn't peed since before I was prepped for the surgery.

A bedpan had been left at the foot of my bed. No one expected me to be able to get out of bed that first night. I held it in as long as I could. Years of having to hold my pee in public for fear of using the bathrooms had strengthened my tolerance for full bladder pains, but it was past the thirteen hour mark and I had to go. That made me cry.

I could barely reach far enough to scoot my underwear down past my ass. Mom had to reach under the sheets and help get them down to my knees. I couldn't even reach to get the bedpan under me. But after some maneuvering, with Mom's help we got it in place. It was cold and it hurt to sit on. Mom was going to have to wipe me or I'd have to drip dry. That made my bladder clench up. I tried to pee but nothing would come out. I was afraid I'd bust a kidney. It hurt so much I wanted to scream.

Right then I wanted to pee more than anything in the world. But no, it was useless. Mom kept saying she didn't mind and I kept crying that I didn't want her to wipe me. But I had to pee so bad. Round and round we went for a half hour and then I gave up and scooted off the bedpan.

Mom helped me get my underwear back up and I lay in the bed trying to convince myself I could hold it until morning.

After another fifteen minutes of bladder torture I realized I had to get out of the bed and walk down the hall to the bathroom. It took like ten minutes just to maneuver past the pain into a seated position with my feet on the floor. I was still hooked up to an IV bag and I glared at it, resenting it for slowly filling me with saline that converted to urine.

I thought I'd feel lighter after the surgery, but I felt heavier. It felt like I had a 50 pound rock hanging by threads attached to my muscles, ribs and lungs. If I lay down it was crushing me. If I stood up it pulled at me. If I moved too fast or leaned too far it felt like I was being stabbed with steak knives. But I had to pee. Holding my breath as long as I could, I bit down on my lip to stifle my screams and shuffled one foot in front of the other until I reached a toilet.

Everything in the clinic looked different in the dark. The longer I walked/shuffled the further away the bathroom seemed to get. When I finally made it inside and got to the toilet, I couldn't figure out how to sit down without straining and causing more pain. The shock sent up my body from my butt plopping down on the hard seat almost made me piss myself anyway.

I refused to pee until Mom left the room. I wiped and took care of my underwear on my own. It hurt, but I'm really private and stubborn. While I was in a bathroom I unhooked the canteen-like bag at the end of the tubes still draining fluid and emptied it out. It looked like someone had bled into a spittoon. Yuck. By the time I got back to bed the whole ordeal had taken over half an hour. I was finally exhausted enough to sleep a bit.

I woke up around three am having to pee again. Damn IV. This time it only took about twenty minutes. I ate a few more animal crackers and went back to sleep.

The next morning the surgeon looked me over. By the time he got in I'd already been out of bed three times to pee, empty the fluid collector and brush my teeth. The staff was amazed that I was up and moving around. He said everything looked good but I'd have to keep the tubes in me for a few more days. Drats. I tried to get a look at myself while the bandages were off but I needed a mirror to see everything. "They" were sure as hell gone though and that's all that mattered.

Mom had to be shown how to change my bandages since we were going back to our hotel room for the next few days. I'd be back in three days for one more check-up. Then we'd go home.

The cab ride back to the hotel was torture. I think I cried the entire time from the pain of being bounced around. The Tylenol was doing squat.

I spent the next three days in bed watching TV and sleeping when I could. I still hadn't seen what I looked like under the bandages because I wanted to be alone when I did and as of yet I still didn't have the reach to change them by myself The pain receded gradually. So now, instead of feeling like my top half was on fire I just felt like I'd recently been on fire. If I moved too fast or bent too far it felt like someone was putting a pack of cigarettes out on my skin, grinding them into my flesh and muscles

I had to wear button-up shirts for the next few weeks because I wasn't allowed to lift my arms up over my head. Due to the pain, I could barely lift them high enough to feed myself or brush my teeth anyway. Mom had to wash my hair in the sink. I couldn't shower. Thank god for Old Spice Pure Sport deodorant and air conditioning. If I had been sweating, that hotel room would have been very funky by the time we left.

On my final check-up before going home the surgeon decided I was still too swollen and draining too much fluid for the tubes to come out. Most people have the tubes in for two to twelve hours, sometime up to two days. I was going to have them in another ten days for a total of two weeks. He showed Mom which stitches she'd have to cut to be able to take them out and sent us home with a scalpel. I'd have to keep my recovery binder on for another month.

The cab rides to the surgeon's office and then to the train station were still very painful. Everyone in New York drives like a total douche, stomping on the gas and then stomping on the brakes. Penn Station was quite a site, and the train ride home was my first time on Amtrak.

I was sad watching the city fade away behind us. My body left, but part of my heart stayed. I was sort of looking forward to going home though. When you feel like crap there's no place like home. And I still felt like crap that had been set on fire and then had the flames stomped out. Some quiet time and familiarity would be nice. I wished the train would either stop rocking or that Jesus would show up and transform my Tylenol into Vicodin.

Coming home

My first night home I locked the door to my bedroom and sat on the floor next to my bed across from a full length mirror. Finally alone for the first time in days, I was going to unhook my spandex binder and peel some bandages back to get a look at myself. I slowly stretched the cotton bandages and gauze away from my front. To my horror my right nipple stuck to one of the compresses and peeled half-way off my body, revealing a red semi circle hole of raw flesh. It took all my strength not to faint. My vision went black and I swooned a little, but I'm pretty certain I remained conscious. A tearless gasp of anguish at what I'd had to do to myself to move on with my life escaped me. I pressed my nipple and all the bandages back in place and hoped for the best.

After a few more days I insisted on taking a shower and changing the bandages myself. I still wore button-up shirts and slept sitting up with a pile of pillows behind me, but I was slowly regaining my independence. The pain was gradually lessening as well. It still hurt twenty-four hours a day, but more often than not it was a dull throb rather than a stabbing, burning feeling.

Mom went back to work and I spent my days inside enjoying the air conditioning, watching TV, and chatting online. It was the same as when I'd been homeschooling but without the false pretenses that I was learning something.

It was another week before Mom cut the stitches holding the two ten-inch drainage tubes and pulled them out. The goo they drained was less viscous now and a soft pink color instead of alternating red, brown, and orange so it was time for them to come out. Her arthritic hands were shaking slightly and the glasses on her face seemed thicker than I remembered them being. I was so afraid she was going to slip and cut me with that scalpel. I yelled and whined and backpedaled away from her for as long as I could, my dignity replaced by fear. Fortunately she didn't slip and everything came out fine. That had been the scariest part of the entire experience.

Before summer school started Mom took me to the town hall to get a copy of my amended birth certificate. Weeks earlier Mom had sent in a letter from the surgeon in New York which stated I had completed all surgical requirements to officially change my gender. I can't remember if it was because I was still a minor or if the city where I was born was just cool that way, but whatever the reason the new birth certificate would supposedly say it had been altered. However, it would not state what specifically had been changed. I thought that was pretty cool. The lady who worked there seemed nice and when she gave us copies of my new birth certificate it didn't say anywhere on it that it had been altered. Not on the long or short form. She pressed the town seal into the papers and for all legal purposes I was now male. This was the last step in burying Marie in the past. As far as the government was concerned not only did she no longer exist, but it was as if she never had. That clerk hadn't handed me some papers, she had handed me my life. I walked out of that building feeling free.

Summer School

Sooner than I was prepared for, it was time to begin summer school. A taxi-cab paid for by the town picked me up at the condo and drove me to school. The first day of school is always hard. I don't care how old you are. But this was my first day at school in over two years. The school was new, the city was new, the taxi was new, the students and teachers were new and I was new.

I still viewed summer school as a punishment for a crime I didn't commit. My nervousness at the newness of everything was outshined by my anger at the injustice of having to be there and, to spite myself, my curiosity. My only fear was a student recognizing me as Marie. The school was in a town between a city and town where I had attended elementary and middle school. I had gone to summer camps near there and played sports as a kid at the YMCA one more city over. Dad worked in the electronics department of a large department store in the mall there. Almost every teenager for a twenty mile radius had bought a stereo or CD from him at some point. Being recognized would ruin everything I had worked for. And now because of my recent stay in a mental hospital I had to stay at this school no matter what. I tried not to think about all this as I entered the building.

Classes were held in one room on the top floor of one building. Most of the other rooms in the building and the building next door were empty and locked because it was summer. There was no air conditioning and the few windows that would open only opened a few inches. I was glad school let out by lunch time. At 8:30 am in July it was already warm and humid. By noon you'd be able to grab fistfuls of air and wring the water out of them in this stuffy room.

There were two teachers and an aid for five students. I was in the youngest one of the small bunch. For the first half of the morning we had English which consisted of creative writing and reading on our own. The books assigned were detective mysteries and I enjoyed them although the reading level was young adult and not very challenging. The second half of the morning was Science and since all the materials were at about a fifth grade level I already knew everything we were being taught.

I was told before attending this school that the other students weren't learning disabled but were in special ed because they had emotional and behavioral issues. When I first saw our learning materials I sort of doubted that. By the end of the first day I realized these kids weren't dumb, they just didn't give a crap. All they wanted to do was hang out listening to rap music, smoking cigarettes and complaining. I hated rap music but I loved smoking and complaining. I couldn't smoke until my stitches were all healed though, so I just drank iced coffee or soda, drinking in the situation with my caffeine, grateful no one there knew me.

I got along ok with the other students. Academically I was the most advanced of the group but I played dumb so I wouldn't stand out. Much like the kids I had befriended in the psychiatric treatment program, these teenagers seemed older than their years. They weren't emotionally more mature than sixteen or seventeen, but experience can age you even if you don't learn or grow from it. They were a lot harder, meaner and more distrusting than average high school students. I impressed them though with my knowledge of drugs, experience with violence and rebellion, sarcastic whit and insatiable anger- especially toward authority.

Back to New York

A couple weeks into school, I had to go back to New York for a follow up with the surgeon. I got to get out of school for a day because of it. I told the other students I was invited to go with one of my friends and his mom while she attended some business there.

The friend I went with was another FTM teenager who was three years older than me and had his upper surgery with the same surgeon a few days before I had. We met through Diane. His name was Thomas. We got along okay. Besides the obvious we didn't have much in common and we lived far apart. He was the first gay trans man I had ever met and the first gay man I had spoken with at any length.

Part of me wondered why if you were previously a woman and attracted to men you were trans instead of just being a straight woman. But then again, if sexual preference was all that mattered I'd just be a lesbian. And I've never felt that was right for me. You are who you are. And Thomas was definitely a guy and very happy. He was starting college in the fall at Brown. I can't remember what his major was going to be but he was brilliant. He was looking forward to jogging with his shirt off after he had healed. That made me more jealous than I'd thought it would.

Thomas was athletic and trim so his surgery hadn't needed many stitches or left much scarring. He'd basically had chest lipo and his nipples were resized and grafted. His surgery took less than half the time mine had, he had less than a fifth of the stitches I had. His drainage tubes had come out the same day.

Maybe if I hadn't let myself get so fat things could have been easy for me like they had been for Thomas, but it was too late to change that now. Even if I lost enough weight to not be embarrassed by my gut to go topless, I'd never be rid of my hideous scars. I doubted I'd ever know what the sun felt like on my bare back and shoulders.

I went to the city with Thomas and his mother because Mom needed to save her PTO. It was also cheaper for me to tag along. Thomas' mother paid for all our cab rides and our lunch. She was very generous.

Same as when I went with Mom, we took the bus into the city and the train back. It was hotter in July than it had been in June, but Thomas and his mother got us cabs everywhere so I didn't have to walk far in the heat. The check-up went well. To my surprise my right nipple hadn't rotted off. In fact everything seemed to be healing fine. The surgeon removed my non-dissolving stitches. I thought it would hurt, but my skin around the incision was numb. The pain I'd felt from the surgery had been deep tissue pain. All the nerves near the surface were severed and dead. Thirteen years later I still have big areas on my chest and sides where my skin doesn't feel anything.

It was hard to say goodbye to the city again. At the train station I thought about Charlotte, the girl I talked to online from upstate New York. Her family lived less than 90 minutes from the city yet she'd never been here once in her life. I found that incredible. The Metro North line ran right through her town. As far as I was concerned New York City was the most amazing place in the world. How anyone could be so close and manage to ignore its allure was beyond me.

Betsie and Luca, age 1 week

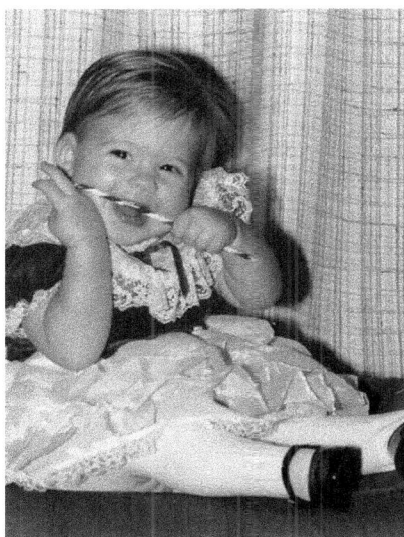

First Christmas, 1983

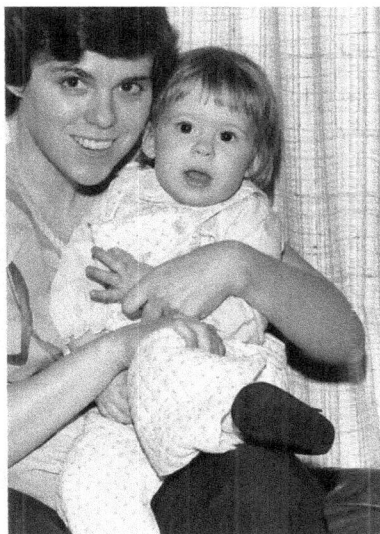

Betsie and Luca, age 15 months

Halloween, 1988

Halloween 1990

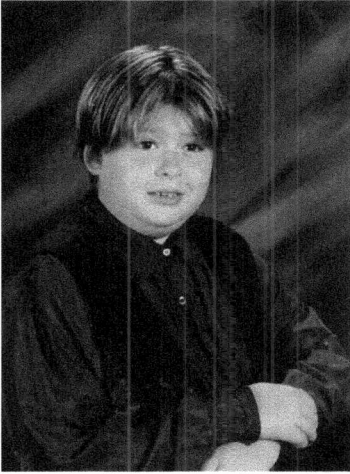

5th grade school photo
Obviously not winning any
beauty contests that year

Just home from Space Camp

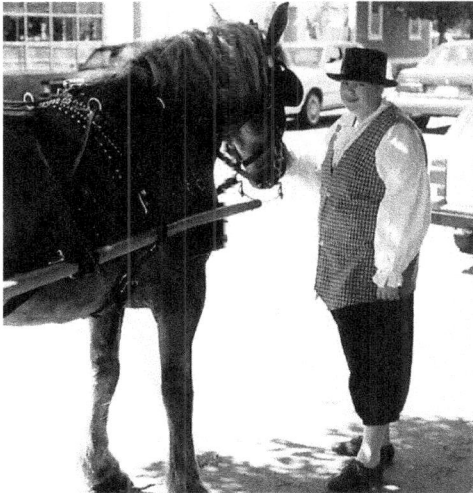

1st job, carriage footman, 1996

1997, Boston, beginning transition and wearing a binder

November 1998, 5 months after surgery

May 1999, just before BAGLY Prom, 1 year post-op

Christmas 1999, 19 months post-op, just over 2 years on testosterone and still getting lots of acne

September 2001, driving around Virginia, in my first car, sporting all the facial hair I could muster

June 2002, Charlotte's Prom

Shitty cell phone picture, taken on my 24th birthday, 2007

Even shittier cell phone picture, taken at night - March 2007, with a chin-strap beard that took 9 ½ years of testosterone to grow

Glacier Bay, Alaska, May 2007, with Charlotte
She was trying to steal my body heat, but it wasn't working

Luca, Charlotte, Betsie in Glacier Bay

October 2007, Charlotte and our fabulous cake at our wedding

Charlotte, Luca, Betsie, Brooks

I still can't believe she likes me

This is about as good as it gets

Chapter Twenty-Two

"He's Really A Girl!"

By Betsie

With everything that had taken place during the first eight months of the year, I needed some R and R. My sisters and their kids had gotten together in Ogunquit, Maine for the week. I had a few commitments I couldn't get out of, so I had arrived two days after everyone else. I was thrilled to hear Luca had made some friends and my nephew Will had been there to keep him company.

Brooks had gone to the grocery store and I was by myself in the trailer making homemade coleslaw. The rest of the family was outside waiting for burgers to be ready. The sound of everyone talking at once was like a peaceful hum.

Without warning the screen door swung open and my niece Ann-Marie yelled, "He's going to kill me! Quick. Hide me. He's going to kill me!"

"Who's going to kill you?" I asked nervously.

"Luca."

"Ann-Marie, what the hell have you done!"

"I told his friends that he's really a girl."

I snapped.

"Jesus Christ! Do you have any idea what you just did?"

"You need to hide me."

Throwing the coleslaw in the sink and pounding my fist on the kitchen counter I yelled, "I hope the hell he finds you and kills you!"

Kicking the screen door open and stepping outside, I gave the door a good slam behind me.

"God damn, why did she do this?" I asked no one in particular. "What the hell am I going to do now? I don't even know where he is!"

"He's down by the pool," Ann-Marie sobbed.

"He's probably going to drown himself."

"You stay here and calm down," my sister Maryanne told me. "I'll go look for him."

"If anything happens to him I'm going to kill you myself!" I yelled at my niece.

I was enraged over Ann-Marie's hurtful words.

"Why the hell did she do this? I don't know what I'll do if anything happens to him."

"You have every right to be upset but you need to calm down," Louise said.

"How the hell am I supposed to calm down? Why the hell did she have to do this?" I sobbed on Louise's shoulder.

"I'm sorry," Ann-Marie cried. "I didn't mean it."

"Do you have any idea what you may have done?"

"He'll be alright," Louise said, with the usual calmness in her voice.

"Jesus Christ, how many times have you had to say that to me?"

I stormed back inside. Louise followed. Picking up handfuls of clothes at a time and throwing them into trash bags I was sobbing faster than I could catch my breath.

"As soon as Maryanne finds Luca and Brooks returns from the store, we'll be leaving," I cried. "I don't understand why we can't just have a good time. Why can't I ever relax and have a good time? Shit like this always seems to happen. I don't even know if Maryanne found him."

"She would have come right back."

"But what if something is wrong and she can't come right back?"

Minutes passed. Maryanne returned alone.

"Did you find him? Is he okay?" I frantically asked.

"He's down by the pool and he's fine. Give him a few more minutes."

"What did he say?"

"That he wanted to throw a rock at Ann-Marie's head. I talked him out of it."

"Maybe we should leave anyway."

"Give him a chance. Just wait a few more minutes."

About ten minutes later Luca returned.

"I'm sorry Hon," I told him. "I threw everything into bags and as soon as your father gets back we'll be leaving."

"I don't want to leave," Luca said surprising me. "I told everyone Anne-Marie was just kidding and they're fine with it. We're going to the movies."

It took me the rest of the evening to calm down. My mind knew everything had turned out okay but every time I thought of Luca possibly trying to run away or drown himself, my body trembled and the tears would start again. Maybe I should have trusted Luca a little bit more but my reaction had been based on years of experience.

"He's Really A Girl!"

By Luca

I was getting into the swing of summer school. It was nice to have a reason to get up in the morning and have a place to go, even just for half a day. Two of the students were becoming good buddies to me and I liked my teachers a lot. But when my family decided to go camping in Ogunquit, Maine, I figured I deserved a break.

Many of my all-time favorite memories are of going to this campground with my family. One of my aunts owned a sort of time-share for a cabin there. My whole family; aunts, uncles and cousins would pile into one medium sized cabin for a week, often sharing one bathroom. It was a blast. We'd cook outside and go swimming every day. I hadn't gone for a couple of years because since I started transitioning I liked to stay out of view.

I was also still hurting every day from my breakup with Michelle. There was a lot going on in my life and a lot of things had changed in a few months, but whenever I slowed down it was hard to live one moment to the next without thinking of her. A family vacation might be a nice reprieve.

So I packed up what little homework I had and went up to the camp-site with my family. My parents would be up in a few days for a long weekend; until then I tagged along with Will. He was now nineteen. He'd been out of high school for a year and working full-time along with traveling with the heavy metal band he was in. He had a white Firebird and if he got it up over 120 miles per hour, the sunroof would make a weird humming noise. I felt cooler just being near him.

Before my surgery I had bleached my hair a blonde so platinum it was white. It was shaved up underneath to the top of my scalp and when I didn't pull it back it fell down past my chin. I also had three piercings in each ear. But with my body type and clothes I didn't look feminine, just alternative. I was excited to have some family vacation photos with me in them that I didn't hate. My weight was under 215 pounds, a loss of almost 35pounds. And I was far along enough in healing that I could wear t-shirts again. All in all I thought I looked pretty good.

After the first day at the campsite Will had to drive back to Massachusetts to go to work, but he'd be back soon. So I was on my own for a bit. Since my time in the mental hospital Will was the only one in my family who didn't treat me differently. I loved my family and wanted to take this time to re-build my relationship with a lot of them, but it was too hard to be around them for an extended period of time. Now that I was in summer classes at a school for rejects, I felt more like a fuck-up and disappointment than usual. I wanted to spend time with them so badly but without Will or my parents there as a buffer, it was just too hard. The silences that used to be comfortable now felt so strained. I was embarrassed of myself so I took off to explore the campsite alone.

After the mental hospital and summer school I wasn't used to being without peers during the day. So wearing my Jnco jean shorts and a black Smashing Pumpkins t-shirt I wandered down to the arcade in search of other teenagers.

I found a girl my age wearing a Bush t-shirt and cargo pants playing

Top-Skater. Bush was my favorite band and Top-Skater was my favorite arcade game. I watched her for a bit, wanting to say something but too shy. It's hard with girls. I was afraid she'd think I was hitting on her and tell me to fuck off in disgust. She was way hot and probably used to guys hitting on her wherever she went. I may have looked better than I did four months ago but I was nowhere near this girl's league. It wasn't a trans thing, just a fat thing. So I knew romance was out, but I was still bored and lonely and terrified of spending time with my family. While I was busy pondering all this, the girl had finished her video game and said something to me.

"I'm sorry, what?"

"I said I like your shirt."

And just like that we started a conversation. This was my first time talking to someone who wasn't forced to be near me for an extended period of time since my transition. In the hospital and at summer school I had said some stupid things and had many un-cool moments but people didn't instantly bail on me because there was nowhere to go and no one else to talk to. On the outside I felt I needed to be as cool as possible 100% of the time or people would write me off. This led to over-analyzing everything I wanted to say and resulted in many abbreviated and aloof remarks. But this worked for me.

The girl's name was Anya. She was here with her two younger sisters and their father. Her family was from Connecticut and like me she loved them all dearly but was actively avoiding them. It turns out avoiding your family for no discernible reason is common teenage behavior.

We hit it off really well and spent the rest of the day together exploring the woods and camp ground, loitering in the camp store and pool area and hooking up with other teens. Anya was much more outgoing than me and paved the way of introductions to half a dozen other cool teens I never would have talked to on my own.

Will came back that night and I introduced him to the other people I'd been hanging out with. They all instantly adored him because his entire persona screamed original badass, yet he's friendly and funny. It took less than two minutes for everyone to decide they liked him more than me but this didn't surprise me. I liked him more than I liked me. Plus he was the oldest of the group and the only one with a car and a tattoo.

The next day my family went to a water park. I couldn't swim because of my stitches so I stayed behind. I finished my homework for the week by mid-morning and ate lunch with Anya in my family's cabin. After that we hit the arcade again and played mini-golf with two other teenage girls on vacation from western Massachusetts. I had remembered that I was supposed to meet my family for dinner, but had sort of lost track of time.

I was sitting on a picnic table near the pool with Anya, the two girls we'd played golf with and another guy when my eight year old cousin came looking for me. She had been pretty pissy with me since I'd arrived with Will two days earlier. She hadn't taken my transitioning too well and handled my having been a mental patient even worse. I couldn't pick up a knife to eat without her asking if I was going to cut myself with it. What could I say? The scars on my arms were too visible to deny. So she inferred I was crazy while I inferred she was an annoying bitch. Harsh criticism of a child but lately she brought out the asshole in me. So the conversation went like this.

"What are you doing?"

"Nothing. Hanging out. Why?"

"You're supposed to be at the cabin for dinner. They sent me to get you."

"Okay, I'll come back in a couple minutes."

"No, you have to come back right now! Plus your friends are smoking. I'm telling."

"Fuck off."

"Did you know he used to be a girl?"

Well that shut me up. I was stunned. I couldn't believe my cousin would do this to me. Then I couldn't believe how stupid I was to think she wouldn't do this to me. Everyone at the picnic table studied me. I could feel the color draining from my face as I fought not to shake. Suddenly my mouth felt very dry and my bladder felt full enough to burst. Anya was the first one to speak.

"Yeah right."

"It's true!"

"He doesn't even look like a girl."

I finally remembered how to speak.

"Get your fat fucking ass back to the cabin before I kick it all the way back!"

I felt bad calling my cousin fat. She had struggled with her weight ever since her parents got divorced and was really sensitive about it. I knew how bad it felt to be the fat girl. It's one of the loneliest feelings in the world. But I couldn't think of what else to say that would upset her enough to get her to leave. She was stubborn and could withstand almost any insult you threw at her unless it was about her weight. She took off crying back toward the cabin.

I stood there feeling like an asshole and a fool. No one looks cool threatening small children. I was unnerved. I was sure everyone could see right through me now. I'd have to go home as soon as possible. My vacation was ruined. The friends I'd made would be making fun of me behind my back as soon as I was out of earshot. The whole campground would know about the he/she on site by morning. Fuck fuck fuck.

My friends excused themselves and took off very quickly, including Anya. I was suddenly alone and feeling angrier than I'd ever been. I figured I could get Mom to drive me home. It would suck for her to have to turn around since she just got there, but she'd understand. In the meantime I'd hang out by the pool. I couldn't go back to the cabin because my family would be waiting to ream me out for sending my cousin back crying and I wasn't in the mood for a scream fest. The pool was deserted because it was dinner time. The air smelled like charcoal and hamburgers. It overwhelmed the smell of sun-block and chlorine but I was too angry to be hungry now.

I kept thinking about how people all over the camp would be gathered around for dinner with their families and talking about me. I felt sick. I shouldn't have come up here. I shouldn't have left my nice safe environment at home where all my friends were online and no one could out me. I wanted to go back to the hospital. I wanted to hurt myself. What was the point of my painful surgery, all those hormone shots, and all the shit I'd been through if even 150 miles from home people I'd never met before would still see me as a gay-dyke-weirdo he/she? I hated my life.

I picked up a huge rock and sat it on the glass table in front of me. I decided the first mother fucker who called me a name was getting this embedded in their brain. As I was musing over thoughts of bludgeoning people my aunt approached me.

"So is the rock you've picked out for my daughter's head?"

"She deserves it you know."

"Yeah," my aunt sighed and sat down across from me. "I know."

We sat there in a hot, thick awkward silence for a minute. I was angry and heartbroken at the same time. I kept staring at the rock on the table until my vision blurred and I had to blink a couple of scalding tears out of my eyes to see again.

My aunt broke the silence.

"She told me what she said. I'm so sorry she did this to you. I have no idea why she does shit like this. Sometimes she drives me fucking crazy. It's not just you. She gives me and her father hell too. She gets in trouble at school all the time. She has a hard time making friends. I try to tell her this is why but she's so young she doesn't understand. She's sorry, you know. She knows what she said was awful and now she feels terrible. I don't blame you for wanting to take a rock to her head, but I'd consider it a favor if you didn't. She is my daughter."

I thought about what my aunt said for a bit. I knew I wasn't the only one who had it rough. My cousin got picked on, too. But it wasn't fair for her to out me like that. Then again my aunt had always been good to me and done a lot for me. When I started transitioning she took me clothes shopping and the last time I saw Michelle, my aunt had been the one who took us into Boston so Michelle could get a bus back to her family in Sturbridge. I owed my aunt any favor she asked of me. And I could see the situation was hurting her. I guess I didn't want to be the one who ruined everyone's vacation so I told her I'd let it go but only because she asked me.

My aunt left to go back and comfort her daughter. I lingered for a while, giving my family time to finish eating before I went back to the cabin to pack my things. Deciding not to fight with my cousin still hadn't undone what she'd said in front of my new friends.

I was walking back to the cabin when Anya caught up with me. She acted as if nothing strange had happened. This caught me off guard but I tried to act cool.

"I was coming to find you. *There's Something About Mary* is playing in town tonight and I thought we could go together. What are you doing skulking around by yourself? Did you get in trouble for making your cousin cry?"

"I don't think I'm in too much trouble. I haven't actually gone back yet to find out."

"So don't go back. Let's go see the movie."

"Is anyone else coming?"

"Janine and Theresa want to come too."

I couldn't believe the people who had been there when my cousin outed me still wanted to hang out. I didn't know if they didn't care or if I passed so well they thought my cousin was full of shit. Eight year olds are seldom taken seriously anyway. There was no way to find out without outing myself all over again so I had to agonize in wonder. I did sneak back to my family's cabin to invite Will to go to the movie too. He drove us all in his Firebird.

In the dark theatre the air conditioning was running full blast. I was cold so I tucked my arms up into my t-shirt. I felt one of my itchier stitches poking out a little. It felt like a hard plastic fishing line. I couldn't imagine this was a dissolvable stitch and thought maybe the surgeon had missed one. I kept flicking it and scratching it and eventually decided to pull on it. My t-shirt was loose so I had plenty of space to stretch out my arm. I pulled the plasticky stitch out three or four inches and let it go. It snaked back inside me. So I pulled on it again. I just kept pulling and pulling. There was no blood or pain but I was becoming sickened by how long it was. I had it out at least a foot in front of me when I felt a sharp sudden pain under my left armpit. Jesus! Is that how far back this thing went inside me? Christ! I dropped it, gagging and wincing. I figured when I got back to the campsite I'd find a pair of scissors and cut it so the end wouldn't poke out any more and scratch me or tempt me to play with it. Then to my horror the whole thing snaked slowly back all the way inside me. I couldn't find the end anymore to pull it out and cut it. I decided not to say anything about it and hope if I ignored it, it would go away.

Mom was furious Ann-Marie had outed me. I think she figured I'd be crying and wanting to go home or sharpening a knife somewhere to exact my revenge. She definitely didn't expect to find me in a good mood. I was still angry at my cousin and cautious of the situation, but I was having too much fun with Will, Anya and the other people we'd met to go home.

Mom had brought me a letter I received at home from Charlotte, the girl from New York. I read it when I was alone. The smell of her stationary eased my anxiety. She was always so sweet to me. While I was camping with my family she was at an all-girls Christian summer camp. She wrote that she missed me, meaning she missed talking online or on the phone with me. We'd never met face to face. She was no Michelle. She wasn't as exciting as the kids I'd met at the campgrounds either. Still, it was nice to have someone somewhere miss me.

I spent the rest of the week with Will, our cousin Leigh who's only a year younger than me, Anya and a couple other kids we met. We went to Old Orchard Beach, Ogunquit Beach, and Perkins Cove by day. At night we hung out building fires after our families had gone off to bed. We'd stay out until three am talking and telling stories or jokes. It was nice to be happy and belong.

When it was time to leave, Anya gave me her phone number and email. I was glad to have someone to talk to when I got home who was a real friend, not a faceless name in a chat-room online. I had lots of pictures of me with my family and my new friends. For once, I was smiling in all of them.

Chapter Twenty-Three

Emergency Stop

By Betsie

Luca and I had to make one more trip to New York to see Dr. Johnson for some minor touch-ups. I was told it would not be a long procedure and we would be in and out of the office quickly. Minutes turned into hours and I knew there was more going on than what the doctor had discussed with me. I was passing time in the waiting room with a very nosy patient and felt bad when the receptionist told her she needed to reschedule because Luca's "touch-up" was taking longer than anticipated.

When Luca finally came out of the anesthesia the surgeon asked if we had driven or were taking a cab back to our hotel.

"We're taking the bus back to the train station," I informed him. "We have no money for cab fare."

"I can't believe you're not staying the night," Dr. Johnson's voice was stern with me.

"When I called to make the appointment I was told we would be in and out of here quickly. There would be no need to stay."

"I'm not comfortable with Luca going home," Dr. Johnson replied with anger in his voice. "It took a lot more anesthesia than I had planned. He should stay."

"We can't stay. I have to be back at work tomorrow morning. I'm out of vacation days."

"You should have planned this better," he yelled at me. "There's no way Luca can take a bus to the train station. I'll give you cab money."

His infuriation took me by surprise. I wanted to crawl under a rock.

"We need to get going. I have to catch the six pm train. It will be about four hours on the train and then another hour drive home."

With that, Dr. Johnson handed me a twenty dollar bill and his receptionist hailed a cab.

Oh my god was I glad to be out of his office, no longer the target of his ranting.

We arrived at Amtrak just in time and raced to board the train.

We had been on the train for a little over an hour when Luca said, "Mom, my side feels wet."

The side of Luca's shirt was soaked.

Luca took some napkins and put them inside his shirt. Taking them back out, they were soaked in blood.

I tried my best to remain calm but panic set in pretty quickly. Leaving Luca, I walked the length of the car to ask an attendant for gauze from a first-aid kit. After checking all three kits onboard, she informed me none of them contained any gauze. She then made an announcement over the loud speaker asking if anyone onboard was a doctor would they please come to the front of the car.

The first person to offer help was a nurse. Although there wasn't much she could do, having her take charge of the situation put me a little more at ease. A doctor also came to Luca's aid but once he realized he couldn't help, he asked the Amtrak attendant to call ahead to the next stop and have an ambulance waiting to take us to the New Haven, Connecticut Hospital. It would be another twenty minutes before we made the unscheduled stop. By the time we exited the train a small bucket had been filled with Luca's bloody paper towels.

When we finally got to see the doctor, you could tell right away she clearly didn't want to touch my child. Like someone who was afraid of catching the plague.

"Mrs. Harvie," the doctor shouted. "How could you let someone do this to your daughter? How could you let her be butchered like this?"

"He hasn't been butchered. He just had some touch-up surgery. We need to get the bleeding stopped."

"I should report you and the surgeon for doing this," she yelled again. "This borders on child abuse."

Jesus Christ! Could things get any worse? Would she actually report me for child abuse?

She kept reaming me out, her voice getting louder with each accusation. Everyone in the emergency room could hear her.

I was now in a fight or flight mode. However, I was sure fighting would mean losing my son. She meant business. I had to get out of there as quickly as possible.

Luca's bleeding started to slow down. He wouldn't need any stitches. It was a good thing because I don't believe this doctor had any intention on touching him.

Running out of horrible things to say, she slapped a bandage on Luca's side and discharged us.

She had to get in the last word though.

"God will punish you for this!" she yelled for all to hear as we opened the door to leave.

Every nerve in my body knew how Marie must have felt when she had been bullied out on the school yard. It had been a frightening experience. One endured at the hands of the medical profession.

It was after nine pm when we boarded the train again in New Haven. We were both tired. My nerves had calmed down but not my anger. I had witnessed first-hand unimaginable persecution towards my son. MY SON! My child who wanted nothing more than to be treated with dignity.

We slumped into our seats, leaned against one another and fell asleep. We still had another two and a half hours to go before the train made its last stop.

Emergency Stop

By Luca

At the end of August I had to go back to see the surgeon in New York for some touch- ups. This time we'd be taking the train round trip because it was faster getting there. I would see the surgeon before lunch and take a train back the same night.

Mom was with me. We had to leave the house around five am to catch the train. I tried sleeping on the Amtrak, but I couldn't stop thinking about school. Summer school was already over and in less than two weeks I'd be going for full days instead of half days. I had done okay with the two teachers and the small handful of students I'd met, but in September there'd be over a dozen teachers and upwards of seventy or even eighty students. Eighty hard-core kids proven too troubled and unruly for conventional education. I reasoned these kids would be worse than the bullies who tortured me into wanting to kill myself in public school, since even those bullies hadn't been deemed too hopeless for regular school.

The age limit at the alternative school was twenty-three so a lot of the students could be much older than me. I feared they'd be bigger and stronger, too. There was also a greater chance that someone would recognize me from my not so distant previous life as Marie. This could be bad. I tried to be positive though. As long as I was careful about when I went to the bathroom, maybe after this second surgery I'd be lucky and just get picked on for being an unusual and unpopular guy, rather than an unusual and unpopular "it". If anyone found out I was trans they'd stomp me to death, especially in a bathroom. Being a boyish girl will get you picked on and beat up; being a half-boy half-girl will get you killed. Don't believe me? Look up Brandon Teena or google "trans murder rates". It's horrifying.

If summer school had taught me anything it was that if I wanted to blend in I'd either have to start liking rap music, build a longer rap sheet or get into way heavier drugs than pot and alcohol. So I spent the train ride in plotting a survival strategy to camouflage this black sheep from wolves.

We arrived in the city and made it to the surgeon's easily. He put me under and re-opened some of the incisions on my chest to give me a little more lipo. So much had been during the first surgery, and I'd been such a wreck to begin with from being obese and binding so tightly, it was difficult to predict how the outcome would look. My chest was pretty flat now, but after eight weeks of healing the swelling had gone down and was some noticeable sagging from left over boobage. I hadn't mentioned the fishing-line-like stitch I had almost yanked out a couple weeks prior and he didn't mention finding any surprises while he was back in there.

I wasn't under as much anesthesia as last time, but for some reason they were having a hard time bringing me around. Mom kept shaking me and trying to sit me up and I'd come to long enough to mumble something and look around before passing back out. She was worried we'd miss our train back to Boston. Since my first surgery in June I hadn't been eating much because I couldn't throw it back up without risking my stitches. In fact, all summer I was hardly eating at all. I threw out most of my food when no one was looking. I depended on iced coffee with extra cream and sugar to keep me going most days. My protein and nutrient deprivation might have contributed to the strong affect the anesthesia was having on me, but I wasn't going to say so. Somehow I found my feet and got dressed. I didn't fully awaken until I was in the cab heading to the train station. Once again we had a crazy cabbie who bounced and slammed us all the way across town. The terror and agony had me fully awake and wired by the time we reached the train station.

We were lucky to find seats together on the crowded train. It departed on time and I laid my head back, listening to Veruca Salt on my portable CD player. After a while Mom got us some Cokes from the club car. I still had my eyes closed when I felt something wet on my side. I couldn't tell if it was warm or cold because the surgery had damaged so many nerves. The air conditioning on the train, my exhaustion and remnants of anesthesia had me confused as well. I sat up and took my headphones off.

"Mom, did you spill some of your coke on me?"

"No, it's been sitting on my tray. I haven't touched it. Why?"

"I'm wet."

The shirt I was wearing was black so I couldn't tell what was on me from the color. I grabbed a couple of napkins and dabbed at my shirt. They came away red. Crap.

"I'm bleeding."

"What?!"

"It doesn't hurt. Some stitches must be loose or something. Do you have any more napkins?"

Mom got up to look for more napkins. By the time she came back I was bleeding into my pants and on the seat. It had started flowing much heavier despite my attempts to be still. Mom became distraught. I was only worried about drawing attention to myself. I didn't want people staring at me or asking questions. But if I didn't get some fresh bandages or something I was going to start bleeding on the floor.

Mom asked a train attendant for some bandages from the first aid kit. Funny thing, not a single first aid kit on the train was stocked.

An announcement was made over the train speakers that if there were any doctors on board with a medical bag could they please make their way to where I was sitting. This much attention felt as embarrassing as a stranger pointing out that you have toilet paper stuck to your shoe. Four good samaritans responded. One doctor, two nurses and a dentist who had medical training. They were all very nice but none of them had any equipment or supplies with them. The first person to reach me was a nurse who put on a pair of gloves and kept applying handfuls of napkins to my side and holding pressure on it. The other three left when they realized there was nothing they could do to help. All I told anyone was I had some stitches that were bleeding. I didn't say how I acquired them and no one asked.

A decision had been made to stop the train in Connecticut and let Mom and me off. An ambulance would be waiting to take us to the hospital. It was announced over the speakers that we would be making a brief unscheduled stop. The collective groan from the other passengers felt like a bucket of shit being poured into my lap. The stares of curiosity I'd been receiving turned into glares of accusation and annoyance. Concern quickly morphs into hostility when your problems spill over onto other people.

The train stopped in New Haven, Connecticut. A stretcher and two

EMTs were waiting for me. I wanted to walk, but they insisted I lay down. As they were strapping me down the train pulled away. I saw hundreds of faces pressed against the glass windows, all eyes on me. I wanted to flip everyone off but restrained myself.

I felt bad watching Mom struggle to carry her stuff and mine throughout the deserted train station. I felt worse watching the EMTs struggle to push me up and down long winding ramps, no elevators in sight.

This was my first ride in an ambulance. It wasn't fun. Just awkward. At least they didn't use the sirens.

In the Emergency Room I was wheeled past the waiting area and straight into the back. Once the EMTs were gone I peeled off my shirt to see the damage. It wasn't so bad, just a few loose stitches on the left. The flesh in between looked like uncooked sirloin, tough and red. It didn't hurt though. It didn't even have pins and needles. I don't know how to describe being attached to something you can't feel. When the dentist gives you Novocain the numbness makes your tongue and face feel bigger. This felt like it wasn't there anymore. Parts of my chest still feel this way, but I don't mind.

In the brighter light the blood didn't seem so dark and thick anymore. I didn't feel as light headed or nauseous as I thought I would from so much blood loss either. In fact, other than annoyed, I felt okay.

When the doctor came in and read my chart she looked at me as if I had horns and a glowing pentagram on my forehead. She looked at Mom with the chilly, snide, superior contempt a woman might give a mistress of Satan. I thought she was going to walk right back out without helping me.

She examined me with all the interest and concern of a babysitter changing a diaper. Apparently most of what I'd lost wasn't blood, but saline pumped in during the brief surgery. There was blood in it, making it red, but the effects of it leaking out weren't dire.

She refused to add any stitches or even give me a butterfly bandage to temporarily pull the skin tighter. She refused to treat the incision in any way. All she would do was slap a bandage on me that had a water-tight clear plastic window on it. It was about 3x5 inches and although I'd still leak saline and blood, this would trap it against me so I wouldn't leak all over my clothes and what not. And even then she wouldn't give me the bandage until she was done tearing Mom a second ass for letting some surgeon butcher a clearly confused child, AKA me.

I'd heard this song and dance plenty of times. *I'm too young to know what I want. It's a phase. God made me a girl and He doesn't make mistakes. Transsexualism isn't real. I need mental help. I should be taken away from my parents. I'll change my mind in five or ten years and regret this.* Blah,blah-effin-blah. Just because you and your kids were idiots when young and changed your minds about stupid shit and chased every fad doesn't give you the right to put your narrow minded problems on me. NEWS FLASH: I'M NOT YOU! I'M NOT YOUR KID! YOU DON'T KNOW ME AND YOU DON'T KNOW SHIT ABOUT ME! You don't know God either or what his plans are for me. If he doesn't like what I'm doing he'll call me or email me or take out a commercial during the Super Bowl if he feels like it. He has a big enough budget to get his own messages across and doesn't need your help. You know who knows about transsexualism and whether or not it's a crock or a mistake? ME! BECAUSE I AM ONE! I won't tell you how to be you and you don't tell me how to be me. OK? OK.

So once the sermon was over I got my bandage and one for the road. Then we caught a cab back to the station and waited for the next train out of that hellhole.

Chapter Twenty-Four

First Day of Alternative High School

By Betsie

I'm not sure why I was so nervous dropping Luca off at school. He had attended summer school at the same location, but somehow this was different.

Maybe it was all the tough-looking, cigarette-smoking teens hanging around the doorsteps. Maybe it was because I knew how Luca struggled with anger issues and wondered how many of these kids harbored outbursts of rage. After all, there had to be a reason why they were all attending this school.

Of course my mind was thinking about Luca using the men's room. That was always on my mind. What would happen if someone recognized him? Did he and the school counselors have the skills needed to handle a potentially explosive situation?

Luca and I were both scared. There were too many bad scenarios we could play in our heads. But not wanting to frighten one another, neither of us spoke of our fears. We tried to pretend there was nothing to be afraid of. But it was like attending the same horror movie. We both understood the villains were there.

With my stomach tied up in knots, Luca exited the car. He hesitated for a moment, gathered his courage, and headed towards the teens crowding around the stairway.

A new school year had begun and with it came a new set of challenges. The one thing that had remained the same was the constant worrying by a weary mother.

First Day of Alternative High School

By Luca

Mom drove me to school on her way to work. The full time session started earlier in the day and the school wasn't too far out of the way.

It was fall, but September on the North Shore can be as hot as August. My stitches itched, making me wince with the effort of not scratching them in front of the crowd of students milling around outside. There were a couple dozen teens talking and smoking, loitering on the staircase and blocking the entrance. I didn't know any of them. From the bits of conversations I picked up as I weaved through them I decided I didn't want to know them. I was wearing a black "Life of Agony" t shirt and had my long hair pulled back under a Harley Davidson bandana that I'd cherished since childhood. By the time I'd reached the door at least three people had made fun of my bandana. One started laughing and asked where my motorcycle was parked. I took the bandana off and stuffed it in my pocket by the time I reached the office to get my homeroom assignment and class schedule.

I sat down in an empty classroom. No teacher or other students. They trickled in after the bell. I learned that it wasn't cool to show up early. If you were cool you stood around in the smoking area chilling and talking shit until it was time to go in. We were allowed to talk during homeroom. One of the girls who sat in front of me had been on the stairs when I'd walked in. She asked me where my bandana was. I told her it was too hot to wear it and she told me I should wear it if I liked it, and the fuckers outside could kiss my ass. I liked this girl.

In math class there were only eight students, including myself. We were each given a workbook and learned at our own pace. If we had a problem the teacher would help us, but the books were instructional. Since they didn't have any books advanced enough for me I was allowed to listen to my portable CD player and read the newspaper.

Science class had more students. The teacher admitted to us he didn't know much about science but he'd taken biology 101 and political science in college. I didn't think this school would make me smarter, I was afraid it would make me dumber. The science teacher was also the sports program head coach. He asked me if I played any sports. I told him how I'd played basketball and soccer at my last school and he was all over me to come out for football. I was hesitant, but when he said it would get me out of gym class I figured it was worth looking in to.

Finally in English class I was taught something. The materials were all eighth grade level and I was earning tenth grade credits. My English skills, especially my spelling and vocabulary, were very rusty and remedial. This was perfect. I felt the English program was solid, although a little sad. The school library resided in a closet of the English teacher's classroom and was comprised of randomly donated books that no one ever borrowed. If we all had to read the same book for class the teacher had to buy a copy himself and Xerox it for us. We had no access to computers so everything we did, even reports, were hand written on loose leaf.

At lunch I didn't want to eat anything. I was still trying to lose weight. Jackie, one of the girls I'd made friends with in summer school had been in my math class and she insisted I sit outside with her during the breaks. On our side of the school the outdoor break area had two picnic tables and a fire escape for kids to sit at and talk, eat or smoke cigarettes. Being at a school where smoking was allowed, even if you're under eighteen, was amazing. Everyone who was cool smoked. I knew as soon as my stitches were dissolved I'd have to pick the habit back up.

Jackie wasn't very popular but she introduced me to some other students. One of them was Matt. He was almost twenty-one, blonde, hilarious and a total trouble maker. Matt showed me how it was easier to shoplift NyQuil than to buy alcohol when you're underage. Smart guy.

I was also introduced to Ashley. She was younger than me, only fourteen, but she hung out with the twenty-plus crowd. I thought she was kind of cute because she was goth. Ashley and Jackie were nice to each other's face but would talk a ton of crap about each other when the other wasn't there. That's how I learned Ashley had come to the school from a mental hospital the previous year. Apparently she was nuts. Stupidly I thought this made her hotter and gave us something in common.

I did make it over to the football field. I was a lot lighter than I used to be, but the running was making me sick. I refused to let it show though. Not because I was afraid I wouldn't make the team, it was open to anyone. I refused to show weakness in front of the other students. I was still self conscious about blending in as a guy. On top of that, two of the guys on the football team had monitoring anklets from court. I didn't know what crimes they'd committed but assault or possession were good guesses. Some of the other guys had spent time in juvy, and a few who were over eighteen had been in real prisons. If I wanted to survive I was going to have to walk the walk. That meant never letting them see you're hurting, no matter what.

When it came time to scrimmage I had to tell the coach about my stitches. It's one thing to run with them, but getting hit and busting a few would not be good. To my horror instead of having me sit out he announced to everyone that "Puke-a," as he liked to call me, "has some stitches so don't hit him too hard." That earned me some sideways glances. Gordon, a familiar face from summer school, asked me why I had stitches. I told him I'd been stabbed in a fight. A bunch of other dudes had been listening in and they were all openly impressed. I couldn't believe that lie worked, but given the circumstances of how many people ended up at this school my story was totally plausible. Besides, if anyone called me out on my bullshit it would open them to being called out on theirs. The world of guys is convenient that way.

Matt was the quarterback. He was the oldest guy in the school and had been playing football the longest, so it made sense. Although I had stitches the coach placed me as center. I'd never played football before and didn't fully understand what was going on. This was just flag football but a lot of contact was still allowed.

My job was to hike the ball to Matt and then keep him from getting hit before he could pass the ball. In short distances I can move pretty fast. I'd also grown another inch and a half during the summer. At five feet, nine inches, and 210lbs it was hard to get around me. Matt was pleased with me as the center and took time after the game to explain the rules until I understood them and practice some passes with me. I decided I liked this game. More importantly, all the guys who had been making snide remarks or jokes at my expense when I first walked up the steps that morning held their tongues when Matt was around. It was a good way to finish the first day. A taxi was waiting to take me home.

High School wasn't nearly as terrifying as I'd expected it to be. I didn't make a lot of friends right off as I had in the psychiatric programs, but I wasn't afraid to walk the halls like I had been in elementary and middle school. The school days were short and the homework was minimal to non-existent. I was friendly enough with people, but I was secretive. I never shared anything meaningful about myself with anyone. So I had a few buddies, but no real friends.

For my electives I picked football, art, guitar and student council/student store.

Football

I was thrilled football counted as gym class credits. I wasn't amazing at it but I did try my hardest. The coach seemed happy with my efforts and put me on the starting string as center as soon as my stitches healed. He still called me "Puke-a," even in science class, but I figured earning a nickname meant he liked me.

Our first football game against another team was at the end of September. There were only a few games in the season. We played against three other alternative schools and two juvenile correction centers. The games against juvy's were always away games for obvious reasons. For our first game we drove almost an hour away to a corrections center in Chelmsford, MA. I got to skip science and English to go because it was so early in the day. I was surprised more kids didn't want to play just to skip classes.

The field was muddy and the juvy kids were all in matching gray sweats. They were supposed to be under eighteen, but they all looked big. In flag football you wear flags attached to a belt and if a player on the opposite team pulls off a flag that ends the play, but you're still allowed to hit and block below the neck and above the waist. So there's an intense amount of contact but no pads or helmets are worn. On a field full of thugs, what could possibly go wrong?

Our team won the coin toss so after returning the punt I was put in as center. I hiked the ball to Matt and blocked for him, but he had handed the ball off pretty quick. Since the QB was no longer in possession of the ball I turned my attention up field where the play was happening. That's when a player from the other team ran into me at full speed. This dude outweighed me by at least forty or fifty pounds. It was all fat, not muscle, but that didn't cushion the blow. I went flying and landed on my back with mud up to my ears. I couldn't hear anything through the mud and I couldn't speak because all the wind had been knocked out of me. I was still pretty stunned when my teammates hauled me to my feet. The juvy kids were laughing their asses off at me.

I convinced myself I wasn't hurt badly and persuaded the coach to let me stay in. On the next play the guy did it again. Long after the ball was gone and headed up the field he ran at me from the side and knocked me on my back. This time I saw a few stars before getting back on my feet. I'd bitten my cheek when my head smacked the ground and my butt was numb from the cold mud that was leaking through my jeans and into my underwear. But now I'd figured out this guys plan. He wasn't trying to "sack" the QB, he was in it to hurt and humiliate me. I didn't think it was personal. I could have been anyone. But he was the fat kid on a team of criminals and knocking someone else in the mud would earn him respect.

On the next play I was ready for him. I saw him on the far left of the defensive line and sure enough when the ball was gone instead of following it he followed me. I gave him my side and let him come at me full speed, but at the last second I turned and threw my right elbow up. It caught him in the throat. He still knocked me to my knees, but he sat out the next few plays and wouldn't come near me the rest of the game. Matt had seen what I'd done and thought it was hilarious.

After the game we had lunch at McDonalds. I don't remember if we won or not, I just remember being glad people were joking about my elbow and not the mud on my ass. It's such a different feeling when people are laughing with you, not at you. I was cold, sore, cut, bruised, tired, hungry, and covered in mud but I was beginning to feel safe. My status as a guy, and a tough guy at that, was secure.

Chapter Twenty-Five

The View

By Betsie

Luca had pissed me off when he refused to go to his therapist appointment. If he didn't see his therapist he wouldn't get his Paxil. Thinking about the consequences of him not taking his anti-depressant made me snap. I escalated from just screaming to hitting him. He still sat on his bed refusing to move. I tried grabbing and pulling him. He wouldn't budge.

"This is how you fucking repay me for everything I've done?" I screamed one more time before storming out of his room, giving the door a good slam behind me.

My body tensed as I pulled angry fists towards my chest, screaming at the top of my lungs.

I was tired of arguing. Tired of being tired.

Sitting at the dining room table my fists relaxed as the tears flowed.

The following day was Saturday. Although our condo was small we avoided one another at every opportunity. After lunch, I tried speaking to Luca but our anger kept getting in the way. I wanted him to know how upset I was for having to pay for an appointment he never went to. We ended up having another screaming match and he went to his room. I went back to crying.

Now someone was knocking at my door. Neighbors had probably complained to the security guard about the screaming and slamming of doors. Tough. They could knock all they wanted, I wasn't going to answer. The knocking became louder. I hoped they would go away. Fists were now banging on the door.

"Mrs. Harvie, come quickly. Your son is about to jump from the ledge!" the building's security officer was yelling.

Tears stopped instantly. The dining room chair flew backwards as I ran toward the door.

The officer jumped aside as I suddenly pulled the door open and ran past him.

As I reached the set of doors at the end of the first hallway he yelled again, "We've already called the police. They should be here any moment."

Then I heard them; the sounds of sirens as they came to an abrupt halt.

Turning the corner at the security desk I stopped dead in my tracks. Luca was standing outside on the fifth floor ledge, the balls of his sneakers extending over the side. I can't remember a time before or since when I was so terrified.

The condo was built into the side of a hill and as you entered from the parking lot you were actually on the fifth floor. From the security desk to the entrance thirty feet away, the entire right side of the hallway was glass from floor to ceiling. When you looked out the window you were looking down at the community pool and neighboring golf course. Directly below Luca were concrete steps. He was standing outside on a very narrow ledge with his back against the glass.

Luca was angry with me. What if the sight of me made him jump? What if I startled him and he lost his balance?

I had to take the chance. Running to the last door, I swung it open just as a young police officer was coming inside. The security guard wasn't far behind me.

"This is the child's mother," the guard said to the officer.

More sirens.

Two ambulances had arrived. One stayed up on the parking lot level while one drove down the hill and behind the building to be stationed below.

I was panicking.

The police officer was about to ask me questions when a woman who lived a few floors above me approached.

"He's been out there for quite some time. I tried to talk him into coming back over the railing but he says he likes the view. I don't think he wants to jump. I'm more afraid of him falling off."

More sirens.

State police arrived with their negotiator.

So far my brain had not been able to put anything coherent together.

The young officer began asking me all the usual questions. "Name? Age? Any mental health problems? Ever tried anything like this before? Does he take any drugs? Does he have any journals?"

Finally a question that made sense.

"He writes in his journal every day but I think it's more for school."

"Can you retrieve it?

"I'd rather stay here."

"But he may have written something that the negotiator can use," the officer insisted.

"Give me a minute."

I didn't want to leave. Somehow I felt as long as I was there Luca would be safe. If I left, the unthinkable might happen.

I ran as fast as I could but the rubber in my legs was slowing me down. My heart was pounding heavily by the time I reached our door. Luca's room was at the end of our short hallway. His journal was on his bed. Grabbing it, I hurriedly exited the condo and was quickly handing the officer Luca's journal.

Trembling, I tried desperately to call Diane. No answer.

This wasn't like watching a movie where the mother shows up and talks the son off the ledge. This was my son. And he was angry with me. One wrong word. One mistaken action. One misguided emotion and my life would end.

Frantic, I called my sister Louise. Through my heaving crying and gasping for air, I was amazed my niece Ellen could even understand me. Louise was not home but my niece promised to get in touch with her.

The local and state police both wanted to be in charge and were constantly bombarding me with questions. My thoughts were all scrambled. Was I even answering them with anything that made sense?

Sounds became muffled as the ringing in my ears grew louder and the pulsating in my head intensified. My legs gave way and I slumped to the pavement.

Officer Daniels, the same young officer I had given the journal to, came running towards me.

"Are you okay?"

"What the hell is going on? I need to know what's going on. Why can't anyone tell me anything?"

"The negotiator is talking with your son. We can't take the chance of interrupting him. He'll let us know when it's safe."

"If we can get Luca to come back over the railing, what's going to happen to him?"

"I won't sugar coat it. He'll be thrown to the ground and handcuffed."

"Even if he's making no attempt to run?"

"It's just procedure."

A crowd was gathering. People were everywhere.

Where was my sister?

My nephew, Will, niece, Ellen, and her boyfriend, Charles, arrived. Speed records must have been broken to get them there so quickly.

They wanted to know what was going on. Why in the world was Luca standing out on the ledge?

I had no answers.

Minutes passed.

A State Police Officer approached. "Your son is requesting to speak with someone named Charles."

"That's me," Charles answered.

"Does your son have a good relationship with this guy?"

"I think Luca looks up to him. Anything is worth a try."

Charles disappeared around the corner. With Ellen's help I stood up.

Police barricaded the parking lot with yellow crime scene tape. They began holding back angry neighbors, yelling because they weren't allowed to move their cars. One neighbor was told if she crossed the line again she would be arrested. I watched all the chaos as if I wasn't part of it.

Although my vision was focused on the corner of the building, I spotted my sister Louise and her husband Bill scooting under the yellow tape.

"So what's going on?" Louise asked in her typically composed voice.

"Charles is speaking with Luca right now. They've been talking for quite some time. I don't think Charles is getting very far."

"Luca will be alright," Louise said, trying to reassure me.

I didn't believe her. Not this time. Today her words couldn't calm my storm.

We stood in silence as minutes passed.

"Luca must be scared out of his mind. Can't we promise nothing will happen to him when he comes over the railing?" I questioned a nearby officer.

"We'll back off," the officer said, signaling for two others to stand around the corner where Luca couldn't see them.

Oh my God what was taking so long? What the hell were they talking about?

Then I saw him. Luca stepped onto the pavement. Safe. I wasn't even given the chance to be relieved. Within seconds, officers had pounced on him. He was on the ground.

"But you promised. You promised!" I screamed.

Louise went to Luca's rescue.

Luca and I never made eye contact. Once he was back on his feet,

Louise escorted him to the waiting ambulance. With Luca safely inside, Louise climbed in.

"Where are you taking him?" I asked the driver.

"North Shore Children's."

The ambulance pulled away and with it went my spirit. Every ounce of me had been depleted. I had reached my breaking point.

"Come on Betsie, I'll drive you to the hospital," my brother-in-law, Bill, said.

"I'm not going. I'm done," I sobbed.

"You have to. He's your kid."

"Not any more. Let someone else take him."

I had had enough. What more could possibly be expected from me?

"You have to go to the hospital," Bill kept insisting.

And what about Brooks? I had to call him. It had only been six months since his heart attack. How was he going to take this? Would this incense him to the point of another heart attack? Would I now have both of them hospitalized?

I wanted to crawl into bed, pull the blanket over my head, and stay where I felt safe. Why did I always need to be the strong one?

"Let me call Brooks and then I'll go with you. But God damn it, Bill, I'm telling you right now, I don't want any part of this."

Brooks was with a customer, taking forever to get to the phone. Through heavy sobs I explained the situation the best I could.

"Why the hell didn't you call me?" Brooks yelled.

"There wasn't enough time. Besides with your big mouth always having to be in charge you would have made the situation worse. I couldn't deal with what was going on and deal with you at the same time."

"The important thing is he's safe," Brooks replied a little bit calmer. "He hates me right now. We haven't been on speaking terms for weeks.

Don't you think the sight of me at the hospital will make things worse?"

"I don't know. I don't know anything anymore," I answered. "You're probably right. I'll go with Bill and call you from the hospital."

We drove in silence as unforgettable scenes occupied my mind. Helplessness, hopelessness and confusion had taken over. I started carrying on a conversation with myself.

"I don't want to do this."

"You have to."

"I can't take his shit any longer."

"But you know you will. You always do."

"Not this time. Let the state take over."

"It won't be that easy."

"I was raging mad and hit him. They can find me unfit."

"Is that what you really want?"

"I don't know any longer what I really want."

"WHY THE HELL DID HE DO THIS?"

No answer. Silence.

Then the vision of Luca on the ledge would start it all over again.

Arriving at the hospital I was greeted by Officer Daniels. He'd stuck by me through this ordeal. His concern seemed genuine.

"I brought your son's journal. Thought he'd want it back," he told me.

"Thanks."

"Your sister is waiting for you."

"She can come out here. I'm not going in there," I said, stooping down to sit on a curb.

"But your son needs you."

"Bullshit."

"You know you don't mean that. You've both been through a very traumatic event. You should be thankful he didn't jump. We would be having a much different conversation."

"You don't understand," I told him. "I've had enough."

"I know you've had problems. I've responded to your unit a few times."

A nurse came outside and joined in the conversation.

"We need you to come in and fill out paperwork."

"Nope," I answered.

Officer Daniels and the nurse went back inside. I sat there, elbows on knees and head resting on my hands for about ten minutes. It was getting cold. I could see my breath. Why couldn't anyone understand? I just didn't want to deal with this.

Officer Daniels came back out.

"Come on, Mrs. Harvie. We need you inside. I'll help you up," he said, extending his hand.

It took a minute before I finally gave in.

Officer Daniels escorted me to the waiting area, a room I had previously spent many hours in. Will had dropped Ellen and Charles off at home and had continued on to the hospital. He was sitting next to Louise. I sank into the chair next to her.

"He's okay," Louise told me.

It was almost like we were talking about someone else's child. I was glad Luca was alright but I couldn't find it in me to care. I would never want anything to happen to him but I didn't have the strength to fight any longer.

An attending physician came out to let me know Luca had calmed down but they needed my permission to call local adolescent psych units. I knew this drill all too well.

Luca was heading back to minimum security at Boston Regional. Will took Bill home and Louise drove me in her car. Our conversation kept going around and around as to why Luca had been out on that ledge. Why now? After everything he had gone through?

Louise and I finally made it to Boston Regional and waited for Luca to arrive and be admitted. After about an hour, the emergency room physician came out to speak with me.

I still had Luca's journal. When the physician spotted it, he asked if he could see it. I had already glanced through it and hadn't noticed anything out of the ordinary. Mostly song lyrics. But this guy should know what to look for so I said yes. He walked away with Luca's journal in hand. I waited patiently for his return.

It was now around ten pm. It had been a long, agonizing day. Without warning Luca was standing in front of me and yelling.

"I hate you! How could you do this to me?"

"What the hell are you talking about?"

"You gave him my journal. How could you?"

"I thought it would help. I'm sorry."

"I hate you!" he was still yelling as he turned the corner and walked back down the hallway.

My dismay was interrupted by a loud commotion coming from Luca's direction. Louise and I ran to the corner of the open waiting area in time to see two security officers tackling Luca to the floor.

The admitting physician was yelling something about Luca attempting to run.

"Get the hell off him!" I screamed. "He wasn't running, he was yelling. Not running."

It was too late. They were already dragging Luca around the next corner.

"Mrs. Harvie, go back to the waiting area. I'll be with you shortly," the doctor demanded.

My entire body ached as if wounded in battle. I slowly retreated to the waiting room.

"I'm so angry with him but all I want to do is throw my arms around him," I told Louise.

"Poor kid," Louise replied. "I know he's angry but I've never seen him like this."

"I don't know what to do. I'm so scared."

"They'll calm him down. Just be patient."

"You must be exhausted."

"Don't worry about me. You have enough to think about," Louise said.

Louise put her arm around me and pulled my head towards her shoulders.

"Close your eyes, Hon. It might be awhile before they send him upstairs."

I gladly closed my eyes, but it brought me no relief. Every muscle, every nerve, was in stress mode.

Eventually the doctor came back and told me Luca was being put in maximum security. Evidently he was too much of a threat to himself. Boston Regional had no rooms available but they had found an opening in Concord, New Hampshire. Luca had been sedated and would asleep for quite some time. I should go home.

"I want his journal back. I should never have given it to you."

"Mrs. Harvie, you did the right thing," he answered, handing me the journal. "Someone will call you in the morning."

Louise and I left Boston Regional around midnight. She still had to drop me off at my house before she could head home to her own bed. She hadn't said much all day. She didn't need to. Just her presence had helped me through those harrowing hours.

Arriving home, and wanting to be alone, I went directly to Luca's room. Shock and disbelief crept into bed with me. Nightmares were not far behind.

The phone ringing at eight am quickly brought me back to where I had left off the previous night. *Jesus Christ*, I thought. *I forgot to call work.*

"Hello," I whispered with a tired, raspy voice.

"Mrs. Harvie, this is Officer Daniels. Sorry for calling so early. I wanted to be sure you were okay."

"As okay as I'm going to be. It was a pretty rough day."

"What was the outcome?"

"Luca was transported to Concord, New Hampshire. That's all I know."

"Well, I'm sorry you had to go through all that. Just wanted you to know we're here for you."

"Thanks for all your help yesterday."

I knew Brooks was up when the sound of music lifted the fog in my head. I didn't want to talk but had no choice.

"What the hell happened yesterday?" Brooks asked. "And who was on the phone?"

"Officer Daniels from the police department. He was checking up on me," I replied.

"Sorry I couldn't be there. Hope you understand."

"It was horrible. You couldn't have handled the stress."

"Is he at Boston Regional?"

"No, he's in Concord, New Hampshire," I respond. "There's no way in hell I'm driving up there."

"Did he say why he was out on the ledge?"

"If he did, no one told me. I'm so angry with him. I thought all the bad shit was behind us."

"What was going on before he left the house?"

"I was trying to tell him how upset I was about him not going to his appointment Friday night. We had another yelling match and he went to his room. I never heard him leave the house."

We were interrupted by the phone ringing. After a brief conversation with the hospital, Brooks and I continued our talk.

"Luca is still sleeping. They'll call us back tonight with a better update," I told him.

"I always feel left out you know," Brooks said. "Luca hasn't let me meet any of his friends. The two of you are always doing things without consulting me."

"You can't meet his friends until you can stop saying "she." We have to do things without you because you're never around and when you are you don't seem to care."

"I'm sorry. I'll make it a point to pay more attention."

"Look, I don't want to fight," I said. "I'm going back to bed."

I withdrew back to Luca's room. I don't know why. Maybe I thought I could find solace there. All I found were continuing nightmares.

Luca had now been in New Hampshire for three nights. He was going to be transported back to Boston Regional and needed clean clothes. Three days had not been long enough for me to get over my hurt and anger. I wouldn't make the trip. Brooks drove the two hours up but was unable to see Luca. Leaving a clean change of clothes and Luca's journal, he turned around and made the two hour drive home.

Tuesday afternoon I received the phone call from Boston Regional. Luca had been placed back in minimum security and we could see him anytime. I immediately called Luca's principal, Kendal Tanner.

He was stunned when I called him the previous day to tell him what had happened over the weekend.

"He's back in minimum security. You can see him anytime you want," I told Principal Tanner."

"If you go up tonight, let him know we're all thinking of him."

"I won't be going for a while. I still don't want to see him and I'm not sure he wants to see me."

"Oh come on. I can't believe that. With everything the two of you have been through?"

"I don't know what I'll do when he gets released. I don't want him home."

"Well if you think he wouldn't mind, I'll visit him in a few days. Do you want me to tell him anything for you?"

"No. Thanks anyway."

Over the next few days I also had conversations with the hospital psychologist. He told me without directly telling me, "I told you so." But I still stood by Luca. I knew the decision for surgery had been the right one. This doctor needed to find out what was going on without blaming it on the transgender issue. He thought it would be best for Luca, Brooks, and I to sit down together. I still wanted no part of it.

I don't remember when Kendal called me back. Staff members had gone to see Luca but he had been off-site at the day center. So there wasn't any news to report.

"Why don't you come with us Monday?" Kendal asked me. "We can help break the ice between you and Luca. Instead of meeting him at the hospital we're going to see him at the day center. I think you should come."

"I'll think about it."

I did think about it. It was time. I left work early Monday and met Kendal at the day center. When Luca walked into the room there was immediate tension. He was genuinely glad to see Kendal but surprised to see me. There were no big hugs. No saying "I'm sorry."

We kept the conversation light, Kendal doing most of the talking. When Kendal left, so did I.

That quick fifteen minute visit at least brought me to my senses. The anger that had kept me from crying melted away. Luca was still my son and I owed him more than I was giving. He may have been trying to act tough but he was hurting. Tears of regret stayed with me all the way home. I would be going back.

Over the next week, tensions between Luca and me eased. He would be released from Boston Regional shortly but I wasn't ready for him to come home. Although I was no longer angry and hurt, I was still on edge. This experience had been a major quake in my life and my ground was still shaking.

I was given a little relief when my sister Maryanne agreed to have Luca stay with her. Maryanne was no-nonsense. If Luca misbehaved, he would be out.

Luca spent Sunday through Thursday nights at Maryanne's and Friday and Saturday nights at home. This gave us a few weekends to see how things would go before coming home permanently. By the time Luca was ready to come home, Brooks and I really wanted him there.

This incident shook me like no other. I thought I was going to watch my son fall to his death. I realize how close we came and how fortunate I am to still have Luca near me. Secrets had almost torn us apart. Anger had almost kept us apart. Now we tell each other everything; knowing that understanding comes through unconditional love.

The View

By Luca

Since I hadn't grown close to anyone at school, and my friends from the psychiatric unit were scattered in the wind, I still spent most of my time at home on AOL. I didn't talk to Charlotte much anymore. Since starting school I'd developed an even more rebellious attitude. Charlotte's sheltered life and Christian values no longer interested me.

Mom and I were barely on speaking terms. Our health insurance company had assigned me a psychologist who I was supposed to meet with weekly for psychotherapy and prescriptions. I hated the guy though and refused to go. Mom had put her foot down and tried to assert her authority. I still refused. She tried crying and begging, but I couldn't be bothered. Then she'd tried threats and hitting me. She'd slapped me and choked me, but I pushed her out of my room and locked the door. She screamed this was a pretty shitty way to repay her for everything she'd done for me. That was probably true, but whatever. I was sick of being told what to do.

Between Trazadone to sleep, coffee to wake up, Paxil to help my brain hold on to happy-time feel-good juices, Benadryl in the afternoon to keep me docile, massive amounts of testosterone to overwhelm my teenage female biology, and my lack of nutrition from vomiting, I barely knew up from down. As long as I kept swallowing the pills they put in front of me, I didn't see why I needed to talk to some condescending prick on the night new Buffy episodes aired. And as long as I went to school and did my work, I didn't see what Mom had to complain about.

I still didn't talk to Michelle, but I did talk to a couple of her friends who had become my friends back when we'd been dating.

One sunny Saturday, I started the day with a walk to enjoy some fresh air and smoke a joint I had bought at school. This left me with the munchies so I had a large lunch, which I threw up in my bathroom sink. After that I went online and talked to a girl who used to be Michelle's best friend, but had been cast aside when Michelle and Alan had started dating a few months back. This girl was complaining to me about how Michelle had become such a skank and the only time she called anymore was to complain about how sore she was from banging Alan twice a day. I think deep down some part of me had known Michelle was having sex with her new boyfriend, Alan, but having the news paraded in front of me hurt more than I would have expected.

All of those feelings of inadequacies came rushing back. Feelings that if I'd had a penis Michelle would still be with me. Jealousy and rage filled me. I went to my room and opened a bottle of Robitussin I'd had hidden. I sat on my bed drinking it and leafing through old love letters from Michelle. The edges of the stationery were all worn and frayed from being thumbed so many times. By the time I reached the bottom of the bottle and had a good Dextromethorphan high going on, I'd convinced myself I'd never find true love again and life was shit. Thinking about your true love in the arms of another man hurts. Thinking about your true love in the arms of another man because he can offer her something she obviously desires but you don't have- thinking about her being sore from another man's dick and her loving it- well that hurt more than I have words for.

I knew I needed a change of scenery. I needed to look at this from a different point of view. And I knew where the perfect view for this was. So without saying a word I walked outside, around to the side of the condo's lobby and hopped over a railing that led to a drop of over seventy-five feet to the concrete patio of the in-ground pool below. It wasn't as high as jumping off the roof, but it was high enough.

So what to do now? Will I ever get over Michelle? Will I meet someone new? How do I date a girl long-term when I don't have a penis? Lower surgery is expensive and dangerous. Mom and Dad could never afford it. How will I ever get the money to get it on my own? How long will it take to get the money? How do I get by until then? Am I doomed to live a half life? Having my top surgery and going to high school as a guy, but not being able to let anyone close to me was like being released from a dungeon, having the sun on my face for the first time in my life, but not being able to feel it. In some ways it was almost worse. I didn't have anyone to talk to who knew how I felt. Everywhere my mind turned there were more questions and no answers.

Maybe someday things would be awesome for me. I could make some friends. Go to college. Have a job, an apartment, a car and a girlfriend. I could move away to the west coast like I'd dreamed of as a child. I could move to New York. I could grow old and have laugh lines. But did I have it in me to be who I wanted to be? Could I make it through high school? Would it be easier to just walk forward and fall? I might miss out on some good things to come, but at least the ground would catch me. The embrace would be eternal for sure, but it might be nice to be held by something other than my own arms for a change. I wouldn't have to think anymore. I wouldn't have to hurt anymore.

I looked out at the trees, my toes edging closer to the empty space before me. Then a Cooper's Hawk flew into view. Hawks had been gone from the North Shore since before I was born, but amazingly around the time I'd started transitioning a Cooper's Hawk had started nesting in the surrounding woods and flying by from time to time. At first I'd thought it was a sign, like a symbol of pride and strength sent to encourage me. I tried to hold on to that as the hawk circled above.

Then a small voice from behind me asked what I was doing. I'd been spotted by one of the elderly residents. She eyed me with open concern.

"I'm watching the hawk up there. See?" I pointed.

"You could see him from this side of the railing as well."

"I'm happy where I am, thank you."

"Yes, but I'm afraid you might fall."

"Well, that's my problem, isn't it?"

I scooted further sideways down the ledge. I still hadn't made up my mind about what I was going to do, but knowing I had an audience for my decision making process annoyed me.

I was still thinking: high-school, college, surgery, Michelle; round and round, when the fire truck arrived. Some police cruisers and an ambulance had arrived too. In fact they blocked off the whole parking area. Residents were flocking to their patios and the glass fronted lobby to watch. I felt like a fish in a fishbowl.

I hadn't wanted the attention. It felt like an invasion of privacy. Orchestrating your own death should be private. Not a spectacle. Now if I chose to come back over the railing I'd have to live knowing I was a source of amusement for all these people. It made jumping seem that much more appealing.

A police officer came over to talk to me. He swore he wasn't going to touch me, just talk. I wasn't in a very talkative mood. The attention I was receiving made me more confused. Then the cop made a grab for my shoulder. I twisted back out of reach and screamed at him to get away from me. I wanted to spit at him but the wind was against me. I was feeling I couldn't trust anyone and my options were dwindling.

Then I saw my cousin Will's white Thunderbird streak into the driveway. I wanted desperately to talk to him but couldn't. He was always there for me to lean on; always accepted me. But surely this was too much. I'd gone too far this time. I respected him too much to face him. My Aunt Louise was there, too, along with my cousin Ellen and her boyfriend, Charles. Christ, how long had I been out here? It felt like minutes, but the sun had moved a long distance in the sky.

Shit. I thought jumping off this ledge would be an easy way to stop hating myself. But I didn't want to do it in front of half my family.

But if I'm not going to jump, how am I going to get out of this? The cop who'd made a grab for me was pacing and staring at me. He looked pissed. The condo security looked pissed. The firefighters looked pissed. I was always pissing people off. But this was a grander scale than I was used to.

I yelled to one of the cops. I wanted to talk to Ellen's boyfriend, Charles. Over the summer, while renovating my aunt's house, he'd shown me how to pull up floor boards, remove insulation and use a nail-gun. He smoked cigarettes and joked around a lot. Sometimes a butt, a joke and a crowbar in your hand can be very therapeutic. I liked Charles. He'd earned my trust. But at the same time I didn't feel I owed him anything. So he was the person who made me feel the least embarrassed in this situation.

He sauntered on up with a smile on his face and offered me a cigarette as if nothing unusual was happening. It was exactly what I needed to calm and comfort me.

"So what's going on?"

"I come out here to think all the time. Some old lady saw me and panicked. What's up with you? How is it you were so Johnny-on-the spot?"

He grinned wide. "I spent the night with Ellen."

"Alright, alright, I don't want to hear any details."

"So if you just came out here to think, why won't you come back over?"

"See that cop over there? He made a grab for me earlier and now he looks pissed. These cops are going to beat the shit out of me."

"With all these people watching? Nah. They want you to get in that ambulance so you're not their problem anymore. They won't hurt you as long as you're co-operating."

"You think?"

"They told me so before I walked over here."

I thought it over. I was probably going to end up back at the same hospital I was in before. If I co-operated maybe I could get into minimum security instead of maximum security with those "I told you so" douche-bag psych doctors. Minimum security wouldn't be so bad.

"Okay."

Charles stepped back to give me room to climb over. He walked next to me toward the waiting ambulance, but when we rounded the corner of the building four police officers tackled me. They knocked me face down on the pavement and jumped on my back and legs. I wasn't fighting. I just lay there and let them handcuff me behind my back. When I asked why they were doing this, I got a knee in my ribs. My hat had been knocked off, and with my hair in my face I couldn't see anyone's faces.

They dragged me over to the ambulance and threw me in. My handcuffs were redone so I was attached to the gurney. No one had brushed my hair aside so I still couldn't see, but maybe that was for the best. I didn't really want to see other people just then anyway.

Aunt Louise rode up front. I still didn't want Mom near me, not after the other night when she'd hit me and thrown stuff around my room. The ambulance took me to the local children's hospital because it was the closest, although they had no in-patient mental health unit.

Will followed the ambulance to the hospital but he wasn't allowed in to see me. My handcuffs were removed upon arrival and I sat quietly in an examination room, trying to look as calm and normal as possible. The whole thing was surreal. Ending up there wasn't what I'd expected when I woke up that morning. How could things go so wrong, so quickly?

They decided to send me back to the hospital with an inpatient juvenile mental health unit. No surprise there. Since I was still considered to be in a questionable mental state, an ambulance was going to transfer me from one hospital to another. This seemed ridiculous, especially since I was in a perfectly good ambulance an hour ago and could have gone straight there. I went along quietly so I wouldn't be handcuffed again. It seemed as soon as the cuffs went on, my nose would start to itch.

The emergency room doctor at the other hospital remembered me from last time. He interviewed me and I tried my best to downplay the whole situation. He was all set to admit me to minimum security. Mom had arrived with some of my things and the doctor was going to talk to her before sending me up. When he came back he had my journal in his hands. I knew Mom must have found it in my desk and given it to him. I suddenly felt sick. The idea of someone reading my private thoughts made the floor drop out from under me.

The doctor started waving the journal around and accusing me of lying to him. Apparently he'd read it and had put paper clips on pages where I wrote about using drugs and contemplating suicide. I told him he had no right to read it. He told me since Mom gave it to him he could do with it what he wanted. He was going to Xerox it and put the pages in my file for the other doctors to see. Then I could have it back before being sent to maximum security.

I felt more violated than I ever had by Bobby, and more humiliated than I had been confessing what Bobby had done to me. This was a new low in my life. Having my private thoughts leafed through felt like every part of me had been ripped open for scrutiny; naked past my skin and down to the bone. I've always been a secretive person. This was too much.

I stormed out of the examination room. The doctor yelled at me to come back, but I was heading for the waiting room to give Mom a piece of my mind. I knew she was mad at me but I couldn't believe she'd stab me in the back like this. I heard the doctor pick up the hallway phone and call for security, saying I was heading for the exit. I walked right past the automatic doors and turned the corner to the waiting area.

Mom was seated next to Louise. They both looked small and tired.

"I can't believe you'd do this to me!"

"What?!" Mom asked, shocked and bewildered.

"How could you give him my journal?!"

"I thought you'd want it! I brought it with your clothes! I didn't know he'd read it!"

"The motherfucker is down the hall right now making copies of it! I hate you!"

"I didn't know! I'm sorry!"

"Yeah, right. I fucking hate you. I don't want to see you again."

I stormed off, heading back to the examination room. I'd told Mom what I thought about her backstabbing. Now all that was left to do was wait for the inevitable trip upstairs.

I was halfway up the hall, almost back to the examination room when I heard skidding shoes behind me. Three panting security guards were at the end of the hall. Ahead of me the doctor appeared in another doorway.

"That's him!" He shouted to security.

"What's going on?"

"You tried to escape!"

Interesting way to phrase it.

"No, I didn't. I went to talk to my mother. Now I'm here heading back to the room."

"It's too late. We're going to have to restrain you so you can't run again."

"But I didn't run. I walked."

"You can make this easy or you can make this hard."

"This is bullshit!"

The security started up the hall, a human wall closing in.

"Fuck it. Make it hard."

"This was your choice," the doctor sighed.

"Yeah, right."

The security guards came at me. I just stood there watching them approach. When they were almost on me the doctor yelled, "Careful! He plays football!"

That made me laugh. Then they were on me. One came in from either side to get my arms and the one in front of me tried to punch me in the balls. I remember the surprised look on his face when he tried to junk punch me but only swiped air. I threw myself back and managed to knock one of the guards off me and into a wall. The dick-puncher in front of me made another grab for my balls and held onto the empty front of my pants so tightly, he ripped the button off and broke the zipper, when the other guard kicked my knee and dragged me down.

I was face down with grown men on top of me for the second time in one day. This time I'd landed on my arms and fought to keep them under me, not wanting to be cuffed behind my back again. I struggled and ended up with my ankles in shackles, along with my wrists being cuffed behind me. They dragged me into a padded room and restrained me on a gurney by my wrists and ankles, as well as with straps across my chest, stomach and thighs.

I screamed and cursed. Then I rocked the gurney back and forth until it fell over and I was suspended on my side. When a nurse came in to see what the noise was about I spit at her. When some orderlies tried to pick the gurney back up, I thrashed as much as possible and tried to bite anyone who came near my head. This was when they stuck me with the first syringe full of red-colored knockout drugs. I'd seen other kids in full-body straight-jackets get a dose of this. They all fell asleep within minutes and were out for at least twelve hours.

I kept thrashing, screaming, spitting and cursing although my head was starting to feel very heavy and the lights started looking fuzzy. The doctor came back in and asked if I was going to calm down or did he need to stick me again? I told him to fuck himself and his mother. The second syringe was as full as the first. A red liquid plunging into me; then blackness.

Concord, New Hampshire

I woke up in a dark room I'd never seen before in clothes that weren't mine. I didn't know what time it was. My watch was gone and there was no clock in the room. I looked around, letting my eyes adjust to the dark while trying to get my bearings. The window above the bed had wire running through the glass. Not a good sign.

My mouth was dry and my bladder ached. When I stood up to find a bathroom I felt like an old man. My joints groaned and every part of me hurt.

The room had its own bathroom by the door to the hall. The fluorescent lights were practically blinding after so much darkness. I tried to judge how long I'd been out by how much I peed. I guessed it was almost a day.

When I looked in the mirror my hair was lank and greasy. My lips were wrinkled from dehydration and I had a yellow bruise on one cheek. I found other bruises on my arms, back, hip and knees. My skin was pale and my brown eyes looked almost black as they stared back at me. I was wearing a blue and white button up shirt and sweat pants that I didn't recognize. Thankfully my socks and underwear were my own. As I hunted around for my shoes, I wondered who had dressed me.

My shoes weren't in the room. Nothing of mine was. Adrenaline had chased most of the lingering knockout drugs out of my head. I wanted to know where I was. Apprehensively I tried the doorknob and it turned. Wherever I was, I wasn't locked in. Did this mean it wasn't a hospital? Was I not under restriction? Did they think I was still asleep?

I cracked the door open slowly, crouched down and peered out. The hallway was long and deserted. There were other doors but no sounds from behind them. I craned my neck and spied what looked like a nurse's station fifty feet away.

Wearing socks, I was able to walk quietly down the hall, staying close to the wall. I spotted the night nurse before she saw me. I didn't see any security or cameras. I still didn't know where I was. I didn't even know what floor I was on.

The nurse was working on a crossword puzzle. I had to clear my throat to get her to notice me. The clock behind her said 11:30 pm. This meant I'd been out for twenty-four hours.

I learned I was in a psychiatric hospital in New Hampshire. My clothes had been changed because my t-shirt and pants had big tears in them. I told her some big security guards had manhandled me. She just shrugged.

My stomach growled audibly and I was offered a peanut butter sandwich with standard hospital apple juice. At first I didn't want the food but the nurse explained it would help me metabolize whatever drugs were lingering in my system. So I ate and went back to my room. The rest of the patients were asleep. I'd get to meet them in the morning. Goody.

I was still fuming over that a-hole doctor making copies of my journal. That, and thinking about Michelle and Alan, put a pretty big cloud over me. I was sick with rage. I couldn't be bothered to learn the names of the other patients or staff at this new hospital. I didn't care about attending group therapy and earning privileges like TV time, phone time or time outside. All I wanted to do was lie in bed, stare at the ceiling and think angry thoughts.

So for two days I kept to my barren room, void of distractions or amusement of any sort. I left my room at odd times twice a day for peanut butter sandwiches and juice, avoiding having to dine with other patients. Containing my anger took up all my attention and energy. On the outside, I appeared as calm as still waters, but my inner thoughts and fantasies were brutally violent. I did my best to seem apathetic and bored.

In situations like this appearances are everything. I vowed not to have another outburst like the one I'd had in the emergency room. I'd never let them break me again. They'd never know what I was thinking or feeling. I'd build a wall around myself, never letting them see the face of the monster they were creating.

On the third day, some doctor I'd never met came into my room to tell me I was leaving. Since I hadn't expressed any intention of hurting myself or anyone else, I was being transported back to the minimum security ward of the hospital that had sent me here. The other hospital wasn't exactly close to where I lived either but at least it was in the same state.

I got my torn clothes back and changed into them. The zipper on my pants was beyond repair and when I sat down my green underwear was visible through the fly. I didn't care though, it felt better to be in my own clothes.

I was admitted back into the same minimum security psychiatric ward I had left four months earlier. Everyone I had known was gone except for most of the staff. I had to learn all new names and faces but the routine was the same. Dad had delivered a box of my clothes and CDs as I was leaving New Hampshire. The pillow and journal Mom had tried to bring me days before were waiting on the bed of my new room. Seeing the journal again made me grind my teeth.

Being back in the hospital made me feel safe. It was comfortable and familiar. I liked being in an environment where nothing was expected of me. On the other hand being around new people made the experience different.

As before, almost all of the patients had substance abuse issues. The two I grew closest to had been transferred in from a group home and an alternative boarding school/ drug rehab. They showed me how to get high in secure facilities and still pass a urine test, by huffing. On slow nights back at the hospital if there was nothing good on TV, we'd sneak into the supply closet and inhale the fumes or gas of cleaning products. This gives you an instant high by cutting off oxygen to the brain. It also instantly destroys brain cells and can be deadly. I didn't think about what

I was doing to myself. I knew if I wasn't distracted, Michelle and the journal would float back to the surface of my mind. I couldn't let that happen. I couldn't function if that happened.

One evening I came back from the offsite daytime clinic and found a stack of books in my room. My homeroom/English teacher and science teacher/football coach had driven all the way up to visit me while I'd been out. They both brought me books to pass the time and handwritten letters of encouragement. In a way I was glad I'd been out when they came because this unexpected outpouring of concern and encouragement left me stupefied. What would I have said to them? I had no idea anyone gave a crap about me anymore. No one in my family had called or come to visit me. Having teachers that cared was touching but made me acutely embarrassed of my situation. I felt like I'd let them down.

The following week my principal and art teacher drove up to visit me. They showed up at the outpatient clinic with McDonald's food and a copy of *Jonathan Livingston Seagull*. The other patients all seemed pretty jealous of the surreal attention I was getting from high-school teachers. I'd gotten word that morning from my advocate that Mom didn't want me to come home and Dad wasn't saying anything either way. I had very mixed feelings about this and seeing familiar supporting authoritative figures was comforting.

When I was first told I had to go back to high school it seemed like the last place on earth I wanted to be. Now I was certain it was the only place I wanted to be. The teachers cared about me. They'd support me and keep me safe. It would give my life some direction and purpose until I figured out the bigger questions.

If I didn't go home I had to go somewhere that I could still go to New Horizons during the day. I gave my advocate the name and phone number of my only aunt who lived alone during the week. This aunt had come to my rescue many times but I was still surprised when she agreed to take me in. Surprised and glad.

As before, while I was in the hospital I wouldn't admit to anyone why I'd come so close to killing myself. When you're fifteen, wanting to die over love lost is way too embarrassing and emasculating. I couldn't admit I had doubts about my future. I was afraid people would start screaming "I told you so!" and attribute my insecurities to proof I wasn't trans after all. So in therapy I mumbled some vague excuses about school being overwhelming and in group therapy admitted my substance abuse.

I still kept my bulimia and fresh grief over Michelle to myself.

My prescriptions and diagnoses were changed again. I came into the hospital on Paxil for Bipolar Disorder, Benadryl for behavior control and Trazodone as a sleep aid. My amount of Paxil was doubled and my Bipolar was now Borderline Personality Disorder. The Benadryl was taken away and replaced with Depakote to control my mania. It was suggested I might have mild OCD because I'd developed an obsession with touching everything in sight. But I attributed it to being high and suddenly fascinated with textures. I still needed the Trazodone to sleep.

During the day I could busy myself with friends and activities so I didn't have to focus on Michelle and the likeliness I'd never have another girlfriend because I was trans, or deep down how inconsolably lonely I was. Lying in bed at night, alone with nothing to distract me from my thoughts, I'd start having panic attacks which led to insomnia. The Trazodone would knock me out before I reached that point.

Alcoholics Anonymous was recommended for me and a couple other inpatient kids. We were driven to a church one night for our first meeting. Except for our small group, and one other fifteen year old there by court order, the entire assembly consisted of people at least twice my age. The experiences people talked about in the meeting were gut-wrenching. The meeting was humbling, but I had a hard time relating. I'd never lost a job, child, or spouse to alcohol. I'd never been in jail or spent the night on the street because of my addictions. I'd never stolen to support my habit. Their adult problems were on a level I couldn't comprehend yet. I was still in the invincible teenager stages of my drug and alcohol use where consequences didn't exist. The night opened my eyes to where I might be heading, but I figured the road ahead of me to get there was plenty long with lots of twists and turns. I could end up going another way at any time.

When we got back to the hospital, I dropped acid for the first time. Another patient had snuck in some tabs of LSD wrapped in tinfoil and crammed between the pages of a book. The little square of paper she gave me was smaller than a postage stamp and didn't have much of a taste or smell. I didn't think about the consequences, just slid the paper to the back of my tongue not knowing what to expect.

At first I thought it was a joke because I didn't feel anything. I saw some trails here and there, but with all the prescription drugs I was on, I'd been seeing trails for months anyways. It wasn't until I walked through the dining area and Chef Boyardee started talking to me from an empty can of ravioli that I even knew I was high. I took the can into my room where Chef Boyardee philosophized and sang the *Beefaroni* song. That was a long night.

This stay at the hospital was briefer than the last. I was inpatient less than three weeks. During this time, I'd made a few new friends and discovered there were still new and fun things to experience. I didn't want to die just yet. Not everyone in the world was a total asshole as I'd feared when being re-admitted. But on the whole I preferred my chemically altered perception of reality.

Chapter Twenty-Six

You Gotta Have Friends

By Betsie

Luca spent weeknights at my sister's house and weekends at home. I was thankful he could still attend New Horizons while staying in Reading and hoped he would make some friends at school. Instead, he wanted to hang out with two teens he had met while in day treatment. Bob and Henry were always nice to me, but I worried about Luca spending so much time with them. Neither of them had completed high school or held a job. Luca didn't need this kind of influence. He had enough problems. But he needed friends and I needed to back off.

Fighting was the last thing I wanted to do. We had done enough of that already. So when Luca asked to go to Salem's "Haunted Happenings" with Bob and Henry, I hesitantly agreed. After all, I had to start trusting Luca sometime.

While attending a play there, the three of them met another teen named Harmony. Within days, Luca had been invited to Harmony's birthday party. She lived in Somerville and I felt it was a little too fast for Luca to be going to someone's house so far away, especially when he had only met her once.

"But Mom, Henry and Bob will be there too."

"And what about this Harmony? You don't know a thing about her."

"Come on Mom, I haven't been to a party in a long time."

"I suppose I'll have to drive the three of you to the T station and then come back and pick you up."

"I won't be late. I promise," Luca said.

He was so convincing. But then again he always was.

The evening came and I dropped the boys off at the Malden T Station. Luca would call me when he got to Harmony's house and then again when it was time to leave. Receiving a call around eleven pm, I totally expected to be heading back to Malden. Instead Luca said he was going to spend the night at Harmony's house. The kids were having too much fun.

"I don't like this you know," I told him.

"Mom, you can't make me come home. No one else is leaving. I'll look like a baby."

"But I don't even know where you are."

"I promise I'm okay."

"Let me speak with Harmony's mother."

"Her parents are already in bed."

"Luca, I really wish you'd come home," I said, almost begging.

"I'm having too much fun. Mom, I'll call you in the morning."

I was already walking on eggshells with Luca, never knowing what would set him off. I didn't like this. I felt as though I had been cornered into a situation with no easy way out. Demanding he come home would only start another fight. I had no choice but to let him stay.

In the end it all worked out. When I picked Luca up in the morning, he was very happy.

The following week I received a surprise call at work.

"Mom, I met someone at school I think can be a real friend," Luca said enthusiastically.

"What's his name?"

"Brian. Mom I think he's going to be someone I can confide in. Someone besides Diane to talk to. Do you think you could drive us to the movies this weekend?"

"It depends on where he lives."

"About ten minutes from our house."

Well, I had gotten my wish. But I had to remember Luca went to school with some real trouble makers. Was it possible Brian could be a worse influence than Loser Number One and Loser Number Two? I would have to wait to find out. The following day would be Thanksgiving.

We went to my sister's house. One of the best Thanksgivings I could remember. I tried my best not to shoot Luca *"I don't trust you"* glances. Surprisingly, no one else did either. Even Brooks behaved. We all made it through the day unscathed.

On Friday morning Luca told me he had a date with Harmony that evening. What the hell? Where did this come from? I almost hit the roof.

I called Harmony's mother. She said it was okay with her. Harmony knew she couldn't be out late, and Luca could spend the night on the couch. Luca had me just where he wanted me. Afraid of the consequences if I said no. So he had his first date with Harmony that evening.

I guessed it had gone okay. When I picked him up at the T station the following morning, he didn't say much about it either way.

On Sunday afternoon I drove Luca and Brian to the movies. Brian was a little heavy-set with medium length brown hair covering his face. He was neatly dressed and very soft-spoken. I was relieved when immediate laughter came from the back seat of the car. Brian didn't seem like much of a troublemaker. I hoped Luca would see more of him.

You Gotta Have Friends

By Luca

Halloween

During the week I slept on my aunt's living room futon couch in Reading. I spent Friday and Saturday nights at home. Staying with my aunt was a nice way to decompress. It was less tense and hostile than at home. My parents and I could stand to be near each other for short amounts of time but mostly only if no one was talking.

The first few days back at school were awkward. I hadn't talked regularly to many people outside of the football team, but my absence had been noticed. A few rumors were going around about me. I played off my suicide attempt as an accidental drug overdose. People could relate so no one gave me a hard time.

One day, to avoid the rain, I was sitting in the break room for lunch period instead of outside in the smoker's area. I grabbed a newspaper and Alanis Morissette was on the front page. Her album *Supposed Former Infatuation Junkie* had just been released and she was on tour in North America. I'd loved her last album so I turned to the music section to read the reviews but the music section was missing.

"Hey! Who took the entire music section out of the paper?"

A quiet voice from the next table answered, "I did. Sorry. Here."

We saw each other practically all day but this was the first time I'd heard him speak.

The boy's name was Brian and he shared all but one of my classes. While I was in science he worked in the student- staffed coffee shop downstairs.

"I just wanted to read the reviews on Alanis."

"Her new album is really good. I took the article for the pictures. I didn't think anyone else wanted to read it," Brian said.

"Oh, well if you want the pictures I'll give it back to you as soon as I'm done."

"Okay, thanks. Do you like her new album?" Brian asked.

"I haven't heard any of it except the single *Thank You*."

"I got it the day it came out. I can make you a copy if you want."

"Really? That'd be awesome!"

That conversation was the beginning of a tight friendship.

My best friends at the time were a pair of losers I'd met in the hospital. Henry and Bob had both been outpatients at the daytime treatment center. Henry for depression, Bob for heroin. I'd spend most Friday and Saturday night with them drinking fruit punch soda and playing *Dungeons and Dragons*. Neither of them smoked, did drugs, or drank alcohol anymore. But they didn't go to school or have jobs either.

They both seemed content to mooch off their parents from here to eternity. Their hygiene was questionable at best, and being with them in public was sort of embarrassing.

On Halloween, we decided to hang out in Salem and see an operetta. We showed up early to get good seats. Before the show started the guy sitting behind us was yakking our ears off about his girlfriend who was in the show. He was going on and on about how beautiful and talented she was.

"*Yeah right*," I thought.

This guy was a brain dead hippy; no way was he dating an attractive singer. A couple minutes into the show a cute little redhead came onto the side of the stage singing backup soprano. The guy behind us tapped my shoulder and pointed to her. She was sexy with her dark red hair, big brown eyes, smooth white skin and a tight bodice. Henry thought she was sexy too.

During intermission she came out to say hi to her boyfriend. I couldn't believe the guy had been telling the truth. He introduced her to the three of us. Henry took this opportunity to slip the girl his phone number. Henry gave his phone number and email to any girl who crossed his path. But with his greasy hair, creepy neck beard and B.O., he'd never had a girlfriend, except online. She was nice but I doubted she'd call. At least the dipwad she was currently dating had clean hair.

A few nights later Henry called me all excited. Harmony, the girl from the show, had actually called him. The other guy at the show wasn't her boyfriend anymore and Henry had a date lined up with her for Friday.

Their date went well and the next thing I knew I was invited to Harmony's sixteenth birthday party in Somerville. Henry had invited Bob and me so he could show off his new girlfriend. I had no idea where Harmony lived or what to get her for her birthday.

The party was on a Saturday. It was awkward meeting Harmony again. Her entire family was there and a couple of her friends as well. Everyone was new to me except Harmony and Bob, who basically ignored me. Henry was following Harmony around like a lost puppy and Bob was there to be set up with Harmony's best friend Stacy. I felt like a fifth wheel.

As the party moved upstairs Stacy hung back to talk to me. She was pretty with blonde hair and blue eyes but she was shy. I guessed her shyness was from wearing glasses and being a little chubby. Her clothes were loose on her so I surmised it wasn't that long ago she had been a fat girl. She looked good now but probably didn't know it yet. I understood what it was like to undergo a radical change in appearance but still live under the burden of your former self.

Stacy and I had a lot in common. Our personalities were similar; we liked the same music, books and movies. We liked the same foods and activities. But Stacy had been introduced to Bob first and was expected to go on at least one date with him, so I didn't bother hitting on her.

Bob had greasy facial hair and sweaty armpits, but he also had large biceps and chiseled abs. Even girls with glasses and deep personalities will choose the smelly Adonis over the interesting chunky guy every time.

The party turned into a slumber party although no one had a change of clothes or sleeping bag. I thought Mom would be relieved that she didn't have to pick me up from a train station at midnight but instead she sounded shocked and apprehensive. She consented because she didn't have much choice.

I couldn't sleep though. Everyone passed out around three am but Stacy and I stayed up talking and smoking cigarettes. At dawn we walked down to McDonalds for hash-browns, then to Dunkin Donuts to surprise everyone with coffee and donuts when they woke up.

I was the only one who had to go home in the morning. With me gone, Harmony, Stacy, Henry and Bob could go out on their double date later that day. I'd told Mom I'd meet her at the train station in Revere by ten am. At 8:30 Harmony left her guests to walk me to the train station in Davis Square. On the walk over she kept looking at me sideways and smiling. At the station she thanked me for coming and for the coffee and donuts. Then she kissed my cheek and dropped a folded piece of paper in my pocket.

The kiss caught me completely off guard. Other than Michelle I'd never been kissed by a girl, not even on the cheek. I was sort of dazed. I didn't find the paper in my pocket until I was on the train. It said "call me" with a little heart and Harmony's phone number. Now I really didn't know what to think.

First Date

I moved back in with Mom and Dad the Saturday before Thanksgiving. Coming home was bittersweet. On the one hand, I was getting along better with my parents. My commute to school was half the time and I had access to the internet again. On the other hand it had been quieter and simpler staying with my aunt. I had been cut off from my friends during the week at her apartment, but I also hadn't taken any drugs other than my prescriptions or drank any alcohol. I didn't even bring cigarettes to her apartment. Being sober was one of the rules my aunt had set down before I moved in with her. Not drinking or smoking gave me the shakes. I'd listen to the copy of Alanis Morissette's album Brian copied for me and grit my teeth.

Living with my parents was more intense. I had my own room and bathroom to hide in. I could blast my CDs and tie up the phone-line and smoke cigarettes on the balcony patio. But living with my parents made me feel the need to hide and smoke more often than not.

I'd been talking to Brian more at school. He was really funny and liked a lot of the same music I liked. He seemed smart too. Other than being painfully shy, I couldn't figure out why he was at our school. I'd dropped math class in the mornings, and taken up working in the coffee shop for my first period. Brian worked during second period, and most days I skipped science class and hung out with him while it was his turn to pour coffee and toast bagels.

Brian had given me his AOL screen-name and when I went home and signed online, he was there. He sent me an IM, writing with pink print. He said he had a secret to tell me but judging by the pink letters I guessed his secret. He was gay. He said no one in the school knew. His family didn't know either. Suddenly it made sense why he was in an alternative school. He must have been ferociously bullied in public school. I felt humbled and honored that he came out to me. His courage impressed me. It made me feel bad I didn't tell him I was trans. I wanted to tell him though, and that was a new concept to me.

The next day was Thanksgiving. I'd expected to be nervous around my family. The last few times we'd been together had been disastrous for me. After once again being recently released from the booby hatch I figured people would be uncomfortable or rude around me. I hardly noticed the atmosphere though. I was too busy stressing over the thought of coming out to my new friend Brian and simultaneously vexed about what to do with Harmony's number.

Henry was still Harmony's boyfriend and my friend. I couldn't put a move on my friend's girlfriend, could I? I didn't like Henry that much to begin with. Now that I had Brian, a friend I had stuff in common with and was fun to be around, did I even need Henry as my friend? It's one thing to grow apart from your friends, it's another to stab them in the back. Was I that kind of person? Was Harmony even worth it? She was cute but I barely knew her. Was she really into me? What kind of girl moves from guy to guy so quickly? If we tried dating, how long could I realistically hide it from her that I'm trans? Maybe I was seeing signals that weren't there. Some girls are just flirtatious. It doesn't mean anything.

I figured the best way to decide what to do was to call Harmony and see what she wanted. I called her that night when I got home. She seemed excited that I called and we talked for a couple hours. She said the only reason she called Henry was because I hadn't given her my number. She thought I was cute, and after her party she thought I was wicked funny and really nice. I couldn't believe my ears! All thoughts of morality and loyalty to my friend Henry went right out the window.

We made plans to meet Friday night and spend the night at her place. When I arrived at Davis Square the sun had gone down and it was pouring out. I couldn't remember how to get to Harmony's house from the station and by the time she met me I was soaked and shivering. She threw her arms around me and pulled me down for a kiss. Her mouth was warm, and her embrace stopped me from shaking. If she noticed how awkward I was, she didn't show it.

We walked arm in arm back to her house. Her body against mine made my skin tingle. I felt so alive! I couldn't believe this was happening to me. I'd lost forty pounds in the past six months and didn't think I was ugly, but I didn't think I was nearly attractive enough to be in Harmony's league.

We got to her house and went straight up to her room. I sat on the corner of her bed and she sat on my legs with her arms around my neck, her hands in my hair. We were kissing and she let me slide my hands up under her shirt. I thought going for second base not even an hour into a first date was rude of me, but on the other hand who knew how long this would last. I was packing at the time, and if she decided to reach in my pants it'd be all over. Even if I didn't out myself, just trying to stop her would raise all kinds of flags, because guys never say no. I was walking a tight rope.

Just as I slid my hand into her bra the phone rang. Harmony ignored it but then her brother was knocking on the door saying Henry was on the phone. I sat back thinking she'd take the phone and get rid of him quickly. To both our surprises, Henry was calling from a payphone at the redline transfer station. He was on his way over with Bob. Crap.

Henry wasn't a stable person. Harmony hadn't wanted to break up with him in person for fear of how he'd react. I didn't blame her. There was time for me to leave, but Harmony wanted me there as a barrier between her and Henry. She didn't want to break up with him to his face, but she didn't want him hanging on either. The smart thing to do would have been to break up with him over the phone right then. Instead, she called Stacy and asked her to come spend the night too. When Henry and Bob arrived they were both surprised to see me. Harmony said she'd called me after Henry hung up. I said my mom had driven me over and that's why I'd arrived before them. Henry still seemed put out. Bob was happy Stacy was there. Harmony was trying to pretend nothing strange was going on. I was pissed. My date had turned into five's company.

After an uncomfortable pizza dinner with Henry glaring at me the entire time, I decided the best way to get through this was to go to sleep early and leave first thing in the morning. But how to sleep through four rowdy teenagers horsing around? Trazadone to the rescue! I wanted to make sure I took enough to black out through the entire night. Two or three would have done the trick but I took ten to be sure. What followed did not make a good impression on Harmony's parents.

As I lay on the end of Harmony's bed drooling on myself, my eyes wide open but unseeing, Harmony noticed the empty bottle of pills next to me. It took Harmony, her thirteen year old brother, and Bob to drag me into the bathroom. I came to on my knees in front of the toilet with Harmony's mom telling me I needed to puke. I shook her off and lay down on my side, going back to sleep. I woke up again when Harmony's dad came in the room and started yelling that they needed to call an ambulance. I managed to sit up and mumble that I was fine. I was just really tired because I hadn't eaten any of the pizza and I took my medicine on an empty stomach. This was partially true. Then Harmony's parents yelled at each other over whether or not to call an ambulance. I willed myself to keep my eyes open. Harmony was in tears. Her dad finally relented and went downstairs. Her mom brought me a huge glass of milk and said the deal was they wouldn't call an ambulance if I could stay awake. So much for my plan of sleeping through the awkwardness. Now the tension and weirdness was elevated to the tenth power. It was my fault, and I had to sit through it all.

I was wrapped in a blanket on the couch eating cold pizza and drinking milk. Harmony doted on me, ignoring her other guests. When she got up to use the bathroom Henry came in and accused me of doing this on purpose to hog all of his girlfriend's attention. I told him it was an accident but he didn't believe me. Harmony came back in and kicked him out of the room so I could rest. Then the two of them got in a fight over me. After the fight, Harmony came back and we spent the night cuddling under the blanket and talking. It was hard to stay awake. I kept falling asleep and hallucinating with my eyes open. Harmony's mom came to check on me a few times. I felt bad she was up most of the night because of me.

When the sun came up I was finally allowed to go to sleep. A couple hours later Stacy had to go home and Harmony got rid of Henry and Bob, saying her dad wanted the house empty. When I woke up, Harmony said I could stay. But I didn't think I could face her parents again. She walked me back to the train station and kissed me goodbye.

The night had been a wreck. I'd hurt Henry, pissed off Bob, made a terrible impression on Stacy and Harmony's family. I'd made myself incredibly sick. Harmony was so sexy and the thought of being with her had been exciting. But I figured I'd gotten what I deserved. I could still feel her lips on mine all the way home; like a sensual haunting. I knew I'd never call her again though. I'd fucked it up too badly.

Chapter Twenty-Seven

Transgender Convention

By Betsie

There was another transgender convention coming up and I was actually looking forward to this one. Diane had asked Luca and me to be on a panel with her. Because of my nerves, I declined. But I couldn't wait to see Luca speaking to other teens.

Taking a vacation day and getting Luca out of school, we made the trip into Boston. Diane spoke first, giving introductions and a brief overview. Thomas' mother had agreed to take my place and to read a speech which she prepared beforehand. She was eloquent as she spoke about her little girl who was now her son. She not only spoke of immediate family but of extended family and how difficult Thomas' change was for some of them. But throughout her piece, she remained steadfast in her love for her son. Just what every parent there needed to hear. She had been the right choice.

Luca had nothing prepared but answered many questions; from "When did you know?" to "How are you doing in school?" and everything in between. At times he was funny. At times serious. But always hopeful. I was so proud of him!

At the end of the question and answer period, he surprised the audience with a short speech.

"I want you to know I couldn't have gone through any of this without my mom. I know this has been difficult for her, but she's always stood by me. My family has taken on a lot of debt because of me. I want to tell my mom I appreciate everything she's done. Love you Mom."

"Love you too," I managed to say before falling to pieces.

There was no use trying to stop the tears.

Now, with a beet-red face it was my turn to answer a few questions. Strangers praised me saying how wonderful it was Luca had parents who stood by him. Teens asked if I would speak to their parents. I gave my phone number to a few of them.

Within the next few weeks I received two phone calls from teens asking if I would please speak to their parents. One, in particular, needed someone to speak to his father who had abandoned him. It was a privilege. I actually had three phone conversations with his father and was able to reunite them. A feeling of personal accomplishment.

Transgender Convention

By Luca

There was another trans convention coming up in Boston. A much smaller one being held at a hotel instead of a convention center. Mom and I were both invited to speak on panels. I was nervous and excited.

The convention only lasted one day. There were FTM's, MTF's, doctors, surgeons and SOFA's (Significant Others Friends and Allies) in attendance. Besides Vanessa, the peer counselor I had spoken to when I first came out as trans, I'd never seen or spoken with other trans women. I expected them to all be sweet and overly feminine, but some of them were grouchy and catty. There were nice, pretty, trans women, but a few seemed like they lived their lives in permanent menopause. I guess constant persecution, ridicule and hormone craziness will do that to a person. It made me glad I'd transitioned so young and blended so well.

My panel was trans youth, which consisted of Diane, me and Thomas' mom. I hadn't prepared anything to say so mostly I fielded questions. More people were interested in what I had to say than I had expected. They asked me how old I was when I first knew I was trans. Did I have any regrets? How did my family react? How's school? Do I have any friends? Do I date? Will I get more surgery? What's it like to go through this so young? Etc, etc. I talked about my depression. My suicide attempts as a young kid. Being bullied. Being alone. And how, after I transitioned and had surgery, I went back to school and now have friends and even date.

When asked if my dates knew I was trans, I said my last girlfriend was cool with it; which was a lie. I'd never told Michelle, but I didn't want to seem like a deceitful scumbag. A number of people told me I was lucky to have such an awesome mom. Almost all of the adult trans people told me they were jealous I got to go to high-school as a guy and it was so cool that I had a girlfriend and played football.

I was glad to answer questions from parents whose kids might be trans and were unsure what to do. Mom ended up answering questions too. It was really funny because when she talks in front of crowds her face turns scarlet.

By the time I'd left the convention, I'd decided I was going to tell Brian I was trans. It's not the same as being gay, but I thought he'd understand.

The only other friend I'd ever told was Jenny. She had been cool with it, but recently we'd kind of grown apart. We went to different high-schools in different cities and went months without seeing each other. I hoped Brian would soon be my new best friend. I felt it was important that I be honest with him.

He caught a cab ride with me back to my house after school, and while we were smoking cigarettes on the balcony, I told him. I was so nervous my hands were shaking and I felt like I had a hornet's nest in my stomach. He took the news in stride, but since Brian hadn't known me from before, he had a lot of questions. We went inside and I showed him pictures of me as a little girl in pink dresses with white tights and basketball trophies that said "Marie".

I kept waiting for him to laugh, but he never did. I told him about the suicide attempts and the hormone shots. I mentioned surgery, but I didn't go into detail about it. Gay guys are still guys and I didn't want him to think less of me. It's one thing to be a guy who used to be a girl, but even gay men wouldn't consider you a man if you didn't have a penis. I didn't feel bad about that omission. I'd spilled my guts plenty as it was. It's not like Brian had to go into gory detail to tell me he was gay. I felt we were even. More importantly I felt our friendship had become much deeper and stronger. I knew telling him had been a good decision.

Chapter Twenty-Eight

Harmony

By Betsie

I was finally going to meet Harmony and was sitting at the subway station waiting for her to step off the train. Watching from my car, the moment she stepped onto the platform she gave Luca a big hug. *"Oh my god,"* I thought. *"Please don't let us be in another ride like the one with Michelle."*

Harmony's personality was as flamboyant as her flaming red hair. She said more to me in our thirty-minute ride back to the condo than Michelle had ever said to me, even after spending time at our house. I liked Harmony right away.

When it was time for her to go home, I drove her back to Somerville. About a forty-five minute drive from our house. I wanted to meet her parents. Harmony's mother was very welcoming. We sat and talked for quite some time.

I now had to find my way out of Somerville and back to Route 93. After passing a few places more than once, I finally made it to the highway.

Another one hundred times and it became much easier.

Harmony

By Luca

I may not have called Harmony back, but that didn't stop her from calling me. She and Henry were through. She hadn't heard from him in two weeks. I hadn't heard from him either and I knew I'd lost a friend but it didn't bother me. There was a time when I would have been remorseful about losing a friend or betraying one. I didn't know who I was anymore, but it was obvious I'd changed. Being accepted in the world as a normal guy and seen as datable by attractive girls had changed my priorities.

Harmony and I met in Boston and had a normal date. We took the train to Cambridge and checked out some book stores, hit up Newbury

Street in Boston for some music stores and ate dinner in Quincy Market.

By then it was snowing and we strolled through the Boston Gardens. I liked watching the flakes melt on Harmony's eyelashes as she smiled up at me. It was amazing having someone to hold hands with and just feel comfortable. It wasn't desperate or earth shattering. Just two teenagers who were a little unsure and a little brave, getting to know one another.

The next weekend Harmony spent the night at my house. Mom and I picked her up from the train station. It was the first time they met and I think they hit it off okay. Harmony was sweet and polite. I wanted her to spend some time on my turf and meet Mom and Brian. It was so much easier having people over for the night and not having to stay in a binder the whole time. I still had to pack and sleep with it in but that was way easier. Harmony slept on my bed, I slept on the floor with Brian.

Harmony and Brian got along well. She knew he was gay before she met him so that wasn't a hurdle. I was encouraged by how open-minded Harmony was toward gays.

The following weekend Harmony had to stay home and watch her younger brother and sister who were ten and thirteen. With her parent's permission I spent the night and hung out with her siblings. The brother was into wresting, the little sister was into the Spice Girls. I'm an only child so spending time with youngins was intriguing to me. It was sort of hectic having three people vying for my attention and pulling me in different directions.

The kids were both extremely well-behaved and independent, but I was new and interesting to them. They jumped all over me and dragged me from one room to the net all day and all night. Harmony thought it was hilarious I hip-hop danced with her sister and let her brother toss me around the living room in fake wrestling matches. It was nice feeling part of a family. I loved my family, but so much had happened in the last year, I was always self-conscious around them and the atmosphere was strained. Harmony's family didn't know about my suicide attempts. They'd never seen me after I'd cut myself or been in a fight with Dad.

Being with Harmony's family was a chance to start over and invent myself as normal and loveable.

I didn't know how to ask Harmony to be my girlfriend. I'd never been in a real dating situation before and it was nerve wracking. I liked her a lot and the thought of her seeing other people while dating me upset me. I didn't want to seem clingy or demanding though. Her sister solved the problem for me.

"So are you Harmony's boyfriend?"

"I don't know." I looked over at Harmony. "Am I?"

She replied, "Well duh! What do you think!"

And that was that. I had a real live girlfriend. One who I could call and not get billed long distance. A girlfriend I could see more than once a year. Yippee!

The day after Christmas, Harmony came to spend the night at my house again. This was our fifth weekend in a row together. Dad was at work and Mom was out. We were alone on my bed kissing, when Harmony told me she wanted to have sex with me. She'd dropped hints before but with her family or mine always around I'd been able to put her off. She made it plain she would not be put off this time.

"I can't" I said feebly.

"Why not?"

"It's hard to say."

"You're gay." She said looking crushed.

"What?! I'm not gay!"

"Then what is it? You don't want me?"

"Of course I do! It's not you."

"Just tell me. Whatever it is I won't care. I love you." Now she was pleading with me.

"You do?" This was news to me.

"Yes!"

"I love you too." Actually I wasn't sure how I felt but it seemed like the right thing to say.

"So tell me what's wrong."

"Okay. I can't say it, but I can write it."

She watched me write in a marbled notebook with a green pen. She was patient at first but by the time I reached my third page she was starting to look unsure I was terrified.

Telling Brian had been easy compared to this. Hell anything I'd ever done had been easier than this. What if she laughed? What if she cried? What if she got pissed and started trashing my room? What if she wanted to go home? What if she hated me and never wanted to see me again? A lot of horrible what if's went through my mind, not once thinking what if she was okay with this, because I was sure that was impossible. She thought she loved me but within minutes she'd know I'm unlovable. No sixteen-year-old, straight bio girl could be okay with this. But Harmony had been good to me and she deserved the truth. Telling Brian had worked out and I found a small part of me wanted people to know the truth. I wanted it to be okay for me to be me.

I wrote her a long letter telling her I was sorry for not telling her sooner about myself. I told her I was trans. That I had been born a man trapped in a girl's body. It wasn't a joke and it wasn't my fault. Every moment I'd lived as a girl had been hell. I'd had sex reassignment surgery but only on my top half. I'd get the other surgery soon but my parents couldn't afford it right now. I was sorry if she felt deceived and understood if she didn't want anything to do with me anymore. Then I put the letter in her lap and walked out of the room.

I didn't know where to go. I debated going outside but then figured I should be there when she asked for a phone to call her parents to come pick her up. I paced the living room for a while, circled the kitchen and ended up crouched under the dining room table.

After fifteen minutes or so, she came out of my room and called my name. I didn't answer. I was trying to gauge her response before I gave away my position. If she seemed pissed maybe I could sneak out.

Harmony looked around the living room, went through the kitchen and came up behind me in the dining room. She squatted down next to me.

"Luca?"

I scooted further under the table. She sighed.

"Will you please come out?"

I didn't move.

"I want to talk to you."

"You can talk to me from there."

"But I can't see your face."

"You don't need to see my face to break up with me."

"I'm not breaking up with you."

I still didn't move. Part of me wanted to go to her, but the other part couldn't believe her. It didn't make sense. It had to be some kind of trick. When it became obvious I wasn't coming out from under the table, she crawled under after me. With her hand under my chin she turned my face to hers.

"Hi." she said.

"Hi." I said back.

"I'm not breaking up with you."

"Why not?"

"Why should I?"

I shrugged.

"Do you want me to break up with you?"

I shook my head and she hugged me.

"Then please come back to your room with me."

Harmony got up and headed back to my room. Cautiously I followed. She shut the door behind us and locked it, then sat on my bed.

"Come here," she pulled me down next to her. "So what does this mean? You don't have a penis?"

"No." I mumbled.

"Then what do you have?"

"What do you think?"

"Show me."

"Why? Are you bisexual?"

"No. But I want to see. I want to see all of you."

Harmony lay back on my bed and took her clothes off. All of them.

"No secrets. I won't judge you."

She got to her knees and started unbuttoning my shirt. I was glad the light was dim, but even so my scars burned angry red against my white skin. Harmony sucked her breath in through her teeth.

"They look painful."

"Not anymore."

"I'm sorry you had to go through that."

"Me too."

"Take your pants off." Her hands undid my belt.

Nervously my fingers stumbled with my button and zipper. Then I was just in my teal briefs.

"What's that?" She pointed at my crotch. I'd been packing since we'd met. I pulled it out to show her and she laughed. My face turned red and my jaw clenched. I rigidly stood up and turned my back to her.

"Wait!" She jumped up and hugged me from behind. "I wasn't laughing at you. I just think it's funny in a cute way what you went through to impress me. Lay back down with me. I want to feel your skin on my skin."

I was hesitant. Her laughter had stung. But she was offering me what I'd dreamed of for so long – to hold someone and be held in return with nothing between us.

I climbed back into bed and we held one another. Then we touched. She was the first person to see me naked in my adult life. I expected it to be disarming, but Harmony treated me in a way that made it feel liberating. She treated me like a man.

Chapter Twenty-Nine

Luca Turns Sixteen

By Betsie

At times I thought I would never see Luca turn sixteen. He finally had friends and could have a real party. Something he had not had since the fourth grade. He deserved it.

I rented the community hall in our building and supplied the usual party food and soda. No drugs or alcohol were allowed and with Brian and Harmony there, I knew the kids would keep it that way.

Not wanting to hover over them, I just made appearances every fifteen to twenty minutes. Things were going great and the kids were having a wonderful time.

Brian knocked on the door and asked to use the phone. He wasn't going to stay. It was late, but with some of Luca's friends still there, I couldn't drive him home. He had to call his grandmother. I felt bad. Harmony was also supposed to spend the night but went home when her parents came to pick up her brother. Something wasn't right.

I questioned Luca but of course never got a straight answer.

I've read Luca's accounting of what actually happened the night of his sixteenth birthday party. It makes me sick thinking of what the outcome could have been. And where was I? I must have stepped into that function hall twelve to fifteen times that night, never noticing anything out of place.

Luca Turns Sixteen

By Luca

For my sixteenth birthday I wanted to have a big party. I hadn't had a birthday party for a few years due to a lack of friends to attend. Now I had lots of friends and a cute girlfriend. I wanted to live it up and show off.

In the last month at school I'd become more popular. I think having a girlfriend and best friend who both accepted me as I was gave me confidence to make more friends. I was set to have over twenty people at my party.

Harmony and I had been dating for almost two months when my birthday rolled around. I invited her brother to the party as well since we were close and only two years apart. Harmony invited her friend Stacy who invited her boyfriend Bob who pretended he wasn't mad at me anymore.

Harmony and Brian didn't drink or do drugs, but strangely all of their friends did. So while the two people closest to me abstained, they didn't criticize my growing problem.

Harmony had confronted me about my intentionally vomiting up food and I tried to stop. It took weeks to be able to eat without gagging afterword. I hadn't expected the feeling of food in my belly to be so nauseating. I had to retrain my body to eat and not get sick. It's a good thing I wasn't thin; otherwise I might have been in real trouble. Now that I wasn't destroying my esophagus and tooth enamel to stay under 200 pounds I figured I should watch my food intake. That meant no more drugs that gave me the munchies. Alcohol, LSD, ecstasy, pain killers and cough syrup were still in.

I don't know why I was suddenly so into drugs. Things were going good for me. But the more you get high the more it seems like the normal state of things. When I wasn't high on something I felt out of place and bored. It seemed like altering my brain chemistry allowed me to experience the best me possible. I was happier, friendlier and easier going. It wasn't just me who preferred me high, everyone around me liked me better if I was stoned on something or other. Drugs make everything better; until they don't.

Harmony asked me to stay sober for the night since her parents were stopping by with her younger sister to drop her, her brother, Stacy and Bob off at the party and pick them up later. She didn't want me wasted in front of her siblings or parents. I promised I'd stay straight but early on one of my friends gave me a tab of E for my birthday and like the asshole that I am, I swallowed it without thinking twice. I figured it was just one so I'd barely be rolling. No one would notice. I probably would have gotten away with it if my friend hadn't been obviously toasted and casting suspicion on me by association.

Harmony cornered me and asked if I was high. I didn't say anything but my aversion was answer enough. She was pissed. She crossed the room and wouldn't talk to me. For some reason, my stupid stoned-ass self, thought that was funny and I laughed it off. Brian was with me and he just shook his head in dismay. I figured it was a party and couldn't understand why they were both being so stuck up. Everyone else was having a good time.

A little while after that my bud Gordon from summer school and the football team was dropped off by some of his friends. Mom stuck her head in the door to tell me she wanted these guys to go because they looked like trouble. Brian looked pissed and Harmony looked beyond furious. I explained the guys were leaving; only Gordon was staying. That satisfied Mom. Brian said if Gordon was staying he was leaving. Since I'd invited Gordon and his ride was gone, I didn't see what choice I had but to let him stay.

Brian left the party to call for a ride home. I went to talk to Gordon because I felt bad that Brian and Harmony had been so rude to him. That's when Gordon suggested I use my birthday money to buy beer. He said he knew a store that would sell to him. I thought it was a good idea but I didn't have a car. Some of my other friends were listening in and they were really excited about the prospect of beer. Some had been planning on leaving soon but now that alcohol was a possibility they all wanted to stay. I felt put on the spot. I wanted to be a good host so I caved in and set myself to the task of finding a car for Gordon to drive to the store.

Mom would notice in a heartbeat if her car was missing because you could see it from our living room. Dad's car was parked underground in the garage but it was a stick shift. My neighbors were out of town and left me a key to their condo so I could feed their cat. I knew they left their car key by the entry way. I also should have known this was a bad idea but when you're high you make bad decisions.

I went upstairs and got the key, and then Gordon and I snuck down to the garage to find the car. It was a new Cadillac Seville. I couldn't believe I was giving Gordon the key to my neighbor's car and all my birthday money. Part of me was scared but part of me thought it was funny.

I went back to my party and tried to make up with Harmony. She asked where I'd been and I told her Gordon left to go pick up his girlfriend. She seemed happier. She sat on my lap on a couch watching my friend Sarah shark people out of their money at cards. We were listening to music and having a good time until Gordon came back. He gestured that he needed me to follow him and Harmony looked suspicious. Gordon said he got me a birthday present and needed help carrying it. I told Harmony I'd be right back and followed him out. When he popped the trunk of the car there were six six-packs of glass Heinekens. Gordon's girlfriend was with him and we each grabbed two packs of beer. I turned to walk back in and Harmony was in the doorway. She looked at me and what was in my hands, and then turned on her heel and left.

We snuck the beer into my room and went downstairs to tell whoever was left where it was. Harmony was on the floor in the hallway with her head between her knees sobbing, Stacy was rubbing her back. Neither of them would look at me as I walked past.

While I was gone, Harmony's brother had folded up all the tables and chairs. The party was basically over. I said goodnight to everyone who was leaving and headed upstairs with those who were staying the night. Harmony's brother looked upset and stopped me to ask why his sister was crying. I said she was just pissed at me but she'd be over it by tomorrow. He looked uncertain and I thanked him for coming and helping clean up before brushing past him and out the door. I didn't bother saying goodnight to Harmony and Brian was already gone.

Back in my room, Gordon and his girlfriend took my bed. I stayed on the floor with some other people, knocking back beer and pizza. I didn't know that alcohol and E can make you extremely ill. It can cause severe dehydration and make your body overheat. Luckily I only had three beers before I passed out, but I woke up sick as a dog the next day.

My clothes were soaked in sweat and I was too exhausted to shiver. My mouth was dry; my tongue felt like sand paper and the inside of my head was like my own private fireworks display. Worse, I realized no one in my room was really my friend. They only stayed for the beer. The people who actually cared about me I'd pissed off and pushed away the night before. I was a lonely wreck. When I thought about how I'd basically conspired with some kid I barely knew to steal my neighbor's car and buy alcohol for a bunch of minors, I was a scared lonely wreck.

Aftermath

After my birthday party it took me the rest of the weekend to recover from my hangover. I tried talking to Harmony. We were having a standoff in our relationship. She wanted me to give up drugs and alcohol. I thought that might be a good idea but refused to admit it out loud. I didn't want Harmony to think I was willing to give up something or change just for her.

It was important to me at the time that no one would have authority over me unless I respected them and it was my choice. I wouldn't be cowed with threats or ultimatums. Harmony could take me as I was or forget me. When I was with Michelle she had always had all the power in our relationship. I had a feeling Harmony wanted me more than I wanted her and that she'd back down and take whatever crap I shoveled her way to keep me.

Intentionally treating another person this way was sick but intoxicating. Knowing you can drag another person through hell over and over and that they'll keep letting you; keep proving their love for you, because whatever the pain and grief you're worth it to them, is a self-esteem rush. For a young, newly transitioned and formerly friendless, dateless, hopeless loser who hated himself as much as I did, self-esteem was in high demand. Maybe if I hadn't spent the majority of my life being treated as sub-human I wouldn't feel the need to prove something to myself at the cost of someone else's self-esteem. Maybe if I hadn't been taught to hate myself for being different I wouldn't harbor secret cravings to destroy myself with drugs and alcohol.

Maybe.

I spent the weekend alone in my room. There were still unopened bottles of Heineken clinking around in my clothes drawers. I'd taken the empties down to the recycling bin while Mom had been grocery shopping, but I needed to get rid of the full ones before I got caught with them.

I decided to hide them in plain sight. I wrapped each bottle in newspaper and crammed them into a cardboard box. You couldn't hear the glass clink unless you REALLY shook it. Then I wrapped the box in leftover birthday wrapping paper, put a bow on top and brought it to school on Monday. I walked right into home-room with it before school started and sold the unopened box to another student for $15. I used the money to buy Brian a CD in hopes that he'd forgive me for blowing him off at my party.

Brian did forgive me. But only on the condition that I quit drugs and alcohol. It was the same talk Harmony had given me, but with Brian I took it more seriously because I was afraid he meant it. I needed Brian. He was the funniest, coolest, smartest guy I knew. The thought of him not being my friend anymore sent icicles up my spine and into my heart. Choosing between Brian and drugs was like deciding over a hundred dollar bill wrapped in dog shit or a million dollars clean and free. I picked Brian.

At home my drug stash was pretty low so getting rid of it was easy. I poured the NyQuil down the drain and flushed the Ritalin I'd been planning on crushing and snorting. One of my friends from the hospital had mailed me some of her Ritalin for that purpose along with a tab of acid for my birthday. I took the acid and some marijuana I'd been holding to school.

The pot I sold no problem before school even started. At the end of the school day I gave the LSD away to a girl who went to all the football games and was fairly popular. Apparently she got caught with it at her group home later and no one from school ever saw her again. I felt awful. It seemed like I was never the one to pay the price of my indulgence. It wasn't fair. I was such a scummy douche yet I never got caught or was held responsible. The guilt ate at me for a long time.

I vowed to never go near illegal drugs again. Harmony thought I'd come around and given them up for her. I kept my mouth shut and let her believe it. I was weary of making life harder for everyone around me.

Chapter Thirty

April 20th

By Betsie

"Jesus Christ Luca. Where the hell are you?" I said out loud as I paced the living-room floor. Luca should have called by now. It was April school vacation and he had gone to Boston to meet up with some friends. He had done this a few times but always called me to pick him up at the Malden subway station. It was now after seven pm and he hadn't called.

I gave Brian a call hoping he knew where Luca was. Brian hadn't heard from him.

I had no option but to sit by the phone and worry. I turned on the television only to find out two students from Colorado had shot and killed classmates. It was still too early for details.

Eight pm, nine pm, ten pm. "*Where the hell are you Luca?*" I kept asking myself.

The news about Columbine High School was devastating. My emotions were running high when the phone rang.

"Mrs. Harvie?"

"Yes."

"This is Sergeant Riley from the MBTA police department. We have your son Luca in custody."

"What did he do?"

"He attacked a police officer."

His words startled me. Luca may have done many stupid things including hurting himself, but it was totally out of character for him to attack a police officer.

"Where is he?"

"He's being held at the Roxbury precinct."

"Where's that?"

I listened to what the officer said but it was like he was speaking to someone else and I was overhearing the conversation. None of this made sense.

Within minutes Brooks would be home from work and we would have to drive into Roxbury to get Luca.

"Luca got in trouble in Boston. He's been arrested for attacking a police officer," I blurted out as Brooks walked through the door.

"What the hell?" Brooks replied.

"The police wouldn't give me any further information. We have to drive to Roxbury to pick him up."

"Do you even know how to get there?"

"No. I have the directions but they don't mean anything to me."

"Jesus Christ, I can't believe the trouble he gets into. This morning I begged him not to go to Boston. I had a feeling something was going to happen. He never listens to me and this is the kind of shit we have to deal with."

"I'm too upset to drive. I'm calling Maryanne. She knows Boston. Maybe she knows how to get there."

"At this hour?"

"I don't know what else to do. Unless you can drive."

"Go ahead and give her a call."

Thank God my sister agreed to help us out.

Resting my head against the car window, I was too distraught for conversation. I kept asking myself, "*How is Luca being treated at the police station? Did they find out he is biologically a female? Will they do anything to hurt him? Is he in with other men who will hurt him? Why the hell would he attack a police officer?*" I couldn't get to the precinct fast enough.

It was scary walking into the police station at eleven pm. It was deserted except for an officer sitting at a desk behind dark glass. It took a while for him to acknowledge us.

"I'm Mrs. Harvie. You have my son Luca. I'm here to pick him up.

Can you explain to me what happened?"

"I'll have one of the arresting officers speak to you. It'll be a few minutes."

It seemed like it took more than just a few minutes.

The door opened and Luca came running out.

"Mom, you have to get Mike out. He's hurt. They're hurting him."

My sister was so angry Luca had not even thanked us, she slapped his face.

That's when we saw his bruises.

"What the hell is this all about? Why is your lip cut?" I asked trying to remain calm in front of the female officer who had appeared out of nowhere.

"Why is his face so bruised?" I asked her.

"He and some friends jumped the turn-style at the subway station. When we went to question them, your son went after my partner with a broken beer bottle. He was thrown to the ground."

"Mom, she's lying. They're all lying," Luca said with a hoarse voice. "We did nothing wrong except not pay. But right now you have to get Mike out. Don't let him stay in there any longer. He's hurt and probably needs stitches. Please, please."

"Why can't his parents come and get him?"

"I don't know. But he doesn't have the bail money. You have to bail him out."

"Why does he need bail money? You didn't need bail money."

"Because he's not a juvenile."

Luca was so upset. Something wasn't right. Although I had never met Mike, I took the twenty-five dollars from an ATM and bailed him out.

Now we had to wait to give Mike a ride back to a T station.

When Mike came through the doors he looked pretty roughed up.

The female officer would not offer any further information.

We were given an order to show up for a hearing early the next morning in Boston. The five of us left the police station.

Maryanne drove to the nearest T stop. Without ever saying a word, Mike got out. This pissed Brooks off.

"Luca, he never thanked your mother for spending twenty five dollars to bail him out. Now he doesn't even thank your aunt for dropping him off. Maybe we should have left him there."

Luca was agitated.

"You can yell at me all you want. At least Mike is out of there and they can't hurt him anymore. I don't know what they told you, but it's all a lie. I never attacked a police officer. We didn't even have bottles of beer with us," Luca said, his voice barely audible.

"Luca," Maryanne said. "Today some students went into a high school and shot a lot of kids and maybe even teachers. We're all on edge."

"Sorry, I didn't know. But don't take it out on me. Mom, when the big male officer grabbed me he threw me to the ground, I think I passed out. I need to see a doctor to document these cuts and bruises."

I put my arm around Luca and pulled him close.

"Well first we have to go to court in the morning. This is such a mess."

All the way home I listened to how the kids were all roughed up. How the officers used excessive force. How Luca was being charged with attacking an officer with a deadly weapon; a glass bottle that didn't exist.

What a fucking mess.

The Arraignment

The courthouse in Boston was big and confusing. I was immediately panic-stricken. Once upstairs, we bumped into Mike and his father. Mike was a mess. His father was dressed in a work uniform. He thanked me for bailing Mike out the previous night. He never offered to repay me but I guessed he just didn't have the money.

From there we had to meet with a Department of Juvenile Justice Officer. He was a large, intimidating man with cold eyes. He wasn't going to put up with any juvenile's shit. Now I was scared. Was this guy going to recommend juvenile hall for Luca? I had to make sure that didn't happen.

I told the officer Luca was a good kid and attended school regularly. He had good grades and never got into any trouble. He would be my responsibility. Of course I didn't mention trying to steal my car, running away, or mental institutions.

The officer ordered a CHINS (child in need of services) warrant. This meant if Luca got into any trouble, he would be arrested and put into juvenile custody. My heart sped up. I couldn't believe this was happening. I knew juvenile custody would kill my son. We left his office and headed for the courtroom in search of our appointed attorney. I was wide awake yet walking through a nightmare.

Then I saw Jane, Luca's co-defendant. I couldn't believe this is what Luca had been hanging out with. She was dressed in torn fishnet stockings, high black boots, a short black skirt, and a long sleeve black blouse with holes. Her white face makeup, black eyeliner, black lipstick and black nails would frighten anyone.

We met with our Suffolk Law School intern. She asked very few questions, not seeming to care for answers. She explained how the arresting officer would give his testimony and the judge would decide whether to dismiss the charges or have it go to trial. We wouldn't even be given a chance to speak. When she said Jane and Luca would go before the judge together I knew we were in trouble.

I sat dumbfounded as the arresting officer gave his testimony. This was clearly not my child he was speaking about. How could he sit there and say this bullshit and have the judge believe him? Why couldn't Luca testify? Why was this all one sided? What about Luca's bruised cheek, the cut on his lip or his torn clothes? Didn't any of this matter?

The officer wasn't harmed in any way. Why couldn't the judge see he was lying?

The judge ordered Luca and Jane to stay out of trouble for three months. The charges against him could carry a three year minimum detention.

We were dismissed but I couldn't find my legs. I couldn't find my mind. The attorney helped me to my feet, but I had to sit back down.

"Don't worry," she said.

Yeah right! Don't worry. This wasn't over. Maybe she had heard these stories too many times to care. Luca was in real trouble and I knew it.

"This was just preliminary," she continued. "The judge had to give you the worse scenario. Luca has never been in trouble with the law. I'll try to get the charges of attacking with a broken bottle dismissed. They can't prove it. The charges of not paying the subway fare will be dropped."

Why didn't I believe her?

We drove directly to Luca's pediatrician's office to document Luca's bruises. Luca was a lot worse off than I thought. He had been complaining of a headache. But wouldn't anyone who's head hit the ground with such force? I'd never given a concussion a thought. His back and neck were killing him. He would have to see a physical therapist and chiropractor.

Luca and I went to his first chiropractor visit together. No wonder he was in so much pain Luca's hip was out of alignment along with pinched nerves in his back. The damage done by the MBTA Police would take months of painful therapy.

April 20th

By Luca

Harmony and I dated another three months. We had a lot of amazing times together, fun, romantic and sweet. We also had a lot of fights. In the end the only times we weren't fighting was during sex, and even then we fought a few time. Mostly we'd just argue and yell at each other but if she hit me I had a hard time not hitting back. Once she grabbed my hair and started bashing my head off her bedroom wall so I grabbed her by the throat and lifted her up until her face went from red to purplish and I dropped her on the floor. Brian was there at the time and I think his yelling is what made me let her go. Oddly that incident isn't what broke us up. I broke up with her a few weeks after that.

I never imagined I'd be capable of treating someone the way I treated Harmony. I thought I'd be so grateful to have an attractive, hetero girlfriend who accepted me only half transitioned, that I'd treat her like a princess until the end of days. But that wasn't the case. Part of me was punishing her for not being Michelle. Part of me wanted to love Harmony the way she loved me, but I just didn't feel that deep connection to her. I'd blame her for that too. Being with her and being mad all the time or always caught up in drama was changing me into someone I feared. I blamed Harmony for that as well. Finally I couldn't take hating myself for hating her and I broke it off for good. It was hard because I'd never had to break up with someone before. It's an awkward and nauseating experience. It didn't matter how mad I was at her, in the end I just felt guilty for breaking her heart and making her cry.

Around the time I was breaking up with Harmony I'd hooked up with a girl named Jane. We met through mutual acquaintances from the mental hospital. I'd heard Jane had been picked up from living on the streets and prostituting herself to feed her heroin addiction at the age of thirteen. She never denied any of these rumors.

Now, almost fifteen, and recently released from an addiction recovery group home, she was living with her parents in Brookline. Jane had over a dozen tattoos, pierced tongue and pierced clitoris hood. Her hair was a nest of dreadlocks dyed black, her face was caked in white foundation and black eyeliner and she was clad from throat to toes in torn black fishnet. She'd had boyfriends and girlfriends and was rumored to have had sex with both at the same time, participating in threesomes and foursomes. I was fascinated by her.

Brian didn't care for Jane at all. I thought it was funny that although she had an allowance she panhandled on Newbury Street, asking people for dollars and cigarettes. Brian thought it was embarrassing. She definitely wasn't classy but I thought being with her was fun. Her friends liked to hang out on park benches all day doing drugs or paying hobos to buy alcohol so they could get drunk. I thought they were nice. Brian thought they were losers. After spending a few Saturdays with these goth-burnouts Brian had had enough. I hadn't.

Jane had made out with me a few times and liked to sit in my lap when we were together. She'd lean her head back against my chest or nuzzle my neck and my heart would thunder like a freight train, the world narrowing down to her cool skin and the smell of patchouli in her hair. Every guy wanted to be with her and they'd stare longingly as Jane twirled my hair in her fingers. I didn't care that all anyone did was get high and loaf around in public. All that mattered was Jane's narrow body against mine.

I was still on the drug free wagon and passed up every joint and pill that was offered to me by Jane and her friends. On April 20th, I broke down and went in on some alcohol to celebrate the holiday. It was a Tuesday, but that week of April is school vacation week in Massachusetts. I caught the train into Boston and set to getting buzzed and flipping off tourists with my new friends.

None of us really got drunk that day. Six people shared a couple packs of beer and wine coolers and a cheese pizza in the park for a few hours. It was a beautiful lazy sunny day and none of us had a care in the world. After lunch Jane and I decided to go back to her house. Our friend Mike was heading the same way so the three of us walked to the Hynes Convention Center T stop together.

By now we were all sober but I still had two cans of beer in my backpack. Jane led the way downstairs and I followed. Mike brought up the rear. At the turnstiles we parted briefly. Mike went to use his train pass to get through. Being out of money, Jane and I planned to pull the turnstile bars back halfway, then sneak through. We didn't get five paces past the turnstiles before two transportation police stepped out and whistled at us.

One of the transit cops was huge; six feet four at least and over 220 solid pounds. The other was a short black woman with a kind face and curly hair. They motioned for Jane and me to come over to them. We walked over grudgingly. We both knew we'd been seen fare skipping. I was nervous about being in trouble, but not scared. It wasn't that bad a thing to get busted for. I thought the worst part would be explaining it to Mom later.

The big guy pulled out a notebook and pen and asked us for our names, ages and addresses. I told him my information but Jane gave a fake name and said she was homeless. The cop didn't believe her and started to seem agitated. Mike walked over at this point to see what was keeping Jane and me. The cop asked Mike for his name and address as well. Mike protested that he hadn't done anything.

"You're all fare skippers," the cop barked at Mike. Jane and I said he wasn't with us and Mike pulled out his monthly T pass to show the cop, but it was no good. Then we heard the lady in the token booth yelling that Mike had showed her his pass and that he'd paid the fare. The cop told the woman in the token booth this didn't concern her. That's when I started to become afraid. Whatever was happening wasn't making sense.

The cops had been circling us during the conversation and now our backs were to the wall with them in front of us. The male officer had been doing all the talking; the woman stayed by his side and followed his lead but looked uncomfortable.

The male officer stared hard at each of us in turn before saying, "Let's stop kidding around here. I know you have drugs on you. Just hand over whatever you have and you can go. Make this easy."

I was completely taken aback by this statement. I was glad I'd stopped doing drugs and I knew that Mike was drug free as well. Jane did all kinds of drugs but I was fairly certain she didn't have anything on her at that moment. My brain raced to the two cans of light beer in my backpack and I worried a little more but reason told me having alcohol underage wouldn't be as bad as drugs. If he searched me I might have to go to court and attend AA again or do some community service, but that was it. Kids drink underage all the time and I'd never been in legal trouble before.

Then Jane started crying. She reached for me and I put my arm across her shoulders.

"Step away from him!" The cop bellowed.

I let her go and Jane backed up.

"What did you just try to sneak in his pocket?!"

Jane hadn't put anything in my pocket. I started to say as much but the words caught in my throat when I noticed the female officer was no longer looking at us. She was looking nervously over her shoulder at the token booth attendant and the commuters filing past.

Why won't she look at us? I thought.

Then the male cop slammed into me. It felt like being hit by a car. He'd tackled me from the side and crushed me against the brick floor My body spasmned in pain and confusion. I guess the cop took this for struggling and kneeled on my back, wrenching my arm up behind me. He had me pinned face down. My lip and forehead split open from the pressure. I tried to turn my head, blood flowing into my mouth and left eye. The cop readjust his weight so his knee was on my neck. Black spots appeared in my vision. I could hear Jane screaming but it sounded far away. As the oxygen left my brain my fear and pain seemed to seep away, and then the blackness swallowed me as I was choked out of consciousness.

I came to choking, my lungs trying to suck in big gulps of air, my throat burning and tightening involuntarily. I drew in a few shaky breaths and drooled blood onto the cold urine-reeking bricks beneath me. I was still face down on the floor but now my hands were cuffed behind my back. When my vision cleared and my ears stopped ringing, tentatively, I turned my head, wincing at the deep throb in my neck, and peered through my hair at the chaos around me. Jane was sobbing, crumpled into a heap against the wall, thin streams of blood running from her mouth and down her chin and neck. My backpack and Jane's purse were lying empty on the floor, their contents scattered and broken. I could hear Mike screaming but he was behind me and I couldn't see him. "I didn't do anything!" he yelled over and over again hysterically.

The futility of it made me want to cry. I didn't know how much time had passed while I was unconscious. It couldn't have been much, but the devastation around me made me uncertain. Surely things couldn't have fallen to shit in less than a minute or two?

Other transit police were on the scene. They smiled big and congratulated one another, even patted each other on the back for such a good bust. They had my two cans of beer and two sandwich baggies from Mike's backpack that contained sea salt and herbs. Mike was a Pagan and although I thought it was silly, he was very serious about it. I knew he always had candles and herbs in his bag. The cops must have thought they were drugs.

After what felt like an eternity gone in the blink of an eye, I was hauled to my feet. We were being ushered out and a nameless cop had his hand between my shoulders, giving me periodic hard shoves. Mike was ahead of me and at the exit turnstiles he made his final stand by refusing to go through them until someone told him what he was being charged with. Two cops grabbed him by the back of his pants and tossed him up and over the turnstile bar. Mike's hands were cuffed behind his back and he fell head first onto the stone floor.

A muffled gurgling scream came from behind me. I looked over my shoulder at Jane whose eyes were wide with terror but her bleeding mouth was still clamped shut. I noticed her lips were swollen and the side of her jaw seemed to be growing darker by the second. The cops who'd dumped Mike now yanked him to his feet. Dazed, they dragged him up the stairs. Fear swept over me and clouded out my sanity.

Outside there were four transit police cars and even more transit cops milling around. I couldn't believe the enormity of the authority display they'd laid out for us. It seemed ridiculous. Rationality chased back some of my fear and as a cop was going through my pockets; discarding my lighter, train schedule and the photographs in my wallet into the street.

I piped up, "Aren't you supposed to read me my rights?"

"Ha. You watch too much fuckin T.V." was the only response I got.

Anger flared. It helped me keep a brave face when they threw me into the back of a car with Mike.

My hands had gone from painful to numb. The cuffs had long ago cut off circulation and when I tried to wiggle my fingers I couldn't tell if they moved or not. I tried to lean forward and not crush them behind me, but the driver slammed down the gas and brake pedals at every opportunity, bouncing Mike and me around.

Mike wasn't talking. His eyes were fluttering open and closed but when they were open he didn't seem to see anything. The cops up front kept asking us if we were in a trench coat mafia. I had no idea what he was talking about so I kept quiet. When he started calling us "fucking Satanists" I guessed he was mad because Mike, Jane and I had all been dressed in black with black bags and dyed black hair. I'd been dressing all in black for a few years because the look was slimming and I was sensitive about my appearance.

When it became fashionable for goth and metal heads to dress in black I was grateful to no longer stand out because of my clothes. Now our uniformity was biting me in the ass.

At the station, Mike and I were herded into the drunk tank. I still tried to be brave. The cops undid our handcuffs and I momentarily felt better until they spoke.

"Take off your shoes and your pants."

"Wha..what?" I stammered, incredulous.

"Take off your shoes and your pants!" The cop screamed in my face.

"My... my pants?"

He made a grab for me and I hopped back.

"I can do it!" I said, my voice so high with terror it cracked.

I looked over at Mike. He had slumped down on a concrete slab bench and a cop had torn off his sneakers and begun pulling down his jeans. I slid out of my sneakers and fumbled at my belt buckle, my purple fingers searing with the pain of recirculation.

I hadn't been packing that day because I was wearing boxers. Now down to socks, underwear and a t-shirt in a room full of strangers I was glad my shirt was extra long. Mike and I were handcuffed to the concrete bench, our ankles were shackled. The cops exited the room and we were left defenseless in a freezing room with two drunk, homeless men who stank of beer, piss and B.O.. I'd never been so panicked in all my life. I could feel my sanity shrinking under the crushing terror. The other men in the tank were asleep, snoring loudly. I was so afraid they'd wake up and see Mike and I were helpless prey. It took all my willpower to keep from crying.

Mike stirred and groaned a little, and then he sat up straight and looked around as if seeing the room for the first time.

"Hey man, are you alright?" I whispered.

When he turned and looked at me, I could see the blood soaked in his dark hair and shirt. My stomach did a flip flop.

"My head is killing me. Fucking pigs. Where's Jane?"

"I don't know. I haven't seen her since they put us in the car.

They must keep the girls somewhere else."

"Maybe they took her to a hospital. Back at the train station when you were on the ground and stopped moving, Jane started screaming.

"The big cop was kicking you in the back over and over and when you didn't move Jane and I thought you were dead. She wouldn't stop screaming so that fucker punched her WHAM right in the face. I heard something crack. It might have been her jaw, I don't know."

"Jesus Christ!"

"They say what they're charging us with?"

"No. They wouldn't say anything to me. But they think the stuff in your bag was drugs."

"Ha! They're going to be disappointed when they test it. Don't worry man they don't have anything on us."

I did worry though. It felt like we were left there for hours, but with no clock or natural light, I couldn't tell. My watch had been taken from me but it didn't matter, they'd smashed it first. I thought about the big deal they were making over skipping train fare and two beers. I didn't imagine planting drugs on us when they discovered Mike's were harmless herbs was a big stretch. Why weren't they talking to us? Why weren't our parents here? Why did they take our pants and restrain us when the other men in here were fully clothed and unrestrained? I pondered this while watching bruises bloom on my wrists and arms.

Two officers undid our restraints and threw our pants at us. I couldn't believe my good fortune to get my pants back without being outed as trans. They were moving us to cells. I debated outing myself out of fear of being placed with ambulatory adult male criminals. I didn't know if they'd put me in with the women or by myself but I was pretty certain that if I went in with men I'd get hurt or bust a kidney holding my pee. I decided I was more afraid of these transit police than I was of other prisoners and wisely kept my mouth shut, accepting my fate.

Since Mike was seventeen, he was being put in an adult cell. I was sixteen so they brought me to my own juvenile cell. I almost got down on my knees to thank God I was alone; alone meant safe for now.

The cell had solid, windowless, concrete walls, concrete floor, and a metal door. You couldn't lay down in any direction without curling up. There was no toilet; only a rusty drain in the floor. I hadn't had anything to eat or drink in hours and I was never offered access to a toilet. I curled up in the back of the cell hugging my knees to my chest and concentrated on my breathing and my pulse, trying to keep insanity at bay. I could hear muffled crying coming from the cell next to me and thought it might be Jane but I was too afraid to call out to her.

The black police woman came to get me and bring me to booking. She still wouldn't look at me. I told her I needed to urinate and she told my feet there was nothing she could do. I wanted my mom.

In booking they photographed me and took my fingerprints, all the while asking me if I was a faggot or if I was banging the little whore with dreadlocks that came in with me. When I wouldn't rise to the bait, they suggested Mike and I were both faggots and that we blew each other while Jane watched. I'd never been called a faggot. Before transitioning, people would call me a dyke or lesbo. I thought being called a fag would be more dignifying because at least it was gender appropriate, but it wasn't.

After the photos and fingerprints I was brought to the lieutenant for information gathering. I thought I'd be questioned about what happened or how I was doing but all he wanted was my name, address and phone number.

"Can I call my mom?"

"No. We'll call her."

"When?"

"After you give me your information."

"I already told all this stuff to the other officer."

"Hey, if you don't want to co-operate I can take my dinner break and we can come back to this in a few hours. But no one's calling your parents until I get your name and address."

My throat burned, my lips were crusted with blood and my head was swimming from pain and terror. It hurt to talk. It hurt to concentrate.

"Hey kid," another officer who had been at the scene whispered to me with a smirk on his face, "You hear about that guy in Nebraska last week who was corn-holed with a plunger by cops? He wasn't very cooperative either."

A handful of officers laughed at this. The lieutenant grinned. I shrunk into my seat. The bastard who was taunting me pointed at a broom in the corner.

"You can pick splinters out of your ass all night or you can tell this man what he wants to hear and go home."

It was so surreal. They already had all my information. I knew that. It wasn't about my name and address, it was about them getting what they wanted. I made swallowing motions to try and work up enough spit to talk above a whisper.

"Luca Harvie. L U.."

"Speak up boy! I can't hear you!"

I sat up straight and spoke as loud as I could without choking. A couple cops were laughing. I got the impression somehow I was the joke. When I was done I asked if he'd call my mom.

"I'll call after I eat my dinner."

The black officer was there to take me back to my cell. She nudged my elbow and I stood up.

"Hey," The lieutenant snorted; "I just did you a favor son. Now what do you say?"

I swallowed hard. "Thank you," I said to the floor.

"Thank you what?"

What? What does he want from me? "Thank you Sir."

He nodded and motioned for me to be led out. The other officers burst into laughter. As I was being taken back to my cell I saw Jane's parents in the lobby. If it was her in the cell next to mine she'd be gone soon and safe from these assholes.

I felt much safer back in my empty cell. I saw a clock while I was being questioned and it was after nine pm. I'd been in custody almost seven hours. I was starting to think I'd be here over-night. The crying from the cell next door had stopped so I guessed Jane was gone. Mike had to be bailed out and didn't have the twenty-five dollars on him. I knew he'd use his phone call to call his dad and wondered if he was out yet. Was I the last one here?

At 11pm the black officer and the officer who had threatened to anally rape me with a broom came into my cell and tossed my sneakers at me. I didn't want to go with him but he said he was taking me to my parents. Exhausted, I summoned all my courage and got to my feet.

When the door to the lobby was in sight a desperate mania born of fear and relief swept over me. The end was in sight. Once I was through those doors they wouldn't be able to threaten me or call me names, I'd be safe in my parent's presence. But what about Mike?

"Is my friend still here?" I asked the black police woman.

Finally she spoke to me. "He's still here. If no one brings him bail he's going to spend the night."

Oh God! Mike needs a doctor! He can't stay the night! What if the police attack him again? What if he gets an infection? Oh God, oh God, oh God.

The anal rape officer opened the door to the lobby and I burst through at full speed.

"Mom!" I practically ran into her. "Mom! You have to bail out Mike! He can't stay here! It's not safe! Mom you need to do something. You need to help him!"

I was hysterically pleading and almost clawing at her when a hand flew at my face and slapped me so hard it spun me half around. That's when I saw my father and my aunt. I hadn't even noticed they were there.

"You ungrateful little shit! Do you know what you've put your mother through having to come down here? The first thing out of your mouth should be thank you! How dare you make demands of her to help your criminal friends right now!" My aunt shouted in my face.

I stepped back, hurt and confused. Obviously the three of them were pissed at me. I had no idea what the police had told them but I surmised it didn't paint a pretty picture of me or my friends. I had to make them understand that leaving Mike behind wasn't an option. I took a deep breath and tried to choose my words carefully. Out of habit I reached up to push my hair out of my face and behind my ear. That's when they saw my face. My aunt gasped and stepped back, the fight going out of her eyes.

"I'm sorry," she mumbled; "I didn't know."

Her slap had started my lip bleeding again. My mother's eyes widened and even Dad looked concerned. I must have really looked like shit.

"They're torturing us. Please, you can yell at me and punish me, I don't care. I won't fight back. But you have to get him out. He's hurt and it's not safe."

Reluctantly Mom withdrew the cash from the lobby ATM and bailed out Mike. My aunt had driven my parents to Roxbury to come get me. She gave Mike a ride to a train station so he could get home. Mike was acting kind of stupid and not like himself at all. He didn't say thank you for the bail or the ride. Mom thought he was ungrateful and rude. I thought he was delirious.

After Mike was gone from the car my aunt let in on me again. I was just glad she was driving and couldn't reach behind to slap me.

Earlier in the day while my friends and I had been out acting like carefree jackasses two teenage boys in Columbine, Colorado who dressed all in black and listened to heavy metal music, had gone into their school and opened fire on their fellow students. It was being called the Columbine Massacre. And while the nation had been shocked and mourning, my friends and I had been completely unaware. It was the most publicized tragedy since the Oklahoma City Bombings and every adult in the car thought I was mocking it by being dressed all in black and associating with goth metal heads.

"We didn't know..." was all I could stammer out in response to the heavy news. It was scary to think a couple of kids had gone so fucking nuts and needlessly destroyed so many lives.

Then again it wasn't that long ago that I fantasized about doing the same thing. I'd dreamed about going to my local middle-school cafeteria at lunch time with a gun and shooting my bullies in cold blood. I'd written short stories about it and smiled when I imagined their parents balling their eyes out over the corpses of the demonic bastards they'd unleashed to torment me. You can only push people so far before they decide to push back. I was just grateful to have been saved from the utter hell of public school and the evil allowed to breed there. I was lucky I'd gotten out before murder had been the only way to protect myself.

The Arraignment

I was due in court at nine am the following morning for arraignment. By the time I'd stripped off my grimy clothes and showered, I barely got five hours of sleep. When I'd looked at my reflection in the mirror before going to bed I'd noticed my pupils were two different sizes. That couldn't have been good but I was too exhausted to care.

Mom had to take the day off from work to escort me to the Boston courthouse. We caught a train from Malden a little after seven am. There wasn't time for breakfast, but who could eat under these circumstances?

The only button-up dress shirt I had was long sleeved. It was hot that day and the wrist cuffs kept chafing my bruises. My body was one itchy ache shambling into the courthouse.

The courthouse scared me more than the police station had. The events that had taken place at the police station had been so unexpected and surreal they were like a graphic nightmare. In the light of day the court and what it represented was far more real and terrifying. It was like a day-mare I couldn't wake up from.

The sudden anxiety either temporarily broke my sanity or jolted leftover LSD up my spinal column and into my brain. As we crossed the interior entryway I started hallucinating, seeing flashes of light and pools of dark fluid swirling across the floor. I tried to chase the hallucinations away and stay in the here and now. It was important that I have my wits and a clear understanding of my surroundings but I was too exhausted and frightened to focus. I could feel sweat breaking out on my back and sucking my shirt to my skin. Suddenly my necktie felt like a noose.

We were directed upstairs and on the ride up my whole body quaked with cold sweat shivers. I had to grind my teeth to keep them from chattering. Mom and I turned a corner toward the juvenile family courts and bumped into Mike. Seeing him snapped me back into myself. He hadn't been to bed yet and was still wearing the clothes he had on from last night. By the time he'd reached a hospital it was too late for stitches. It took seven staples to close the gash on his head. He was badly concussed and the E.R. doctors had wanted to admit him for observation but he was afraid of missing his court time. The drug possession charges hadn't stuck because his drugs had just been herbs, but they were charging him with assault and resisting arrest. I wished him luck on his way to adult court.

I never saw Mike again.

I couldn't believe he had been charged with assault. At no point had any of us raised a hand in our own defense. Maybe he had taken a swing at a cop after we'd been separated. I doubted it though.

Jane was in the halls of the family courts with her dad. She was dressed in the same clothes she'd been wearing the day before as well. Since this was the only outfit I'd ever seen her in I couldn't tell if it was because she hadn't had a chance to change or if she just didn't give a shit. I wanted to ask her but she wasn't up for talking. The punch from the big transit cop had loosened most of her front teeth and dislocated her jaw. I wasn't anxious to stand before a judge with a co-defendant who dressed like a junkie prostitute, but I wasn't anxious to stand up there alone either.

Before meeting my court appointed attorney I met with a Department of Juvenile Justice (DJJ) officer. He interviewed me to determine if it was safe for me to go home with Mom and await my trial should a petition of delinquency be brought up against me, or if I was a runaway risk who would need to be monitored or detained until the trial date. This guy was the scariest motherfucker I'd encountered yet. He didn't look at me like I was a criminal; he looked through me as if I weren't a real person. His black eyes were as pitiless as a shark's. Mom was in the room and she told him about my good grades at school and that I was good at home. I think she saved my bacon because I was too scared to speak. Detention for a trans person is a death sentence. Knowing that was a possibility curdled my blood and dried up my voice.

The DJJ officer was finally swayed that I didn't need to be detained but he was confident a petition of delinquency would go through against me and that there'd be a trial down the road. To make sure I was present for that trial he drew up papers for a Child in Need of Services (CHINS) warrant. This meant if I ran away, stayed out past curfew, skipped school, failed a drug test or even failed any classes at school between now and my court date, I'd be picked up on the warrant and detained under custody of Family Services. This was some scary bullshit.

I met my court-appointed attorney minutes before being called in, which was hours after I'd arrived. She wasn't very interested in my side of the tale or my many cuts and bruises. She wasn't interested in whether I was innocent or guilty. Judging by her demeanor I assumed she thought I was a good-for-nothing piece of trash who was probably guilty. Maybe she was just over-worked.

She explained that at an arraignment all that happens was the petition was read aloud along with the arresting officer's testimony of events. The judge will then decide whether to dismiss the petition or proceed to trial. There is no jury in family court. The bad news was I wouldn't be judged by my peers. The good news is whether this went to trial or not I'd most likely be going home with Mom today.

I was called into court at the same time as Jane. We stood side by side as the colossal transit cop who'd beaten us to pulp the previous night sat in a chair by the judge and calmly read his report of the arrest. It started out normal enough; Jane and I skipped the fare and he approached us. When he got to asking us for our personal information he claimed Jane leaned into me and passed a beer bottle from her purse to my hands which I then broke against a wall and attacked him with. He claimed to have wrestled the beer bottle from my hands and then sustained multiple blows to his face from my fists before he gently restrained me. While he was restraining me Jane and Mike attacked his partner as she called for backup. Two other officers arrived on scene and the three of us were taken into custody and transported separately. Upon arrival at the station, Jane's and my parents were called and after booking we were promptly released into their care. The broken bottle was lost in the scuffle but two beer cans were recovered from my possession.

It was incredible. He sat up there cool as a cucumber and lied his ass off. I wondered why the judge didn't notice the transit cop didn't have a scratch on him, yet Jane and I were covered in scabs and bruises and her jaw was swollen. Why wasn't anyone asking about the six hour gap from when we reached the station to when our parents were called? Why didn't my attorney ask why I was denied medical attention, food, water or access to a toilet? How was I being charged with assault of a police officer with a deadly weapon when the weapon was nowhere to be seen? What the fuck? I didn't know whether to laugh or scream. Obviously, this was all a big joke; so why was everyone acting so seriously?

I was allowed to enter a plea of not guilty. I thought that with the complete lack of evidence or witnesses to the assault the judge would dismiss the petition. Nope. Jane and I would be back for a trial in June. Assault with a deadly weapon is a serious, violent felony. I'd be facing three years minimum. Given that I was sixteen, some of those years could be served in an adult penitentiary. Trans people were raped and murdered all the time in prison. Being raped as a kid was bad enough. There was no fucking way I'd allow myself to be raped as an adult. And being beaten to death wasn't my ideal way to die either. If I was found guilty I was going to have to kill myself. There'd be no confusion or attention-garnering half-hearted attempts this time. This was the real deal.

As we left the courthouse to head home, I silently consigned myself to the fact I may only have ten weeks to live. I might never graduate high-school, drive a car, go on a road trip or discover who I really was. The system may decide I need to die before I see seventeen, but doing the deed myself was the only way to preserve my dignity and ensure I die a man. I had ten weeks to experience all I could in life; then I'd tie a belt around my neck in some detention center bathroom and break my mother's heart for good.

From the courthouse in Boston, we went straight to my pediatrician's office. X-rays were ordered of my head and neck. Photographs were taken of the abrasions and bruises on my wrists, forehead, face, back and ribs. The back of my head had been throbbing non-stop and was hideously painful to the touch. The doctor speculated my head was struck against the ground so hard it bruised my skull. I'd definitely been concussed and may have suffered unknown brain damage from being choked out of consciousness. Referrals were written up for physical therapy and chiropractic services for my neck and back.

I saw a chiropractor first because the physical therapist had a wait list. The chiropractor examined my neck and back. My spine was out of alignment and he concluded the arresting officer had repeatedly kicked me so hard they'd rotated my right hip bone forward. This injury was straining the hell out of my back muscles and causing me to limp, because my right foot now hung over and inch lower than my left. I had pinched nerves in my lower back from this injury too. It felt like I was being electrocuted and stabbed at the same time. It took months for the inflammation to go down.

The agony I languished in from those injuries was day and night torture. I was constantly being reminded of the ordeal those fake cops had put me through. The sessions with the chiropractor were so painful I'd often faint. Brian had to come along to help Mom get me back in the car.

I had to drop out of all sports programs at school. The back-brace I was prescribed to wear throughout the day had so many magnets in it I couldn't go near computers. The physical therapy wasn't any better.

The stretches I was forced to do made tears squirt out of my eyes, and when I ran out of physical therapy referrals I still couldn't stand up straight or walk without limping.

My plan to live life to its fullest for ten weeks got off to a disappointing start. I was afraid of public transportation now so I never wanted to go anywhere. I couldn't walk long distances or stay on my feet for more than a few minutes. I was single again and all my remaining friends were sick of my down-trodden attitude.

And because my CHINS warrant had gone through I'd been assigned a Department of Mental Health social worker who was very nice but decided that although I was on the honor roll for my good grades I'd have to attend summer school again. Staying in school year round gave me less of a chance to get into trouble. So now even if I beat my trial in June I had summer school to look forward to. I'll admit that when I'd been arrested I had started out the day being up to no good but it seemed to me the punishments surpassed my crimes.

Chapter Thirty-One

Joy Riding

By Betsie

I was furious when I came home from work and Luca wasn't there. He knew the rules of his CHINS warrant. He was to come right home from school. It was after five pm. Before long I found myself speaking with Officer Lewis from the Danvers Police Department.

"We have Luca in custody," he told me.

"Oh my God! What now?"

"I'll tell you everything when you get here."

"It'll take me about twenty minutes. I'm on my way."

What kind of trouble had Luca gotten himself into this time? He still had a few more weeks left on his CHINS warrant. This could be the catalyst to have him put away.

I honestly don't remember driving to the police station. But I do remember the fear I felt about him being "discovered." There was always that nagging fear.

Officer Lewis greeted me.

"Luca and some friends stole a car and had an accident. Then they left the scene."

"Luca wouldn't do that. He doesn't have any friends who would do that."

"Do you know this boy Jason?"

"He's a class-mate. Luca has only said a few things about him. I guess he got his driver's license a few months ago."

"Actually, Mrs. Harvie, Jason doesn't have his license. He took his mother's car without her permission."

"But Luca didn't take the car. He wasn't even driving."

"Doesn't make any difference. He's still an accessory to grand theft auto."

"Is he alright?"

"He's fine. He'll be out in a minute. We don't think he had anything to do with this except being in the wrong place at the wrong time."

Then, to my disbelief the officer said, "Mrs. Harvie, I know this is difficult for you but is there any way you can drive to Lynn and pick up Jason's mother? She can't get here without her car."

"You've got to be kidding! Jason gets my son in all this trouble and you want me to help him get out of here?"

"I guess it is asking a lot."

"I'll go if it's okay with Luca. But Jason's mother has to give me really good driving directions. I don't know Lynn very well."

This wasn't like the time in Roxbury. When Luca came through the doors there were no cuts, scratches or the anxiety he had suffered before. He gave the okay to drive to Lynn and we were on our way. A decision that still gets my blood boiling.

Luca told me everything that happened. It seemed Jason was only bragging about his license. He didn't actually have one. The car he had been driving for weeks wasn't his but his mom's. The police were looking for Brian because Jason had said Brian was driving. There would be a warrant issued for his arrest. When they caught up with him he would be charged as an adult. Brian was seventeen.

"You do realize we now have to go to juvenile court in the morning. They may be able to see you have a previous case against you," I said to Luca. "And what happens when we go back to Boston and they see this?"

"Maybe my counselor, Mary, can help. She thinks Jason has his license and has seen him driving for months."

"I don't know Luca. I just don't know. This scares the hell out of me."

"How do you think I feel? I don't even do this shit and I always get into trouble. Maybe Boston and Salem aren't linked together."

After a few wrong turns I found Jason's house. I got out of the car and looked around. It didn't seem like anyone was home. I banged on the door. No answer.

"I think there's a grocery store down the street. Let's go call the house," I said to Luca as we got back into the car.

I drove a few miles down the road to a pay phone and called Jason's house. No answer.

Now I had to drive all the way back to the Danvers Police Station to let them know I wasn't able to get in touch with Jason's mom.

"Mrs. Harvie, we appreciate you going out of your way to get Jason's mom. I guess she decided not to wait for you and asked a neighbor to drive her. Jason has already been released."

I was beyond angry. Scared to death and angry.

Once again, Luca, Brooks and I headed for Juvenile Court and the fear of an unfair system. Would the judge realize Luca had nothing to do with this? Or would he see a prior outstanding record and send him away?

We found our way through the busy hallways and took a seat. And then a ray of hope walked in. Luca's school therapist came to lend her support. If necessary she would testify how everyone at school thought Jason had his license. How even the teachers thought the car was his.

Then Jason and his mother walked in. Jesus Christ! She was dressed in a very tight, short, leather skirt, and there wasn't much of a bra under her sheer white blouse. Plastic white boots completed her ensemble. Her teased hair stood high atop her head, and her large hoop earrings looked like they would hurt.

Jason's mom stopped to apologize to me for not waiting the previous night. I crossed my arms and looked away, keeping my mouth shut in fear of starting a fight. This was my child's life we were here for. I could still hear "I'm sorry," as she reached the end of the hallway.

I kept getting up, trying to shake off my nerves. But they wouldn't go away. We were assigned another attorney. She listened intently to Luca's side of the story. Even with a prior unresolved record she felt things would be alright. Just having Luca's therapist there would pull a lot of weight. We would be called next.

The judge listened. Actually listened. He could see Luca was clearly not at fault and was impressed with the amount of support Luca had. Not just by family but by the staff at New Horizons High School.

There was still the issue of the CHINS warrant. Luca had clearly violated the stipulations of that warrant. Now we had to see a family court judge who would make the decision whether or not Luca would be released. In situations like this you can never see the light. Darkness floods your brain. The worst case scenario always plays out in your mind. Fear never left my side as we waited those three hours.

The judge was very quick in his decision to let Luca be released. However, the incident would be reported to the juvenile system in Boston. Shit!

Joy Riding

By Luca

Toward the end of May when school was winding down and I only had a few weeks left before my trial, I decided to step outside my comfort zone and try to befriend someone with a driver's license so I could get out of the house for a bit. As it happened, a kid named Jason who worked the student-run coffee shop with Brian, had been bragging that he'd gotten his license. He offered to drive over after school and take Brian and me to the mall. Brian was apprehensive but I was dying to go anywhere with anyone. I'd been cooped up too long.

When Jason arrived at my house Brian was agitated and didn't want to go out with us. I talked him into it, though. The mall wasn't far from Brian's house so if he wasn't having fun he could walk home.

Jason took us for a little joyriding first. He definitely wanted to show off his new car. I didn't think he was that bad of a driver. It was obvious he was new but he went the speed limit and used his turn signals. I felt safe enough. And then near the mall we came to a halt behind a Jetta at a stop sign for a busy street. There was a large break in traffic and the Jetta sped up, but suddenly came to a complete stop mid-intersection. Jason hadn't noticed the Jetta had stopped though; he'd seen them go and had his eye on oncoming traffic. Since no cars were coming he gunned it and plowed into the back of the Jetta.

The passengers in the Jetta got out. The four men were probably ten years older than us and way bigger. Their eyes were all bloodshot and I could hear the empties rattling around when they exited the car. The driver looked really pissed. Jason backed up and shouted out the window that he was just moving his car out of the way of traffic; then to Brian's and my surprise Jason sped up and took off down the street.

We had no idea where he was taking us. Brian was screaming from the backseat that this was stupid and we were fucked. Jason was laughing at the guys we'd left back at the intersection. I was worried those guys would catch up with us.

At the end of the street Jason pulled into a retirement village and parked the car. Brian and I bolted out and told Jason he should just drive home. He lived two cities over and probably wouldn't be found there. To my confusion, Jason got out of the car too and started to follow me and Brian. He seemed to think he could just walk away and come back for the car later. This was the dumbest thing I'd ever heard but we couldn't seem to shake him. He was probably scared and didn't want to be alone. I was afraid if we went to Brian's house the other guys or the cops would follow us there so I told him to go on alone. He'd been in the backseat and it was unlikely anyone would recognize him. I figured letting him go was the least I could do since I'd gotten him into this mess.

Jason and I headed to the mall. I thought with enough people there we could get lost in the crowd and wait it out until Mom got out of work and I could call her for a ride. On the way, Jason decided maybe it would be smarter for him to just go home but he'd only go if I went with him. Fine. Mom could pick me up at this house later instead of the mall. We doubled back to his car but before we were even in view of it two of the guys from the Jetta jumped out of the trees behind us. They'd parked their car behind Jason's, blocking him in. We were ushered back to the

cars. Afraid I was about to get the shit kicked out of me I said that I'd been in the passenger seat and Jason had been in the back seat; the driver had pulled over and ditched the car and we didn't know where he was. The four guys were so wasted they'd believed my story. I couldn't believe they didn't recognize Jason. But the driver of the Jetta was determined to wait by the car until the owner came back and insisted we wait with him. Just when I thought this charade couldn't possibly go on any longer and that someone would sober up, recognize Jason, and kick both our asses, a police cruiser pulled up behind the Jetta.

Some old folks in the retirement village were scared of the boys in the parking lot who looked like hooligans and had called the cops. I was both relieved and disappointed when the police showed up. I figured it was better to be arrested than be stomped on by the guys in the Jetta, but I was utterly disappointed in myself and disheartened to be arrested for the second time in a few weeks. I knew I hadn't done anything wrong and I wasn't a bad kid, but the circumstances I seemed to keep landing in painted a different picture.

I wasn't surprised when the handcuffs went on. The officer had been firm but polite so I co-operated easily and quietly. I was surprised however, when the drunken pot heads from the Jetta were allowed to drive off after giving brief, jumbled statements, empties still clinking and rattling as they sped away.

Jason was cuffed and put in back of the cruiser with me. He was relieved to have avoided having his ass handed to him by the pissed off guys from the Jetta as well. He was even grinning. I thought he was lucky but he was also a fucking idiot to be smiling at a time like this and I must be a moron for being here with him.

The staff at my high-school knew I was trans. Brian knew along with one other student we were friends with. None of the other students knew, including Jason, and I wanted it to stay that way. At the police station we'd been separated and that suited me just fine. We were both being held for accessory to a hit and run and I didn't know what was going to happen. But if any of my past came up during questioning I wanted Jason far away from me.

During questioning I stuck to my story that Jason had been in the backseat and I'd been in the passenger seat, because I didn't want to be a snitch. But I also didn't know what else to say. The two officers interviewing me had been courteous but since I wouldn't give up the name of the driver I was shown to a cell.

I sat for a while with my feet curled up under me on a metal bench in a concrete cell wishing I didn't have to pee. Eventually Jason was brought in to share my cell. He was giving the same story I was so everything was at a standstill. Jason still thought this was funny and really believed he was going to get away with it. I couldn't believe I was trapped with such a fucknut. Of course he wasn't getting away with it! All they had to do was open the car and look at the registration! God, how could he be so stupid?!

At five pm we were brought McDonalds happy meals for dinner. I thought maybe this was a jab at how childish Jason and I were acting by sticking to our stories which were obviously lies. I ate my food in contemptuous silence. The only sound in the room was Jason chewing with his mouth open. Suddenly everything he did and everything about him was driving me crazy. This was ridiculous! I wanted to go home. The cops would figure it out sooner or later. Why wouldn't Jason just confess so we could get out of here?

After our meal Jason was taken out again for more questioning. He seemed to match the description of the driver given by all four witnesses and the car was registered to Jason's mother. Finally! They have him by the balls! I should be out of here any time now.

Nope. Jason came back to the cell grinning wider than ever.

"So are we out of here or what?" I asked.

"Almost. They saw the car is registered to my mom but I told them Brian was driving. That should get us out of here soon."

"What?!"

"Come on! He ditched us! It's not fair for us to take all the heat."

"No, it's not fair for Brian to take any of it! He didn't do anything!

You're the fuckup who was driving!"

"Hey! Keep it down, man!"

"Jason, I swear to God. When that cop comes back if you don't tell him the truth I'm going to kill you."

"Seriously?"

"Give it up! They caught you! If you push this, Brian and I will just say you were driving anyway."

"Fine. But you're a rat. Punk ass bitch..."

The cop came back to question me again. This time I told the truth.

"Jason was driving! Brian went home because he didn't have anything to do with it. He was sitting in the backseat and he didn't even want to be there. He only came along because I begged him."

"Relax. We know Jason was the driver. Do you think we're stupid?"

"No. I knew you'd put it together once you opened the car."

"So why did you lie?"

"We started lying because those older guys on the scene, the ones whose car we hit, were threatening to beat up the driver. I kept lying because I didn't want to be a snitch, you know? I thought Jason would confess and save me the trouble."

"This Jason guy isn't your friend. Before he gave us Brian's name he told us you were the driver."

"What??"

"Don't worry. You're not even close to the driver description. Plus, the witnesses all put you in the passenger seat. We knew he was lying. We just let him because we thought eventually he'd drop the name of the third person in the car. And he did."

"Yeah but I told you Brian wasn't driving. He was the one who told Jason to go back when he was trying to drive away from the accident."

"The accident isn't that big a deal. The problem is that Jason stole the car from his mother, which makes you and Brian accessories to car theft."

"No way! The car is his!"

"Nope. The car is his mother's. She was at work and never gave him permission to take it. She couldn't have anyway because Jason doesn't have a license."

"He does too! He's been bragging about it all over school! He's driven his car to school for months!"

"Did you ask to see his license?"

"Well no, but do you ask to see your friends' licenses or do you just take them at their word?"

"Ok. So you didn't know that all he had was a permit and you didn't know he took the car without asking?"

"No. I swear I thought he had a driver's license and I thought the car was his. Ask my teachers at school. They've seen him driving it."

"Well we'll still need to talk to this Brian kid just to make sure his statement matches yours."

The next day Mom had to take me to the arraignment hearing in Salem. It was closer than Boston so we'd gotten to sleep-in a little. The added sleep had not improved Mom's mood. She was pissed but at least she wasn't pissed at me. The cops at the station had explained to her that Jason had lied non-stop since being taken into custody and they felt certain one hundred percent of the blame was on him. I was grateful to have an authority figure take my side for once.

Jason and I were arraigned separately. This worked for me because every time I looked at him all I saw was red. If I was forced to stand beside him I might throw a punch, courtroom be damned!

Since my principal, Kendal Tanner, and two other teachers called the police station and swore Jason had driven to school and been bragging about getting his license, the accessory charges against me were dropped. However, since being arrested had violated my CHINS warrant I had to go to family court and plead with a judge to let me stay home and not in a detention center. I was facing steeper punishment than Jason and he'd been the one driving!

It took three hours to get in to see the judge who spent three minutes hearing the police testify that Jason had deceived me. I hadn't been too worried about the outcome because so many adults had been on my side. The judge agreed to let me go home but warned me that this incident had to be forwarded to my DJJ officer in Boston. Crap.

After being threatened with a warrant, Brian went down to the station that afternoon with his grandmother and father to give a statement. His statement had matched mine and his grandmother had given the police an earful. Brian's charges were dropped too but his grandmother didn't seem happy to see me the next time I came around.

Jason wound up with 120 hours of community service since he was a first time juvenile offender. He stopped working the coffee shop, though, which was probably for the best. Brian and I were so mad at him I don't know what would have happened if the three of us had been confined to close quarters together with many heavy, sharp objects at hand. Half the student body and a fair amount of teachers were pissed at Jason too for getting Brian and me in trouble. But I had to let it go.

Even though Jason had been an idiotic, spineless liar, any retaliation would only get me in deeper trouble with my CHINS warrant and upcoming trial in Boston. I took solace knowing the entire time Jason and I were locked up together he hadn't learned I was trans. Also, Mom and my teachers backed me up and believed I hadn't been the cause of the trouble. Even better, for once it was true. Maybe there was still time for me to grow up a little and be a better person.

Chapter Thirty-Two

Boston Juvenile Court

By Betsie

Brooks, Luca and I arrived early to speak with our public defender, Miss Dunkin. I was armed with what I thought would be our ammunition against the lying officers and the complacent judge. Not only did I have detailed medical reports but I also had photographs of the injuries Luca sustained at the hands of overly aggressive MBTA officers.

Miss Dunkin gave us some half-ass excuse about why my evidence would not be used in court. Then she disappeared, leaving us alone in the hallway for over two hours. When she returned she had a plea offer. If Luca would plead no contest to assaulting the police officer, he would only get probation. The charges would be sealed and would go away after the age of eighteen.

We gave our okay to Miss Dunkin. We accepted the plea bargain. She left to give the information to the prosecutor.

The three of us were standing on the second floor landing, a four-foot tall banister separating us from the twenty foot drop below, when Miss Dunkin appeared.

"Luca," she said. "I'm sorry but the prosecutor has learned of the stolen car in Danvers. He's insisting you serve a minimum of six months in juvenile lockup."

The open landing started closing in on me. Blackness surrounded my vision. I grabbed a hold of the twenty foot column I had been leaning against. I felt dizzy. When I opened my eyes the room slowly shifted to the right. I swallowed hard.

"It's out of our hands," Miss Dunkin was saying. "It will now be up to the judge.'

We were quickly ushered into the courtroom.

The prosecutor presented his side. He made reference to the stolen car incident and said he would like to see Luca serve six months.

Miss Dunkin gave our side. She questioned where the broken beer bottle was. She made reference to the mistreatment of Luca and Jane. She explained how the charges of being an accessory to a stolen car had been dropped.

Then, completely taken by surprise I heard, "Mrs. Harvie, would you please rise and face the court."

Having difficulty standing, I used the bench in front of me to push myself up.

"What kind of school is this New Horizons? It seems Luca has a lot of support from his teachers."

"The school is for kids with emotional problems. Kids who just need a little more help than what public school can give them."

"I have to say, it is nice to see Luca has both parents here," the judge continued.

"Luca has a lot of family support your honor," I answered, not sure if the judge had expected a reply.

"I'm recommending six months of probation. Luca, if I see you back in my court, I promise I will not be so lenient."

Collapsing back into my seat, I bent forward, putting my head between my knees and breathed deeply. I had come too close to losing my son.

I was only given a minute to compose myself before Luca and Brooks helped me to my feet. The courtroom had to be cleared for the next defendant who may or may not be guilty of the charges against him.

Boston Juvenile Court

By Luca

I'd had plenty of time to prepare for my trial but it still seemed to catch me off guard. The day before, my cousin Ellen had cut and dyed my hair so it looked normal. Mom had bought me a short-sleeved blue dress-shirt and a grey tie. She'd even bought me dress shoes which squeaked as much as they shined. I looked clean cut and all American.

But did I look innocent? I didn't think so.

Mom had brought letters written by my principal, guidance counselor and multiple teachers testifying to my upstanding character and moral integrity. The defender took these letters but seemed bewildered as to what she was supposed to do with them. This did not raise my confidence. Where was my defense? Why were there no witnesses or evidence? I had proof from medical doctors that I'd been badly abused while in custody. Didn't anyone care?

Jane appeared with her father again. We shared the same defender. For our arraignment I'd been slightly comforted to have Jane at my side. I wasn't as enthused to be seen with her now. I'd gone through a considerable effort to appear presentable; she seemed to have employed the same effort in the opposite direction. The knot in my stomach was getting tighter. I tried to keep a brave face in front of Mom but I was fairly certain I was screwed. I suddenly knew how a caged animal feels on the way to slaughter, adrenaline raised but completely hopeless.

Morning waned into noon at an agonizingly slow pace. The hallways to the courts bustled with movement but I sat glued to a slatted wooden bench, my butt cheeks numb. I hadn't eaten breakfast and couldn't bring myself to face lunch. The thought of food made me gag. It seemed too akin to a last meal before execution. I didn't want the last food I ate to come from a courthouse convenience store.

Finally, well into the afternoon my defender appeared again. She seemed in a better mood. Jane and I were presented in turn with a plea offer from the district attorney. If we were to plead no contest to assault of a police officer, the district attorney would recommend probation only. The judge still had to approve the plea if submitted, but since the judge was a golfing buddy of Jane's father it seemed likely he'd approve.

On paper this sounded nice. Probation isn't so bad. But I'd still be confessing to a felony I didn't commit. A serious felony at that!

What if this came up when I applied for college or a job? I shouldn't be pleading no contest. Those officers should be pleading to keep their own butts out of jail for what they did to us! The whole department should be up on charges! If I accept guilt now they'll never have to answer for what they did.

Jane was all set to accept the plea. I was on the fence about it. I was given about ten minutes to make up my mind before entering the court. My public defender assured me the charges would never be able to follow me into my adult life because this was family court. She swore everything would be sealed and would disappear after I turned eighteen. She also said if I chose to fight this I'd almost certainly lose and wind up incarcerated for years. Well nothing like having your back up against a wall and no hopeful alternative when making a major life altering decision.

I decided my life was more valuable than my pride and agreed to take the plea. I was all set to go into the court and lie about my guilt when my public defender was called away again. She returned flabbergasted. The district attorney had gotten wind of my hit and run accessory arrest and had changed his mind about my plea. He didn't want me to serve a full sentence but thought I should serve at least six months because it was obvious I was a habitual offender. Are you fucking kidding me? If they lock me up for six months I'll make sure I survive it just so I can come back out and kill Jason. Why is the world always shitting on me?

"I'm not pleading to any charges if they're going to lock me up! Those accessory charges were dropped! Even the cops who arrested me took my side in court last month!"

"Let me see what I can do."

Wow. Was my public defender going to actually defend me in something? Mom looked ill.

My defender came back and said it was out of her hands. It was all up to the judge; but she strongly suggested I stick to the plea and hope for leniency. Jane seemed totally complacent and unconcerned about my possible detention. Sometimes I hate everyone.

I entered the court in silence. My insides felt full of small critters barfing fire in my organs and gnawing on my bones. I plead no contest, but speaking the words felt like pulling the trigger in Russian roulette. I gave them everything they wanted. Now would I be sent home or dragged to hell?

The entire charade lasted less than five minutes. Jane and I were both sentenced to six months probation. I certainly felt the punishment handed down reflected the absence of any real crime. The court acknowledged my innocence while coinciding with the perpetual victimization of young people at the hands of the law. It's a terribly cruel and unjust system.

I met with the appointed probation officer once. He upheld the stipulations of my CHINS warrant and then transferred my case to Salem. The Salem probation officer was supposed to check up on me every two weeks. It shouldn't have been hard because a number of his other charges were fellow students of mine. He'd just come down to the school on a weekday and catch us all at once. Instead he called me at home and told me he didn't have time for me because he didn't view me as a viable threat to society. My attendance and behavioral record at school was impeccable and my living situation wasn't high risk.

After all that grandstanding, fussing, and scaring the holy Jesus out of me in the Boston courts, now I wasn't even worthy of a checkup from a probation officer. He said if I got into trouble again I'd hear from him. But I'd been scared pretty straight. I never spoke with a probation officer again. After six months I received an unsigned form letter from the Salem office stating my probation period was up. It seemed like a joke. If I hadn't been so mad I probably would have laughed.

Two years after my arrest I was approached to join a class action suit against the Boston Transit Police. There were almost forty other plaintiffs who had been abused during arrest, all juveniles. The suit was seeking millions in punitive damages. The lawyers wanted to set a precedent addressing the departmental sanctioned targeting of minors for assault, battery, and trumped up charges by its police force. I was all for it. The thought of seeing my arresting officers and their lieutenant answering for their crimes made me giddy.

As the trial date grew closer, myself and thirty other kids were dropped from the suit. It had become clear the only way to take on the MBTA was in a smaller claims court. It's sad what happened to me wasn't considered bad enough to be worthy of the suit. Mom and Dad had met with parents of other plaintiffs and their stories had been worse than mine. Their case settled in 2003 for $70,000. It was far from the millions initially sought, but I guess it made a point.

As for me I still have a scar on my lip and under my hairline near my forehead. Years of walking with my hip and back out of alignment has compacted the cartilage in my knees and compressed three discs in my spine. The damage to my spinal cord from these compressed discs has led to strange and unpredictable nerve responses and chronic pain. I'd also developed injury- induced arthritis in my back by the age of twenty. I've lost many a night's sleep and missed a fair amount of work days from the pain.

I still live with debilitating back, hip and leg pain every day of my life from the injuries inflicted on me by the MTBA police. But best of all, those felony charges that were supposed to be sealed and then disappear have cost me two jobs in my adult life and keep me from applying for a great many more because I fear the background investigations. I'm certain my defense attorney knew the charges would never disappear because it was a violent felony but lied to me to lighten her work load. And to think I imagined having a sex change would be the biggest obstacle in my life.

Chapter Thirty-Three

Junior Prom

By Betsie

Oh my God was I excited. Luca had been asked to be the blind date of a classmate's cousin to her Junior Prom. My son was going to get dressed up for the first time. I couldn't wait. April would be wearing a purple dress so we set out to find something that would match.

Not being able to afford to rent a tux, I took Luca to a men's store where they sold them fairly inexpensively. Because of Luca's size they didn't have many to choose from. But when he walked out of the dressing room, I was overwhelmed. It wasn't just seeing him dressed in a tux. It was watching him admiring himself in it. My little boy had grown up. An overpowering moment for any mother.

We purchased a black cumber-bun with purple hi-lights to match April's dress. A new pair of dress socks and we were all set. Luca had his new shoes from his day in court.

The day arrived and I left work early. I wanted to give myself plenty of time to take photos of Luca and drive him to Reading. From there his friend Jackie's mom would drive the four of them to the prom.

We arrived at Jackie's on time but no one else was ready. Luca met April for the first time. She was in a mint green dress. I was livid. Not only had Luca asked Jackie about the color of April's dress, I had asked her to please make one more call to her cousin so we would be sure April's dress would be purple. I could see Luca's disappointment.

The chaos at Jackie's house was distressing. Jackie couldn't find her shoes. Her baby sister wouldn't stop crying. Jackie's father wasn't able to get out of work. He wouldn't make it home in time to watch the baby so Jackie's mom could drive the kids. Jackie's date hadn't shown up. I had gone from being excited to angry within an hour.

My heart was broken when April refused to have her photo taken with Luca. What was supposed to be a fun night for me and my son was turning out to be a disaster.

It was getting late. There was no way the kids were going to make it to the prom in time for dinner. The note from the school said if they were not there by a certain hour they would not be allowed in at all. We were running out of time so I volunteered to drive the kids.

I got the kids to the prom just before they were closing the doors. Now I had plenty of time to calm down during the long, lonely ride home.

Junior Prom

By Luca

I think going to Prom might be every gay and trans kid's fantasy. Proms are uber hyped up across the board in our culture. New Horizons didn't have school dances for any of its students and there was no way I'd go to a prom at my hometown high-school. When Jackie asked me if I'd be her cousin's date for a prom in Reading, I was very interested. Sure it'd be a blind date, and the fact the girl, April, couldn't find a date on her own, wasn't a good omen; but when was I ever going to get invited to a prom again?

Mom seemed pretty excited for me. We went shopping for a tuxedo at a discounted formal clothing warehouse store. The clothes were all new but the selection was last year's look or older. I didn't care though. I was eager to be looking at gender appropriate formal wear that wasn't for a court appearance. A small part of me had secretly yearned for a tuxedo since I was a kid. What boy doesn't have fleeting fantasies about being dashing and debonair in a black tux like James Bond or Bruce Wayne? I'd spent most of my life believing I'd never be allowed to don a man's suit outside my house. This was cool.

It was hard to find dress clothes that didn't need to be altered because of my odd size. I was big in the shoulders and chest, even bigger in the stomach but short of height. I did manage to find one tuxedo close to my size, 46S. It was plain black with a shiny black stripe down the pant legs. The shoulders were squared off, the jacket a touch long, but I thought the look was flattering. All in all, I thought I looked pretty good. With a black and purple cumber-bun to match April's dress, white shirt, and my shiny court shoes, I was all set.

When Mom drove me over to Jackie's house I met my date for the first time. She was wearing a mint green dress. We didn't match at all. I had expected her to be woefully unattractive but she wasn't bad looking; just a few pounds overweight and with thick glasses. April was excessively shy and nervous. She barely made eye contact with me and blushed whenever I stood near her. It amused me to meet someone shyer than myself but I was sympathetic. I remembered how it felt to be the fat girl in a small town. April had probably been wearing glasses since elementary school as well. She wasn't nearly as unattractive as her schoolmates had undoubtedly made her believe. I thought that was sad and went out of my way to be extra nice to her, but as the evening wore on, all my attempts to be kind were rebuffed.

Jackie was in the same grade as her cousin so this was her junior prom as well. She and her boyfriend Tony were double-dating with April and me. Mom drove us all to the dance and would be back to pick us up later.

We'd arrived too late for the meal. I was too nervous to eat anyway so that was good. April let me get her a soda but when I sat down next to her with our Cokes, she scooted her chair away from me a bit. Jackie and Tony talked to me but April wouldn't even look at me. I wondered if she was disappointed in me. I knew I wasn't handsome or built, but hey, she was the one who couldn't get a date, not me.

I'd asked April to dance to a slower song. She was stiff and awkward in my arms. I'd been afraid I'd be a terrible dancer because I hadn't slow danced much, just a few times with Harmony. Compared to April I was Fred Astaire. If she had relaxed a little it might not have been so bad. When the song was over and a faster hip-hop song came on, April danced with me for a minute before she froze up again and blurted out, "I'm sorry I just can't do this!" And then ran off the dance floor, leaving me alone and bewildered.

Jackie's boyfriend Tony wouldn't dance either so Jackie and I danced to a few hip-hop songs. I knew some other people who were there from New Horizons, two from the hospital and a few from spending time in downtown Reading while living with my aunt. When Jackie got too hot I stayed on the dance floor with some of the other people I knew. After a while though I felt bad about ignoring my date, even though she'd ditched me, and found my way back to our table.

"I'm sorry I freaked out on you. There were just so many people. I was feeling claustrophobic. I didn't realize you had friends in Reading," April said.

"Yeah Tyler goes to my high-school during the week and Rowena and I go back a while. Do you know them?"

"Not really. I don't talk to many people at school. Do you want to have our picture taken? I think the photographer is leaving soon."

"Sure."

Mom had given me money to pay for the portraits. April seemed a little more mellow and approachable now. Maybe someday I'd want a picture to remember this.

After the portrait we sat down again with Jackie and Tony. It was almost eleven and Mom would be expecting us outside soon.

"Before we go can I get your phone number?" I asked April.

"Why?"

"So I can call you?"

"Umm... what for?"

The look she gave me was distrustful with a hint of revulsion. I had no idea what I'd done for her to dislike me so much. I'd never had a girl send out such mixed signals to me. One minute she ignores me, then she's apologetic and friendly, then cold and annoyed. Maybe she thought because I'd agreed to a blind date I was a sex crazed maniac; which I was but since I couldn't act on it, it doesn't count. Or maybe she thought because I went to an alternative school and was friends with her cousin, I was a loser. That was probably true too. Then why was I asked here in the first place?

"Nevermind."

"Yeah. Okay. Excuse me."

April got up. I assumed it was to use the restroom but when it was time to leave and we all headed outside she informed me she'd called her mom from a payphone to pick her up.

"Do you want me to wait with you?"

"No thanks. I'm fine," she said curtly.

"Okay. Well I had a nice time. Thanks for inviting me."

"Mmmhmm."

I walked off and left her shivering alone on the sidewalk. It was against my nature and everything Mom had taught me about how to treat a friend or date. But April had made it clear she was neither to me. Still I supposed I'd had a nice enough time with my friends. It hardly seemed worth the effort though and I hadn't sensed any of the magic I'd been led to believe happened at proms. But I went to a prom. No one could ever take that away from me.

Chapter Thirty-Four

Ashley

By Luca

So far I'd maintained a strict policy of not dating anyone I went to New Horizons with. My friends Brian and Sarah knew I was trans but they could keep a secret. I wasn't ashamed of who I was and I'd grown comfortable enough to not be afraid of the other students hurting me. I just didn't want my high school experience more awkward than it needed to be. I wanted to have fun and keep things light. Then Amanda came to school.

Amanda was enrolled as the school year was almost at an end. The principal had asked me to show her and her family around before they made a final decision in her attending. Amanda was a year younger than me. She dressed all in black with black lipstick and black nail polish. She had black hair and dark brown eyes. I thought she was cute. But being a potential student made her off limits for me.

As I tried to ignore my attraction to Amanda she tried to fan the flames. Having a girl blatantly pursuing me was a new and flattering experience. I tried to play it off and pretend we weren't going on dates by inviting Brian and Sarah whenever I hung out with Amanda. She was so forward I was almost afraid to be alone with her.

The first moment Amanda and I were alone, she kissed me. We were in her backyard. Brian was out front smoking a cigarette and Sarah was inside using the bathroom. The kiss wasn't bad. She seemed genuinely passionate, but I didn't feel anything special. I tried to pull away when I heard Brian coming back but Amanda attached herself to me and gave me a huge black hickey on my neck. She'd bitten me and it actually hurt. I guess some people are into that, but I was more surprised and embarrassed. I didn't have anything to cover it with. Brian and Sarah just raised their eyebrows.

At school the next day I was teased mercilessly by every teacher and student I came in contact with. The hickey had drawn a lot of negative attention. But on the other hand, nothing makes a girl want you more than another girl who also wants you. I don't know why that is but it's totally true. And this is where Ashley entered the mix.

I had a crush on Ashley at the beginning of the year before she had been pulled from school to live in a rehab center. She was back now and the day after I came to school with a hickey Ashley decided to make a move on me. I tried to hang out with her just as friends without telling Amanda. That had been a mistake.

I suppose my brief relationship with Ashley had been doomed from the start for a few reasons. For one it broke my rule of not dating other students. Two; it was founded on deceit as I tried to hide Ashley and Amanda from each other. Three; dating someone fresh out of rehab is never a good idea. Four; Ashley was fucking nuts.

The first time I hung out with Ashley outside of school we bumped into Amanda at a park. Brian was there and the two of us hung back while Ashley and Amanda got into a huge fight over me. I'd never been fought over before. It wasn't flattering. It was scary. Ashley won because although she was smaller, she was crazier. Amanda avoided me completely after that. I tried to tell myself Amanda and I had never agreed to any sort of commitment but I still felt like shit about it. Worse I felt like I owed Ashley something because she'd "won" me.

Brian and Sarah thought going out with Ashley was a terrible idea; but the more I spent time with her the more I started to like her. Sure, she was insane and still doing drugs, but underneath was a highly smart and capable woman.

Ashley was very open minded, liberal, intelligent, and a self-admitted bisexual. If we were going to keep spending time together I thought I should tell her about me. I told her in person at my house after school. She took the news casually and swore she'd keep it to herself. She even said she thought it made me sexier, more exotic. She wasted no time telling me she wanted to be my girlfriend. I was elated. But the first time we kissed she told me I kissed like a girl. She said boys were much sloppier kissers than me. What did she want? For me to drool on her face? I'd never been told I was a feminine kisser before and it kind of hurt my feelings.

Ashley made a lot of weird little comments that indicated she felt I was feminine, which slowly chipped away at my self-esteem. We barely dated two weeks, which meant we were still together a week after I'd grown sick of her. Before going out with me, Ashley had been extremely promiscuous and loose. But while we were dating she was prude and frigid. I didn't feel like I was missing out on anything because I suspected she was trading sexual favors for drugs to some guy at school. Suspicions which turned out to be totally right by her own admission. So we broke up.

I thought she'd be okay with the breakup. Ashley seemed to like me plenty before we started dating but after about two days she seemed bored with me. I thought the feelings of lost interest were mutual and we could move on and just be friends. But I had forgotten Ashley was crazy.

The first thing she did was try to tell my closest friends Brian and Sarah that I was trans. But they already knew. Their indifference to what Ashley had hoped would be shocking news infuriated her. She tried to expand her rumor by telling other students. This had me sick with nerves for a while. One of my worst nightmares come to life. The students that she'd told, even the most popular and badass ones, all confronted me with what Ashley had said.

"She's saying you're a he/she and that you don't have a dick."

"Ha. She wishes. She's just mad because I wouldn't fuck her. After I found out she was blowing Fernando for pot and screwing his brother for E, I wouldn't touch her. Can you blame me? That girl is hella skanky. I'm just glad I found out before we did anything together. She probably has hep C or some shit."

"Yo, for real. I couldn't believe you were with her nasty ass at all, Dawg. You definitely dodged getting an STD by dropping her. What a lying ho. We all knew she was totally making that shit up about you. Bitch is crazy."

"Truth."

I couldn't believe how many people were taking my side. But from an outside perspective Ashley was known to be crazy. And a teenage transsexual at our small school sounded ludicrous. No one believed a word she said; or if they did, they never acted like it. Instead the gossip turned to Ashley being a lying cracked-out whore.

When turning my friends against me and trying to get the student body to hate me hadn't worked, Ashley went over the edge with rage. She rushed me at break time, trying to take a swing at me, but Sarah caught her and threw her on the ground.

Students were laughing and clapping as Ashley was being dragged away, but she was screaming, "I'll get you. You sick dickless freak! This isn't over! Fuck you! Fuck all of you! Freak lovers!"

Ashley was suspended for a week from school, but she never came back. No one missed her.

Target

There was a Target store opening at our local mall. In 1999 the suburbs I'd grown up in had yet to be affected by the Target/Walmart blight. I'd never seen a giant box store before and was naively excited. Brian and I both decided to apply for jobs there.

I was scared filling out the job application.

Have you ever gone by another name?

I'd rather not get the job than open that can of worms. They can't find out anyway. Can they?

Have you ever been convicted of a felony?

I'm going to go ahead and assume "adjudication" doesn't count...

I was offered a job in the "food alley" section of Target for $.50 over minimum wage. Brian wasn't hired though and that surprised the hell out of me. I could only guess he'd been pegged as a homosexual by the interviewer. Brian wasn't flaming but his voice was high pitched and he gestured with his hands a lot. All I can say is it was the store's loss. Honestly and truly.

I sat through training seminars with handfuls of other teenagers. It was kind of exciting. The store wasn't open yet so everything was shiny and new. Like many of my co-workers I was only sixteen, but we were being treated like adults. Oddly no one was hired from the town I lived in. As always, fears of being recognized as Marie lurked behind every corner for me. But I guess the rich lazy jerkoffs from my home town didn't need after school jobs.

Working with "fast food" has a lot of negative stigma surrounding it. I thought it was a blast. My co-workers were amazing; some of them are still my friends. On sunny days I'd ride my skateboard to work after school. Usually my boss would find me in the parking lot and ask if I wanted to start my shift early. I'd always say yes. I worked a lot of thirty-five to forty hour weeks and never felt tired. In the time I worked there, I received two raises. I had more money than I knew how to spend. I met all kinds of new and fun people my age from working at the mall.

Unfortunately, in a small town where every teen who works at the mall knows every other teen, it didn't take long for word to reach Ashley that I worked there. Since she'd dropped out of high-school she had a lot of free time on her hands. Time she used to hang out with other drop-outs and stalk me. Sometimes when I was walking to work a car would drive up next to me and the passengers would throw trash, lit cigarettes, or soda at me. As they sped off I'd always recognize at least one as a friend of Ashley's.

Ashley would come into my work and sit in the food court area staring at me. I told my co-workers she was a jealous ex who was also psychotic. They started spitting in her food whenever she deigned to order something. I refused to wait on her. A few times this pissed her off so much she kicked things over and caused a scene, having to be removed by security. Eventually, she was banned from the store.

I thought I'd get some peace at work after that, but Ashley took to stalking me through the mall on my way to start my shift. She knew my schedule and that was creepy. In the mall she'd scream and throw things at me. When I ignored her she threw herself at me, knocking me into a sunglasses cart and sending half the merchandise to the floor. The police were called and the officers who'd arrested me for the hit and run in May responded. They were both super nice to me. Ashley ended up being banned from the entire mall.

After this I never saw Ashley again. I thought it was because she'd been banned from the mall but I heard later it was because she'd tried to drink rubbing alcohol and was locked up in psychiatric care again.

Now I thought I'd be left alone at work for sure. Nope. One of Ashley's cousins was a cashier at Target. When I'd gone through training, she had been in my group and was really friendly with me. Now she wouldn't even look at me. I was okay with that, until she started telling my co-workers I was a hermaphrodite.

"Luca, is it true you're a shim?"

"A what?"

"A she him. Shim."

"No! Where on Earth did you hear that?!"

"Rebecca."

"And you believed her?"

"Well not at first, but a lot of other people are saying it too."

"What do you want me to do? Whip out my dick at work?"

"No man, don't be crazy. I just thought you should know what people are saying."

I tried to act angry but underneath I was scared. I loved my job and I loved the independence that came from having my own money. I wasn't ready to let all that go. Worse, what if these rumors reached my school? It would be hard to squash them down twice. Shit.

I tried to approach Rebecca but the look she gave me told me not to waste my breath. I knew I couldn't threaten or blackmail her into silence. Ashley had once told me when she and her cousin Rebecca got drunk they sometimes went down on one another. That was a pretty juicy rumor but I didn't think starting a new one would make people forget what was said about me.

Fortunately, when you make friends with people from psychiatric facilities, rehabs and alternative schools, you can usually find someone who's not afraid to be a bigger badass than whatever trash is giving you trouble. My friend Jasmine was very upset when she heard someone was harassing me at work and spreading terrible lies about me (to be fair I'm not a hermaphrodite so it was a lie). Very, very, upset. Jasmine was nineteen, older than me and Rebecca, and though strikingly beautiful, a delicate flower she was not.

Jasmine drove me, Brian and Sarah over to Target on one of my days off. I watched with Brian and Sarah as Jasmine walked right through a flock of Rebecca's friends and approached her. Rebecca tried to turn away but Jasmine's hand flew out and held Rebecca's upper arm in place. We couldn't hear what Jasmine was saying but all of Rebecca's friends slowly backed away as the color drained from her face.

"She won't bother you anymore," Jasmine announced with calm confidence.

"Are you sure?"

"OH YEAH."

The next time I went to work Rebecca actually came up to me and apologized. It must have been killing her inside to do it, but she hid it well. She even went so far as to tell people she'd been totally wrong about me and that it was a stupid prank. I was astonished. Jasmine never did tell me what she said to Rebecca. But after Rebecca set things right at work, she quit two weeks later. I never saw her again and the teens who had been throwing things at me from moving cars vanished as well. The rest of the summer was quiet after that.

Chapter Thirty-Five

BAGLY Youth Prom

By Betsie

At the end of the school year it's difficult for gay, lesbian and transgender kids to attend their own high school prom with the date of their choice. That's where BAGLY (Boston Alliance of Gay Lesbian Bisexual and Transgender Youth) comes in. They were holding a prom and Luca and Brian insisted on attending.

I was scared. Something like this was going to create unfriendly crowds. I didn't want Luca and Brian to get caught in anything violent. But it wasn't fair to make them stay home.

All kinds of frightening images were racing through my head so I put on the early news. They showed the religious protesters, even interviewing a few of them to get their point of view. They also showed the police protecting the kids as they arrived. The news didn't show any major outbreaks of fighting so I was reassured the kids had made it there safely.

At 11:30 pm I anxiously drove back to the T station to pick them up.

"Mom, we bumped into Jenny and her date," Luca said.

"What?"

"Jenny was there with her date."

It was late and I was tired. My shock would have to wait for another day.

BAGLY Prom

By Luca

My last big hurrah before summer school started was attending the BAGLY LGBT Youth Prom in Boston. Although Brian's gay, I practically had to beg him to come. Maybe it was because he wasn't out to his family. Maybe it was his hatred of crowds. Or he was sick of people mistaking the two of us for a couple. But when we exited the subway station at Government Center and had to walk past a line of Christian protestors, I had a better understanding of why he wanted to stay home.

The dance was for people under twenty-three. Some kids were as young as fourteen. Whatever the age, we all had to make our way past dozens of adults with signs telling us we'd burn in hell. The police were present to make sure the protestors stayed a few hundred feet from the door of the event. But if you took the train in, as many of us had, you were guaranteed to have to walk past them. I tried to laugh it off and put on a brave face but I felt very vulnerable.

I'd been told I was straying from God's path a few times before. But walking past people waving giant signs of painted hell-fires and screaming "*God hates you!*" while cartoon pamphlets of "sodomites" rained down on me was a new level of intimidation and hatred. I was just glad no one pulled out a gun or threw a bomb as these whackos were known to do from time to time.

Reaching the dance was worth crossing the line of bigots.

I had no idea so many GLBTQ youth existed in the Boston area, although they weren't all from Boston. I traveled over twenty-five miles to attend. Some kids had come from New Hampshire, Connecticut and Rhode Island to be there. The place was packed to the rafters with hundreds of young, warm bodies. Some of them seemed nervous; some were very confident and proud. The outfits ranged from t-shirts and jeans to tuxes and gowns. But whatever the attire, **everyone** was beautiful. The excitement and energy in the air was so palpable I felt enveloped by it. There was no fighting. No one was rolling his or her eyes, or making snide remarks about anyone; just acceptance, love, and a feeling of unity blanketed by loud techno dance music.

Not everyone who attended was gay. I tried to find other trans youth but either I was the only one or they blended into the crowd as I did. Everyone I talked to thought I was a bio straight guy there with his friends. There were other hetero people at the dance as well but not many guys. That left some insanely hot hetero girls who'd come with their gays friends having no one to dance with but me. I took advantage of the situation and danced with as many gorgeous girls as possible.

I bumped into my friend Jenny on the dance floor. We hadn't spoken in a while because high-school and life had been pulling us in two different directions. Even though we'd been friends since the third grade and she'd known me before, during, and after my transition, I had no idea she was gay.

Jenny introduced me to her girlfriend, a heavy-set older woman with a shaved head, wearing men's clothing. I tried to keep the surprise off my face. For once I knew how it felt to be on the other side of a "coming out." With Brian it hadn't been a big deal because I'd figured it out on my own. But now someone I'd known half my life had caught me completely off guard. I had less than a second to totally rearrange how I understood and related to her before the situation got awkward. Obviously, I didn't have a problem with my friend or anyone being a lesbian. But with Brian I'd always known him as gay. With Jenny this was all new and I had some questions.

How long have you known you were gay? How do you know you're gay? Are you really gay or just bisexual? Is this a phase? Who else knows? Are you scared? Do you feel safe at school? Are you happy? Why didn't you tell me?

I finally knew how it felt to be on the other side of the questioning. I'd always loathed people doubting my sincerity and certainty about being trans. Somehow I thought transitioning would make me immune to feeling speculation or disbelief for other's gender identity or sexual preference. I guess I was wrong.

I never asked any of my questions. Asking the questions aloud would have been admitting I knew so little about my friend. I didn't want to scare her off or put her on the defensive. I only wanted to enjoy catching up with Jenny and having a nice time together.

Brian and I had to leave before the dance was over so we could meet Mom at the train station before midnight. On the walk back to Government Center I threw condoms at the few remaining protestors. It may not have been the mature thing to do, but I was sixteen and they were assholes.

Despite the Christan right-wing douchebags outside the prom, I'd had a truly magical and profound evening. Being surrounded by GLBTQ of my generation and seeing how diverse, strong and supportive we were, strengthened my hope for a better future. Having fun with so many awesome people and unexpectedly reaffirming my friendship with someone I loved and cared about, had been amazing. I may not have been kissed or voted prom king, but I finally understood what all the awe and anticipation was about regarding this holiest of teenage traditions.

Chapter Thirty-Six

Saying Goodbye / Boys Don't Cry

By Betsie

Luca was growing up and maturing. He was doing great in school and had close friends who accepted him for who he was. However, when he told me he wanted to stop seeing Diane, I had my reservations. We had stopped therapy many times in the past and it always ended poorly. But he insisted he was no longer getting anything from the sessions.

This was difficult for me. Diane had brought us through the worst of the worst. With her help I had a happy son. We now had a future. Something I had never allowed myself to look forward to.

But in the end, it was time to part ways. Luca was ready to spread his wings.

Boys Don't Cry

Naively believing the movie *Boys Don't Cry* was like a documentary with a happy ending, I had agreed to make the trip to Cambridge to see it with Luca. I watched in silence as in scene after scene Brandon Teena dealt with many of the same issues Luca had dealt with.

When Brandon was raped I cried for my nine-year-old daughter and my sixteen-year-old son. Luca had already survived one rape. The thought of him being brutally attacked just for who he was horrified me.

I had to close my eyes as gunfire rang out and Brandon was murdered. It felt like a personal attack on me and my son. The bullets hit too close to home. The reality of what Luca's future could hold terrified me, leaving me speechless.

The credits starting rolling. The heaviness of fear had me pinned to my seat. I sat in silence, incapable of assimilating what I had just witnessed. It was all too real. Luca helped me to my feet. Walking slowly toward the exit, I was grateful the theater was still dark as I wiped away tears.

Unable to look at Luca without crying, we made our long, cold, silent trek back to the subway station. It was another forty minutes before we reached my car and I was able to speak.

"I'm sorry Hon. I don't know what to say."

"I'm sorry Mom."

"Did you know it would end this way? It felt like you were being hit with those bullets."

"Yeah I knew," Luca said giving me a hug. "I'm sorry I didn't tell you, but I promise I'll be alright."

Fear engulfed me for days. After seeing the needless death of Brandon, it was difficult to believe Luca would be alright.

Saying Goodbye / Boys Don't Cry

By Luca

Summer of 1999 was fun. I didn't mind going to summer school that year because more of my friends were in attendance, including Sarah. After school, on days I didn't work, Sarah would usually drive me over to Brian's house and we'd either go swimming in his grandmother's pool or drive to the beach. I still wore a t-shirt in the water, but being fat gave me a good excuse to do so.

My family went camping in Ogunquit, Maine again that August. I got out of summer school for the week and Brian came with me. Anya and her family were there. I hung out with her, Brian, and a couple other teens we'd made friends with. My cousin Will drove us around when we didn't feel like walking or taking the trolley. Every night we'd make a fire or lie out on the empty camp basketball courts and watch for shooting stars. My younger cousin didn't try to out me that year. I didn't have creepy, long stitches poking out, and I'd lost twenty five pounds since the summer before. As far as I was concerned everything was perfect. It was the best summer vacation I'd ever had.

When Fall rolled around and school started up again, I was in a great place mentally and emotionally. I hadn't been smoking, drinking, or doing drugs for a while. I hadn't cut myself or thought of hurting myself since my trial. I wasn't fighting with my parents or anyone else. Things finally felt right. I was good.

So I told Mom I didn't think I needed to see Diane anymore. It was a hard decision. Diane wasn't just a therapist. She'd been a remarkable advocate and extraordinary ally. She'd saved me when no one else could. Diane had led me down the path to understanding myself and in doing so freed me to notice the world around me. For the first time since I was a toddler, when I looked around I didn't see my own misery or feel my own pain. I saw what was in front of me and felt wonder and joy for all the possibilities surrounding me. Everything was new and waiting to be discovered. I wanted to make this part of my journey on my own.

Saying goodbye to Diane had been difficult. It meant part of my life was over and I was on my own. But it felt like the right thing to do so I moved forward with my head up and didn't look back.

In school I was still in music and art class, but instead of working in the coffee shop I took up woodshop. I liked shop because it was a great new way to be creative, and despite girls being in the class, it also made me feel manlier. Instead of playing football, I joined drama. Brian hated sports and we'd become practically inseparable so I wanted to join an elective he was in. This meant once a week I had to attend a gym class. But being 190 pounds instead of 244 made physical education much easier. It wasn't a hard gym class anyway. Most of the other kids had been outcasts in their public schools so P.E. had been torture for them as well. In this gym period no one was ever picked on and we alternated who was chosen first and last for teams. It wasn't so bad.

Drama had become very interesting to me. As a kid I'd liked musicals and had been interested in acting, but I always refused to play feminine roles so nothing ever came of my few acting classes. Brian had been a volunteer usher at the North Shore Music Theatre for two seasons and knew a lot about Broadway musicals. He'd introduced me to *Into the Woods, Hair, Phantom of the Opera, Miss Saigon* and my favorite; *Rent*. Anything that had to do with the stage suddenly fascinated me.

I loved our drama teacher, Deedie. Her constant sunny and cheerful disposition was both abrasive and contagious. Sometimes people wouldn't take her seriously because her endless optimism made her seem more like a character than a real person. But underneath was a passionate, savvy woman I hoped to learn a lot from.

When the movie *Boys Don't Cry* came out I knew why I needed drama in my life. The stage wasn't just for entertainment; it was a way to reach people. Theater was a way to share your experiences and messages in a more emotional and captivating way than printed words alone. It was more intimate, more moving and more powerful. Someday I'd have a message to get across and Deedie would help prepare me to deliver it. Where the Brandon Teena story had been one of dark tragedy, my story would be of beating the odds and having the happy ending we all deserved.

Boys Don't Cry

Boys Don't Cry had premiered at a New York film festival in October of 1999. At first I was absolutely floored a major motion picture had been made about a transsexual man. This was a chance for us to shine in the media, opposed to our usual presence as a joke on Jerry Springer. Dignity! Respect! Acceptance! This was big. This was bigger than big. This was beyond words.

I wanted to see the movie. I knew how the movie would end before I went in and that it was going to depress the hell out of me, but I still had to go. The only place showing it in my area was all the way in Cambridge. Mom drove us to a redline station and we took the train in. It was a long, dark, freezing walk to the theater and I debated turning back. I was afraid the movie would affect me like watching Holocaust footage. It would be too personal, too dark. But if Brandon had to experience it, the least I could do was sit through a re-enactment.

The acting was truly amazing. Within seconds you forgot Hillary Swank was a hetero woman. All the performances were utterly convincing. Watching the character Brandon date unknowing girls, get chased by hillbillies, fall in love, narrowly avoid being outed, and allowing himself to get caught up in illegal activities trying to prove himself and make friends, was all very reminiscent of my life.

The brief rape scene was painful to endure. The uncaring response of the police more so. Of course the movie ends with his murder which was a heartbreaking warning to trans people everywhere.

What was the warning though? That we need to be more forthcoming and have a stronger public presence, hopefully leading to improved public awareness and understanding? Or do we need to be more secretive and hide ourselves even better than we already do? Should we never date or fall in love unless we're 100% post-op? Or do we just avoid Nebraska? Fuck if I knew.

Boys Don't Cry hurt me inside in a way I couldn't describe, but I still thought it was the most incredible movie ever. Twice, Brian and I made plans to see it. But both times he bailed on me at the last minute, coming up with excuses why he couldn't travel to Cambridge. Then Hillary Swank won an Oscar for her performance and the movie was more widely released.

When it finally came to our local theater Brian broke down and told me the real reason he didn't want to see it. It took me by surprise. We were waiting at the bus stop and he started screaming how he couldn't bear to see someone depicted in a movie, who reminded him so much of me, be brutalized and murdered. I was touched. I felt guilty. What kind of effect had the movie had on Mom?

Even though the movie was probably the biggest thing to happen for trans awareness, I didn't try to make anyone else watch it.

Chapter Thirty-Seven

Seventeenth Birthday / Spring Break

By Betsie

Luca was turning seventeen. Once again I rented the function room at the condo for a small party. This time Luca had real friends to invite. Not kids he had met in psych wards.

Neighbors were complaining about the noise so I went downstairs to tell the kids their music was too loud. They welcomed me in, even asking me to stay for a few minutes. Then, as if in unison, they insisted I dance with Luca.

I was elated. Luca took my hand, and in front of his friends we had our first dance as mother and son. Looking into Luca's eyes, there was no shadow of Marie. In her place was a mature, seventeen-year-old young man. Laughter had replaced years of misery. Instead of contempt suffered at the hands of former classmates, he now valued the respect of his peers. Luca no longer dwelt in the past; he looked forward to his future. It had taken years, but happiness had defeated depression.

I had changed too. Contentment had overcome sadness. A smile was found where tears once resided. My constant worrying about Luca's future had disappeared.

All too soon the music ended. But in those three short minutes, joy reflected back in the twinkling eyes I had gazed into.

Spring Break

Luca was doing great in school. Because he had attended summer school twice, if he agreed to attend again at the end of the school year they were going to let him graduate a year early.

There was so much to do. We thought we'd have another year to prepare him for SAT's. Now we only had months. New Horizons had never had any student take SAT's. I was thrilled when my old high school allowed him to take the test with their students.

Then there was a prom. New Horizons had never given the students a prom. They felt it wouldn't be safe because so many of the students had disciplinary problems. This made Luca even more determined to have one. Although it was months away, I rented out the party room and we started making plans.

The last big idea Luca had was to visit Charlotte in New York. Even with all the time she and Luca had spent talking, her mother, Joanne and I had never spoken. I gave her a call and arranged for Luca and me to go to New York for a few days so we could all meet.

After our three hour drive to a local motel, Joanne picked us up and brought us back to their apartment for dinner. Although not as intimidating as meeting Michelle's parents, it was still awkward. However, Charlotte, her mother, father and sister were quite gracious to the strangers in their home.

The following day Joanne drove us to a mall in Danbury, Connecticut. We strolled around going in and out of a few stores and stopping for lunch. Luca and Charlotte tried to get away but Joanne was a little apprehensive. The kids had to stay in our sight.

All of a sudden, out of nowhere, Luca invited Charlotte to his prom. This took Joanne and me both by surprise. Joanne had never driven to Massachusetts and wasn't sure Charlotte's dad would want to either. But as always, when Luca gets something in his head he doesn't give up easily. Next thing I knew we were shopping for prom gowns. We only went to one store. When Charlotte stepped out of the dressing-room in a teal and black gown, her smile told us this was the one. Luca now had a date to his prom.

Seventeenth Birthday/Spring Break

By Luca

Christmas had come and gone. The new millennium and my birthday were approaching. I'd had a girlfriend at Christmas but we broke up shortly after. She was a friend of Sarah's that I'd met at a Halloween party. For Christmas I'd bought her a green thong from Victoria's Secret. Purchasing it had been awkward. It was my first time alone in a lingerie store. My neck, face and ears turned bright red and prickly with heat. I was afraid to look up from the floor so I bought the first thing an associate put in my hand. The sales lady was nice but I felt certain everyone assumed I was a pervert and my girlfriend was fictitious.

I'd liked this girl a lot and we'd had fun dates together. But I never told her I was trans and was glad I hadn't. She'd been the third girlfriend I'd had cheat on me for free drugs. I didn't break up with her so much as I stopped returning her calls and avoided her. She took this about as well as one may expect. I really needed to start dating classier girls.

My seventeenth birthday wasn't nearly as over the top crazy as my sixteenth had been. It was just a small party with a dozen friends. We had loud music and dancing but no drugs, alcohol or grand theft auto. The only remarkable thing to occur around my birthday was a decision I'd been presented with.

It came to the attention of my home town's special education admins that my summer schooling had racked up a lot of extra credits. In fact, if I attended summer school for one more session I could graduate in 2000 instead of 2001. I'd like to think when the admins approached me they weren't motivated by the money the town would save on tuition if I graduated a year early. Or the headache I'd caused them when another student from my home town had wanted to attend New Horizons but had been turned away by Kendal when I expressed my fear of being outed. I'm sure they only had my best interest at heart.

Graduating early was tempting. My closest friends Brian and Sarah would be graduating in 2000 and the thought of being left behind without them made me sad. On the other hand, was I ready to go out into the world beyond high school? I'd barely begun to get comfortable as it was.

I chose to pursue graduating early. As much as I loved high school, I had to admit a big part of why I loved it was because my friends were there. Sure, I had other friends, but not like Brian and Sarah. I could be ready for college in eight months, right?

Spring Break

Being bumped from a Junior to a Senior overnight meant I had to get the ball rolling on a lot of things. I had to think about SATs, colleges, scholarships and how to get the most from the time I had left.

I dove into art class with more fervor so I could bang out a portfolio to show colleges. I joined the JV basketball team in order to drop gym and utilize that time and energy elsewhere. In drama I rallied the other students to push for approval to perform an edgy play called *Bang Bang You're Dead* about a school shooting. I even recruited other students from wood-shop and the basketball team to help fill out the cast. I was more active in student council than ever before. In 1999 I'd spearheaded the first teacher appreciation awards ceremony through the student council. This year I wanted to step it up a notch. The teacher appreciation ceremony would be bigger but I thought the students deserved something too. We deserved a prom.

I had the right to attend a prom at my local public high-school but I didn't hate myself that much. I doubted I was the only kid at an alternative school who felt that way. After graduation I'd miss my high-school and the people who'd made the experience so unique and fun. I felt we needed a New Horizons prom to commemorate and reflect on our time together as students. I had less than four months to coordinate the first dance in our school's history; and find a date.

Cass

I did meet a classier girl than the ones I'd been dating. Her name was Cass and she'd found me online by searching AOL profiles for people in her area who shared her taste in music. Cass was eighteen, a college student, and lived at home. Her major was liberal arts but she was taking classes in women's studies. Women's studies included sexuality and gender identity. While I loathe my condition being lumped in with women's issues, it was refreshing to go on a date with someone who understood "transsexual" without my having to explain it.

I don't know if it was Cass' college education or because I met her online, which has a certain amount of anonymity built in, but I was comfortable telling her about me. She still had a few questions. Cass had read an entire book on gender identity disorders but had never met a trans person. I was glad to tell her anything she wanted to know. It was nice getting it all out in the open before we had a first date. She even wrote a paper from the information I gave her.

Mom had to drive me almost twenty miles to a movie theater in Cass' town. I don't remember the movie, but I remember her very kissable lips and long, dark, silky hair.

Cass and her mother drove up to my neck of the woods a few times while I was working at the bookstore and later at Starbucks. She got to meet Brian and the two formed an instant connection. Every fag needs his hag (this may sound derogatory but I assure you "fag hag" is a slang term that denotes deep affection and respect.)

Cass and I went out on a half dozen or so dates. She was far and away the most intellectual and mature girl I'd dated. But while we were going out, Charlotte had written me a letter. Her family had moved and instead of parochial school she was attending public high-school in a little town that bordered Connecticut. From her letter, Charlotte seemed changed; happier, wiser. She also had a boyfriend. Some guy she went to school with. Well, just as nothing makes a girl want you more than another girl wanting you, nothing makes a girl seem more interesting than knowing she's unavailable.

Spring Break in New York

All spring I'd busted my butt studying for my SATs and composing essays for college applications. I'd toured Montserrat College of Art with my art teacher, and Salem State and Emerson College with Brian and my guidance counselor, Mary. My drama teacher Deedie had taken me to the Hasty Pudding show at Harvard and suggested I check out their drama program. As much as Deedie had faith in me, I felt it was out of my reach. But I had a good application in at Salem State and they had a great drama department. I'd also managed to score a 1050 on my SATs which wasn't exactly dazzling, but I'd been the only student at my school to take them. I definitely earned that 1050 and deserved a spring break.

For weeks, I'd bugged Mom to take me to Brewster, New York. So Mom rented a motel room for half a week and made the drive down, with me as co-pilot.

When Charlotte and I had stopped writing each other in 1998 I always felt something was left unfinished between us. I didn't agree with the strong religious points of view she'd had in the past and stopped talking to her when it became obvious we were from two different places and moving in different directions. Charlotte had been so innocent and pure. Just knowing she existed forced me to realize what a shit-bag I was in comparison.

At the time, I'd been into drugs, metal music, atheism and rebellion of any kind. I'd told myself blowing her off had been for her own good. Still, something about her drove me nuts. I couldn't say exactly what it was but this girl really got under my skin. Opening her letter back in March, written on real stationary and smelling faintly of warm brown sugar, had filled me with a longing I hadn't known I was still capable of feeling.

Charlotte lived 185 miles away from me, but through email, instant messaging, letters and phone calls, it didn't take long for her to become an integral part of my life. I never asked her to break up with her boyfriend but I was thrilled when she did. It must be hard to have someone dump you for someone they've never met in person. I didn't know how that felt but I'd stopped seeing Cass shortly after Charlotte was single again.

Dropping Cass had been a scummy thing to do. She'd been great to me. I asked her to be my date to my prom and a week later stopped returning her calls. Cass was a classy girl. I was a skeeze. I didn't deserve her. I didn't deserve Charlotte either, but Charlotte didn't know that yet.

Charlotte didn't know I was trans. I decided that even after telling Ashley had blown up in my face, I didn't want to hide myself from whomever I was dating. If a girl couldn't handle the real me, then we didn't belong together anyway. No more hiding. If I was serious about wanting to visit Charlotte and her family, and possibly starting a relationship, I wanted to start it off right. But like a huge wuss who's afraid of rejection, instead of telling her over the phone I emailed her.

Charlotte, being a sentimental pack rat actually saved a copy of the email for over a decade and now I'm able to offer you a peek at a genuine coming out, bad grammar and all.

"March 07, 2000

i have some stuff to tell you. i dont know how else to say it except just blurting it out. i know, huh? for once i dont have a poetic way to be confusing so enjoy it. i hope you're sitting down...

Charlotte... i am a transexual. two years ago when i went to NY for those surgeries... thats what i was having done. i hope that this info makes alot of my past more clear to you. why i was always depressed. why i lied to you. why i tried to kill myself. why i dropped out of school. why i had to take time to re incert myself into society... i had to literally start ALL over again at the age of 15... i had no contact with my former friends except one... my family had to get to know me all over again.

i had to have my birth certificate changed. new SS card. everything. and everyone i tell the truth kind of flips out on me. so i get lonely alot of the time... but there you have it. when you met me, in the eyes of society, on the outside i was a girl. but inside i've always been me. you were a big part of the real me coming through. so thank you... and if you dont email me back or whatever, i'll understand..."

Charlotte had thanked me for telling her, and seemed understanding and accepting. I knew that since attending public school, her opinions had become more liberal and she'd left the Catholic faith. She was for gay rights and all that, but verbally supporting a movement can be easier than dating it. We decided not to tell her family I was trans. They were very religious and conservative. It was bad enough they assumed I was a weirdo because Charlotte had met me on the evil internet. No need to fan the flames of paranoia.

Now, after a long drive, Mom and I were waiting outside on a cold moss-covered stone bench for Charlotte and her mother to pick us up. The air was permeated with mildew and a nearby ashcan. I hoped the smells wouldn't settle into my clothes.

I was excited and scared to meet Charlotte. She knew what I looked like from pictures I'd sent her, but what if she was disappointed anyway? I'd put some weight back on, and was up to 200 pounds again. What if my physique disgusted her? If she thought I was gross I'd be thoroughly crushed. I tried to focus on remaining calm and acting cool, but when Charlotte and her mother, Joanne, drove into the motel parking lot I lost all my confidence.

Charlotte hopped out of her mother's car and stole my breath away. She had long, frothy chestnut hair that shimmered like spun copper in the fading sun. Her eyes were large shiny green pools set among classic features in a pale olive complexion. At five feet one inch, and barely one hundred pounds, her petite frame looked dainty and delicate. She was wearing a white blouse under a pale blue sweater and a skirt that hung past her knees. I know it sounds cliché but as she ran toward me she looked like an angel off a tree. I was in love before she even reached me.

When Michelle and I had embraced each other it always felt like clinging to a life-preserver in a storm; passionate but desperate. Charlotte's arms felt like walking through your front door after the commute from hell; peaceful and safe. I pressed my face into Charlotte's raspberry-vanilla scented neck and felt home.

Throughout the entire vacation, I couldn't stop staring at her. Whatever we were supposed to be doing, she was always more interesting. This might have annoyed her when we were eating or seeing a movie but I couldn't help myself.

I didn't bother packing around Charlotte. I hadn't been specific as to what surgeries I'd had done. Was an omission the same as a lie? She was too beyond virginal to notice such things anyway. And yet we were hardly alone together. Joanne insisted on chaperoning us wherever we went. Between her and my mother we had two sets of eyes on us at all times. But we did manage to sneak off for a short walk and had our first kiss on a bridge near her home. I didn't see fireworks the first time we kissed because I'd been too busy trying to figure her out.

Charlotte was so shy I couldn't tell if she wanted to be kissed or not. After we kissed, she'd looked about ready to cry. That scared me. I thought she'd changed her mind about being okay with a trans guy; after all, she was just fifteen and I was only the second guy she'd kissed. But she insisted she was happy and I wanted to believe her. Later that night we stole out onto her porch and she sat upon my lap. I rested my head on her chest and listened to her heart beating; utterly still and content.

The second day I was there I asked Charlotte to be my date to my prom. She said yes; her mom said no way. But on the last day of my trip we all found ourselves in a mall and Charlotte was trying on a teal formal evening dress. She looked so incredible in this slim off the shoulder gown that her mother's resolve melted away. Next thing I knew Joanne was buying the gown and I had a date.

It was hard saying goodbye to Charlotte. Mom was getting annoyed because she had a long drive ahead of her but I kept lingering by Charlotte's side. I knew I'd see her again but it wouldn't be soon enough.

Chapter Thirty-Eight

Bang Bang You're Dead

By Betsie

"Jesus Christ" I thought. *"Was the school serious?"*

New Horizons wanted to put on a play where a teenage gunman kills his parents and five students and they wanted Luca to play the gunman.

During our two years of home-schooling, Luca had informed me of his "hit list." He had planned on bringing a gun into the lunchroom of his middle school and one by one taking out the students who had harassed him. Now I was being asked to watch this play-out before my eyes.

Would this bring back old demons, setting us back years? And what about my emotions? Could I handle this?

I didn't want to mess this up. Brooks thought Luca had come a long way and would be fine. Speaking with Luca, he assured me he was okay and was looking forward to doing it. I spoke to his school therapist and she thought it would actually be good for him. Principal Tanner was onboard. So reluctantly, I gave my permission.

The day arrived for parents and teachers to see the play. Brooks couldn't get out of work so I went by myself. I stopped to pick up a bouquet of flowers for the kids to give Deedie, the director, and a few "Congratulations" balloons for the stars of the play.

Luca had put a lot of work into this and I was looking forward to watching him. But the closer I got to the school, the more my stomach told me I didn't want to attend. I was the first to arrive and could have taken any seat I wanted. I chose to sit near an exit door just in case I couldn't handle it. Principal Tanner sat next to me.

As the play began, I was aware of eyes watching me. The teaching staff knew how difficult this was for me.

Luca's composure had me mesmerized.

Bang! The gun is fired and the father is dead. Bang! And the mother is dead.

My heart started racing.

Pop, pop, pop. Five students lie dead on the stage.

I eyed the exit.

The play takes a turn. As ghosts, the five dead students start haunting the gunman.

"Why me?" one of them asks.

"You should have figured that when you pushed me," the gunman replies.

"I had my whole life before me," another one says.

"Sometimes I hate being alive, but I'm afraid to be dead."

"I'll never be nineteen the way I always dreamed about." "I'll never go to college and have a double major." "I'll never be married in a white dress and have a huge wedding." "I'll never learn all mom's recipes." "I'll never have a chance to make dad proud of me." "I'll never cry at my children's graduation." "I will never, I will never . . ."

Each statement is gut-wrenching.

I wanted to leave.

The ghosts are relentless in their verbal attacks.

They finally get through to the gunman and he realizes what he has done.

Feeling the hopelessness of lives lost and knowing there was no one to console the gunman was painful. I wanted to run to my son.

The gunman concludes his monologue with, "Is this the rest of my life?" He falls to his knees and calls out, "Oh God."

The play thankfully ends.

It took a minute for me to catch my breath.

I went to the stage and gave Luca the flowers to give his teacher, then made a quick exit. Sitting alone on the fire-escape steps, I sobbed What if Luca really had been the shooter? All those innocent lives lost.

I was only outside for a few minutes. I knew I had to get to my son.

Wiping my eyes and shaking off my uneasiness, I opened the door. Luca was receiving a lot of well-deserved praise. But what Luca needed the most, and what I needed to give, was a hug from a very proud mother. Eventually I had to release my hold. Taking a step back, I stood in awe as I watched Luca enjoy his moment.

To the audience, Luca's performance that afternoon may have been just that. A performance. To me it was more. Realizing what his life could have been still scares the hell out of me.

Bang, Bang, You're Dead

By Luca

The play *Bang, Bang, You're Dead* was the first stage performance our school had put on in three years. Drama wasn't very popular. In fact, that semester the elective had started out with only four students; Brian, Sarah, myself and one other girl. When Deedie showed me the script for *Bang Bang You're Dead* I talked seven other students and one guidance counselor into joining the cast so we could represent every character needed. Two students and the shop teacher built the props.

It had been such a grueling rehearsal schedule, usually focused on emotionally difficult scripts, Sarah and Brian dropped out. It hurt me when they wouldn't commit to something so many people, including myself, had worked so hard for. But we pushed through with some people doubling up on characters.

At first the boy is indifferent to his crimes; almost proud of them. But when the spirits of the dead haunt him in his jail cell he's confronted with the irreversible devastation he's caused. The character transitions from a self-involved victim, to a boy who finally realizes the world doesn't revolve around him. The play ends with the boy sobbing on his knees alone in his cell with his guilt and regret.

It was a strange experience to act out on stage something I'd once dreamed of doing. I didn't want to kill my parents but shooting kids from my public school who'd made my life hell had sounded very appealing. It wasn't seeing where the road not taken could have landed me, primarily prison, that was eye opening or therapeutic. Nor was it considering the other lives I could have destroyed by murdering my bullies. What got to me was realizing I didn't feel that way anymore. I no longer felt victimized or angry. I didn't harbor any hate or wishes to hurt anyone. After all the name calling, tears, backwards glances over my shoulder and years of living in fear, I was finally free. They couldn't hurt me anymore and I didn't have room in my life to dwell on the past. I was living in the now. And the now was good.

Chapter Thirty-Nine

New Horizons Prom

By Betsie

Together, Luca and I had worked hard to give the students at New Horizons their first- ever prom. Once again we utilized the function room at the condo. Luca was in charge of the music. I was left with the decorations, food and security. The security bothered me the most. After all, a few of the students had behavior problems. Could I trust everyone?

My wonderful family came to the rescue. Between family members volunteering as chaperones and Charlotte's mother agreeing to stay, I felt we had everything under control.

Once in the function room there was no going outside until it was time to leave. No sneaking a joint or drinking alcohol. No leaving to make a phone call. Ellen's boyfriend Charles was in charge of the smoking area, making sure no one snuck out the back door. These kids were my responsibility and I didn't want any trouble.

With my family members watching every move the kids made, I was able to take photos of each couple. We had set up a room with a banner reading New Horizons. The students stood under the banner and I snapped away. I was having a blast. It was so much fun seeing the kids dressed up.

The night progressed without a flaw. The kids didn't eat much and most of them didn't dance, but they were all having lots of laughs. I was exhausted, but thrilled our hard work and months of planning had paid off. Before the evening ended we took a group photo of the twenty teens. Their smiles told a story of a wonderful night.

New Horizons Prom

By Luca

Two weeks before graduation we had our New Horizons prom. It wasn't just open to seniors. I sold tickets to anyone who wanted to come. When I'd approached the school about the dance I was told that for security reasons, they couldn't support me legally; but if I wanted to throw a dance off campus they couldn't stop me. So Mom and I planned the entire thing on a shoestring budget.

For a twenty dollar refundable deposit our function room would provide twenty-four-hour access to a full kitchen, dance floor, lounge area, and folding banquet tables and chairs.

We bought table-cloths and center pieces from the Christmas Tree Shop for mere dollars. Party City blew up a few dozen blue and silver balloons (our school colors) for pennies apiece. I crisscrossed blue Christmas lights over the dance floor. The food was buffet style platters of cold cuts, chicken tenders, cheese, veggies with dip, and fruit trays from a local grocery store deli. The desert was a Costco sheet-cake.

Mom, a former professional photographer, set up a portrait area and volunteered to take pictures. The DJ was a friend I'd met while working at Target. He'd bring professional speakers, a catalog of thousands of songs, a disco ball, and spin tunes all night for half of what most DJs charged. Everything was in place to have a kickass little dance. It was exciting for me to have my family involved. I was looking forward to the big night.

With no overhead or need for profits, I was able to sell tickets to the prom, which included a meal and portraits, for only eighteen dollars. Compared to the eighty dollar public school prom tickets, ours was a bargain. We ended up with less than thirty tickets sold. The prom would be small and intimate. Instead of a faceless party machine, people would be able to make a connection with each other.

Jenny came as Brian's date and showed up early to help me and Mom set everything up. Charlotte's parents drove her and her sister up from New York the day before. They stayed at a motel in town through the weekend. I was thrilled Charlotte would be able to meet some of my family and friends. She was important to me and I wanted everyone to know it.

The girls looked beautiful in their gowns with their hair done up. The guys looked handsome in shirts and ties. People did more mingling than dancing but as long as they had fun that's all that mattered. The DJ was a big hit. Because he was still a high-school student himself, people were comfortable chatting with him and were impressed with his setup.

Charlotte was shy and sort of clung to me most of the night. She looked beautiful in her teal dress with black trim and matching accessories, but because of her tiny figure people thought she was only thirteen or fourteen years old. I felt bad no one went out of their way to talk to her, but my classmates were sort of cliquey when it came to outsiders. More surprising, my friends were a little chilly toward her as well. I think their passive aggressiveness was their way of being protective of me, which was nice, I guess. I knew if they gave her a chance they'd like her. But memories of Ashley still hung in the air, and to a lesser extent Cass and all the rest of my ex's. I think my friends, especially Brian, were sick of getting acquainted with girls who would either try to ruin my life or disappear from it with little warning.

I tried my best to ignore my friends' standoffishness and show Charlotte a nice time. After seeing her dress in New York, Mom and I had bought a matching black bowtie and vest that shimmered teal when I moved. It looked really nice and matched Charlotte's dress well. I thought the two of us looked good together although I outweighed her by almost one hundred pounds. She didn't seem to care though. Probably because years of having the thickest glasses in her small classrooms and being the youngest, therefore smallest and flattest girl in her grade had slowly destroyed most of her self-esteem.

The up-side was she had no idea how attractive she actually was, and she was able to look beyond physical appearance in others. Her loss was my gain. It's the only way I could explain her being satisfied with me. We danced to a couple of slow songs and posed for some pictures together. I didn't try to kiss her because both of our mothers were present, but it was killing me not to.

Near the end of the evening we had a vote for prom king and queen. Since I was running the show I got to count the ballots. More people had voted for me than I would have imagined but I took those out so it wouldn't seem rigged. Brian had a fair amount of votes as well, but the guy with the most votes was a popular jock type. The girl who won prom queen was a very sweet and stylish senior. She seemed touched and that made me happy. Later, for our school yearbook, she was quoted saying being crowned prom queen was her favorite high school memory.

Since the king and queen hadn't come together no one asked them to dance with each other. Instead they had a short spotlight dance with their own dates. It was a nice moment. Shortly after that the party started to break up. Charlotte and her mother went back to their motel while I was left with Mom and my aunts to clean up, but I didn't mind. It gave me time to reminisce on the great night I'd had and what a milestone accomplishment it had been.

Visiting with Charlotte's Family

Coming to Massachusetts was the farthest Charlotte had ever traveled. This was only the second time she had left New York (not including the six mile drive to Danbury, Connecticut.) It blew my mind how sheltered she was and how much I took for granted.

Mom did her best to play tour guide for Charlotte and her family. In the morning we took them to Salem so her family could see some local museums and Pickering Wharf. Charlotte had never seen the ocean before. I thought this was funny and a little sad.

We took the commuter train from Salem to Boston, shopped around Quincy Market and ate lunch inside Faneuil Hall. Walking to Government Center to catch the T, we passed by the decorations for the annual BAGLY youth prom. I'd forgotten it was tonight. I showed Charlotte a flyer and explained to her what it was. She got really excited and I had the brilliant idea that we could go to two proms in two nights. Her mom firmly objected.

My mother let me do almost anything I wanted, few questions asked. Seeing how conservative other parents were gave me a headache. But we only had a few hours left together and I wanted them to be happy so I tried to let it go.

Our next stop was the Museum of Fine Arts. Charlotte had never been to an art museum and this one is world class. I'd been a few times myself, and though it still impressed me, her reaction was more memorable than the art. We walked hand in hand through the many hallways and exhibits, Charlotte reveling in the beauty, history and culture of it all; me reveling in her fascination and smiles. I was pleased I'd taken her somewhere she'd enjoyed and would make a lasting impression.

Being with her made me see things with fresh eyes. Her excitement made the commonplace interesting and the dull beautiful. I loved how everywhere we went she'd notice little things other people, including myself, had overlooked. Without any pretenses or effort, just being herself, Charlotte was fun and stimulating to be around. I wanted to go everywhere with her.

After the museum and dinner, Charlotte came back to my house so we could be alone for an hour or two. Her mother had not been keen on the idea, but after much protesting and begging she'd allowed it; though her jaw was clenched tight when she said okay.

I'd never been alone with Charlotte. She couldn't get over how my bedroom door had a lock on it and we were allowed in my room together. I couldn't imagine not having privacy or the liberty to do whatever I wanted with whomever in my room.

The two of us stretched out on my bed and watched a movie. I don't think Charlotte had ever seen an R rated movie without cable TV edits. She constantly baffled me by how sheltered she was.

I thought this would be my chance to fool around a little before she went back to New York. She wasn't having any of it. No girl had ever told me no before or pulled my hand off her. Then again I'd never been with a girl who hadn't done everything under the sun long before I reached her. It was confusing, frustrating, and made me feel like a would-be date rapist.

I didn't get what the big deal was. My hormones were raging. But Charlotte was a good girl. It was infuriating but also admirable. I wondered if it was hard for her to say no to me, and then felt bad about the position I'd put her in. I respected her enough to drop it. I'd just have to wait until she was ready. I doubted that would be a problem though. I liked Charlotte a lot and was in it for the long haul.

Mom drove me over to Denny's the next morning to have breakfast and say goodbye. It was harder to let her go than it had been in April. Watching as her family pulled away left me cold inside, and the emptiness was growing. I didn't know when I'd see Charlotte again, but I knew attending college in New York suddenly sounded brilliant.

Chapter Forty

Luca Graduates

By Betsie

Luca had fought hard for this day. Not just academically, but in defeating demons that had reared their ugly heads at every opportunity. He had overcome addictions, won friends, and gained confidence.

It wasn't until meeting Kendal Tanner that I had even allowed myself to dream of Luca graduating from high school. There was a time when I honestly believed my son would be dead before the age of seventeen. Working with the staff at New Horizons for the past two years had changed everything. I was thankful for their dedication and grateful I had been given the opportunity of seeing my dream come true.

I was too excited to stay at home. Brooks and I arrived at the restaurant for the graduation lunch forty-five minutes early. Luca was going to give the class speech, and wanting the best advantage point, I changed our seats three times. As Principal Tanner set up rows and rows of trophies, he had to tell me more than once to stop asking if Luca was getting one.

My anxiety rose as students, family, and friends started taking their seats. The head of the Special Education Department of our local school arrived. He stopped to tell me how proud he was of Luca, and how excited he was to be a part of Luca's special day.

For this small, informal graduation, students were not wearing caps and gowns. That is, all the students except one. Wanting the entire graduation experience, Luca had insisted on having a cap and gown. I offered to help the other graduates order one, but no one took me up on it. Luca also had a custom-made high school ring. He was every bit the graduating senior.

Principal Tanner welcomed everyone and gave a brief speech. Then it was time for the awards. The first one was for Best Actor. Luca was presented the award for his performance in *Bang Bang You're Dead*. He received a standing ovation from the students, teachers, and of course, me. There was at least one trophy for each student. No one was left out.

Mary got up to give a few words. She spoke about a special parent who had gone above and beyond for the two years her son had attended New Horizons. This parent had gotten involved in the school: everything from baking cakes for special occasions and always being the designated driver, to giving the students a first-ever prom.

I knew Mary was speaking about me. My face became red. My nerves took over, and my ears started ringing. I didn't hear the rest of her speech. I was too busy thinking about not tripping on my way up to receive the beautiful bouquet of flowers Mary was holding. What an unexpected honor! Not only did I get to attend my son's graduation, but I was made a part of it by receiving the "Mother of the Year" award. I thought the day couldn't get any better.

There was still one more award on the table. Deedie, Luca's drama teacher got up to say how much this particular student had contributed to New Horizons: orchestrating the first ever New Horizons teachers' awards, collecting cans for charities, and volunteering with younger, disabled students. Once, when called into the principal's office, this student called the principal "Poopy Face."

Only Luca could get away with that one.

Deedie went on to say how this "Student of the Year" award was being given to a student who had not only made a difference to the school but to the teaching staff as well.

Once again, Luca received his award to the applause of students, teachers and guests.

Then it was time for diplomas. I was so proud, I could barely contain myself. When Luca stopped to give Mary a hug instead of the usual handshake, tears welled in my eyes. She had been instrumental in making sure he graduated from high school. Mary had stood up for him in Juvenile Court, and had taken many short walks with him when Luca needed someone to talk to. It was going to be difficult for Luca and me to say good-bye.

After Principal Tanner said a few more words to the graduates, Luca was called to the podium. Watching him walk up and confidently take his position was more emotionally charged than anything I could have expected.

All through elementary school, with Marie's straight A's we always thought she would become Valedictorian of her graduating class. She was going to become a doctor. Drugs, alcohol and life had gotten in her way. Yet there we were. Luca may not have been top of his class at a major public high school, but he was top of his class at New Horizons High School. A school that taught more than the three R's. There was a fourth R. Respect. Not just respect of others but respect of oneself.

Luca had not practiced his speech in front of anyone. In fact, even the teachers had no idea what he was going to say. I don't remember his exact words, but I do remember the tears.

Giving me a gentle nudge, my sister, Dorothy said, "Look around. There isn't a dry eye in here."

When Luca returned to our table I stood up to give him a hug. It didn't matter that I cried on his shoulder in front of a room full of strangers. Together, we had journeyed down the path of our "*Yellow Brick Road*," with all its demons and beauty. We deserved this moment.

New Horizons Graduation

By Luca

Although I wouldn't receive my diploma from my hometown until I completed my third summer-school session, I was on the list of graduating seniors at New Horizons. It was the largest graduating class to date for the school; thirteen seniors.

I'd been approached by Principal Tanner to speak at the ceremony. I spent two weeks preparing my speech for the event. I wanted to convey my thanks to my family and teachers for their wisdom, guidance, and support. I also wanted to thank my fellow students, even the ones I wasn't overly fond of, for their individuality and spirit.

Our student body was an eclectic one and getting along with everyone was a challenging learning experience unto itself. As students and young people entering the world it was important we respect each other and value each other's talents and contributions. With the stigma of special education over our heads, we needed to constantly raise the bar of expectations in ourselves. Our teachers would no longer be at our backs. It was up to us to remind ourselves how intelligent and capable we were; to believe in ourselves when we were underestimated and life was kicking our asses.

I hoped my sentiments would get through.

When the big day came I showed up in a silver graduation gown and cap with a blue tassel. I was the only graduate in a gown, but since I wouldn't be attending a public school graduation I wanted the cap and gown photos. The ceremony was on a week-day but both my parents took time from work to attend. Two of my aunts, my cousins Will and Ellen and my two youngest cousins also came.

Sometimes I wondered what my baby cousins thought about me. They were both born before I transitioned, but not much before. The youngest had always known me as Luca but her older brother might have a few memories of Marie. I was the only person in my family to attend an alternative school. Did this make my cousins think I was stupid or a troublemaker? I think some of my fellow students scared them a little. But it was nice to have them there.

Before diplomas were given out, academic achievement awards and sports awards were presented. I was given an award for drama, English, music, and player of the year in softball. I'd joined softball in the spring when basketball ended. The award was for effort, not skill, I assure you. I also received the overall academic student of the year award.

Mom was singled out for a "mother of the year" award for all her volunteering and support at the school. It was the first time an award had been given to a parent. It was a surprise to me as well as Mom. She totally deserved some recognition for all she did to help people. I was proud she was my mother. Plus, it was funny to see her blush in public.

I gave my speech right before lunch was served. It received mixed responses. Some people seemed moved and others wanted me to shut up so they could eat. The next day at school though, a number of students, particularly those I hadn't gotten along with during the year, came and thanked me for my words. Connecting to other humans and conveying admiration and respect, especially to people you have little in common with and can barely stand to be near, is difficult and humbling. I was astounded and thrilled that I'd reached them.

There were plenty of hugs, tears and photos to commemorate the occasion. I'd expected to feel something like pride, joy, anticipation or reverence. But everything was happening so fast I didn't have time to feel much of anything. I was grateful for my family, teachers and friends but that was no different than any other day. I still had another week of school and two months of summer school ahead of me so it didn't feel like anything was over yet. I suppose I just felt stunned.

The transformation I had undergone in recent years was unbelievable. I'd gone from Marie; the friendless, sad, lonely, fat, ugly, useless girl who wanted to kill herself almost as badly as her classmates wanted her dead, and became Luca; sort of happy, sort of popular, in a relationship with a smart hot girl and graduating high-school a year early with many honors.

My high-school experience hadn't been perfect. There'd been many ups and downs, disappointments, confusions and heart-aches. But the bad and the good had evened out to what I felt was a normal middle ground. There was a time when I'd thought I'd never experience anything normal, so to me normal was awesome. If someone had told me in middle school that I'd have friends, a girlfriend, and enjoy high-school, I'd have never believed it.

New York, New York

On the last day of school I found out Principal Tanner had been let go. It felt like the Kennedy assassination of my generation. Kendal was like a second father to all of his students. I'd never respected or loved another man as much as I did him. Sure he'd suspended me once or twice for fighting, but that's because he was fair. He didn't play favorites. We were all his favorites. It wouldn't have affected me since I was moving on, but that was hardly the point. They had removed the most loved, trusted and competent man in the building. A good amount of students cried when they heard the news, possibly parents as well.

My mother and a number of other parents formed a group, appealing the decision. Kendal was the only person they entrusted with their children's futures. Some parents of graduates joined the group, stating that without Kendal's guidance their kids would never have completed high school. I thought about the principal of the other alternative school who had wanted to out me to the entire student body, and my hometown elementary and junior high principals who had turned blind eyes when I was being tortured.

I knew beyond a shadow of doubt, were it not for Kendal, I'd never have completed high school; I'd be lucky to have a GED. My guidance counselor and other teachers had made a huge difference; but if Kendal wasn't who he was, I may not have even enrolled. I owed him so much it bummed me out there was little I could do for him now. I prayed Mom and the other parents would get the matter resolved before summer school started.

Meanwhile, for over a month, Brian and I had been planning a trip to New York. I'd saved up money from working after school and Brian had a good chunk of change from graduation gifts. Mom made us reservations at the same hotel I'd stayed at for my surgery. One of the bond traders from New York mom worked with bought Brian and me tickets to see *CATS* as a graduation gift. Brian and I were thrilled. While in New York, I was going to take the train north one afternoon to visit Charlotte, and I'd get to see my first Broadway musical. This was wicked exciting.

I packed a small duffle bag and grabbed a backpack for my Discman, CDs and maps. With $400 transferred from my savings to my checking account, I braced myself to enter the world unsupervised.

When we stepped out of the bus terminal and onto the streets of downtown Manhattan, I watched Brian's face as he took it all in. Manhattan on a slow day is like Boston during the marathon, the last game of the World Series and the weekend before Christmas all at the same time.

This was Brian's first time here. He hadn't been allowed to smoke on the bus or inside the station and was craving a cigarette pretty bad, but he still had a huge grin on his face. If he could smile while he was fiending, I knew he was happy.

Instead of dining out at touristy restaurants, Brian and I got most of our food from convenience stores and street carts. Hostess cupcakes and falafel - nutrition at its best. We walked the streets well past midnight and took pictures of the fronts of all the sex shops and strip clubs, which were novelties to us. Each night we'd go to a different fancy bar on Broadway, sit in the window overlooking the street and split an appetizer because that's all we could afford. It probably drove the servers nuts.

On our second day in the city, I left Brian behind while I took the Metro North line to Brewster. The train tickets were over $20. That put a bigger hole in my wallet than I'd planned for. I caught a cab to Charlotte's house from the Brewster train station.

Charlotte answered the door with a huge smile and threw her arms around my neck. I momentarily lost myself in the sweet smell of her hair.

Charlotte's parents were out but her older sister was home. It made our all-afternoon make out session awkward, but not enough to deter us. Hormones can overcome almost anything.

I skipped lunch and dinner while at Charlotte's. Partly because I didn't want to waste our precious time together by doing something as mundane as eating, but also because she made me so nervous and excited my stomach did flip flops around her.

When her mother got home from work she seemed pissed Charlotte and I had been in Charlotte's room with the door closed. If she thought that was bad, she should have asked my mother how she liked waiting for me or my dates to put on clothes before we answered the door. I was smart enough not to suggest it though. Charlotte was so shy and chaste she'd barely let me sneak a peek at her boobs, which were the best set of boobs I'd ever seen and totally worth my travel and fuss. I thought her mom should cut her some slack. But I managed to keep my mouth shut, even as Joanne was ushering me to her car to drive me back to the train station and away from her home as quickly as possible.

It was painful to say goodbye to Charlotte. I wished I could whisk her away to the city with me for the next two nights. If she thought the Museum of Fine Arts was awesome, the Metropolitan Museum of Art would rock her world. I wanted to show her Fifth Avenue, Times Square, the lights of Broadway and the Empire State Building at dusk.

I felt guilty leaving Charlotte behind in a dead-end town like Brewster. I wanted to attend college in New York City so I could visit her more often and hopefully she could visit the city with me. When I returned to the hotel, I'd get started convincing Brian to move to New York with me.

When I got back to the city Brian was sort of pissy that I'd left him alone all day. I offered to pay for his admission to the Empire State Building to make it up to him.

Street level in July, the city was hot and suffocating, even late at night. Up past the 100th floor you could finally feel a breeze. We lingered at the top of the Empire State Building until closing, for the view as well as the cool air. Brian and I were on the last elevator full of tourists forced to head down for the night. It was rad not having to worry about being back at a certain time so Mom could get us at a train station or getting in before Brian's grandmother was in bed. Not wanting the night to end, we went for coffee at midnight and walked around for another hour discussing our dreams of moving here.

Our last night in the city we saw *CATS*. I'd never listened to any of the songs from the show and didn't know what to expect other than *cats*, of course. But the show had been a staple on Broadway for most of my lifetime so I figured it would be good.

Our seats were incredible. Front and center. Mom's broker friend really spoiled Brian and me. Seats this good were way beyond our reach on our own. For two kids from a small town with big city dreams this was breathtakingly stupendous. Of course we giggled like schoolgirls at our amazing fortunes, showing ourselves for the rubes we were to the sophisticated city dwellers around us.

As advertised, the show was about cats. The stage was really cool but I thought the characters were annoying and the songs were superficial. How this show remained popular was beyond me. It pretty much relied on *"Memory"* to redeem it. Thankfully, the woman who sang it f'n nailed it. The performance was haunting. I'll never forget it.

The next morning we lamentingly packed our bags and checked out of the hotel. Our bus home didn't leave for another eight hours so we planned to visit the Metropolitan Museum of Art until we left. When we stepped outside the weather had changed drastically from the previous three days. It was pouring buckets, the sky was charcoal gray and the streets were a moving ocean of uniform black umbrellas. With no rain gear of our own, Brian and I were drenched to the skin before we reached the end of the block.

After buying admission to the Metropolitan Museum of Art we couldn't afford lunch. I purchased a gift for Charlotte in the gift shop, and then couldn't afford dinner later either. The air conditioning on our soaked clothes and wet skin made our teeth chatter and our lips turn blue. Our sneakers squeaked loudly in the large halls and we left little puddles behind us throughout three exhibits before calling it quits and heading to the bus station early. We split a refillable cup of coffee before braving the dreaded public transportation system. We'd reached our tolerance level for being wet and figured what's the worst that could happen on the train? Maybe someone could pick our empty pockets.

The subway turned out to be cheap, cleanish and no more confusing or dangerous than Boston's. Brian and I made it to the bus station quickly and easily, and then kicked ourselves for not taking the train earlier instead of walking around getting soaked.

I was flat broke, waterlogged and freezing. I dug around in my bag for some dry clothes, not caring if they were dirty. The chill had sunk through to my bones. But everything in my duffle bag was as wet as what I had on.

We made it back to Boston unscathed, leaving soggy ass-prints on the seat cushions of the bust for the next lucky passengers. Without enough money for the train tickets back to the North Shore, Brian's dad had to drive into Boston to pick us up. He reached us just as Brian's cigarettes ran out. Thank goodness, otherwise things might have gotten ugly.

Overall, Brian and I had a great trip, although our friendship had been tested a few times and it was obvious we needed to learn to better manage our money. I'd lost eight pounds in three and a half days from all the walking and lack of food. Brian lost eleven. We couldn't wait to go back.

Chapter Forty-One

Going Nowhere

By Betsie

Luca had been accepted to Salem State College under their Special Education program. Instead of seeing the positive side and all the possibilities, he felt insulted. Nothing I could do or say was going to change his mind. After everything we had gone through for him to graduate high school, it broke my heart when he gave up so quickly.

A local women's clothing warehouse hired both Luca and Brian to do data entry. I'll never forget the day Luca surprised me with the most beautiful white evening dress. Hundreds of hand-sewn beads and pearls adorned the laced scooped-neck and bodice. A scalloped pattern finished off the short, lace sleeves. Fine, soft silk was layered over the three-quarter length satin skirt. I absolutely fell in love with it.

Employees of the women's warehouse were able to purchase samples. To someone else it may have been a sales sample, but to me it was a gown fit for royalty. Although the dress was a few sizes too small for me, I kept it hanging in my closet, still in the plastic wrapping, for over five years. I had to lose fifty pounds to fit into it, but when it zipped up and I could still breathe, I felt like a queen.

Luca liked his job, but now his mind was set on living in New York and attending college there. I found the Kingsborough Community College in Brooklyn. Luca and I even flew to New York to visit and tour the school. We submitted an application and Luca was accepted for the winter semester.

Brian had agreed to move to New York with Luca but just a few weeks before they were scheduled to leave, he had second thoughts. We had to cancel everything. Now, not only was Luca not going to attend college but he wanted nothing to do with his best friend.

To help Luca get out of his depression, I suggested he try out for a part in a local production of *Mame*. He was given two small parts. For the last performance I purchased tickets for my family and the teachers from New Horizons. Luca and his father had been fighting and he specifically asked me not to let his father attend. Brooks wanted to go so I went ahead and purchased a ticket for him. Luca stopped speaking to me.

When fights broke out between Brooks and me, Luca would always take my side, sometimes even wanting to hurt his father. I would tell him it wasn't worth it. Then Luca and I would argue over my complacency. I was trying to keep Luca safe. I didn't want him getting in the middle and hating his father. In actuality, he already hated him. I should have left Brooks years earlier and the fighting between all of us would have ended; a victory achieved with no winners at the end of the finish line.

The following day Luca had a dental appointment. He promised me he would find a ride.

Before leaving work, I called the dentist's office to let Luca know I was on my way.

"Mrs. Harvie, Luca never showed up for his appointment," the receptionist told me.

I called the house. No answer. I called the motel where Luca was working. They hadn't seen him. I called Brian. He had no idea where Luca was. I headed home.

Checking Luca's room, I realized some of his things were missing: pillow, duffle bag and backpack. He was gone. What the hell? With everything I had done for him, how could he do this to me? An angry knot formed in my stomach.

Going Nowhere

By Luca

After my trip to New York with Brian, a lot of things happened quickly. Kendal wasn't reinstated at New Horizons. I, my parents, other students and parents held a small protest on the sidewalk in front of the school. We received a tiny write-up in a local paper. All this accomplished was making summer school more awkward and me being banned from school grounds upon my completion of the summer session. I finally received my high-school diploma but it was too late to enroll in colleges for the fall semester.

Stuck in a small town, rather than twiddle my thumbs until winter college registration I got a job. Brian and I both ended up working at a mail-order women's clothing warehouse. It was a good job. I made $10 an hour handling most of the filing and data entry for the receiving department. I didn't feel I was living up to my potential though.

Salem State College had accepted my application for a late admission under special education guidelines. I didn't understand what that meant; to be in special education in a college. After high-school I had a wild hair across my ass about being perceived as less than equal and didn't want anything further to do with special education. I decided not to pursue higher learning at Salem State. This was probably a huge mistake. Getting into a state school with my background was a great opportunity, no matter what standards they held me to. I could have proven myself equal, but alas, I was seventeen, bitter and stupid. Besides, I had dreams of a bigger city.

Toward the end of July I'd been at Hampton Beach with Dad and had bumped into Stacy, my ex-girlfriend Harmony's former best friend. Stacy and I spent the next two days catching up. After the third time we hung out, she kissed me goodnight. I honestly hadn't seen it coming but I couldn't deny that Stacy and I had tremendous chemistry. When I told Charlotte about it over the phone we broke up. I regretted it instantly, but what could I do? I'd allowed myself to be a victim of circumstance.

Charlotte was impossibly far away and still had two years of high-school ahead of her. She was barely more than a girl and her parents kept her on a tight leash. Stacy was a short train ride away, three years older and wiser than Charlotte. As much as I loved Charlotte, Stacy was more my equal.

Of course things didn't work out with Stacy. She'd known I was trans and none of that had been an issue. Stacy and I shared a deep connection but our personalities were too much alike. It felt like dating my twin sister. This freaked me out. In typical Luca fashion, instead of breaking up with her, I waited until she went off to college and stopped returning her calls. From then on I threw myself into work, pulling fifty-six to sixty hour weeks and banking all my paychecks. I just wanted everything to go by quickly until Christmas was over and winter registration started for colleges.

Mom and I found a great community college in Brooklyn, New York near Coney Island. It was in a quiet neighborhood and had a comprehensive theatre department. In September we visited the campus and checked out apartment agents in the area. My application was accepted and we put down a deposit on a small one bedroom apartment for me and Brian that rented for $750 a month. He'd have the bedroom and I'd sleep in the living room. One of my aunts bought me a really nice futon to celebrate. I was all set.

Two weeks before Christmas I put in my notice at work. I wanted to be free to celebrate the holiday with my family and have time to pack before moving to Brooklyn. But on Christmas Eve, Brian and I had a small fight and his family convinced him not to move to New York. I couldn't afford the apartment by myself for more than a few months and was afraid I wouldn't find a roommate I could trust. So two weeks before I was supposed to move I had to call everything off.

I had no college prospects, no girlfriend and no job. I would have begged for my job back at the warehouse but I'd trained my replacement before leaving so I knew that bridge was burned. Plus, I didn't want my former co-workers to know I'd failed so miserably at trying to get out of there. I took a part-time job with my cousin Will, selling sunglasses from a cart at the mall. It was awesome of him to get me the job but every day I had to watch teenagers coming and going, excited about the life ahead of them while mine was passing me by. I fell into a deep depression and started starving myself. I stole my mom's prescription Darvocet to fill the void in me.

I couldn't stand working at the mall and being surrounded by happy young people, so I applied for a job as a desk clerk at a sleazy motel. I felt more comfortable selling overpriced rooms with moldy carpeting, exposed wiring, cable-less televisions, and dirty sheets to hookers and drug addicts. My only other co-workers were a twenty-year-old girl and our twenty-one-year-old manager. I worked seven days a week, sometimes pulling twelve and sixteen hour shifts if the manager wanted time off. I loved my job though. The guests were usually regulars and they'd buy me food and cigarettes. People would come down to the lobby to hang out and talk all the time. At night I'd lock the doors and watch T.V.

I moved into the motel so I wouldn't have to commute home to sleep during the day. But instead of sleeping, I'd mix cough syrup and Sudafed (before they took the pseudoephedrine out of it) and trip balls all day. I was still wickedly depressed and preferred the hallucinations brought on by insomnia and over the counter drugs to reality. Sometimes while I was awake and alone, instead of watching the room grow larger and blacker around me, I'd write Charlotte long tear stained letters of insane ramblings. I never mailed them.

In the spring I joined a local theatre company and their production of *Mame*. It broke up the monotony of pain killers, pseudoephedrine, dextromethorphan and self-loathing. It was also a good distraction from the fighting going on between me and my parents.

On Mother's Day, after the final production, I attended the cast party. My boss at the motel had called and left a message for me to come in early so she could go to a Mother's Day party for her mom. I ignored her. I'd gone in early plenty of times. The play was done with its short run and we'd only be having a cast party once. I'd grown fond of a few fellow actors and lamented parting with them for what could be the last time.

I made it to work two hours early, but not the four hours early my boss had wanted. She screamed at me in the parking lot on her way out, calling me a selfish piece of shit and what not. Marie would have taken that kind of verbal abuse. Not Luca. The next day I decided to call out of work and see how my boss liked working a twelve hour shift since she had no problem dishing them out. Besides, I hadn't had a day off since February.

I knew she'd be mad but I didn't expect her to freak the fuck out. She screamed a string of curses at me so loud and so long I thought her head would explode. I hung up on her mid-rant but she called me right back. I let the machine pick it up.

"You little motherfucker. I had plans to go to the beach with my boyfriend this afternoon! When Cheryl gets here I'm coming straight to your house to kick your ass!"

Are you kidding me? Who was I working for, Ashley? If you scratch the surface, are all girls this psychotic?

Mom and I hadn't spoken for days. Weeks earlier, she and Dad had a huge fight, and he'd thrown something at her. This pissed me off and I went after him. Before I could reach him, Mom caught up with me and blamed me for everything, even though their fight had nothing to do with me. Her leg was bleeding, but she insisted it had been an accident and I was the asshole for getting mad. Okay. Sure. I'd had my fill of this Dad-yells-at-Mom-so-Mom-yells-at-me bullshit.

My relationship with everyone I knew was strained at best. Since my boss was on her way to my house to attack me, I figured I was unemployed again. I thought, "Fuck this noise. I'm out of here." I packed a bag and called a cab.

Chapter Forty-Two

Virginia – Country Mouse

By Betsie

My anger over Luca taking off the previous day quickly turned into a sickening fear when I awoke the following morning and he still wasn't home. There were just too many scenarios playing out in my head. Remembering the movie *Boys Don't Cry* sent me into a panic. Where the hell was he? Why hadn't he called? Was he in trouble?

I would have lost my mind if I stayed at home. Brooks was going to be working the late shift so I went to work. At least one of us would be home if Luca called.

Concentrating was difficult. Every time my phone rang I thought the worst.

A co-worker suggested I call our bank. If Luca withdrew his money, maybe he said something. I called and asked for the manager.

"My son and I have a joint account. Can you tell me if there's any money left in it?"

"Mrs. Harvie, almost all the funds were drawn out yesterday."

"May I speak with the teller?"

"Did she do anything wrong?" the manager asked.

"No, all the funds belonged to my son. I'm just wondering if he said anything to her."

The teller came to the phone.

"Mrs. Harvie, your son said something about going to Virginia."

"Thanks. That's all I needed. And don't worry, he had the right to take his money."

Luca had been chatting on-line with someone from Virginia. I didn't know much about her except she was married and had a son. What the hell had she told him that would make him withdraw the thousands of dollars he had worked so hard to save?

I couldn't wait to leave work. A few weeks earlier Luca had actually spoken to this person over the phone. Hopefully, I could find the bill with her number.

Sure enough, there were a few calls to a Virginia number. So I dialed.

"Hello," a young male voice answered.

"Hi. I'm looking for Luca."

"He's with my mom at the hotel. Here's the number."

"By the way, what's your mom's name?"

"Gwen."

"Thanks."

Were things at home so bad he felt the need to flee all the way to Virginia?

With the heaviness of feeling betrayed, I called the hotel.

"I'm looking for Luca Harvie," I told the desk clerk.

"I'll connect you."

I wished the spinning on this nauseating carnival ride would stop.

"Hello," a female voice answered.

"I want to speak to Luca."

"He doesn't want to speak with you."

"Listen. I'm only going to say this once and I mean it," I told the unfamiliar voice. "If anything, AND I MEAN ANYTHING, happens to my son, I'll hold you personally responsible. If you or your husband hurt him in any way, I'll kill both of you."

I slammed down the receiver, not giving her a chance to respond.

Why had Luca done this to me? Had I broken him to the point he felt he had to leave? I was inconsolable and spent most nights sleeping in Luca's bedroom crying myself to sleep.

Not speaking with him was killing me. It took me a few weeks, but I put aside my pride and called Luca to be sure he was alright. He couldn't talk for long but insisted everything was okay. The sadness in his voice told me otherwise.

I tried calling Luca many times over the next few weeks, but it seemed there was always something going on, always a reason he couldn't speak with me. Then, one day, he surprised me.

"Mom, I want to come home. Will you come and get me?"

He had finally come to his senses. Brooks and I made the long drive down to Virginia.

Oh my God. What a freakin' mess. The smell of cat urine and garbage were overpowering. I refused to go in any further than the other side of the door. Brooks refused to go in at all.

Gwen was at work. We'd meet her later. After loading the trunk with Luca's bags, Brooks and I headed for the hotel. We needed a rest before meeting this Gwen person at a local Chinese Buffett.

It was difficult being nice to her. After all, she was responsible for Luca leaving everything behind and running to Virginia. She was also rude. Either no one had taught her manners or she chose not to use them. She must have left her please-and-thank-yous back in the filth of the rented duplex. When I asked Luca how come Gwen was eating so much, he said they hadn't eaten a decent meal in days.

What the hell had Luca gotten himself into?

Brooks, Luca and I left the following day for our long drive back to Massachusetts. I thought we had gone to Virginia to bring Luca home for good. My anger reared its ugly head when he told us he was just coming back to get his driver's license. Why did I bother driving 800 miles to get him? Brooks and I both tried convincing Luca he owed Gwen nothing and begged him not to go back. The fighting began again.

Arriving home the following day, our answering machine was filled with messages and the phone was ringing. It was Gwen. She was relentless. More than once I had to tell her to stop calling. Luca stopped answering the phone. It did no good.

We left the phone unplugged for a day figuring Gwen would get the message. Nope. As soon as the phone was plugged back in, the ringing began. After speaking to Gwen, Luca told us he would be going back to Virginia as soon as he had his license. I held my tongue. Once again, I would have to put my broken heart back together.

Luca was so unhappy. I couldn't believe he would take living with that slob, in dirty surroundings, over living at home. I still couldn't accept the fact Luca had left because he felt he had no other choice. Perceptions are everything. I didn't think Brooks was that bad. I had become used to his rantings.

One day, while speaking with Luca over the phone, I told him to go and look for a car. I wanted him to know when things got really bad he could just pack up and drive out of hell.

Christmas was coming, and I wanted Luca to have something reminding him of home. Something comforting. I sent him his Christmas stocking from his first Christmas. A friend had made it when Marie was born. When he changed his name, I had taken the time to carefully remove Marie's name and sew in Luca's name. Sending it to Virginia would turn out to be a regrettable action for me.

On Christmas morning, I tried calling Luca but Gwen wouldn't let him come to the phone. Then, a few hours later, I received a call.

"Mom, I'm on my way home."

Words I had waited months to hear.

Snow was falling from Washington, D.C. right up through New England. I begged Luca to stay in a motel for the night. He insisted he would be okay. He just wanted to get home. I sat by the window watching the snow accumulate and worrying.

Finally, around two a.m., the living room door opened. Luca was home. Best Christmas gift ever.

Luca had been home for a few weeks when the unthinkable happened. Gwen convinced him to go back to Virginia.

I didn't know how much more of this I could take. Luca was unhappy, but I couldn't do anything about it. Each time I had the chance to speak to him, I begged him to come home.

Then, the Saturday before Easter, I got an early morning phone call.

"Mom, I've left my job. I think I'm coming home."

"Luca, just get in your car and drive."

"Mom, I love you."

"Love you too, Hon."

My phone started ringing a few hours later, but it wasn't Luca. It was Gwen. She wanted to know where he was. She was stuck at work and had no way of getting back to the farm house they had rented.

"Gwen, I really don't know what to tell you. I don't know where Luca is. You'll have to ask some friends for a ride."

"He better not be on his way to Massachusetts."

"Gwen, go home."

About an hour later, my phone rang again. I hoped it would be Luca. But no, it was Gwen.

"I need to know where Luca is."

"I've already told you, I don't know."

"I can't live here without him. I'm going to lose my job. He needs to come back."

"Gwen, when I hear from him, I'll call you."

Late that night, Luca called me. He was heading to Charlotte's house in New York. If he could make it there, he would be safe for the night.

"Call me when you get there. I don't care how late it is."

I was up past midnight but no phone call. Knowing how tired Luca must have been made it difficult to convince myself he was alright.

It was a long night. The following morning, I tried calling Charlotte's house but couldn't get through.

When my phone rang, I raced to answer it. But it wasn't Luca. I felt sick. It was Gwen. She wanted to know what was going on.

"Luca is on his way to Massachusetts. He was supposed to go to Charlotte's, but I don't know if he made it. I'll let you know when I hear from him."

Finally, Sunday morning Luca called. His weary voice awakened my tears. He'd be home soon.

I contacted Gwen. She unloaded her anger on me. Even with everything she had done, I felt sorry for her.

It was a beautiful Easter afternoon when Luca walked through the doorway at my sister's house. There were no words. Just hugs and more tears. My nightmare was over. Luca was home.

Virginia – Country Mouse

By Luca

The cab picked me up and pulled out of the driveway just as my boss from Super 8 was turning in. I couldn't believe she'd actually shown up for a throw-down. Did she expect me to trade blows with her in the parking lot or something? I slumped in the backseat of the taxi until we were down the road a bit.

The first stop was the bank so I could empty out my savings account. I'd saved thousands of dollars and even in hundreds the envelope full of cash was too big to fold. This was crazy.

Next stop was the train station in Salem. I tipped the driver and waited with my duffle-bag, backpack, and wad of cash, for a train to Boston. From North Station, I took the subway to South Station.

I knew a woman in Southwestern Virginia from a chat-room on AOL. She was nine years older than me, married and had a son eight years younger than me. She was interested in me romantically even though she knew my age and that I was trans. I figured what the hell. I paid cash for an Amtrak ticket to Richmond.

Second, third, fourth, and fiftieth thoughts about leaving for a place I'd never been to, to be with a woman I'd never met, swirled around my head. The wait for my train was almost three hours. Mom would be home from work by now and wondering where I went. Brian was going to be pissed that I'd left without saying anything. My whole family would think I was nuts. I decided to call someone to kill time and calm my nerves.

I called Stacy at her apartment near college. She thought I was making a huge mistake and begged me to stay with her for a while instead. She was in a relationship with a woman now but said I could stay on their couch for a few weeks. It was very tempting. I could crash in a liberal college town and meet other intelligent, intellectual types.

But Gwen, the woman in Virginia, was already expecting me. I'd phoned her before leaving the condo and she'd set to work kicking out her husband. I didn't owe her anything but felt I did since she'd up-heaved her home life at my request. I was also afraid if I went to Stacy's I'd end up back with my parents again and never really escape. Reluctantly, I hung up on Stacy and continued to wait for my train.

It was a thirteen hour train ride to Richmond, followed by a cab ride and a four hour bus trip to where Gwen lived. I hadn't slept at all. The money in my back pocket made me too nervous to get comfortable. This was the farthest I'd ever traveled on my own after transitioning. I was deep in bible thumping Confederate territory. Not a safe place for a young trans boy alone.

I met Gwen at a hotel. We wanted to be alone to get to know one another before I went to her house and met her son. I walked into the air-conditioned room and the only light inside came from the TV. At first I couldn't see Gwen. When my eyes adjusted to the dark I saw the glow of a Newport 100 wedged between pudgy fingers with huge acrylic nails. My insides were screaming at me to turn around and leave. But I'd come too far and had nowhere else to run. I knew I'd made a mistake. All I could do now was grin and bear it.

The first thing that bothered me was how needy and clingy she was. We'd just met and she couldn't stand for me to be out of her sight. She didn't even want me to close the door when I went to the bathroom. We compromised; I'd shut the door but not lock it. Then as soon as I had started to pee she busted in and struck up a conversation. I'd never had my privacy and independence so smothered before. I was instantly uncomfortable. I'd only been with Gwen two hours before I wondered how much more I could take.

In Manhattan, I'd felt like a country mouse visiting the city. In Virginia, everywhere I went I felt like a city mouse. I saw all kinds of people and customs that made me want to run back to Boston and kiss its sidewalks.

There were a few differences between New England and this pocket of Virginia I couldn't reconcile. One was their tolerance of domestic violence. **Every** woman I met either had a man or ex that smacked the shit out of her. Then there was the blatant racism, illiteracy, anti-choice and religious billboards everywhere. But strangely there were more gay bars and gay book stores in small town Virginia than the entire "liberal" North Shore where I grew up. It was an odd contrast. I liked having more access to "queer" culture than I did in Massachusetts, but I was never going to be able to call the South home.

Things in Virginia never went well for me. Even when I was out having a good time; driving the Blue Ridge Parkway, walking the Appalachian trail, going out to dinner or the movies, people pegged me as a "Yankee," as soon as I opened my mouth. Their demeanor toward me changed instantly.

Growing up outside Boston, I had no idea people down south were still upset about losing "the war." Even at the local gay bar, drag queens and gays would spit the word "Yankee" at me as if it was a curse. I was constantly surrounded by rebel flags and insistences that the south will rise again.

I'd thought being trans would be my biggest hurdle, but it turned out to be my accent.

Another setback was their public transportation system. It didn't really exist. If I wanted to leave the house and get more than a mile or two I'd have to get a driver's license. I thought it would be easier to go back to Massachusetts so I could test on streets I knew. After five weeks without me, my parents were prepared to drive the 800 miles between us to visit and take me home for a week.

Gwen and her son weren't into housework. If Jody spilled something, the thought of cleaning it wouldn't cross his mind or Gwen's minds. So the interior of the townhouse Gwen rented was covered in stains. The walls were tinged a nice yellow from the millions of Newports she and her husband had smoked. The trash barrel and sink had maggots from never being cleaned or emptied in a timely manner. The kitchen floor housed an army of ants marching back and forth from sticky maple syrup to a soda spill or piece of forgotten food. The flowers along the side of the house were dead from Jody pissing on them rather than climbing the stairs to use the bathroom like a human. The ashtrays were always full so Gwen would resort to whatever was at hand for her cigarette butts: an empty can of soda, a glass of water, a plate of food she was finished with. The carpet had fleas from their mangy cats. The furniture smelled like Jody's ass because he went weeks at a time without bathing. When I first moved in I did my best to clean but it was impossible to keep up.

The first thing Dad said when he and Mom walked in the door was, "Pack your things. You're not staying here."

Mom and Dad knew I wasn't living the high life but were shocked to see how far I'd fallen. I was embarrassed myself. Gwen hadn't wanted me to get my license in Massachusetts. She didn't want me to go back there at all or for my parents to visit. She only agreed to let me go if I got her name tattooed on me. This hardly seemed fair or smart but it was impossible to win an argument with Gwen. The tattoo I got on my wrist was small, black and easily covered with my watch. I was sad my first tattoo hadn't been something cool. Gwen was pissed my watch covered it. My parents were just pissed.

For most of the drive north, my parents tried to convince me not to go back to Virginia. Their throats went hoarse by the time we reached the George Washington Bridge and the subject was finally dropped.

It was tempting to move back in with them. My standards of living had fallen considerably since leaving home. But after a day with my parents I remembered why I left in the first place.

I was home for about a week. After a driving lesson with Mom and one with a professional, I took the road test and got my license. I marveled at how simple it was this time for me to obtain official identity documentation that reflected my right name and gender. For a moment I felt proud. Then it was back to Virginia.

Since I hadn't known how to drive, Gwen had been driving us around in her husband's car although her driver's license had been revoked years earlier. After my return, we gave the car to her husband and let him take over the payments.

Mom bought me a modest car. Now I needed a job to pay the car insurance and the rest of my bills. My savings had gone quickly in the short time I'd been unemployed and living with Gwen. We'd moved out of the townhouse and into a string of rundown motels. The motels had been deplorable and costly compared to rent.

I got a job at the same warehouse where Gwen worked. It was awful. Gwen worked in the office. I worked on the warehouse floor packing and shipping mail order products. I was introduced to mandatory overtime, spending twelve to fifteen hours a day on my feet stooped over a dusty concrete floor, moving boxes. My feet barked and my back screamed. The injury to my hips and lower back from the MBTA beating made my job hell. Gwen introduced me to amphetamines which blocked out the pain and gave me an energy boost, unlike opioids which left me drained and fuzzy. Soon I couldn't work a shift without them.

My home life was dreadful. After Gwen's son Jody got us kicked out of our third motel, I got in a fight with Gwen about it. Exasperated, I was drinking at night and cutting my upper arms under my t-shirt sleeves to vent my frustration.

Jody was out of control. My only experience with kids was with my cousins. None of them had been half as bad or difficult as Jody. I was eighteen and didn't know shit about parenting, but Jody never took me seriously anyway. He also walked all over Gwen. I wished the people back home who thought I treated my mother like crap could see this dysfunctional family.

Jody made me look like an angel as a kid. I'd tried being nice. I'd bribed him, begged him, threatened him, reasoned with him - none of it had any effect.

He constantly yelled, threw temper tantrums, called Gwen names, picked fights with other kids, stole things and lied. He refused to do schoolwork, bathe, brush his teeth, change his clothes, pee in a toilet or watch what he ate. He had type- two diabetes and his glucose levels were always way too high. And he stunk.

We'd left the flea-ridden townhouse after he'd gotten into a fight with the neighbor's kids that resulted in the parents threatening me with a gun. Now we were leaving another motel because Jody had been caught stealing from the guests next door.

When packing our things to move again, I lost my temper and grabbed Jody by the throat. Gwen pried my fingers off his neck. He fell to the floor and I started kicking him. In that moment I blamed him for all my unhappiness, all my failings. I hated what my life had become and what I'd allowed myself to be trapped into. When I realized how dangerous I was in that situation and how close I was to seriously injuring Jody, I stopped kicking him and left the room.

I spent the night in my car, reflecting on how I'd become like my father. My response to stress was violence and then abandonment. At home Dad would explode at the slightest provocation and then take off, leaving Mom and me to clean up and sort through the humiliation.

I was drinking to escape my reality like Dad used to, taking drugs, and ignoring my domestic obligations. I let Gwen cover for me and blame Jody whenever I got upset. Basically everything I'd run from in Massachusetts I'd re-created in Virginia. And on top of everything, if I'd injured Jody I would be arrested and my life would be forfeited. What the hell was I doing?

The next day I went back and told Gwen I was leaving. Jody was a bastard, but he didn't deserve me beating on him. Yet I couldn't be around him without becoming violent. Like any good mother, her response was to call CPS and put him in foster care. She chose me over her son. I wished she hadn't. It disgusted me. But Gwen put it on me that she'd kicked out her husband, given up her car and her townhouse for me. Now she was giving up her son. With all these sacrifices, if I left she'd have nothing. I was too young to realize how I'd been manipulated. So without Jody, Gwen and I rented a farmhouse on the side of a mountain.

Before hooking up with Gwen I'd had plenty of dating experience with other teenagers, but not with an adult. I'd never lived with someone I was dating. Being younger and less experienced than Gwen put me at a disadvantage in our relationship. Geographically, I was far removed from my family and friends, my surroundings were new and unfamiliar to me.

Gwen had lived in this part of Virginia for most of her life. She knew short cuts to get everywhere and never needed a map. For me, the small, unpaved, twisting rural roads were confusing and scary. Working the same shift at the same warehouse meant we carpooled and spent our breaks together at work. No matter what time of day or what I was doing, Gwen always had her eye on me. It took me a while to notice how effectively she'd boxed me in and cut me off from reaching out to anyone but her.

At work I wasn't allowed to talk to any of my co-workers unless Gwen was already friends with them. At home I wasn't allowed to have any hobbies she couldn't participate in. I stopped playing guitar, drawing, and skateboarding and relied on reading or watching movies to pass the time. I gained a lot of weight. Any self-esteem I'd had left, vaporized.

I could never get online because Gwen was **always** using our home computer. If I picked up the phone she came up with a chore I suddenly needed to do. If Mom or Brian called, Gwen would hover over me, listening in on my conversation. After a few minutes she'd come up with a reason we needed to leave the house, thus ending my phone call. If I wanted to talk to my family I had to sneak away from the floor at work and use a payphone.

One day I called my aunt Louise from a work payphone. Before moving to Virginia I'd been taking my testosterone from a topical gel I applied once a day. It made me itchy but the doses were steadier and it freed me from depending on someone else for injections. Gwen didn't approve of the gel because it meant I had to keep an undershirt on at night or else risk some of the testosterone rubbing off on her. She liked me to sleep naked or in underwear, although when I undressed she made fun of my acne, my scars and my hair.

Gwen decided I'd be going back on testosterone injections and she'd be administering them because she had experience giving Jody his insulin injections. I explained how the needle had to go into a muscle, and the meat on my thigh was the best spot. She nodded her head but once my back was turned she stuck the needle in my buttocks. This wasn't only painful but bled a lot. The second time she gave me an injection my hamstring seized up like a charlie-horse for three days. I screamed from the pain. The third time I'm not certain what she did, but I swear she stabbed a bone. The pain made me grind my teeth and see stars at the corners of my vision. I'd decided I needed to ask Aunt Louise for advice on how to give myself the shots.

Louise seemed surprised I'd called her during the middle of the day from a payphone. I didn't know how to tell her I couldn't call from home because my girlfriend was so controlling. Instead I made up a lame but believable excuse about the phone being out at home. Louise took it in stride and reminded me about rubbing the injection site with an alcohol wipe and making sure there weren't any air bubbles in the syringe.

That night I went home and locked myself in the bathroom. Gwen was outside the door yelling that she needed to give me a shot. I told her to shut up and wait until I was done taking a crap.

Then with nervous, trembling hands, I filled the syringe myself and sat on the toilet lid with my jeans down. I couldn't bear to see the needle enter my skin so I injected myself on the side of my right thigh using my right hand. On my own, it took me much longer than Louise or Gwen to push the needle in and fully depress the plunger. But when I pulled it out there wasn't much bleeding. I'd finally given myself an injection of testosterone. I wanted to be happy or at least proud, but I knew Gwen would be displeased. When I came out of the bathroom she'd been waiting for me. I told her I'd given myself the shot. She got so angry she wouldn't talk to me for the rest of the night.

I left Gwen on Christmas day. We'd had a fight after she wouldn't let me talk on the phone to Mom. I'd reached my limit of being controlled. I drove from Virginia to Massachusetts by myself. In northern Pennsylvania I started to get a little tired and called Charlotte's house from a gas station. Charlotte answered but she didn't recognize my voice. I'd spent all Christmas, my first away from home, battling snow and icy roads alone in my car. The lack of recognition from Charlotte made me feel lonelier than I had all day. I asked to talk to her mom. Joanne came on the line and I asked if she knew any safe places in their area I could park my car and rest for an hour or two. She sounded very put out by my call and basically told me I was on my own.

Rest stops are scary enough when you're alone. Alone in the middle of the night when it's snowing, they're infinitely creepier. For a woman I imagine they're terrifying. On the outside, I may appear safer because of my gender. But I didn't forget being trans made me vulnerable, if not for what's between my legs then because being trans meant I was smaller and had less muscle mass than average men. Bathrooms at rest stops and truck stops can be dicey for someone like me, especially alone. This was before cell phones were popular, so no one who cared about me knew where I was. It was not a comforting position to be in. I tried taking a short nap at a rest area in Connecticut. Every noise I heard made me jump in alarm. After an hour I gave up and pressed on.

I was exhausted when I reached the North Shore. My eyes were bleary and it was hard to keep the car on the road. I made it to my parents' condo at two am, almost fourteen hours after I'd left Virginia I was tired and sad that I'd missed Christmas but glad I was okay.

Brian seemed happy to see me. I'd missed him more than I had words for. We hung out for a few days spending his Christmas money. It was neat having the freedom of a car. Brian and I drove all over; visiting Hampton Beach in New Hampshire, our friend Robin in Framingham, and my favorite places in Boston.

On my third day home, while Brian and I were in Boston, I thought

I saw Charlotte crossing Newbury Street. I knew it couldn't be her because she was in New York. My eyes were seeing what my heart wanted, but my brain knew Charlotte was lost to me.

After that, I realized I had to go back to Virginia. Mom and Dad offered to let me move back in but I'd signed a lease on the farmhouse and my job was back there. If I stayed, Gwen would rob me of everything I'd left behind and abandon the house. I'd get stuck with six months of rent. With no job to pay for it, my credit would be ruined. I finally returned Gwen's numerous messages and made arrangements to go back.

Gwen apologized for running me off by smothering me. She agreed to let me make friends with a pair of lesbian women close to my own age who worked in my department and lived nearby. This probably wasn't because she cared about my happiness, but so I'd overlook the $900 phone bill she'd racked up in my name while I was gone. Still, it was nice having friends again, but no one could replace Brian.

In February, Gwen and I took a couple days off from work to attend the *True Spirit* convention for trans men, in Washington, D.C. Besides Gwen, the only person in Virginia who knew I was trans was Gwen's mother. She thought it meant I wanted to become a woman. I guess that's when you really know you're passing. In Massachusetts my whole family and half of my friends had known I was trans. It's not the only thing that makes me **me**, but it did feel weird no one around me knew. The last time I'd attended a trans convention I was fifteen and had a hard time relating to the other people in attendance. Now, nineteen and almost a grown-up, I thought maybe I'd make some friends if I met the right people.

Being too poor to stay near where the convention was being held, we stayed at a fleabag motel in Alexandria and took the train in. When they held mixers and movie screenings in the hotel at night, this really separated me from the rest of the attendees. I couldn't stay because it took over an hour to get back to my motel.

The other thing that separated me from the attendees was Gwen. She'd sworn to ease off and let me do my own thing when we'd gotten back together, but her promise didn't last. It was embarrassing having to explain to her in a crowd full of people that she couldn't attend all the same workshops as me. Some of them were for trans men only. Others, well, it was just hard to concentrate or talk to people with her breathing down my neck and clinging to my arm.

I met my first intersexuals (previously known as hermaphrodites) at the convention. I guess it's not uncommon for intersexuals to also end up transsexuals because there's a chance their parents chose the wrong gender for them. I also met my first transqueer person (now known as genderqueer I guess.) Transqueer people don't feel entirely male or female but rather go back and forth fluidly about their gender. It's sort of like Almond Joys and Mounds - sometimes you feel like a nut, sometimes you don't. Usually transqueer people don't take hormones, have surgery or legally change their gender because they can never fully commit to one gender.

This made little and less sense to me. If you feel like a woman sometimes and a man sometimes then why are you at an FTM convention? I've suffered physical and emotional agony to express my gender. I've sacrificed friends, relationships, educational opportunities and bundles of my parent's money. It's not easy or safe changing your gender. It takes a LOT of commitment. I'm not saying their life is easy, but I couldn't relate to being transqueer at all. I wanted to tell the transqueer person to get their own convention and stop wasting my time, but I couldn't think of a nice way to say it.

I participated in a trans only surgery show-and-tell. By far, my scars were the gnarliest, but in overall shape and contour people seemed to admire my results. Being topless in public, and in front of a hundred people or so to boot, was scary and liberating. I felt bad I was so fat and jiggley, but no one made fun of me. Well, not to my face anyway.

A week later I found out a Baptist minister had attended the convention to expose us "perverts" "sinners" and "women pretending to be men." He called the surgery show and tell a "freakshow" and the participants "grotesqueries." That felt nice.

I had a good time at *True Spirit* and met awesome people but once they met Gwen they sort of shied away from me. Maybe it was her swastika tattoos or her open hostility toward any female under the age of forty. I don't know. I just knew with Gwen around, even though I was surrounded by other trans men, once again I felt utterly alone.

Gwen and I tried to make our relationship work but we always found reasons to fight. She drank heavily and we both mismanaged our money. One or more of our utilities were usually shut off from not paying the bill. On paydays we'd go out to eat but a day or two leading up to them we were often so broke we had to scrounge change for food or go without.

Sometimes I couldn't afford testosterone and I'd miss a few shots. This made my menstruation cycles start and stop suddenly and painfully. It also made me hate myself.

Gwen and I had ugly fights. She knew how to push my buttons and make me insane with rage. I'd never wanted to hit a woman so badly before and I came close a few times. Once I'd almost punched her in the face but turned enough to hit the car headrest instead. Another time a wall. I'd shoved her and made her fall a couple times, attacked her computer with a baseball bat, and trashed her stuff. I left her on the side of the road once to walk home in the snow.

She hit, slapped, pushed me, and threw things at me more times than I could count. She called me names, made fun of me and broke my stuff. Once she pulled all the phone jacks out of the walls, threw the electric breaker to the house, stole my coat and my car; leaving me alone in the dark with no way to call for help.

After a few hours I took off on foot, making my way down the mountain without a flashlight or jacket, being followed by growling dogs I couldn't see. Gwen caught up to me a couple miles down the road. When I wouldn't get in the car she punched me in the face and broke my nose. Another time she tried to push me down a flight of stairs but lost her footing and ended up going down herself, landing in a pile of broken glass meant for me.

I couldn't call the cops or tell anyone about what Gwen did to me because she was a woman and I was a dude. Guys aren't supposed to get beat up by girls, not even girls who outweigh you by thirty pounds or more. I didn't think anyone would believe me, and if they did, I was afraid they'd make fun of me. Living with someone you're afraid of and too ashamed to ask for help is stressful. It changed me. I pitied and frightened myself.

Gwen knew I wasn't happy with her. I'd told her many times. The age difference, her kid, her attitude; it was all too much for me. Secretly I planned to leave her once our lease was up. Until then I needed her income. As that day drew slowly closer, I became more withdrawn. Gwen decided the solution was to get a six inch tattoo of my name on her tit in rainbow colors. I think she was hoping I'd see this as a sign of her love or feel an obligation to her.

I asked her not to get it but she stared me down with hostile eyes and asked, "Why not? You're not planning on leaving me, are you?"

Damn. She'd be impossible to live with if she knew I was leaving in three months. Oh well. I tried. Let it be a lesson for her about the consequences of manipulating people.

In April I was at work when I accidentally over-dosed on a type of amphetamine I'd never taken before. A co-worker found me collapsed on the floor of a bathroom and a friend drove me home. For three days my heart pounded so hard I thought it would explode. Literally. I thought I'd have a heart attack, stroke, or tear an artery and die. I lay on the futon in the living room, unmoving, waiting for death.

On the second day I reflected on my life, my living situation, how low I'd sunk and how disappointed everyone would be in me. I wanted to call Mom but I couldn't think of anything to say that wouldn't scare her. I wanted to call Brian; again I didn't know how to say goodbye. I didn't want my last memory of him to be the disappointment in his voice at what I'd done and who I'd become. Utterly convinced death could come for me at any moment, the only person I wanted to talk to was Charlotte. I didn't care if she was disappointed, angry or disgusted. As long as I got to hear her voice one last time I could go in peace.

Gwen was still at work. Charlotte would be out of school, so it was the perfect time to call. Charlotte wasn't too thrilled I'd called her. I knew better than to tell her I'd called because I'd OD'd on speed and was afraid I'd die. Instead I told her I was home from work because I was sick. She didn't care. I expected her to be standoffish or apathetic but she was more hostile than anything. It was totally unlike the Charlotte I knew. This Charlotte sounded much older, jaded, distrustful, and pissed off. What had happened to her in the last year and a half?

We didn't talk long. I could tell I was boring her. She didn't give a crap about me or what I'd been up to since we last spoke. She wasn't very forthcoming about her life either. Before I said goodbye I asked if I could call her the following day.

"Why?"

God, did she have to sound so tired when she asked that? I wanted to tell her because it would give me a reason to live through the night, but I couldn't.

"I dunno. Because I like talking to you. You sound like you could use a friend and I miss you."

She snorted. It was like a dagger to my heart.

"Give me three good reasons why I should talk to you again."

"Right now?"

"Email them to me. I'm sick of talking."

"Okay. I will. I can't tonight but I'll email you tomorrow morning."

"Whatever."

She hung up. My blood felt cold. A smart man would have taken the hint. Charlotte didn't want anything to do with me. But something was wrong. She sounded weary to the bone. My one consolation about my breakup with Charlotte was knowing she was better off without me. I'd never be comfortable unless I knew she was okay.

"And what if she's not okay? What could you possibly do about it?"

Shut up, brain. I'll think of something.

On my third day home I emailed Charlotte after Gwen left for work. It was hard to find words to tell her my fears and concerns without sounding artificial or condescending. I was afraid whatever I said she'd take the wrong way. I'd never been afraid to say what was on my mind to Charlotte before. This sucked.

I called her again in the afternoon. My email hadn't impressed her but she didn't hang up on me. It disturbed me how nonchalantly she told me she'd just broken up with her boyfriend who hit her and tried to rape her. I asked if she was alright and she laughed at me, deep and bitter. Then, she chided me and told me to stop trying to make a big deal about it. No matter what I said, she made me feel like a fool. It was obvious Charlotte was damaged inside and was doing everything she could to dissuade me from trying to help her or even care about her. I couldn't win, but I wasn't ready to give up.

When Gwen came home she went straight for the computer as usual. It was okay for her to have online friends and chat with them for hours on end while ignoring me, but I wasn't allowed to talk to anyone but her. I laid on the futon where she could see me and buried my face in a book.

A few minutes later, Gwen's mood became very dark. Her face flushed red and her cigarette started trembling. Then she exploded on me, accusing me of cheating and going behind her back and trying to get back with my ex-girlfriend. I tried to keep a calm face, but it angered me that she knew I'd talked to Charlotte. I was careful to use Mom's calling card so I knew the phone record hadn't given me away. I didn't leave my email open. What the fuck? How did she know?

Gwen had installed a secret keystroke program on our computer. She was able to recreate the email I'd sent Charlotte and rub it in my face.

I reminded Gwen I hadn't said anything romantic to Charlotte, only that I wanted to be her friend. It was true I longed to leave Gwen, but I'd never even looked at or thought about another woman sexually the entire time I was with her. Not out of loyalty; more because Gwen had frightened and beaten the passion out of me for all women. Regardless, the point was I was faithful and told her so. Gwen was unmoved. She insisted I was a cheater and a liar and demanded I return to work the next day because she couldn't trust me at home alone.

The following day, I went back to work and resumed my shitty life. I was afraid of amphetamines now and my chest still hurt around my heart. Without drugs, the workload was nearly impossible and excruciatingly painful. After two miserable weeks of having my ass handed to me day in and out at work, I was listening to a Cyndi Lauper song called *"Come on Home"* and decided that's what I needed to do. I may have failed at making a better life for myself by moving out, but that didn't mean I had to continue to fail and be unhappy. I didn't have to prove anything to anyone. I was just a dumb kid who wanted to go home.

I left from work. It was the only way to leave Gwen. I'd tried leaving her earlier on, but when I put my stuff inside the car she'd take it out again before I got anything done. It was childish but effective. She physically kept me from leaving her. But without a car of her own, she'd be trapped at work for another four hours or so, giving me plenty of time to escape.

I stopped at the bank and closed my checking account then drove to the house and hastily gathered some of my things. I didn't have room for my cats, guitar, furniture or most of my clothes. The entire time I was packing, the phone was ringing non-stop. I knew it was Gwen. I had to get out of there quickly before she came after me. The bank account had $836 in it. I left her $800 in an envelope with a note that said I was sorry but I wouldn't be coming back. That left me $36 to reach Massachusetts and my car was almost out of gas.

I called Charlotte from a gas station and asked if I could spend the night in my car in front of her house. I'd been awake from work since 3:30 am. I knew I couldn't make it home before exhaustion got the better of me. It was shitty to ask Charlotte for a favor, but I didn't know who else to ask. She seemed okay with me coming but insisted I sleep inside her house. If I pushed myself I could reach her place by midnight. I called Mom and told her I'd be home sometime the next day. Then, I hit the road.

I was glad to be free of Gwen, that awful job and that shitty state.

Still I felt like a coward, a failure and an asshole for ditching Gwen the way I had. I tried to tell myself I'd had no choice, knowing it wasn't exactly true. I had a choice, I just didn't like it. Gwen had cornered me and turned my life into a hell, but I'd let her. Wasn't I just as guilty? Without me there to drive her to work, she wouldn't be able to keep her job. I was her transportation to the grocery store, the bank, utility payment centers; everything. Without me she'd miss her appointments to visit her son and lose her partial custody of him. Basically, without me she was fucked. She'd made it so I couldn't break up with her without totally dicking her over.

I didn't love Gwen but I didn't wish her any harm or unhappiness either. I know her attempting to control me through my guilt was manipulative and bordering abusive, yet I still felt terrible for screwing her over. We were both drowning. I could only save one of us. I chose me over her. What kind of person did that make me? I was a survivor, but not happy and certainly not proud.

I reached Charlotte's house after midnight. It was weird being there again. It looked the same, even smelled the same, but it felt different. I didn't have to knock; Charlotte heard me coming up the stairs. Her parents were asleep and her sister had moved out. The two of us were the only ones up and moving in the house. The dark and quiet made everything seem much smaller and more intimate. I could barely raise my eyes to look at Charlotte. It felt like the weight of the past year was tangible and crushing my head and shoulders. I was so tired, so ashamed and uncertain. In a few hours the sun would be up and I'd have to face my mistakes in the harsh light of day. I didn't know what the future held for me. I felt guilty, sick, sad, broken-hearted and alone. Leaving Gwen was one of the hardest things I'd done. It left me with nothing; no money, no dignity, no clue how to start over.

When I managed to look Charlotte in the face, I felt old. She was inches from me but we were distant in experience and sorrow. I was looking right at her but felt too far away to see her. We sat on the floor of her room for a while, whispering back and forth to each other's sneakers. But with neither of us willing to talk about the past year there wasn't much to say. Before long I excused myself to go to sleep in the living room. The next morning I left early, not wanting to encroach on her family's Sunday together. I also wasn't ready for non-family members to see me.

Mom was at Aunt Louise's house so that's where I went. Besides a couple glasses of juice at Charlotte's house and a Dr. Pepper I'd bought the day before, I hadn't had anything to eat or drink since Saturday morning. My car coasted into the driveway on fumes. I'd used my last two dollars for the toll on the Massachusetts Turnpike. I was flat broke, dirty, hungry and tired. But I was with family now. I was safe. I was home.

Chapter Forty-Three

Starting Over

By Betsie

Luca was not the same young man who had left home a year earlier. Every time I tried to put my arm around him, he'd duck. I couldn't imagine the hell he had lived through while in Virginia. It took weeks before he told me how Gwen used to hit his head. He'd just gotten used to ducking when she walked by. I held him tighter.

When Luca left Virginia, he left quickly, leaving behind his very first Christmas stocking. Every Christmas I still get mad with myself for sending it. Luca also left without his class ring. New Horizons didn't have class rings and we had this one made just for him. Along with New Horizons and the year at the top of the ring, on one side it had a guitar, on the other, drama masks; things that had been important to him. Gwen had put the ring on one day and refused to give it back. Luca had no choice but to leave with it still on her finger.

Because the ring had been made just for him, I still had all the paperwork. I surprised him at Christmas with a duplicate ring. The ring was exactly the same but I suppose the memories were different. Instead of happy memories of a high school Luca loved, he probably now saw sad memories of a difficult time.

Luca slowly became a happy young adult. He and Charlotte got back together. Luca and Brian picked up right where they had left off. Luca, Charlotte and Brian were like the three amigos, doing everything together. Luca and I hardly ever argued. Even the fighting between him and Brooks eased. There was laughter in our house once again.

When Luca enrolled in our local community college, I knew we were traveling down the right road. I packed the bags of my anxiety demons and left them behind on the curb.

Starting Over

By Luca

Being home meant coming to terms with the huge belly-flop that had been my life, reacquainting myself with my friends and family, seeing a doctor, and getting a job.

The hardest part was getting used to being around people. In Virginia it was just me and Gwen. I wasn't used to more than three or four people in a room at a time. Or to people talking to me, touching, or even looking at me. If someone moved too fast, I'd instinctively duck. If they came up behind me, I'd flinch. When people tried to hug me, I froze. I wasn't used to affection. I was used to being called names and having things thrown at me.

It took a while to get used to food again. In Virginia I'd given up fighting about food and let Gwen decide where we ate or shopped. My diet mirrored hers; hamburger, pizza and fried foods. It'd been months since I'd had fruit of any kind or fresh vegetables. The day I came back I greedily ate over a pound of fresh strawberries Aunt Louise had sliced and left out in a bowl. I decided then to become a vegetarian. Just thinking of all the hot dogs, *Hamburger Helper*, sausage gravy, and chicken fried steaks I'd eaten with Gwen made me sick. Once my body got a taste of some of the nutrients I'd been lacking, I craved fruits and veggies constantly. I dropped over thirty pounds in less than two months.

At night it was hard to sleep without Gwen's knees in my back or her thick fists selfishly clutching all the covers. In the day it was scary to leave the house and hard to make any decisions for myself beyond what I wore. Gwen had forced all her decisions on me: where I went, what I ate, what music I listened to, where I worked, where I shopped, what I did for fun. Living with her had been like being in prison where your body is trapped but your mind is free. Now my body and mind were free, but thinking for myself and planning my day was overload. It took a while to become reacquainted with myself and enjoy my independence.

Meanwhile, Gwen had moved out of the farmhouse in Virginia without paying any rent or utilities. I owed the phone company almost a grand and the electric company three hundred dollars.

Brian and I picked up as if nothing had changed. When I showed up at his grandmother's house to see him, the first thing out of his mouth was, "Wow. You got really fat."

Then we both laughed. I loved that guy. He was my center. Brian kept everything in perspective and me focused. Friends, people you can count on; that's what was important in life. As long as I had my best bud everything else was gravy.

Two weeks after I'd moved back home, Brian made the long journey back to Virginia with me. Mom mailed my landlord a check for the last two month's rent in advance, but he still stole all my possessions Gwen had left behind. All that remained was my cat, starving and living in a pile of trash with a family of possums. One of my friends in Virginia had managed to snatch my guitar and some of my clothes before Gwen had a chance to pawn them. It wasn't much but it was something. At least now I had more than two outfits.

Mom had to buy me clothes so I could fill out applications and go on job interviews. I was soon hired at a hotel in Danvers as a front desk clerk. The pay was a dollar less per hour than I'd been making at the clothing warehouse two years earlier. But a job's a job. If I stayed living in my old room at my parents' condo, I could afford to pay my debts.

Charlotte and I spoke sporadically. She was still one of my favorite people but I was wary of becoming too attached to her. At first I was so withdrawn and emotionally cut off that talking to Charlotte was what slowly rehabilitated me to talking to other people. She was equally withdrawn and emotionally used up. Talking to one another was like taking baby steps to re-enter society for both of us.

It was becoming harder for me to deny my growing romantic feelings for Charlotte. When Brian and I had returned from Virginia with my cat, we'd stopped in Brewster for a few minutes to say hi to her. It was the first time in years I'd really looked at her. She'd grown taller and filled out nicely. Her face was gorgeous and her full-lipped smile haunted me at night. I had a crush on her but Gwen had taught me that even if

Charlotte dated me, once she saw me naked it would be over.

Testosterone hadn't been kind to me the last couple of years. At first the few swirling chest hairs had been cute. Now they covered my chest, stomach, and back, and were reaching for my shoulders. They'd brought some lovely acne with them too. Pimples on your back aren't sexy. If Charlotte saw me with my shirt off she'd probably cry or puke, or both. It was better I should stuff my feelings for her down as deep as they'd go.

This plan went sort of well until Charlotte mentioned her senior prom was coming up and I offered to take her. She had bought a renaissance-style cream colored dress. I was still broke but Mom lent me money to buy the prom tickets and bought me an expensive cream shirt that laced up the front. Louise made me a black vest with antique ivory buttons to match Charlotte's accessories.

I drove down to New York the morning of her prom. The two of us looked pretty snazzy together. The prom itself was held at a country club close to the city. It was over an hour drive away from Brewster. All the other kids arrived in limos or stretch hummers. We showed up in my yellow Kia Rio.

I didn't know any of Charlotte's classmates. With a few exceptions, they all behaved like immature, spoiled jackasses. It had only been two years since I'd graduated. I felt at least a decade removed from everyone there. I was still nineteen, but after my year in Virginia I couldn't relate to kids my age. Their lives seemed so simple and worry free. When Charlotte was ready to go, I was much relieved.

Back at her house, while still in the car, Charlotte kissed me on the cheek before heading inside. The evening had been a lot of hassle for a kiss on the cheek, but it still made my heart flutter.

Two weeks later Charlotte had her graduation. I drove down to attend that as well. It felt kind of weird being the only one there who wasn't family, but I wanted to be there for her big moment.

The night before her graduation, we finally shared our first real kiss in almost two years. It didn't just feel magical, it felt right. Like I was filled with bubbles, fireworks and stars yet it was the most natural thing in the world.

Our relationship progressed agonizingly slow. We only saw each other every other weekend when I drove down from work. After her last boyfriend, Charlotte could barely stand to be touched. I didn't mind being patient because she was totally worth it. And after Gwen, I needed someone to be patient with me as well. Charlotte's lack of commitment bothered me though. I was certain she wasn't seeing anyone else, but whenever I asked her if we were dating exclusively or if I could call her my girlfriend, she'd grow quiet or change the subject. I understood she was afraid of being controlled by someone again. I knew that fear too. Still, it left me unhinged as I did my best to ignore it.

Back home I'd received a promotion at work to assistant accounting manager. It came with an awesome raise and lots of fun new duties and privileges. I thought I was good at it until another front desk employee and the hotel manager conspired to frame me for embezzlement. Together they'd stolen over fifty grand, twelve of it in my name. When the manager confronted me with the transactions that bore my electronic signature and informed me he was calling the police, I fled the state.

I was only in New York a week before I came to my senses. I was terrified beyond expression of going to jail or even a holding cell. But I knew I hadn't taken the money so there must be another explanation. Mom hired an attorney who thought I was guilty. I was able to prove my innocence from time stamped bank deposit slips and lunch cards. The manager and other employee had stolen my computer password and logged in as me to steal the money. I had proof I wasn't present when any money had been taken. No criminal charges were brought against me, but the hotel declined to offer me my job back or even apologize.

I was unemployed, depressed and royally pissed off. It seemed so unfair that I was on the straight and narrow but still finding myself ass deep in trouble. Before, I would have sunk further by drinking or doing drugs and compounding my problems. But Charlotte wouldn't date a loser who did stuff like that, and I'd broken Mom's heart enough already.

I pulled myself together and went back to selling sunglasses at a cart in the mall with my cousin Will. It wasn't glamorous. It wasn't even full time. It was considerably less per hour than I'd made at the hotel. But it was nice of Will to help me out when I really needed it. Plus it gave me the perfect opportunity to go to college.

I registered for veterinary technician classes at the local community college. In the weeks preceding the fall semester my parents and I moved out of the condo and into an apartment near the mall in Peabody. We'd moved so the condo could go on the market.

Charlotte came to visit me for two weeks in August. I was hoping she'd want to move in with me after seeing all the opportunities my area had to offer. There were no colleges and few places to get a job around Brewster. I think she was tempted but still afraid of commitment. Our relationship was in a weird standoff.

For my part, I was still afraid to undress or have Charlotte touch me under my clothes. She refused to concede that we were more than friends with benefits. I was disappointed and annoyed when Charlotte asked me to take her home again but I knew better than to try and keep her from what she wanted to do. Before Gwen, I may have tried to guilt, tempt, beg or threaten Charlotte with ultimatums to get her to stay. Now I didn't have it in me to try and control anyone, even if I thought it was for their own good.

Chapter Forty-Four

Life Happens When No One's Watching

By Betsie

In September, Luca started classes at the community college. There was always the possibility he would be recognized and leave in fear and humiliation. But he sported facial hair and a deeper voice. His head was shaved and his personality was completely different. He was more confident now. When he came home and told me a childhood classmate was in his class but didn't have a clue who he was, I was grateful but not surprised.

During Christmas break, Charlotte came back for another brief visit. She was coming out of her protected shell, and we were comfortable around one another. When the boys weren't around, we would do things together like any mother and daughter would. I even taught Charlotte how to drive. I had the best of both worlds. Son and daughter.

Charlotte returned home for the holiday, and while she was gone, Luca did nothing but talk about marrying her. I told him they were too young. She was only eighteen and he was one month shy of twenty. As much as I loved her, I begged Luca not to make a commitment. Not for his sake, but for Charlotte's. Would she understand what she was committing to? What about never having children? What if strangers discovered Luca's background? Would she be strong enough for that?

Hell, was I strong enough for that?

A few weeks after the new year, Charlotte moved in with us.

Then, within days, Luca said, "Mom, last night I asked Charlotte to marry me. She said yes. I gave her Aunt Hazel's ring."

"Oh, Luca. I wish you'd waited. But I'm behind you if this is what you want. Where is Charlotte now?"

"She's up in the loft."

I went to congratulate the young girl who would someday be my daughter-in-law. She was beaming.

"I'm happy for the two of you," I told her. "And I'm not trying to be mean, but you're both so young. Promise me you won't do anything without thinking it through."

They promised.

Three days shy of his twentieth birthday, we received an early morning phone call from Joanne asking to speak to Luca.

Within minutes Luca came to my bedroom.

"Mom. Charlotte's dad died this morning."

I remember my exact words.

"No fucking way!"

"He died of a massive heart attack."

"But he's only forty-two."

As I held Charlotte tightly, I remembered what it was like to lose a parent and be in too much shock to cry.

Luca purchased clothes for the wake and funeral and drove Charlotte back to New York.

Two days later, Brian and I drove to New York for the funeral. I felt Joanne's, Charlotte's and her sister's loss. They were all so young. Charlotte's dad would never get to see how happy his daughter was. He wouldn't be there to walk either daughter down the aisle.

The day had brought back painful memories of a twenty-one-year-old hearing the echo of taps being played at her own father's funeral. Brian and I only stayed a few hours. I had a long drive ahead of me.

Life Happens When No One's Watching

By Luca

When I started my classes at the community college, I was afraid I'd be recognized as Marie. I bumped into a few students I'd gone to elementary school with, two of whom had sat next to me for years when we were preteens. I even spoke to a couple of them at length, but no signs of recognition came to their faces and no rumors circulated about me. I knew I was passing exceedingly well in my new life, but it was eerie to see that tested. I guess I'd changed more than I knew.

Since leaving public school I'd grown taller and my voice had deepened, but they had changed too. Why was it I recognized them and they didn't me? Probably because Marie was shy with her head down, shoulders slumped, and hair in her face. Luca walked with his head up, made direct eye contact, nodded or verbally greeted everyone he passed, shook hands firmly and believed in himself. Confidence is the key to acceptance. Act like you belong and no one will doubt you.

I found acting confident was a lot easier than actually being confident. I hadn't been in a classroom for two years and most of the texts were over my head. I hadn't taken any real science classes since elementary school. My English and grammar were years behind everyone around me. Yet, there I was taking medical terminology, biology, ethics, small business and accounting classes. I had to read every page about three times to comprehend the material, and my homework took me hours longer than the other students. It was frustrating and hard not to become dismayed. But I made many friends whom I saw during and after class. A few remain close to this day. They made showing up fun and exciting no matter how down I was about the work.

I was studying to be a Vet Tech. The animal care field is largely dominated by women. For the two years I stayed at the community college only two other men took any of the animal care courses. That meant I spent all my time in school surrounded by females.

I considered Charlotte my girlfriend, even if she did not. As far as I was concerned, I was off the market for women. But to my surprise two of my classmates had developed a crush on me.

It was flattering. Being trans, overweight and coming from an alternative school, not many girls had been interested in me. Although one of them was rather attractive and the old schmucky Luca inside me was tempted, I made it clear to both girls I was saving myself for another. But with Charlotte in New York and admittedly unwilling to commit to me, both of the girls seemed to think they still had a shot.

I felt bad because the two of them had started out as friends. Although the circumstances had been different, I'd let Gwen come between me and Brian and hugely regretted it. Seeing friends fighting over a love interest made me sad. I did all I could for a while to dissuade them, but when I lost my job selling sunglasses it became too tempting not to take advantage of the two young women.

The sunglass-cart safe had been robbed twice after my closing shift on weekends. For a time all the carts in the mall had a safe on them that mall security had access to via key. Then a robbery had taken place where multiple carts reported losses. All either changed keys or switched to nightly deposits, except mine. Of course, no one told me this until much later so the first time the money had been taken after I'd closed, I thought somehow it must have been my fault. I borrowed $250 from Mom to cover half the lost money. Will covered the rest and we never told his boss. The second time it went missing I refused to pay for it. I think Will believed I took it and that hurt me deeply. First, I may be a loser in many ways, but I'm not a thief. Second, I would **never** deliberately do something that could get my cousin in trouble. I would have happily taken a bullet for Will anytime. I wasn't about to steal from his work and get him fired. But no one believed me. The owner let me go and held my last paycheck because I wouldn't take a polygraph test.

Now that I was broke, it was too easy to let these two girls try to woo me by buying me food or putting gas in my car. It was a lousy fucking thing to do but the teenager in me thought it was neat. It was fun being liked and having peers one up each other for my company. It created a lot of tension in class though. The girls could barely stand to be near one another anymore.

One afternoon a group of us were at the mall and the two of them came to blows in Sears over who was going to drive me home. I should have intervened but instead ran out the back and walked home. After that, one of them dropped out of the college. I didn't want to believe what I'd done. My need to boost my self-esteem had led down some destructive paths before, but this was a new low. Knowing I was mostly to blame for the humiliation that led to her leaving school plagued me with guilt. I still loathed the bullies who'd made my life hell in the past. Is there anything worse than becoming what you hate? I was deeply ashamed of myself.

I was still driving down to see Charlotte every other weekend. After what had happened in school, I felt I needed to be closer to her. She came to visit for a week before Christmas and I tried harder than ever to show her the benefits of moving in with me.

Besides the distance, our relationship was fairly normal now. Brian had forced her to admit she was my girlfriend. It was childish, but I appreciated it. And our love life was pretty amazing when we were together. She hadn't cried or puked when I took my shirt off. It had been kind of funny and cute when we'd discussed what's going on down below. With all the times she'd sat in my lap, even seen me naked, she wasn't sure if I'd had bottom surgery or not. I should have been more considerate, but it made me laugh.

Testosterone enlarges a clitoris and makes it look like a tiny dick. Since Charlotte had never seen me pee or seen me naked with my legs spread, she thought what I had going on was from some surgery. I explained what was up though and told her that while some trans men enjoy using their "tranny bonus hole" for sexual pleasure, I wasn't one of those people. That's why I hadn't gone to any lengths to disclose it to her. As far as I was concerned, until I had to pee it didn't exist; and even then only begrudgingly. Besides, it was all just temporary.

Charlotte went back home for Christmas but promised she'd return before the New Year. This time she'd be staying indefinitely. I was ecstatic. During the few days she was in New York, I made up my mind I wanted to marry Charlotte. I loved her more than anything. I didn't want to waste any more of my life without it being joined to hers. I could wait for the ceremony and all that until we were done with college and in our twenties, but it was stupid to pretend there was even the slightest chance I'd ever want to be with someone else. My heart belonged to her eternally, and she needed to know.

I told Mom I wanted to propose. She thought I was too young and hadn't been with Charlotte long enough to know what I wanted. I told Brian, and he seemed happy for me but doubtful Charlotte would say yes.

Shortly after New Year's, I was lying in bed with Charlotte, just canoodling and talking.

"I love you, Charlotte."

"I love you too, Luca."

"No. I mean I really, really love you."

"I really, really love you."

"Are you sure?"

"Positive."

"You know I'll always be poor, right? That I'll always be an under-achiever and barely make more than minimum wage. I mean, I'm not a loser who can't hold down a job or anything, I'll always pay my own way, but I'll never be a great provider."

"I don't care."

"I'm serious. And I'll always be close to Brian. Like you could never make me choose you over him."

"I know. He's your friend. I wouldn't want you to choose."

"And I'll probably always be fat. And it could be a while before I can afford more surgery."

"None of that matters to me."

"Well you can't say I didn't warn you."

"Why would I say that?"

"In case we get married. I don't want you to say I tricked you or misled you."

"I'd never say that."

"Do you think you'd want to get married?"

"Someday."

"Well, I didn't mean right this minute. But do you think you'd want to marry me?"

"I don't know. Sure."

"Is that a yes?"

"Are you really asking?"

"I am if you're saying yes."

"Then yes."

"Good. You can have this now."

I gave her a small gold band with an opal and two garnets. The ring was left to me by my Great-aunt Hazel who'd passed when I was a baby but had loved me very much. It was far too small and feminine for me to wear, but I loved it because of where it came from. The ring deserved to be worn and appreciated. It fit Charlotte's finger perfectly and brought me much happiness to see it on her.

That night Charlotte called her mother to tell her we were engaged. I'm sure it sounded crazy. She had turned eighteen just six weeks earlier and I wasn't yet twenty. But we were happy and planning on visiting New York soon so she could tell the rest of her family in person.

Three days before my birthday, the phone rang early in the morning. Mom got me up and called me downstairs to take it. Joanne was on the line. Charlotte's father had passed away from a heart attack that morning. The news was a heavy shock. Her father was only forty-two and wasn't being treated for any heart disease risk factors. He wasn't even fat.

I was thankful Joanne had told me first so I would be slightly better prepared to comfort Charlotte. But the moments between handing her the phone and waiting for her to comprehend the news were sickening. How do you help someone through that kind of grief? What could I do? I had no clue. All I could think to do was start packing some clothes.

When Charlotte hung up, I expected her to collapse into wailing fits of hysteria. Instead, she acted like she'd slept through her alarm clock and been caught unawares for the first day of a new job. She didn't cry. She didn't even want a hug. She just jumped up out of bed, mumbled some nonsense and got into the shower. It took a long time for the shock to wear off.

Mom ran me across the street to the mall so I could buy some appropriate wake and funeral attire. Charlotte packed a black dress suit she'd bought the day before to wear at work. She didn't want to pack much else. I knew she'd be quitting her job and staying in New York for a long time so I packed the rest of her things. We made it to Brewster before dinner but no one wanted to eat.

The next few days were rough. Obviously. I felt out of place and helpless. The day of the wake I turned twenty. I wasn't a teenager anymore. I tried willing myself into a strong, mature and dependable adult on the spot. Charlotte would need a man in her life, and I was now the closest thing she had to that. I couldn't act stupid or behave selfishly or irresponsibly anymore.

Her father was buried without knowing his daughter was engaged. He wouldn't see her graduate college or get married. Charlotte had always been intelligent, kind and pretty. But her dad never saw her grow into the strong, capable and successful woman she became.

I kept thinking how he was on the same prescription testosterone I took. Clearly we were prescribed the medicine for different reasons, but I was susceptible to the same blood pressure and cholesterol raising side effects. I'd finally gotten to see a doctor a few months back when Mom got me on her health insurance, because I was a full time student. My total cholesterol had been 380 and I was diagnosed with stage 2 hypertension. I needed to start taking better care of myself.

It hurt leaving Charlotte in Brewster again. I knew she and Joanne needed to be together. I could drive down and visit once a month; but I'd miss having her next to me at night. Plus I hated to see her cut off from the world again. The next few months were difficult for everyone, to say the least.

Chapter Forty-Five

Life is Good

By Betsie

By the end of spring Charlotte had moved back in with us. I felt she and Luca deserved an engagement party. Nothing special. Just a small get-together at Prince Pizza. Most of my family and many of Luca's and Charlotte's friends attended. Joanne drove up from New York. Mary, Luca's former high school counselor, came.

To celebrate, I made a special heart-shaped cake with pink and white roses. It was a beautiful surprise for my adoring daughter-in-law to be. As our families stood together to have a photo taken, I couldn't imagine a future without Charlotte in it. It had been a perfect afternoon for a perfect couple.

My mother-in-law's estate finally settled and we started looking at houses. The closer it came time for us to move out of the apartment, the more time became my enemy. I loved having the kids around. It kept me young. My dream was to purchase a house where we could all live. Something where Brooks and I could have our own space and the kids could have theirs.

I fell in love with a house in Salem, just north of Boston. Old, original, large panel floor boards. Molding around the entry-ways. Beautiful, original oak kitchen cabinets. And best of all, a partially finished-off basement. With a little work, it could be completed. It even had its own entryway. It was perfect! My bubble burst when our bid was too low. The house would not be ours.

Brooks had spotted a new condo complex in the city of Lynn. I didn't want to move there, but as our time got down to only one month left on the lease, I agreed to purchase the condo.

The place was beautiful. All new everything. But what would I do about the kids? I couldn't leave them out in the cold. Doing what we thought was the next best thing, we bought them their own mobile home. It was terrible. Not just the home, but the idea. I felt I had thrown them to the wolves. They were miserable. I was miserable. They hated

Lynn so much they refused to visit. In fact, I think I think they were there twice. Both times when their water pipes froze.

The condo was cold and uninviting. I hated each day I had to walk through my front door.

Luca had his graduation from the community college in May. He really didn't want to attend. He did it just for me. There were no photos before-hand as he picked up his cap and gown minutes before the ceremony.

A real graduation! It may have been a two-year college but to me it meant a life-time. Keeping my eyes focused on the large-screen TV, I cried when Luca's name was called and I saw him walk across the stage to receive his certificate.

Through the noise I heard them say Luca graduated with honors. If he had known this, he hadn't told me. Maybe he wanted me to be surprised. I was over-the-moon elated. He had worked damn hard for this and I was glad he changed his mind and attended. Even if it was just for me.

After the ceremony, when he found us in the crowd, even Brooks had tears in his eyes.

On a Monday morning in June, 2004, Brooks had quadruple heart by-pass surgery. On Wednesday morning Brian's dad pulled up with a moving truck to move the kids to Arizona. I sadly waved goodbye as Luca's Kia Rio drove out of sight, taking most of my happiness with it. On Thursday I had to put my cat Max to sleep. He was diabetic and had been vomiting a lot. I couldn't have him vomiting in the house when Brooks was released from the hospital.

Hardly able to see the road through my tears, Thursday morning I made the trip to the vet's office. I was so hysterical when I left, they escorted me to the back exit so as not to disturb a waiting-room full of people. I was too angry at Brooks to go to the hospital. I was blaming him for having to put my cat to sleep. I went directly to the kid's empty mobile home. Sitting on the cold linoleum floor and leaning against the wall, I cried until I couldn't cry any longer. Then, using my arms as pillows, I slumped onto the dirty floor and fell asleep. When I awoke two hours later it was time for a trip to the hospital. Brooks would be released the following day.

In September, Luca's best friend Jenny married her sweetheart Jenn in a lovely backyard ceremony. Most of Jenny's family refused to show up. But I loved Jenny. Her happiness was all that mattered. After the ceremony, we were a little melancholy however, when Jenny and I talked about how much we both missed Luca.

Then in October, I received a surprise phone call from Luca.

"Mom, Charlotte and I are going to get married this weekend."

I could barely listen to his words. This should have been a glowing moment for me but instead I felt hurt. It must have been something they had been planning for a while. Why didn't they tell me sooner so I could be a part of it? I choked back my tears and sadness.

"Oh, Luca. Can't you wait? What about Charlotte's mom? She's going to be heartbroken."

"Mom, we want to get married on Halloween. It's going to be very small. We don't have many friends here."

"Luca, I need to feel part of this."

"Mom, I wish you could be here but it's in a few days."

"Then at least let me pay for a dinner afterwards."

"But everything is all set."

"I'm putting one hundred dollars into your checking account. Take your friends out for a great dinner."

"Thanks Mom. We love you."

"Would you at least call me right afterwards? I really need to feel included."

And that was that. The kids got married with no family and only two friends present. It took me a long time to get over this.

Months later, I had a much different phone call.

"Mom, I passed my Commercial Driver's License test. I'm going to drive eighteen- wheelers."

Animal care had not worked out and this was a completely new direction. Luca was excited about seeing the country and driving big rigs like his grandfather had done. I just didn't know if he had it in him to be away from Charlotte for long stretches of time.

When he called and said he would be in Sturbridge for a day, there was no way I wasn't going to see him. Even if it meant driving for hours. The one thing he wanted most was food from the local Thai restaurant in the Salem Mall.

With a packed picnic lunch, Brooks and I drove from Lynn, to Salem, to Sturbridge, just to see Luca for two hours. It was worth every minute. Climbing into the cab of the truck I was blown away by all the equipment Luca had had to learn to operate. If my dad had been given the chance, he would have been a proud grandpa. Then all too soon I was on my way back home and Luca was on his way back to Arizona.

In April 2001, on my birthday, I had been diagnosed with peripheral neuropathy in both feet. The nerves in my feet had started dying and the pain was horrendous. At times it felt like my left foot was in a vice, being squeezed until it would burst. At other times, the feeling was that of a hot branding iron sending electric shocks through my feet. Still having to work, I became depressed from the pain and lack of sleep.

By 2003 my neurologist wanted me to leave work. I wasn't ready. Instead I was put on anti-depressants and pain pills. By the beginning of 2005, I was pretty much addicted to the pain pills. I knew I couldn't go on much longer in this condition. From our many long conversations, Luca knew too.

For months, I kept hearing, "C'mon Mom. Arizona will be so much better for you. The weather will help with your arthritis and should help with your neuropathy."

I still wasn't ready.

Then one night in August, I decided I had had enough. I took a few extra pain pills along with my arthritis and neuropathy meds in hopes of not waking up in the morning. It didn't work. When I told my neurologist I didn't care if I were dead or alive, he insisted I couldn't wait any longer. I had to leave work.

But Brooks had never fully recovered from his by-pass surgery and wasn't working. We couldn't make the mortgage payments on my disability. The only choice we had was to sell the condo and move to Arizona.

In November of 2005 Brooks and I left our comfort zone and moved across the country. The next six months were probably the best time of my life. The kids' apartment was on the other side of the complex from ours. A little bit of a walk, but closer than the other side of the country. I loved walking past the flowing man-made stream, beautiful desert blooms, and humming birds, to reach their apartment.

Brian had moved in with them and each morning I got get up at 4:15 am to pick him up and drive him to work. The stars would still be out and the air crisp. I felt like I was living once again.

My feet and hips were still a mess but I didn't have to get up to go to work every day. Being able to rest when I needed, I was able to wean myself off of pain pills. An accomplishment I'm still proud of.

One of the reasons for moving to Arizona was to have the kids closer to me. We were going to take the proceeds from the sale of the condo and purchase a house big enough for all of us. Including Brian. Pooling all our funds, we'd be able to pay the mortgage and save money at the same time. When it came time to start looking for something, Luca would always put it off. Then one day he told me to just look for something for Brooks and me. There was no way he could live in the same house with his dad. I was deflated once again.

Brooks and I settled on a small mobile home. The kids moved to another apartment in another town. We saw less and less of one another.

Then the unthinkable happened. The kids started talking about moving to Oregon. My insides started screaming, "Don't go. Please don't go." But I never said it out loud. They had to follow their own dreams. Within months, once again, I found myself alone, waving goodbye as the

Penske moving truck pulled away with my dreams quietly packed away in one of their boxes.

Life is Good

By Luca

Charlotte moved back in with me by the end of spring. I finished my first year of college with a 3.86 gpa. Not bad for someone starting out with little more than a middle-school education.

That fall Charlotte and I had a small engagement party. Joanne drove up from New York and the rest of my family and friends got together with us at a pizza parlor. It wasn't high class but it was good food and good company that made the party. It felt all warm and fuzzy having everyone I cared about together to support Charlotte and me.

My deceased grandmother's condo finally sold. Mom paid off my car and gave Charlotte and me enough money to get our own place. We moved into a one bedroom, 480 square foot, tin can on wheels, in a rundown trailer park. It's certainly not the sort of place I imagined myself in, but it was cheap enough that Charlotte and I could pay our bills unassisted, buy her a car and pay for her to start community college too.

Our cozy little home wasn't so bad until winter came. The trailer was virtually un-insulated, the crank windows let in drafts, our pipes froze twice, despite installing electric heat tape and leaving the tap dripping overnight. The snow drifts between tightly packed dwellings buried our cars. It had been an unusually bitter winter that year and with graduation from college approaching, the thought of relocating someplace warmer crossed my mind. This was also on the tail-end of Mom being diagnosed with neuropathy in both her legs on top of the arthritis in her hands and hips. A warmer climate would help her but I knew she'd never move unless I went first and enticed her.

The only place I could think of that would be warm, dry and have job opportunities was Phoenix. Charlotte, Brian and I spent almost two weeks in Tempe after my finals.

I visited Michelle one afternoon while we were there. She'd moved out of her parents' house in Scottsdale and into her own apartment in

Tempe near ASU. I thought she could give me some tips and info on the area. We barely had time to talk about anything. Her drug dealing neighbor stopped by and talked about his pit bull until Michelle's boyfriend came over and threw a hissy fit for me to leave.

The desert was an extreme change from New England. The weather, topography, politics, food and people were vastly different. But I was ready for a change. Charlotte and Brian seemed on board with it, too. We signed papers to rent a two bedroom apartment over-looking a pool in Tempe starting in July.

I graduated from community college with honors. Mom and dad were pretty proud. Charlotte had earned a certificate in restaurant management. Hers had been a one year program but I was proud of her. She's a smart cookie. Together we hoped to make a new start with new careers in Arizona.

As usual, nothing in my life goes according to plan. The drive to Phoenix had been an interesting experience for me. I'd driven in my little Kia Rio alone, with my cat Ito as co-pilot. Charlotte drove her larger car with Joanne and our dog Astrid. Brian was in the moving truck with his Dad.

At first we tried to keep the three vehicles together but it didn't work for long. Alone, I stopped at a rest area in Pennsylvania to pee. When I came out, a man was circling my car, looking at the stickers. I tried to walk past him but he caught my arm and steered me to the back of my car. He asked me what my blue and yellow Human Rights Campaign sticker stood for. But I could tell from the gleam in his eye he already knew. I explained that I believed in equal rights for everyone, including gays, although I myself was straight. He leaned against my driver's side door and proceeded to tell me about all the young guys he'd fucked that month in the cab of his truck. I didn't know how to respond so I called Brian's dad on his cell phone and asked him to stop in the rest area and scare the guy off of my car. After that I scratched the sticker away with my keys.

In Texas, a black Suburban with Bush/Cheney stickers ran me off the road in broad daylight. My John Kerry stickers were the next to get taken off. From then on the drive was much easier and safer.

It's intimidating using bathrooms in truck stops and rest areas when you're alone and trans. Using dozens back-to-back across seven southern states was nerve racking, but I started to get used to it toward the end.

Once we reached Tempe and got settled, it was time to look for work. Charlotte got a job at Outback Steakhouse. I was offered jobs in an animal shelter, a vet office and two upscale pet stores in Scottsdale, but I turned them all down. First, I was only offered early morning shifts. Second, in Massachusetts, vet assistants made $12-14 an hour and kennel workers usually made over ten. In Arizona I was offered about 30-40% above minimum wage, but minimum wage was only $5.25 an hour back then. Not only was I not emotionally prepared to clean dog shit at five am, I wasn't financially prepared to do it for $7 an hour. I needed a new plan.

I don't know if it was desperation or inspiration, but after driving across the country by myself I thought I'd make a good truck driver. This isn't a profession you see many trans or gays in, but being my own boss and traveling, sounded appealing. So I enrolled in CDL (Commercial Driver's License) classes.

Brian wasn't able to find a job he liked so he flew back to Massachusetts. Charlotte and I got stuck paying rent on a two bedroom apartment while I was still unemployed. We'd been living off the savings from the sale of our little trailer. Until I started working, we needed to save money any way possible. It came to our attention that since Charlotte's car was actually in my name, we could save over $50 a month on car insurance by being married. A marriage license only cost $55 so after a month it would pay for itself.

We took a while chewing on the decision. We loved each other and weren't afraid of commitment, but we were flat broke and couldn't afford a wedding. Our parents wouldn't be able to attend on such short notice either. We'd never wanted a big wedding but a cake and some guests would have been nice.

Back in Massachusetts, my childhood friend Jenny was engaged to her lesbian partner. I promised not to get married until they were allowed to marry. It was ridiculous that I, a transsexual, could marry a woman but Jenny could not. I suppose legalities and public displays of affection are some of the perks for hetero trans people. I never hesitated to hold hands or kiss anyone in public who I was dating. I took it for granted that Charlotte and I could obtain a marriage certificate without a problem and our hospital visitation rights or shared assets would never be an issue. If you look at it that way it seemed pretty unfair to gays.

When equal marriage was legalized in Massachusetts, Jenny and her wife had a lovely backyard ceremony. Mom made their cake and favors. Five weeks later Charlotte and I exchanged vows in our living room. One of my friends got ordained online so he could perform the ceremony and sign the certificate. Another friend and her mom took pictures and signed as witnesses. There were no gifts received or songs played. The flowers came from Costco; the cake was a simple chocolate bundt. We'd made our own decorations and wrote our own vows.

Afterwards, my friends bought us dinner at a bar. I hoped Charlotte wasn't too disappointed. I had her and that's all that mattered to me, but she deserved to walk down an aisle in a beautiful dress and have her family ooo and ahh over her.

At the time we were only nineteen and twenty-one. We told ourselves someday we'd renew our vows with our families present.

Truck driving school was a unique learning experience. I met a lot of drop outs and ex-cons but everyone was nice and not what I'd expected. Being behind the wheel of seventy feet and 80,000 pounds was a little boy's grown up dream come true. It took a long time to learn all the different parts of a tractor trailer just to perform a routine safety check. Memorizing the air-brake and hazmat rules was intense but the driving was fun.

The DOT (Department of Transportation) health card was the hardest part for me. I was scared shitless of the hernia check, so my blood pressure sky rocketed. I failed the blood pressure check twice. The third time I went in I'd swallowed almost an entire bottle of aspirin in the morning to thin my blood. I barely squeaked by and was issued a six month card instead of the 12-24 months most drivers got. I'm not sure if the doctor thought I was a lesbian or what, but he didn't ask me to drop my pants and cough. I'd been psyching myself up for days to explain to the doctor I was trans and accept the judgment and embarrassment that would follow. He could make faces and lecture me all he wanted as long as he signed my card. It's not illegal to be trans and I had a right to drive commercially.

But he just asked me to lie on my back while he felt around my lower stomach for hernias. I didn't even have to remove any of my clothes. It was pain and embarrassment free.

The one thing I decided to change about myself to help ensure I passed, and for my own personal safety, was to learn to pee standing up. Well that, and now that I had some facial hair, which came in almost two years after my chest and back hair, I needed to grow some hillbilly sideburns or a chinstrap beard so I'd blend in. But peeing standing up would be equally important down the road.

This isn't a problem any workshop had covered at any of the FTM conventions I'd attended. No one really talked about it. This was years before the "Go Girl" was invented, so I was on my own. I went down to AutoZone and looked at their funnel selection. Nothing would fit quite right and they were all made of hard, unbendable plastics. I bought a couple small to medium funnels and took them home where I set to using a hand saw to reshape and resize them for my needs.

Thank goodness cargo pants were still in style. It's hard to walk around with a plastic funnel in your pocket and not draw attention. I practiced whenever I could, using the funnel to stand and pee, but honestly it took almost a year to be proficient with it. Sometimes the spillover was just a few drops that would run down my thigh and I'd wipe it off with some toilet paper. More than once I had dark wet spots on my inner thighs or the backs of my pants I had to let air dry because I was far from home. A couple times the urine reached my sock. It burned and itched. I just hoped I didn't smell like a hobo. That was a long year but worth it. Now I can pee wherever I need to. I can use most urinals without issue as long as the dividers are big enough. On long drives or hikes I can pee behind my car or a tree. I've even written my name in the snow.

I passed the test to get my CDL with doubles, triples, tanker, and HAZMAT endorsements. Then I was picked up by a long haul company and teamed up with a driver named Jesus for my three week training.

Starting the job was hard. Charlotte and I hadn't been apart a single night in almost two years. It scared me to leave her behind knowing she'd be alone. She had left the restaurant and taken a night job running the COD department for a small shipping company. The thought of her returning home at three am to an empty apartment left a pit in my stomach. It crossed my mind more than once that I'd been selfish in pursuing this career.

Jesus and I drove all over the south, midwest, and the length of the east coast. We stopped in Sturbridge, Massachusetts for a day on our way from Maine to New York. Mom and Dad came out to visit me and we had a picnic lunch at a truck stop.

Charlotte was glad to see me when my training was through, but I wasn't home five days before I was assigned my own truck and sent back out. It was creepier being on my own than I'd imagined. I wished I'd brought my dog for company. Sleeping alone at truck stops scared me a bit. I didn't like to leave the cab after the sun went down, and every noise made me jump. I peed in a lot of empty bottles at night.

You may not imagine a trans guy being a truck driver but I fit right in with all the other fat slobs. Over the road, being vegetarian was harder than being trans.

Yes sir, I thought I'd found my place in life. I missed Charlotte at night but thanks to cell phones and headsets I could call her while I was driving and talk for hours.

I saw thirty-nine states from the truck cab. In Montana I saw a pack of wolves closing on a herd of deer. In Wyoming I saw a grizzly bear sitting on a hill scratching himself. In Utah I saw a tornado. In Texas I saw illegal immigrants running across a desert road to a van. I'd seen snowcapped mountains, valleys, prairies and crossed the Mississippi. I loved the independence of driving on my own. Everything was pretty good until I was sent to Canada.

My dispatch office had forgotten to include bar-code load stickers that United States Customs scans for billing when you cross the bridge back into the United States. It was Memorial Day weekend so no one would answer their phones or return my calls. I couldn't get a temporary pin to buy fuel in Quebec so I had to shut down my truck after Friday. That May was unseasonably warm and the inside of my cab was broiling. I couldn't run the AC or my mini-fridge. I was trapped in a Canadian Customs parking lot from Friday night through Sunday; unable to cross the border. With no choice but to wait until I could cross into the United States and fuel up in Buffalo, New York, I ran out of food and water. I couldn't walk off and leave my truck without facing a recovery charge in excess of $20,000. I had to drink tap water from the bathroom sink in the customs house just to get by.

Sunday night another driver from my company came through with extra copies of the stickers I needed. Before I even crossed the bridge I called Mom and asked her to meet me in Pennsylvania where my company's closest terminal was. I'd had enough of being over the road.

For the rest of 2005 I drove class B street sweepers overnight in Phoenix. In the summer the overnight low for the city is still over 100 degrees, so it wasn't uncommon for me to drink at least a gallon of water per shift. Being able to pee standing up came in very handy at this job. I peed behind trees and dumpsters all along my route.

During this time I saw two surgeons about phalloplasty. I flew all the way to Detroit to meet the first one. The other was in Scottsdale. At the time, I had the cash, approximately eighteen thousand dollars, but procedures had changed. The phallus was no longer constructed in one long operation but rather stretched out over a period of three, each having months between them. Maybe if I'd had an office job this wouldn't have been a problem. I couldn't climb in and out of trucks or operate heavy machinery with stitches and a catheter for three to six months. I couldn't take that much time off without losing my job. I could afford to pay my bills for maybe two to three months and pay for the surgery; but after that I'd be screwed. It's a wonder anyone has this operation anymore.

I was invited to speak on a panel addressing college students about FTM transsexuals at a small private college near Chicago.

My friend Robin was a student at this college and arranged for my airfare, hotel and car rental to be paid. I was also given a $500 stipend which was enough to pay for Charlotte to accompany me. I was pretty nervous. I hadn't spoken in front of an audience about my experiences for almost a decade. I wanted to do a good job so my friend wouldn't be embarrassed, but I became flustered and lost my train of thought many times throughout the presentation. The other three panel members really threw me off my game.

All three of them identified as transqueer, although one of them had transitioned through hormones, name change and top surgery. He now identified as a gay transqueer man. He and his biological male partner had adopted a little girl and were raising her together. He seemed like a dude to me but he insisted he sometimes still felt like a woman.

The other two people confused me even more. They were both college students and were attracted to girls. One of them said he preferred male pronouns and felt comfortable in men's clothing although he didn't want to transition because he still felt like a woman on the inside. My first reaction was that he was simply an extremely butch lesbian looking for extra attention and a way to stand out. But it's not my call to make.

The last panel member wanted to be called by male pronouns and a male name sometimes, female pronouns and a female name other times. Because they went back and forth so often, they weren't interested in transitioning.

They dressed in androgynous clothes and wore no makeup or jewelry, but expected the population at large to know which gender they were projecting and be respectful of it at all times, even when it came time to use a public restroom.

This just sounded exhausting to me. I can't imagine one of my friends demanding I use different names and pronouns for them depending on their mood. I know it's judgmental but all I could think was "give me a break." Then this person said they thought it would be "neat" to experience being pregnant as a guy. That sounded like my worst nightmare. It was obvious I had little in common with my panel members.

I've never felt like a woman. Not ever. If I'm cleaning the house while listening to Cher or Lady Gaga on my Ipod, I still feel like a man cleaning the house and listening to Cher or Lady Gaga. There are certainly things I do that others may perceive to be effeminate or "gay" if done by a man. I never feel maybe I'm sort of a woman or maybe I'm sort of gay or bisexual. I am a straight man. I drive trucks, wear flannel, grow a hick beard, use power tools and take care of my wife.

I also dress my little dog in fuzzy pink outfits, decorate cakes and listen to show tunes. I'm a multidimensional individual but not when it comes to my gender or my sexuality. I'm a man who likes women. That's who I am. End of story.

I wondered how much of the other guests feeling like a man, then a woman, came from external gender expectations rather than internal intuitions. I also wondered how much of it was just attention hounding; like teenage girls who call themselves bisexual because they'll kiss other girls but they're not interested in dating women or eating pussy. You know the ones; the girls that make out at parties to get attention from GUYS. It felt a little like maybe some lesbians were trying to make themselves seem more hip or exotic by honing in on the trans label. They got to seem more complex without making any real commitment. Maybe I was being petty.

I didn't fit in with the other trans panel members that were on the fence or fluid in their gender. My experiences in life had been much different than theirs. It probably would have been easier for me to be a girl while going through middle and high school, then temporarily change into a boy on weekends around my friends in a safe environment. I wouldn't have been bullied or had to out myself to my family. But I didn't get to wait until I went to a private liberal college to come out. My feelings about my gender were too strong and too consistent to move on with my life in any capacity until they were dealt with. I thought more FTM's were like me. Now I wasn't sure. I'm just glad none of these people were around when I was struggling to convince doctors and psychologists that being trans wasn't a phase and my surgery was a necessity. It was awesome to see my friend Robin and visit her liberal college, but I was ready to go home.

Chapter Forty-Six

This is Our Dance

By Betsie

I had been waiting anxiously for this day. Five months earlier, Luca told me how much he and Charlotte wanted to have the wedding they never had. How they wanted to say "I do," in front of family and friends.

As with all families, ours had to have conflict. I was so distraught when my sister Dorothy said she and her family would not be attending, I told her to "Go to hell." Maybe not the best way to handle the situation. But damn it, I was hurt. Wounds so deep they took five years of healing before I could remove the bandages.

My heart ached for Charlotte when her relatives also said they would not be attending. I knew exactly how it felt to have your family tell you, "Family doesn't matter." Family does matter.

The wedding was almost called off because of the pain this caused.

I had to keep telling Luca and Charlotte, "Everyone who loves you and wants to share in your day will be there."

The kids didn't have a lot of money and neither did Joanne or I. For months, I cut forty-percent-off coupons from Michael's. The cake stand, cake pans and other miscellaneous items were all purchased using coupons.

One of Luca's former teachers from New Horizons suggested a church where they could have their ceremony and reception. The cost was reasonable.

I spent two days baking cakes of different sizes and making white frosting roses. Flowers were ordered from the local Stop and Shop grocery store. Luca, Charlotte and Louise spent two days preparing a meal for sixty guests. We rented tables and chairs. Charlotte had made the centerpieces. The bridal party would wear their own dresses and suits. No alcohol would be served.

The day finally arrived. Luca and Brian went to the church early to meet the delivery of the tables and chairs. Charlotte and the bridal party had their hair done. Joanne and I ran back to Michael's for last minute items, then to Stop and Shop to pick up the flowers.

Now we needed to get three cakes, food, pans, plates, cups, flatware, tablecloths, cake- stand, centerpieces, flowers, and ourselves to the church.

My sister Louise got busy preparing the food. Luca and Brian started setting up the tables. I assembled the three tier cake, nestling a "Day of the Dead" skeletal bride and groom among white roses, green leaves, and black sugar sprinkles.

Stepping into the kitchen to check on Louise, I chuckled when I noticed Charlotte in jeans and T shirt, tiara and veil in place, standing at the stove stirring chocolate.

"I think you're a little underdressed. Beautiful, but underdressed," I laughed.

"This chocolate ganache won't behave. It's supposed to go on the sides of the cake but I can't get it to thicken. I'm running out of time."

"You may just have to leave it. Guests are starting to arrive."

Like a magician who could perform great feats of magic, one of Charlotte's friends came into the kitchen and asked if there was anything she could do. She happened to work at a bakery. When she saw Charlotte struggling with the chocolate, she took over, sending the bride on her way to get dressed.

I was still in my jeans and T shirt, putting the finishing touches on the hors d'oeuvres when I noticed the time. I needed to get changed.

I remembered the day Luca brought my dress home from work. He had told me, "Mom, when I saw it on the rack I just knew you had to have it. Maybe someday you'll have a place to wear it."

Little did I know, my someday would be this day. I felt like a queen as I stepped into my white, hand-beaded, silk dress. A dress so beautiful I had lost fifty pounds to get into. A dress having so much meaning to me, I had moved with it three times, keeping it in the plastic wrapping for six years. I wondered if the kids were having a wedding just so I could have a reason to be *"Queen for the Day."*

The ceremony was kept simple. Brooks and I were not escorted down the aisle, but took our seats just before the doors opened.

When Luca walked in and his eyes met mine, a warm rush of adrenaline caught me off guard. He looked every bit his young age of twenty-four yet showed the maturity of his past ten years. Like all mothers who watch their little boys become men, I too had watched Luca become a man. Just yesterday he was dressed as a swashbuckling pirate, complete with an eye patch and sword. Today he is a groom dressed in a tux, complete with tails and top hat.

Jenny was by Luca's side as "Best Woman," their friendship spanned more than a decade. Luca's cousin Will and friend Brian rightfully took their places.

The doors opened.

Luca's outward nervousness gave way to an inward calmness as the love of his life walked toward him. Charlotte was stunning in her long white gown with embroidered small black roses outlining a sweetheart bodice and cascading down to the waist. The band of Swarovski Crystals sparkled in her hair. Her bouquet of white roses with gracefully flowing black ribbons gave a touch of elegance.

Charlotte had stolen my son's heart. But not just for her outward beauty. Her kind, compassionate soul, warmly glowed from within.

Jenny's wife began officiating the service. Charlotte's maid of honor and bridesmaids were friends of both Luca and Charlotte from when they lived in Massachusetts. There they were, standing together, showing how much they cared for one another.

I was too elated to cry as Luca and Charlotte said their vows amongst the love of family and friends. They had each found their soulmate, expressing their love to the world.

As parents, isn't that what we all want for our children? For them to find their one true love? It doesn't matter if they're gay, lesbian or trans. They're part of humanity. Isn't that what we all long for? To find the one person who expands our already giving heart?

The ceremony ended just as the aroma of pasta sauce started filling the air. Louise made the best pasta sauce in the state of Massachusetts.

Louise had been by my side; riding the ups, downs, and sharp curves of my life. She had worked her magic at my daughter's christening. How ironic, today she was working the same magic for my son's wedding. I would never have made it to this day if it were not for her shoulders to cry on. I want the world to know how grateful I am.

After photos were taken, guests were called in for the cutting of the cake. A soft glow from lit candles gave the fondant a feeling of warmth. The misbehaving ganache was now showing off in bold swirls and delicate stripes. Compliments and laughs were heard as guests discovered the "Day of the Dead" bride and groom.

Tears I didn't know I had, found their way to the surface as Luca and Charlotte took to the dance floor dancing to *"Dream a Little Dream of Me,"* by Mama Cass. I realized how fortunate I was to have Charlotte in my life. The daughter I never got to have. Stars and moonbeams *were* shining brightly.

My words of thanks didn't seem enough as Principal Tanner told me how happy he was for the Luca and Charlotte. Their wedding would not have been complete without his high-school principal and teachers. Each held a special place in our lives.

When I finally got to sit down with my family, it was uncomfortably noticeable one sister was missing. However, the love present in the room outweighed my sadness. Nothing would ruin this evening.

Without warning, the guitar music of Israel Kamakawiwo'ole started playing and I felt a tap on my shoulders. "C'mon Mom, this is our dance," Luca said softly.

Taking Luca's hand, together we began our dance as mother and son. It had been twenty years since I first heard, "Life is not worth living if I can't be a boy." Twenty years of heartaches and triumphs. The ending of one life; the beginning of another. Sometimes we traveled together; sometimes alone. But always on the same journey.

The music to *"Somewhere Over the Rainbow/What a Wonderful World,"* played in the background, the lyrics telling our story.

Strength and courage had taken us places we never thought possible.

Yes, I was dancing with my son at his wedding. Somewhere, over that rainbow, dreams that we dared to dream really had come true.

This is Our Dance

By Luca

My parents and mother-in-law Joanne moved to Arizona within two years of me and Charlotte. We had lots of friends, great jobs, and plenty of disposable income. Life was good. So of course I was miserable and wanted to move.

I have no idea what motivated me. I always had this wild hair across my ass that made me hop around. I think it might be from spending so much of my life running to escape problems that I couldn't stay still.

I only lived in Arizona for thirty months. During that time I managed to move in and out of four apartments in three cities and worked four different jobs. I liked a lot of things about Arizona but it was just too different from New England. When Brian suggested I try Oregon, I moved there sight unseen the week of my twenty-fourth birthday.

Overall, compared to Arizona, Oregon has been a better fit for Charlotte and me. The major cities here are far more cultural and liberal. The climate is more akin to New England and I'm closer to the ocean.

While we lived in Arizona one of Charlotte's great aunts passed away. Shortly after moving to Oregon another one passed as well. Her grandparents were getting up there in age and my family wasn't getting younger either. Although we were now fairly broke from the move we decided if we wanted a real wedding it was now or never.

Before moving to Oregon, Charlotte had been promised a transfer within her company but that fell through. I started out driving a bus for mentally disabled adults, but I had to leave when I couldn't pass the background check. I have no felonies or convictions on my record because my juvenile records have been sealed. But Oregon looks into your arrest history. Being guilty or not is irrelevant; just having been arrested has kept me from numerous jobs.

Thanks MBTA.

Charlotte enrolled in college again and worked part-time at a restaurant. I worked two jobs loading and unloading trucks. It was hell on my back. I ended up working night security at an office building for a dollar above minimum wage. The job didn't come with any health benefits or paid time off. We were broke.

We tried not to let the money thing get us down. Neither of us wanted to go too far in debt over the wedding and we knew our families couldn't chip in much either. Instead of getting upset we rose to the challenge.

Charlotte designed and printed our invitations from home. Our wedding colors were black and white, a theme which matched our original Halloween wedding. We were excited about flying back to New England, seeing our families and friends, and renewing our vows with our mothers in attendance.

My high school drama teacher Deedie helped me pick out a location. My former principal, Kendal Tanner, sounded happy to get an invite along with my guidance counselor and shop teacher. Our friends back home were all pretty psyched too. I hadn't seen any of them in three years.

I'd missed Jenny's wedding but now she was going to be my "Best Woman." The rest of the bridal party consisted of our friends from college, Brian and my cousin Will. Having people whom I admired and respected behind me for this occasion was a great confidence builder. Particularly Will. For the majority of my life he'd served as my inspiration of manhood and family values.

Part of becoming a man is looking to other men for traits you wish to emulate; this is especially true for trans men. Marriage is a big step in becoming an adult and taking your place in the world. I was glad someone who'd been by my side from the beginning would be by my side now. So many people who had been influential in my life were on board to see me and Charlotte walk down the aisle. It felt great.

The mood took a turn as the date approached. Some family members were insulted that we wouldn't be having junior bridesmaids or a flower girl; thinking this was a jilt to our younger cousins. Really, the whole wedding and reception were so hastily planned I felt small children in the ceremony would just be a distraction. Other tiffs occurred when people learned I wouldn't be arranging seating, approving guest's dates, or serving alcohol. Some were upset I was serving all vegetarian food.

When Charlotte's family learned it was taking place in Massachusetts and not New York, everyone except Joanne boycotted the wedding; despite Mom offering to pay for their hotel rooms and me offering to transport them roundtrip. It hurt to learn the hard way who really cared about us. We almost called the whole thing off.

After five months of preparations our plane touched down at Logan Airport and we realized we weren't prepared at all. Everything was hectic; people were tired, stressed and cranky. We didn't even have time to unpack before we had to head out and purchase groceries and craft supplies.

Louise's house became the wedding staging headquarters. She slaved away making spaghetti sauce and veggie meatballs for sixty people. Brian, Charlotte and I crouched down on Louise's living room floor assembling favors and centerpieces while Mom baked the cakes. My cousin Ellen became my chauffer for last minute errands. Charlotte's dress had survived the cross country flight but my tuxedo pants were missing. Ellen took me shopping and Mom had to hem the new pants by hand while the cakes were cooling.

Just before the ceremony, my friends and I were setting up chairs and decorations in the church. In place of a band or DJ, we loaded premade mixed CD's into a stereo and a friend cued them up. Another friend flew in from Arizona to fill the role of photographer. The officiator was Jenny's wife. She was incredibly nervous. One of them changed into her dress in an empty church office; I put on my tux in a dim, mirror-less bathroom down the hall. There was no time for a rehearsal.

I wasn't nervous about my vows. Charlotte and I had already officially committed to one another three years earlier so I knew she'd say yes when the moment came. I wasn't afraid of what I'd be getting myself into. My only fear was the whole thing looking and feeing as cheap as it was. I fidgeted a bit by the altar and giggled with my groomsmen, trying to relieve some tension. But when Joanne entered the room with Charlotte on her arm, all my worries melted away.

I already knew what Charlotte's hair would look like. Earlier in the day I'd brought refreshments to her and her girlfriends at the salon. And I'd seen the dress on her because back in Oregon, I was the only one available to take her to fittings. I'd seen her earrings, shoes, bouquet; the whole bit. But I'd never seen her glow like this. I know it's cliché, but she was so beautiful she radiated and lit up the room. I was a lucky man.

Part of my family, and basically all of Charlotte's, were so angry with us they'd chosen not to come; but there in the moment, I didn't even miss them. It was easy to focus on the positive vibes and loving people who did show up and were happy for us.

The fact is, after everything I'd been through, to find someone in this crazy world to love, who loves me back, is miraculous. It's probably better than I deserve and I'm definitely luckier than most. I wasn't an abomination or a freak. I was simply a human being searching for my missing pieces and Charlotte was the last of them. With her I'm complete. I may not have hundreds of people to celebrate my good fortune with but I hold the handful of special people who care about me dearly in my heart. I didn't always think so but I know now that I'm blessed.

Jenny's nervous wife performed brilliantly when the time came. The food was delicious and the cake was beautiful. With everyone's help we'd pulled off a quaint and charming wedding and reception.

Charlotte and I danced our first dance to *"Dream a Little Dream of Me"* by the Mamas and the Papas. This has been our song since it came on the radio in a grocery store parking lot years ago after attending one of Charlotte's office parties in Arizona. We'd gone straight from the party to the store so we both had on evening wear. I hadn't asked her to dance at the party but I was ready now. So, like a pair of crazies we slow danced next to the car in a dark parking lot.

Later in the evening, when things slowed down a bit, Mom and I danced to *"Somewhere Over the Rainbow/What a Wonderful World"* by Israel Kamakawiwo'ole. I knew Mom loved the song so I'd put it on the CD just for her. She looked fantastic in her white beaded dress with a smile plastered to her face. It was the prettiest I'd ever seen her.

The two of us have danced many awkward, sad, and dangerous tangos, across tightropes over dark and deadly emotional precipices. Now we were finally having our calm victory dance; a victory for peace, enduring trust and friendship, finding one's place in the world and unconditional love.

I couldn't help thinking to myself, *"What a wonderful world."*

Epilogue

By Betsie

Our book began when Luca and I became outraged over the comment, "***Gays, lesbians and transsexuals are an abomination on this earth.***" I was saddened my son had to hear such vile words. With teens committing suicide because of such animosity, I knew we had to do something. I had already started writing my stories and asked Luca to join me; telling him to "yell, scream, or holler, but get your words out!" That evening we decided to write our book together.

I hope Luca and I have succeeded in showing how cruel and hateful those words are. Our children are our children. It's not up to us to understand the GLBTQ world, but it is up to us to understand the love of a child. As parents, and as a society, we need to listen and be accepting. We cannot allow our children to feel less than they are. For any reason! One more parent experiencing heartache and guilt, because as a society we allowed a child to feel there was no other way out but to end his or her life, is unacceptable.

I'm one of the fortunate ones. After years of misunderstandings and mistakes, I still have my child. When my daughter was born, all I wanted was a happy, healthy baby. It may have taken twenty-four years, but I now have my content, strong, wonderful son. And best of all, even with all my faults, he still loves me.

As a mother, it doesn't get any better than this.

Epilogue

By Luca

"Rejoice and love yourself today cause baby you were born this way."- Lady Gaga

Since my transition (even since beginning this book) a lot has happened and changed for trans people. The language has changed for a start. A friend of mine told me a while ago she's dating a trans-masculine guy. I was like, "Neat. What's that?" I guess calling yourself FTM is out of fashion. People don't like being called transgendered or transsexual anymore. I've had to learn phrases like "gender non-conforming" and "gender-queer." Likewise "bio" people are now "cisgendered." I think it's great that folks are creating new ways to identify themselves that are more specific, inclusive, and feel right to them. As for me I don't care what you call me; just don't call me late for dinner- ba da boom.

Recently, "Gender Identity Disorder" has been removed from the American Psychiatric Association guide. It's been replaced with "Gender Dysphoria." I still don't agree with it being considered a mental disorder other than it pertaining to the brain. I'm not crazy or developmentally challenged. Okay, well maybe I am a little crazy; but not because I'm trans, dammit. But I think Gender Dysphoria alludes to transitioning (including hormones and surgery) as a cure for most people and that's cool. Maybe the doctors are finally on the right track.

Charlotte and I have been married eight years now. We're still madly in love and disgustingly happy with one another. We live in Oregon where we're total vegan-urban-homesteader-douches. She finished college and has a good job. I'm still an underachiever. We managed to buy a house on our own and I've spent two years working hard to fix it up. My shop teacher Paul would be proud. I think having a wedding brought me some kind of closure because after that I managed to settle down and stay in one place. I no longer feel the need to run from myself. Charlotte has made our house a home where I feel happy and content.

Writing this book has forced me to remember and relive a lot of trauma and needless sorrow. I haven't been in therapy or taken mood stabilizing drugs for over a decade but it's not always easy. I suffered a lot of unnecessary damage before Diane came along all those years ago; some of it my own doing from being so secretive, ashamed, and distrustful.

In a way I feel like a survivor. I try to tell myself the trauma is all behind me, and for the most part it is. Some days I even forget I'm trans. I've been Luca longer than I was Marie and have become so deeply rooted in my new life, no one ever questions me. I don't have to worry about passing anymore. The last few people I've told I'm trans thought I was joking and argued that I couldn't possibly be. But here I am.

I pretty much go wherever I want without fear. I've gone naked under a towel, changed my clothes in men's gym locker rooms, and sunbathed topless at the beach, without even receiving a sideways glance or questioning look. I'm me and I own it. But now and then I awaken in the night plagued by panic attacks and know my past will always be with me.

Sometimes I think I could have done more with my life, achieved more, if being trans hadn't put me at such a disadvantage. I'm old enough now to know that kind of thinking is mostly an excuse. I could go back to college if I had the money, but life has a way of sweeping you up and moving you along from one obstacle to the next. I'm just glad so far I've survived everything that's come my way and maintained most of my dignity. It's my sincere hope other trans children will receive services earlier in life and have better opportunities than I had. It'd be nice if they could avoid wasting as much of their lives hating themselves as I have and seeking acceptance at the bottom of as many bottles as I have. No one should be made to feel ashamed of who they are and miss out on life.

I live my life on my own terms but not without a price. I have scars and regrets. But I also have people I love and I have my pride. No one's life is perfect. Considering how many non-trans people get more shit than stick too, I feel content with my lot.

Thanks for reading my story. I hope it helped you in some small way; whether learning from my many mistakes, gaining some insight, or understanding trans people aren't freaks. Maybe you felt a connection to another human-being, realized you're not alone and things can get better, or just passed along some boredom. Whatever the case, hopefully peeking into my madcap life has shown there's no reason to hate or fear anyone who's trans or GLBQ. We're all just people.

Acknowledgements

Betsie

Thank you Luca for taking this difficult journey back through our past. Your courage never ceases to amaze me.

Thank you Charlotte for stealing my son's heart. You have stolen mine also

A heartfelt thank you, filled with gratitude, to Diane Elleborn. Without your guidance, Luca would not be the man he is today and I would never have experienced the joy in watching my little boy become that man.

Without my family, especially Louise, my ship would have sunk in hurricane-force breakers.

Jenny and Brian – I love you!

Thank you Muriel, George, Dan, Allen, and Rose for giving me time to take a deep breath and just float with the currents.

Thank you friends and co-workers; past and present. You have been my cheering section.

Principal Tanner, Deedie, Mary, and the entire staff at New Horizons; if the education system had more caring teachers like you, our life's story would have been very different.

Thank you Shirley for listening to my stories and convincing me to put them down on paper.

Thank you East Valley Writing Workshop. Your patience, support, and helpful criticisms over the past two years were instrumental in getting me to the last word.

Candice – Your encouragement and friendship mean the world to me.

Acknowledgements

Luca

I'd like to thank Mom for the idea of writing this book and being brave enough to leave her comfort zone and join a writing group. I hope getting up at 4:30 am to write before work and giving up every Sunday for two years to edit was worth it. Like so many things in my life, this wouldn't have been possible without you.

Thank you Diane for ensuring I had a chance at life.

Some other people who deserve props for taking a special interest in me and the man I would become are Mary, Kevin, Harriet, all my teachers from New Horizons, Derek, Betty (thanks for all the rides and a place to stay when things got crazy), Jennifer, Donna, Maryann, Gary, my family, my friends and my Love Bug.

Luca is a post-op transsexual man residing in Oregon with his wife of nine years. After multiple suicide attempts Luca came out to his mother in 1996. He was just thirteen years of age. Fifteen years of adventures later, Luca is ready to tell his story.

Luca is a proud member of PFLAG and a supporter of TransActve. One of his poems and a pencil sketch were published in Dean Kotula's book *The Phallus Palace* (Alyson Publications, 2002.)

Betsie is the proud mother of a trans son. Her greatest joy in life is being a mother and mother-in-law. After heading an alternative family for fifteen years and facing down the challenges that encompasses, she hopes her experiences and commitment to unconditional love will help others.

Leaving the North Shore of Massachusetts for the sunshine of Arizona, Betsie currently resides there with her husband and two cats. She is delighted to be a member of PFLAG and the East Valley Meet-Up Writing Group. Betsie was a contributor to Dean Kotula's book *The Phallus Palace* (Alyson Publications, 2002) while Luca was still pre-op.

Say hi at BetsieHarvie@gmail.com or LucaHarvie@gmailcom.

www.ingramcontent.com/pod-product-compliance
Lightning Source LLC
Chambersburg PA
CBHW062355090426
42740CB00010B/1279